Public Engagement for Public Education

Public Engagement for Public Education

Joining Forces to Revitalize Democracy
and Equalize Schools

Edited by Marion Orr and John Rogers

Stanford University Press
Stanford, California

Stanford University Press
Stanford, California

Printed in the United States of America on acid-free, archival-quality paper

Library of Congress Cataloging-in-Publication Data

Public engagement for public education : joining forces to revitalize democracy and equalize schools / edited by Marion Orr and John Rogers.
    p. cm.
    Includes bibliographical references and index.
    ISBN 978-0-8047-6355-4 (cloth : alk. paper)—ISBN 978-0-8047-6356-1 (pbk. : alk. paper)
    1. Community and school—United States.   2. Public schools—United States—Citizen participation.   3. Education—United States—Citizen participation.   4. Educational equalization—United States.   I. Orr, Marion, 1962–   II. Rogers, John, 1961 Aug. 20–
    LC221.P84   2010
    371.19—dc22   2010013543

Typeset by Westchester Book Group in 10/14 Minion

In memory of Alma Burns and Hannah Williams, who had limited access to public education but nevertheless helped build strong families and communities. —MO

For Ella and Jacob, whose namesakes knew well the power of public engagement, and who remind me daily of the power of learning. —JR

Contents

Foreword   ix
Jeannie Oakes and Wendy Puriefoy

Preface   xiii

1   Unequal Schools, Unequal Voice: The Need for Public
Engagement for Public Education   1
Marion Orr and John Rogers

Part I   **The Context of Public Engagement for
Public Education**

2   A Brief History of Public Engagement in American
Public Education   27
Dennis Shirley

3   The Contemporary Context of Public Engagement:
The New Political Grid   52
Jeffrey R. Henig

Part II   **Streams of Public Engagement for
Public Education**

4   Public Engagement and the Coproduction
of Public Education   89
Donn Worgs

5   Democratic Institutions, Public Engagement, and
    Latinos in American Public Schools   117
    Luis Ricardo Fraga and Ann Frost

6   Community Organizing for Education Reform   139
    Mark R. Warren

7   Broad-based Public Engagement: Alliances and
    Social Movements   173
    Lauren Wells, Jean Anyon, and Jeannie Oakes

Part III   Sites of Public Engagement for
           Public Education

8   Improving Teacher Quality Through
    Public Engagement in Chicago   201
    Sara McAlister, Kavitha Mediratta, and Seema Shah

9   "A Force to Be Reckoned With": The Campaign
    for College Access in Los Angeles   227
    John Rogers and Ernest Morrell

10   "Together We Can" in Mobile: A Coalition Across
     Lines of Race and Class   250
     Brenda J. Turnbull

11   The Prospects for Public Engagement in a
     Market-oriented Public Education System:
     A Case Study of Philadelphia, 2001–2007   276
     Elaine Simon, Eva Gold, and Maia Cucchiara

12   Public Engagement for Public Education:
     Reflections and Prospects   301
     Marion Orr and John Rogers

     Contributors   315
     Index   321

Foreword

Jeannie Oakes and Wendy Puriefoy

DEMOCRACY'S STRENGTH lies in people's ability to understand and participate in decisions that affect them, their families, and their society. In the United States, we look to public education to sustain and reflect the promise of democracy by giving all children, regardless of race or class or language, access to high-quality schooling that prepares them for economic well-being and civic engagement. The links between democracy and public education are so deep that if one of them faces severe problems, as education does today, the other surely will as well. This threat to our social and political values certainly equals the more frequently invoked economic vulnerabilities that are expressed when discussing the shortcomings of public education.

Both Public Education Network (PEN) and the Ford Foundation value public engagement in public institutions as a means to strengthen those institutions and, at the same time, to foster the civic ties that are essential to democracy. Further, both organizations believe that educating all of our children to high standards entails a collective responsibility to move beyond self and parochial interests. Is there an untapped power for reform that could be released by joining these two social values—civic participation and the democratic distribution of educational opportunity? In 2005, PEN and the Ford Foundation convened a group of twenty-six prominent academics representing a wide array of perspectives to explore the relationship between public education reform and civic engagement. Unfortunately, we found frustratingly little in the research literature to support or guide a potential synergy of school reform and public engagement.

x Jeannie Oakes and Wendy Puriefoy

Research on public education reform has focused primarily at the school level. Few studies have explored how to reform public education at the community level—that is, how to engage the community to actively support education reform, demand accountability from elected officials, and push for adequate financial resources. Certainly, much strong organizing and public engagement on behalf of school reform is taking place across the country, but these efforts are underreported and insufficiently analyzed. We have strong indications that public engagement is a promising strategy for school reform, but taking engagement to scale requires far more credibility and visibility. In other words, school reform needs research-based evidence that public engagement can be effective; and it needs that evidence to be brought into focus as an area of inquiry in the arenas of academia, philanthropy, and education reform.

For many years research has accumulated on the limited efficacy of conventional "research, development, and dissemination" reform strategies—especially for improving schools for the nation's most vulnerable young people. Reforms seeking to disrupt historic connections among race, social class, educational opportunities and schooling outcomes consistently have been distorted or abandoned during the implementation process. Accordingly, a growing number of scholars have concluded that successful "equity-focused" change must address political and normative challenges (for example, the power to make decisions along with the beliefs and values that shape those decisions) as well as technical challenges (for example, "best practices" for teaching or novel ways of organizing schools). Some recent studies have looked at the potential impact of including the members of less-powerful communities in formulating, adopting, and implementing reforms, in addition to professionals and elites who typically dominate these processes.

The 2005 convening of the PEN Scholars Forum led to a series of exchanges among social scientists attempting to understand how "community engagement" relates and contributes to better teaching and learning and to political philosophers who view public education as a public good. Over three years, the group reviewed and synthesized the research. They also deliberated about how empirical scholarship could shed light on public engagement when linked to school reform and lead to sustained changes in policy and practice. In sum, the scholars wanted to know if public engagement generates public responsibility for public education and if and how that responsibility matters.

We hope that this work at the nexus of public engagement and education reform will stimulate a field of study—public engagement—that encompasses the research of the forum participants and other scholars drawn to this field. We believe that such research can inform scholarship on education reform, generally, and find particular relevance in the on-the-ground goals and strategies of community-based organizations as they continue to engage the public in school reform, community by community.

We are also pleased that this work comes at a time when policy makers and civic organizations are turning increasingly to public engagement as a strategy for promoting democracy and revitalizing social institutions. Such was the case during the 2008 Obama campaign, in which public engagement was viewed not only as a strategy for winning the election, but also as a way to rebuild public life. Across the nation in "Camp Obamas," Americans became actively engaged in politics—learning concrete ways to organize in their local communities. This citizen engagement and mobilization echoed the abolitionists, suffragettes, labor and civil rights movements, in which public engagement sought to ensure that the rights, benefits, and power of democracy are available to all. At best, such engagement produces structural adjustments, leaving the world no longer as it was. The power of an engaged and mobilized citizenry has changed the order of things.

The challenges facing our current public education system require such fundamental structural changes in our systems of public education. Changes of this magnitude mandate that communities and the public become engaged in ensuring the public benefit. This book represents one step toward understanding how previously marginalized community members come together to take public action in education and what happens when they do. Perhaps it can help marshal the force of an organized citizenry to advance the quality of public education for every child in America. We hope the readers of this volume, both scholars and activists, will find useful insights to continue their work in promoting public engagement in public education. At best, their work can also marshal America's collective intellect and power to create and sustain effective public education and schools and, thereby, strengthen the future of our democracy.

Preface

WHETHER LEFT OR RIGHT OF THE IDEOLOGICAL SPECTRUM, most observers tend to agree that public education works best when students, parents, and community members are engaged in improving the school system. There is however, a troubling aspect of public engagement in public education. Powerful and effective engagement is skewed by race, class, and immigrant status. While everyone wants high-quality education, some are able to advance this interest more effectively than others. Often, students and parents experience unequal opportunities for robust engagement. And frequently, school and elected officials respond to different constituencies differently. This problem of inequality in public engagement—what might be called the "engagement gap"—is critically important to the quality of education *and* civic life. We are interested in how it can be redressed. Hence, the essays in this volume consider how particular political and economic conditions create challenges and opportunities for previously marginalized students, parents, community members, and organizations to come together as powerful publics capable of improving schooling and revitalizing democracy.

What is public engagement? In our highly individualistic culture, it is important to differentiate public engagement from related terms such as *political participation*, *parent involvement*, or *consumer choice*. Public engagement cannot be reduced to individual acts such as voting, speaking with a teacher, or choosing a school. Public engagement emerges as parents, community members, and youth identify common educational problems and work together to address them. Public engagement both builds on and seeks to foster interdependence. Community members take public action as they recognize that the fate of one's own household is tied to the fate of others. In the words of Martin Luther King Jr.: "We are caught in an inescapable network of mutuality, tied in a single garment of destiny." This is the reality from which our focus on public engagement stems. This is the reality by which we take stock of where we are and of the challenges we face.

How exactly should members of the public be engaged in education? Perhaps the response to this question will always remain a contested one, and perhaps in a healthy democracy it should be. But an informed debate about this issue would be well served by a better understanding of public engagement. In this book, we present and explore various forms of public engagement for public education (democratic governance, coproduction, community organizing, alliances, and social movement) and the likely consequences of these forms.

We hope this volume will invigorate scholarly inquiry about public engagement and public education. Over the years, a small but growing number of scholars have taken on this task. Education researchers are increasingly interested in the connection between expanding public engagement and systemic school reform. This interest has been fueled by a growing disenchantment with technical reform efforts that neglect the politics of education as well as recent changes in federal law that have focused new attention on parent involvement as a strategy for educational reform. Scholars in political science, sociology, and urban studies similarly have begun to focus attention on civic engagement and community organizing in education. This interest is fueled by a growing recognition that education is a key site of political mobilization and contestation by marginalized groups. It is our hope that researchers in education, sociology, anthropology, political science and related fields will read this book and begin to systematically explore the promises and challenges of public engagement for public education.

This book examines public engagement for public education through a number of academic disciplines. Our eclectic approach is deliberate. All the contributors to this volume have written extensively on education and inequality, and all of us bring a multidisciplinary orientation to the study of public engagement and public education. It is becoming more and more common for those who study urban education to draw on and build on the research developed not only by education scholars, but also by sociologists, anthropologists, historians, and political scientists. That the editors of this volume are trained in two distinct fields—political science and education—is a testament to the growing recognition among scholars of urban schooling that the interdisciplinary approach brings strength and adds depth to the research enterprise.

This book would not have been written without the impetus of Wendy Puriefoy. Wendy is the president of the Public Education Network (PEN), a national association of local education funds and individuals working to advance public school reform in low-income communities across the United States. Believing in the centrality of community participation in equity educational reform, Wendy sought out research that could inform and deepen the practice of public engagement. She joined the Ford Foundation to convene a diverse group of academics with expertise and research interests in the area of public engagement and public education.

This book grew directly out of meetings of the Scholars Forum on public engagement at the Ford Foundation in 2005 and 2006. The contributors discussed plans for the chapters during a two-day retreat in Los Angeles in February 2007. We met again in October 2008 to present and critique each other's work. The regular meetings of the Scholar's Forum added coherency and depth to this edited collection. In addition to the contributors, several other members of the Scholars' Forum helped us think through some of the broader theoretical and practical implications of pubic engagement for public education. We would like to thank Meredith Honig, Clarence N. Stone, and Joseph Kahne.

We also thank the Ford Foundation for its early and ongoing support of the Scholars' Forum. Janice Petrovich of the Ford Foundation shared Wendy Puriefoy's goal of establishing a body of research that could inform policy makers and practitioners about public engagement and equity reform. She hosted the early meetings of the forum and contributed significantly to the groups' deliberations. In addition to Ford, several other foundations have supported this work, including the Schott Foundation, the Marguerite Casey Foundation, and the Spencer Foundation.

This book benefited from extraordinarily helpful comments from external reviewers who evaluated the manuscript for Stanford University Press. They provided insightful criticism and useful suggestions that enabled the contributors to improve the quality of the book. We also would like to thank the staff at Stanford University Press. Jennifer Hele, former acquisitions editor at SUP, was an early and enthusiastic supporter of our book idea. After Jennifer left, we were very fortunate to have the equally enthusiastic support of SUP's

Executive Editor Kate Wahl, who skillfully shepherded our book through the production process.

We would be remiss if we did not thank those at our home institutions who provided critical support. At Brown University, Brandi Nicole Hinnant, who earned her master's degree in urban education policy and is currently pursuing a PhD in educational studies at Emory University, provided splendid research assistance and helped with the logistics of several of our Scholars' Forum workshops. At UCLA, Martin Lipton contributed immeasurably to the project with his insightful readings of early drafts of the chapters. Carolyn Castelli organized the meeting of the Scholars' Forum at UCLA and later copyedited the draft manuscript, and she did all this with her usual mix of precision and good humor. The multitalented Jessie Castro offered critical technical help in the final stages of production.

We would like to thank our spouses, Ramona Burton and Sharla Fett, and our extended families for all their support. Their love, reassurance, and encouragement lift our spirits and enrich our work.

Finally, we thank the students, parents, and community members chronicled in this book who have joined together as publics to create better and more equitable schools. Their efforts deepen our understanding of educational reform and broaden our sense of democratic possibilities.

1 Unequal Schools, Unequal Voice

The Need for Public Engagement for Public Education

Marion Orr and John Rogers

SOME YEARS AGO Jonathan Kozol (1992) compared wealthy and poor schools located within a few miles of one another. The harsh contrasts of physical surroundings and learning environments—in cities from a variety of states—highlighted just how different school can be for poor and minority-race children as opposed to middle-class and white children. Today, inequality in public education persists across many metropolitan areas (Akiba, LeTendre, and Scribner 2007; Ladson-Billings 2006; Schrag 2003). Some public schools provide first-rate education. In general, these schools enroll students from the most affluent neighborhoods and communities. Their teachers are well trained in the subject areas they teach. Their classrooms have cutting-edge media technology and science laboratories. Their curriculum offers students a wide range of advanced placement (AP) courses. Students who attend these schools are often accepted to the most selective colleges and universities in the country.

Many other schools, however, are much worse off. Their school buildings are older, their classrooms are more outdated, their science laboratories are nonfunctioning, and their curricular offerings seldom, if ever, include AP courses. These schools disproportionately enroll students from low-income, high-poverty, African American, and Latino communities. The inequalities in America's public schools that Kozol wrote about so passionately remain a challenge for the nation (Darling-Hammond 2007; Oakes 2005).

In addition to the issue of unequal schools, there is also the matter of *unequal voice*. In 1960, political scientist E. E. Schattsneider famously observed that "the problem with the pluralist heaven is that the heavenly chorus sings with a decidedly upper class accent" (p. 36). Forty-five years later, a report

1

produced by a group of political scientists affiliated with the American Political Science Association (APSA) reached the same conclusion, arguing that "the voices of American citizens are raised and heard unequally" (American Political Science Association 2004, 1). The highly educated and wealthy hold resources and participate in networks that allow their voices to be heard over the voices of others. The APSA report argued that our democracy is at "risk" because of the "bias in civic engagement that stems from inequalities in material conditions, social status, and political privilege" (Macedo et al. 2005, 99).

Generations of Americans have worked to equalize citizen voice across lines of income, race, and gender. Today, however, the voices of American citizens are raised and heard unequally. The privileged participate more than others and are increasingly well organized to press their demands on government. Public officials, in turn, are much more responsive to the privileged than to average citizens and the least affluent. Citizens with lower or moderate incomes speak with a whisper that is lost on the ears of inattentive government officials, while the advantaged roar with clarity and consistency that policy makers readily hear and routinely follow (American Political Science Association 2004, 1).

Consider, for example, what has happened in Tuscaloosa, Alabama in the years since the federal school desegregation order was lifted in 2000. After three decades of white withdrawal from the public schools, 75 percent of Tuscaloosa's public-school students are African American, although the majority of Tuscaloosa's residents are white. Tuscaloosa's African Americans are seven times as likely as its white residents to be poor, and the city is characterized by continuing patterns of residential segregation (U.S. Census Bureau, 2006–2008). According to Sam Dillon, in early 2005, affluent white parents from the city's "northern enclave" of "mansions and lake homes" began expressing concern about school attendance patterns established by the desegregation order that sent their children to a middle school outside of their neighborhood. "Scores" of parents from the affluent northern section of town attended a school board meeting to complain of overcrowding and discipline problems at the middle school. As Dillon reports, "The white parents clamored for a new middle school closer to their home." Other white parents urged school officials "to consider sending students being bused into northern cluster [elementary] schools back to their own neighborhood." Only three blacks were in attendance—two school board members and a teacher. A few months later, in May 2005, the school board adopted a "sweeping rezoning plan" that "redrew school boundaries in ways that, among other changes, required students from black neighborhoods and from a low-income housing project who had been attending the more integrated elementary schools in the northern zone to leave them for nearly all-black [and low-performing] schools in the west end." The zoning change required few white students to move. Across the country, many public officials are influenced by the kind of public engagement displayed by Tuscaloosa's white and affluent parents (2007, A18).

We believe that the problems of unequal schools and unequal voices are interrelated. Schooling advantages enable the privileged to attain the skills, degrees, and access to power that amplifies their voice. Political advantages in turn allow the privileged to secure preferred educational resources. There is a good deal of ethnographic evidence that highly educated middle-class parents use their social networks and their threat of withdrawal from the public school system to press their interests—interests that often advantage their children at the expense of others (Oakes and Rogers 2006; Wells and Crain 1997). Disrupting this cycle requires working simultaneously to equalize schools and equalize voice. By becoming involved in the process of governing and reforming public education, poor and working-class community members can develop the skills necessary to counteract the elevated voices of the affluent. In short, we believe that public engagement for public education is an essential strategy for equalizing voice and bringing equality to public schools.

This understanding of how to address inequality has not always prevailed. A century ago a major reform idea was to take the public out of public education. In those days, reformers embraced the view that a larger role for professional educators and a freer hand for them in running schools would be the surest path to creating a well-performing system of public education (Tyack 2003). Today that pathway no longer looks so promising. The notion that professional educators could or should operate in isolation from community members has been called into question (Warren 2005). Public engagement is seen as very important to student learning, and many school reformers now look to members of the public to energize students and educators, improve conditions, counter calcified bureaucracies, or secure additional resources.

This book explores how members of the public have come together to equalize schools and equalize voice. The essays in this volume are concerned with public engagement through collective action manifested in coalitions, alliances, public deliberation, and other forms of community collaboration.

The volume includes examples of various kinds of public engagement in communities from Maryland to California. Public engagement for public education includes, for example, the "Grow Your Own" effort in Chicago, in which community members secured public funding for an innovative program that trains residents of low- to moderate-income communities to become fully certified teachers. It also includes efforts of Mobile, Alabama's business and civic leaders, who joined with parents to establish a "community agreement," triggering a series of school improvements, including extra educational resources for Mobile's most troubled public schools. There are also examples of public engagement in Atlanta, Washington, Baltimore, and other inner cities where community groups have developed after-school programs to shore up the inadequacies in the public school systems. Alongside such efforts to bring new resources into the schools, public engagement for public education encompasses efforts to transform the system by developing a critical analysis of its performance, enlisting allies, and seeking to alter public awareness.

These seemingly diverse activities collectively constitute a field we call "public engagement for public education." The field seeks to simultaneously address educational and civic inequality through collective action of parents, community members, youth, and organized civic groups. Before offering a fuller description of this emerging field, we turn first to a discussion of the problems it seeks to address.

Education and Engagement Matters

Over the last two decades, American families have increasingly recognized that economic restructuring at home, heightened economic integration abroad, and an expanding global workforce require their children to compete for an increasingly limited supply of high-skilled and high-paying jobs that characterize the new economy. Globalization and economic restructuring have stamped a premium on technical training, verbal and written communication skills, and higher education credentials (Levy and Murnane 2004). Across the country parents and other community groups are engaged in helping develop and support pathways that would lead their children toward opportunities and careers in an increasingly knowledge-based economy. Few public school systems in the United States have demonstrated that they are ready to meet this new opportunity and challenge alone.

Parents who actively engage the school system—meet with teachers, attend PTA meetings, vote in school board elections, and attend school board meetings—are more likely to obtain information and develop social networks that help their children attain academic success (Horvat, Weininger, and Lareau 2003; Jeynes 2003). Participation in formal political structures, however, is also unequal by class and race—an inequality that stems from factors beyond a lack of interest, minimal concern about public issues, and low levels of political efficacy. Sidney Verba, Kay Lehman Schlozman, and Henry E. Brady provide good evidence that "the resources of time, money, and skills are . . . powerful predictors of political participation in America" (1995b, 285) and these resources amplify the voice of those who have them. According to these political scientists, "the voices of citizens . . . are decidedly not equal" (1995a, 511).

In the area of public education, the affluent and educated middle class has a long history of extensive involvement from the level of the individual household to the activities of such organized stakeholders as the PTA (Crawford and Levitt 1999). Ironically, the affluent middle class is quick to invoke the rhetoric of individual responsibility but is itself highly experienced and skilled in working in groups and in finding ways to become part of the fabric of schools and other public institutions. As a result, teachers and other school officials come to see middle-income and affluent parents as partners in the process of schooling. In addition, the precarious fiscal conditions of many cities and urban school districts and the need to attract and hold on to the dwindling number of white middle-class households is such that public officials are especially eager to listen and respond to parents' concerns in the face of threats to pull their children out of public schools (see Peterson 1981). This heightens the desire of school officials to pay special attention to the needs and concerns of the affluent, essentially giving white and affluent parents more power in determining school policies (Oakes and Rogers 2006).

Don McAdams (2005), a former Houston school board member, described the parents of the largely affluent neighborhoods he represented as being "persistent" in engaging the school system to address the educational needs of their children. McAdams recalled that at one elementary school, it was usual for him to have a monthly breakfast with a group of parents. When these parents had a greater number of concerns, they met more frequently over breakfast and lunch. When those parents engaged the public school system, things changed. For example, if parents complained about a principal, the superintendent usually removed him or her. According to McAdams, "nine times this happened. Nine times principals were removed" (p. 48). Public school officials take seriously the concerns of white and affluent parents and are more likely to act on them.

Race, Class, Culture and the Problem of Unequal Engagement

Education researchers have written extensively about the differences between suburban and urban schools serving middle- and working-class communities, paying a good deal of attention to uneven patterns of parent engagement (Lareau and Weininger 2003; Reay 1998). Much of this literature has focused on presumed deficits of low-income parents of color (Calabrese-Barton et al. 2004). Yet, as long ago as 1981, Sara Lawrence Lightfoot noted that school officials receive different parents differently. According to Lightfoot, "For a long time we have understood that the magic of suburban schools is not merely the relative affluence and abundant resources of the citizens (nor their whiteness), but also the balance of power between families and schools, the sense of responsibility and accountability teachers feel for the educational success of children, and the parents' sense of entitlement in demanding results from schools" (Lightfoot 1981, 101). Hence, Don McAdams (2005, 61) viewed the affluent activist parents in his Houston school board district not as troublemakers but as an asset, noting that "without them it was difficult to build an effective school."

Ethnographic research focusing on inner city schools, however, shows that race, class, culture, and language tend to structure how parents and education activists participate in public schools as individuals and as groups and how they are received by school officials (Rogers 2004; Smrekar and Cohen-Vogel 2001). For example, when parents in a low-income community in the Bronx complained that their children's school lacked basic supplies, the building was in disrepair, and students could not bring textbooks home, the principal took no action. As Medirata and Karp write, "Whenever parents raised these problems individually, teachers and administrators virtually ignored them or reacted defensively." School officials were not only "unresponsive to parents and the community," they "also blamed parents for the school's poor performance" As one parent put it, "They treated us like we were kids—like we were uneducated and knew nothing about anything" (2003, 7). Lareau (2003, 239) compared the interaction between parents and school personnel in a large urban school district and found that "when working-class and poor parents did try to intervene in their children's educational experiences, they often felt ineffectual." One working-class mother in Lareau's study said she "felt bullied and powerless" when she visited teachers and principals (p. 243).

Many low-income parents also encounter a divide between their culture and that of the school. These cultural differences impact how and to what extent parents engage the school system on their children's behalf. In her research on school and community culture, Maria Eulina P. de Carvalho (2000, 12) identified what she called "symbolic violence" taking place between communities and schools, triggered by divergent class and ethnic cultures. "Symbolic violence" is enacted when a parent enters the school and finds that school officials do not value his or her cultural background. This cultural dissonance can lead to discomfort, alienation, and disengagement. Further, many low-income African American parents who had bad experiences with schools when they were students now find that they do not have the "cultural capital" valued in many educational settings. Not surprisingly, they sometimes are reluctant to engage with their children's schools (Lareau and Horvat 1999; Lightfoot 2003).

Parents of inner-city school children often face unequal opportunities to participate meaningfully in public schools. For example, parents of immigrant children want just as much for their children as do other parents. However, many non-English speaking immigrants must confront the huge obstacle of school systems that communicate exclusively in English (Arias and Morillo-Campbell 2008). When letters and announcements are written only in English, these parents have difficulty gaining basic information about the place and time of meetings and announcements about important school matters. English-language learning (ELL) parents also must overcome communication barriers to participate in school meetings. Many school districts still fail to provide translators for Spanish-speaking parents. In his ethnographic study of a predominantly Latino immigrant community, Ramirez (2003, 98) found that "the school board meetings did not offer language support for Spanish speakers. One parent became so frustrated they brought their own translator to the next meeting." Many Latino immigrant parents confront similar communication problems when attending open house and other school meetings. Schools that do not provide adequate translators for Spanish-speaking parents put severe limitations on the level of engagement between immigrant parents and the public schools. Similarly, when school officials consistently schedule meetings that conflict with low-income parents' work schedules, they create barriers to public engagement.

The theoretical implications of the skewed nature of public engagement and the divergent ways in which public officials respond to white affluent parents and low-income minority parents are central to questions of local democracy. For example, in many metropolitan areas, racial stratification and pervasive class inequalities continue to persist (Dreier, Mollenkopf, and Swanstrom 2005; Massey and Denton 1993; Wilson 1987, 1996). Not all segments of society are equally well positioned to claim their role as part of the public and to be heard in that role. Without comparable opportunity for public engagement and equal reaction from school officials, African Americans and Latinos who are in the lower reaches of the system of social stratification, are likely to become marginal participants in public dialogue and political decision making. If professional educators have frequent interaction with affluent whites, then a level of mutual understanding, comfort, and concern can take hold. Others, especially the lower strata, are left out, become subject to stereotyping and, when they mobilize, are viewed as troublemakers to be avoided. For the poor and working class, these problems lead to unequal and inadequate educational conditions; a calcified, unresponsive bureaucracy; and dramatically unequal educational outcomes.

Race, class, culture, and language tend to structure how parents and education activists participate in public schools as individuals and as groups and how they are received by school officials. The problem of public engagement in education is therefore not a general problem of apathy. It is a problem of a sector of the public that has become largely disaffected and disconnected from public life—a disaffection and disconnection based in history, with a concrete and specific sociopolitical foundation. These critical issues about public engagement raise profound questions about democratic institutions of governance.

Public Engagement for Public Education

We view public engagement as a strategy for addressing unequal opportunity, unequal participation, and unequal voice. Public engagement promotes collective action toward shared interests. As John Rogers notes (2006, 633), public engagement "aims to create a vital public sphere capable of generating support for adequate resources and sustaining ongoing improvement." Although there is a strong relationship between various forms of involvement, we use the term "public engagement for public education" to refer to actions that are collective and focused on the interests of *all students*. We emphasize *all students* because advocacy organizations seek to alter public policies considered injurious or unfair to certain groups, especially the historically disadvantaged. These efforts, however, are not always as representative of the varied interests who should rightfully benefit from policy change (Cohen 1999; Hancock 2007; Strolovitch 2006, 2007). For example, Strolovitch (2007) cautioned that race, gender, labor, and other advocacy organizations tend to be substantially less active when it comes to issues affecting the disadvantaged subgroups of their members. As she wrote in 2006, "Labor organizations, for example, are less active when it comes to job discrimination against women and minorities, and issues affecting intersectionally disadvantaged workers" (p. 908). The concerns and issues of the hyper-marginalized subgroup within the advocacy organization claiming to represent a disadvantaged group can be ignored. Cathy Cohen (1999) has shown how interest groups that claim to represent African Americans have nevertheless been reluctant to advocate for "marginalized" African American subgroups such as black HIV-positive gay men. Ange-Marie Hancock's (2007) study of the "public identity" of "welfare queens" is another such example. We are mindful that this is also a challenge for public engagement focused on improving public education. Will the most disadvantaged and marginalized subgroup of students and parents be equal beneficiaries of public engagement efforts?

Although it may grow out of individual concerns and involve actions by individuals, *public* engagement centers on shared interests and collective actions. In this volume, we draw a distinction between individual and collective engagement and between actions focused on individual children and actions that address the interests of students generally. Although there is some overlap, public engagement for public education is not the same area of research and concern as the general topic of political participation explored by Verba, Schlozman, and Brady. Political scientists have long ago employed sophisticated statistical and methodological techniques like causal modeling to determine the individual correlates of political behavior (Campbell et al. 1960). In our conceptualization, public engagement for public education is *not* centered on the actions of atomized individuals. It calls for collective participation to address common concerns. Public engagement for public education is about the public addressing its shared interest in expanding democracy and educational opportunity.

Public engagement for public education is conceptually different from "social capital" (Putnam 2000). Social capital is typically viewed as unconscious interactions among individuals encouraged by a kind of "civic virtue" that develops into trust and reciprocity. Public engagement is about translating shared interests into deliberate collective efforts to promote education equity. The examples of public engagement that we present in this volume are both purposeful and collaborative.

Public engagement has a community context and involves at some level recognition of interdependence—that is, that the fate of one's own household is tied to the fate of others. In the educational arena, public engagement is a collective response to a community-wide concern. It is about more than the education of one's own children. Public engagement for public education is about a shared responsibility to develop the capacities of all young people, even if one's own children are of foremost concern. In light of that responsibility, citizens are not to be thought of as consumers, shopping side by side. Interdependence is real. Public engagement emerges as parents, community members, and youth identify common educational problems and work together to address them. It is the kind of work that people engage in because they believe that their efforts might make a difference to their collective future.

Public engagement takes place deep in the public sphere. It is about communities doing what Harry Boyte (2004, 5) calls "public work," a sustained effort "by a mix of people who solve problems or create goods, material or cultural, of general benefit." As Boyte notes (2004, 21), public work "is grounded in our everyday institutional environments—the places we live and work, go to school, volunteer, participate in communities of faith. It is public-spirited and practical; not utopian or immaculate but part of the messy, difficult, give-and-take process of problem solving." Doing public work in public education requires collective thinking and an understanding of interdependency. Community organizing, social movements, and coalitions and alliances that include civic elites are built on the premise that if residents "develop a sense of collective identity with other residents . . . who share their interests and concerns," they are on their way toward developing the capacity to harness "cooperative action" to achieve their goals (Smock 2004, 87–88). Public engagement for public education is about communities coming together to address issues confronting public schools.

Public Engagement, Schooling, and the Democratic Promise

The need to mark out public engagement for public education as a distinctive category reflects the dual roles of public education in American society. Public schools produce both public and private returns. Public schools help address the shared interests of society to shape the knowledge, skills, and values of community members and future participants in the democratic process. Further, the principle of equal educational opportunity holds that public schooling should mitigate the effects of inherited wealth and promote social improvement by unleashing the capacities of diverse communities in economic, political, and social affairs.

Public schools also play a central role in developing skills and distributing credentials that in turn influence job prospects and private returns. In a highly stratified information-based economy, educational attainment is critically important to the life chances of individual students. Parents, fearing that their child will be left out of the global market place, fight to have their child obtain a place in a highly qualified school. In Houston, Don McAdams found that the middle-income parents in his school district "saw school reform in terms of their child, their school, their neighborhood, this year" (2005, 61). In their case study of a Los Angeles high school, Jeannie Oakes and John Rogers (2006, 28) observed how affluent white parents "applied enormous pressure" to prevent a plan designed to increase the enrollment of Latino and African American students in honors-level courses. The plan would have "fundamentally altered how the school allocated scarce resources," but wealthier white parents feared that it would endanger their children's chances to attend the most competitive college. According to Oakes and Rogers, "the school's reform strategies were strongly supported by the evidence, but when reason met power, power won."

Parents desire educational advantages because they want to set their children on a pathway to achieve the American dream. This is a central paradox of the American dream as it relates public schools. As Jennifer Hochschild and Nathan Scovronick described it (2003, 2), "people naturally wish to give their own children an advantage in attaining wealth or power, and some can do it." Hence, "efforts to promote the collective goals of the American dream through public schooling have run up against almost insurmountable barriers when enough people believe (rightly or wrongly, with evidence or without) that those efforts will endanger the comparative advantage of their children or children like them. At that point the gap arises between their belief that every child deserves a quality education and their actions to benefit their own children over the long run."

As noted above, the educated middle class has a long history of extensive involvement from the level of the individual household to the activities of organized stakeholders such as the PTA. Their voices are heard and responded to disproportionately in the political process. Without comparable opportunity for public engagement, those in the lower reaches of the system of social stratification and at the margins of the American political economy are largely on the outside looking in—and that all too easily becomes a self-perpetuating cycle.

For many disadvantaged communities, believing in the feasibility of achieving education equity and improved educational opportunities is a major step in altering the cycle. Failed attempts at public engagement for public education, raising and then dashing hopes for success, can no doubt have negative consequences. The wide literature on policy feedback illustrates how policies "can influence beliefs about what is possible, desirable, and normal" (Soss and Schram, 2007, 113). Paul Pierson (1993), for instance, writes about political learning as a policy feedback. Political learning is a dynamic process that can produce positive learning conclusions and at other times can engender lessons that generate negative conclusions (Mettler 2002).

Failed attempts in public engagement for public education no doubt could have a negative feedback loop. This is what Jack Buckley and Mark Schneider (2007) found in their study of charter schools in Washington, DC. Although charter school parents began with high levels of satisfaction and enthusiasm, over time these hopes faded, fostering disillusionment. The potential for disillusionment brought on by failed and halfhearted public engagement is real, as is evidenced by several chapters in this volume. For example, we see in Chapter 11 that the Philadelphia youth involved in Students Empowered gain very little from their efforts to create new, small schools. Will they become disillusioned and turn away from the political process? Similarly, Chapter 8 offers a wonderful story about public engagement that brings high-quality teachers to poor communities in Chicago. Yet, as Sara McAlister, Kavitha Mediratta, and Seema Shah note, the number of high-quality teachers that the "Grow Your Own" legislation is designed to put into the pipeline is relatively small. If the numbers of new teachers are so small that only a few poor neighborhoods benefit, the participants in public engagement may turn away from collective action in the future.

We see public engagement as a dynamic process that both produces new capacity and commitment in times of success and undermines public energy when goals are not met. In this volume, we are sympathetic to the goals of public engagement for public education, but we approach each instance of engagement with the empirical question of whether, in the end, "it promotes or discourages citizen involvement in the day-to-day activities of American democracy" (Mettler 2002, 351).

Unequal engagement in public education is of critical importance to educational opportunity. There is a strong relationship between the quantity and quality of public engagement and the opportunities afforded to particular groups of students. Public engagement influences the preferences, expectations, and commitments of both educators and policy makers. These beliefs shape every aspect of schooling from pedagogy to course placement to discipline. Ultimately, public engagement is central to how resources are distributed and how students are treated—which in turn are key determinants of student academic achievement.

We make no assumption that a higher level of public engagement by adults will lead directly to improved academic performance by children. Relationships are much more complex than would be suggested by such a claim. Yet, all the contributors of this volume are interested in determining how and in what ways public engagement for public education can bring us closer to educational equity. We similarly are interested in whether public engagement will lead officials to respond more equally to parents across lines of race, class, and ethnicity. These are issues important for education, but even more broadly they are important for the health of American democracy.

The heart of the democratic challenge on the issue of public education is increasing the involvement and voice of those who are seen as marginal in racial and economic terms. They are often stereotyped as not caring. Many, like the parents in the Bronx, are dismissed as a source of "the problem" (for whatever problem is salient at the time), and they may in fact be politically withdrawn because of past experiences and past treatment. Public engagement for public education is a part of the democratic ideal that all people should have a voice and that a diversity of voices make for better public input and policy outcomes. The premise of democracy is that sufficient understanding can take shape only if everyone is at the table. Indeed, the promise of democracy is that those endowed with much experience, extensive training, and abundant resources will gain understanding by sharing the table with those less well endowed. And this promise is critical to the future of American public schools and our shared public life.

The Streams of Public Engagement for Public Education

We have introduced public engagement for public education as a coherent approach to equalizing educational opportunities and voice. Yet, as we survey practice and scholarship, we see a good deal of diversity in various efforts to reform public education through public action. Public engagement is parents informally working together to create a tutoring program; neighbors convening a forum for school board candidates to communicate their interest in alleviating school overcrowding; members of a community organizing group pressuring district officials to redistribute qualified teachers; civic and business groups forging a concerted campaign to change graduation requirements; grassroots community groups joining labor unions to build a broad-based movement that will ensure all children a high-quality education. Clearly, there are many ways to enact public engagement for public education.

In this volume, we present five streams of public engagement; we call them coproduction, democratic governance, community organizing, alliances, and social movements. We argue that each of these streams reflects a particular understanding of the purpose and practice of public engagement. Although we present the streams as distinct, we recognize that the work of public engagement is fluid. There are many instances in which democratic governance flows into alliance work, community organizing flows into social movement activity, and so on. Our purpose here is heuristic. By highlighting the different conceptions undergirding various forms of public engagement, we aim to give a sense of the diversity within the field. We also wish to assess the opportunities for and challenges to distinct approaches to public engagement. Finally, we are interested in how these different forms of engagement shape and are shaped by particular sociopolitical contexts.

Three questions help to illuminate the distinctions among the five streams of public engagement. First, what is the problem that public engagement seeks to address? What creates and sustains inequalities in education and voice? Second, who constitutes the public that participates in public engagement? Is the public made up of individual parents, residents with certain political rights, members of organizations, or particular sorts of groups? Third, how can an engaged public promote more equal education and voice? What is the theory of change and what does change look like?

Coproduction

In coproduction, parents and community members join together, often in alliance with educators, to design and provide educational services. Coproduction generally focuses on augmenting, rather than transforming, existing services. At times the educational services are provided in public schools, while at other times they are provided in the community. Whether they work inside or outside the school, parents and community members play a direct role in instructing and guiding students. Education is not viewed as the exclusive domain of professionals.

For advocates of coproduction, the problem of public engagement lies in the inadequacies of existing programs for low-income students of color. Too often, educators are disconnected from the communities they serve and hence not able, on their own, to draw on the community's resources. A public emerges to address this problem as individual parents, community members, and members of churches and other voluntary associations recognize that they can produce services that the community wants and needs. Whereas affluent parents turn to the market to secure necessary services, the members of this public create programs through voluntary activity. In this way, coproduction aims to prompt greater public participation in, and ownership of, educational services, leading to better and more equitable schooling.

Democratic Governance

The participation of parents and community members in the governance of public schools has been a long-standing but never fully realized vision of public engagement for democracy. In the mid- to late nineteenth century, so many parents served as school board members that they represented what David Tyack (2003, 130) has referred to as the "largest body of public officials in the world." (Of course, large segments of the community—women, African Americans in the Jim Crow South, and many immigrants—were excluded from this participation.) In the intervening century, the bureaucratization and centralization of school governance has distanced professional educators and elected officials from the communities that they serve. Today, democratic governance aims to reengage community members in the governance process and reconnect them with the elected representatives charged with governing their schools.

Advocates of democratic governance worry that low levels of civic participation in public education and skewed participation by race and class lead to poor governance and unequal schooling. Decisions about resources and their distribution often do not reflect the vital needs of less powerful communities. A public emerges as voters, potential voters, and other members of the community recognize that they can participate in decision making or indirectly influence elected decision makers. This public may take action through school level decision making structures such as local school site councils, or it can participate in electoral campaigns or accountability dialogues between elected officials and community members. The aim of this public action is to foster more representative decision making and more inclusive public discourse, leading to fairer and more responsive educational policy and practice.

Community Organizing

In community organizing, members of grassroots groups act collectively to publicize and seek to transform school inequalities. Susan Stall and Randy Stocker (1998, 732) define community organizing as "the work that occurs in local settings to empower individuals, build relationships, and create action for social change." Similarly, Marshall Ganz (2002) argues that organizing activities seek to create networks that can sustain a new activist community, to frame a story about the network's identity and purpose, and to develop a program of action that mobilizes and expends resources to advance the community's interests. Ganz writes that building relationships, forging common understandings, and taking action in the context of campaigns produces collective power that can secure desired changes.

Advocates of community organizing in education argue that the collective power produced through organizing is needed to confront a political system and public bureaucracy that often are unresponsive to the felt needs and concerns of low-income communities of color. Ernesto Cortes (1996) talks about replacing the power of organized money with the power of organized people. A public emerges as youth and adults negatively impacted by social policies forge shared identities in organizations affiliated with churches, neighborhoods, or community centers. They target issues that represent a set of related grievances felt by the organization's members. Community organizing groups leverage the power of their membership—its size, networks of support, and moral standing—to win tangible policy changes (Orr 2007). In addition to securing resources or more responsive policies, community organizing aims to build sustained power in the community that can foster mutual and respectful relationships between officials and community members.

Alliances

Through alliances, an array of seemingly disparate membership-based organizations join together in broad-based educational reform initiatives. The emergence of alliances is in part a reflection of the increased politicization of public education over the last half century since *Brown v. Board of Education*. The powerful control earlier exerted by superintendents in large urban school districts has given way to greater contestation by various groups at the local level along with more influence from state and federal governments. To effect substantial political change on key policy issues such as school funding or assessment, it is necessary to forge coalitions that stretch across constituencies. Given the heightened importance of education to economic development, alliances can incorporate previously competing interests such as representatives of the business community and more progressive, community-based organizations.

Advocates argue that alliances are needed because the many groups involved in educational reform often are disjoined, uncoordinated, and lacking the connections to powerful inside groups that are needed to win concrete policy reforms. Alliances emerge as members of various groups that previously have not worked together—community organizations, advocacy groups, mainstream parent organizations, and enlightened business leaders—begin to recognize a set of common interests. Much of the initial work of alliances focuses on building coalitions among sometime wary partners. Later, alliances frequently coordinate campaigns and, when they win, oversee implementation of their victories. Alliances generally aim to build coalitions that will be capable of winning and implementing with fidelity overarching policies at the district and state level that enhance the quality and equality of public schooling.

Social Movements

At certain historical moments, people and groups join together around a set of intensely held shared interests, and their actions engender such broad public support that deeply held social convictions are transformed and dramatically new policies are enacted (Payne 1995; Tarrow 1994). In recent decades, social movement activism has changed the way Americans think about issues such as racial segregation and discrimination, gender roles, and the environment. Movements generally build outward from local grassroots organizing efforts, connecting broad constituencies in a shared struggle (Morris 1984). Rather than focusing narrowly on any particular policy victory, social movements seek to effect a broad array of legislative changes that represent a new set of political rights and a new common sense about who is deserving of these rights.

Advocates argue that social movements are necessary because inequalities in schooling and voice are held in place by deeply held norms, beliefs, and policies (Anyon 2005). Other public engagement strategies do not sufficiently challenge the cultural logics that hold inequality in place. Nor do they generate sufficient power to move vested interests. A public for a social movement begins to emerge as members of various organized groups committed to social justice recognize themselves as part of a shared struggle to realize change beyond their local efforts. This initial public then galvanizes the interest of new, previously unaffiliated members, building a wave of public support and interest. As people and groups come together in struggle, they deploy mass mobilization, mass protest, and mass communication strategies. These strategies aim to create a broad-based constituency that can press for egalitarian policies inside and outside the public schools.

Plan of the Book

Part I of the volume examines the context through which public engagement in public education takes place and describes how that context has changed over time. In Chapter 2, Dennis Shirley puts public engagement for public education into historical context, documenting how different streams of public engagement emerged at different historical moments. Shirley also illuminates the countervailing forces that marginalized and excluded different social groups from educational opportunities along the lines of race, class, gender, sex, language, and religion.

In Chapter 3, Jeffrey Henig examines what he calls the changing "political grid." Henig shows how the landscape of the American system of education has been changing. Some of these changes have been steady and incremental—like the changing demands for education in a globalizing economy or inroads by minorities into positions of formal decision making within local education bureaucracies. Others have burst forth more recently and sharply—like the ratcheting up of corporate involvement in the delivery of public education, or the qualitatively different involvement of the national government via No Child Left Behind, or the movement in favor of mayoral control. Changes such as these alter the grid on which groups plan their political strategies. Henig explores the political implications of these changes for public engagement for public education.

Part II provides a more detailed examination of the five streams of public engagement for public education. In Chapter 4, Donn Worgs describes and analyzes coproduction—parents and community members working together with teachers and other education officials to improve the quality of educational services. In the contemporary United States, there are countless cases of citizens coproducing public education that are specifically focused on enhancing equity and learning for students from economically and racially marginalized communities. Drawing on his research in Baltimore; Washington, DC; and Hampton, Virginia, Worgs analyzes parents and other community members as they create supplementary instruction through various after-school or weekend programs and mobilize community resources to establish alternative public schools in the form of "mission-oriented" charter schools. This analysis shows that, through coproduction, lay people can provide professionals with valuable knowledge and schools with additional resources.

In Chapter 5, Luis Fraga and Ann Frost explore how community members come together to engage in the electoral process—a major component of democratic governance. Public engagement in terms of democratic governance is more than voting and elections; it is also about forging strategic relationships with public officials and key private actors. The authors focus on the case of Latino parents to explore the opportunities and challenges of expanding civic participation to non-elites. They consider how communities collectively deploy their civic capacity to make their positions known and, ultimately, to shape official actions.

In Chapter 6, Mark Warren examines community organizing as an avenue for public engagement in public education. Warren draws on the experiences of a variety of community organizing "traditions" and "methods," including faith-based organizing. He shows how community organizing constitutes a distinct tradition that differs in focus from the better-known forms of advocacy group politics and issue mobilization. Rather than advocating "for" people, organizing seeks to develop the capacity of people to be collective agents and leaders for change.

Chapter 7 makes the point that broad political changes require forms of public engagement that extend beyond the reach of coproduction, democratic governance, or community organizing—particularly given the realities of the new political grid that Jeff Henig discusses in Chapter 3. Lauren Wells, Jean Anyon, and Jeannie Oakes explore how and under what conditions diverse groups come together in alliances, and ultimately social movements, to shape educational policy. They explore the characteristics of coalitions and alliances that could be the building blocks of a broad-based social movement for educational equality.

Part III provides empirical evidence from four communities in different regions of the country. Chapters 8, 9, 10, and 11 illuminate what communities seek to change through public engagement, how avenues for public engagement emerge, and how challenges and opportunities shape these efforts. The cases attend to how previously marginalized groups take on new roles in education policy and civic life.

In Chapter 8, Sara McAlister, Kavitha Mediratta, and Seema Shah use Chicago as a case study to explore the emergence of a community-driven initiative for the development of teachers from the local neighborhood. This effort responded to twin challenges of many Chicago schools—the lack of qualified teachers and the alienation of community members from the existing professional staff. The authors consider how community interests coalesced on this issue. They also document how groups used community organizing strategies and alliance building first to win commitments from local schools and later to secure statewide policies related to teacher recruitment, development, and retention.

In Chapter 9, John Rogers and Ernest Morrell examine the efforts of youth organizing groups to create a more robust civic life and better schools in Los Angeles. They consider youth organizing as a powerful context for young people to develop civic knowledge, skills, and commitments. They also explore how youth organizing can be linked to broad-based alliances that build power and win new policies. Rogers and Morrell document how an array of youth organizing groups joined with one another and then allied with more mainstream civic organizations to press for, and ultimately win, a new district-wide policy ensuring all students access to a college-preparatory curriculum.

Chapter 10 is a case study of Mobile, Alabama. It is an in-depth examination of community-wide public engagement, incorporating elites and grass roots. Brenda Turnbull documents and explains how civic and community leaders in Mobile organized a broad-based public engagement effort in which residents articulated a vision for the education of all children, pressed for school improvement aligned with that vision, and monitored the system's progress.

Chapter 11 examines public engagement in a school public system increasingly dominated by market values. Elaine Simon, Eva Gold, and Maia Cucchiara show that as contracting has become the prevailing vehicle for participation in Philadelphia schools, market-oriented nonprofits and private and for-profit groups have gained ground, while community organizing groups are struggling to find ways to ensure that programs and agendas reflect the needs and aspirations of their constituents.

In the concluding chapter, we draw on the cases of Chicago, Los Angeles, Mobile, and Philadelphia to consider what makes public engagement a distinctive approach to equity educational reform. We articulate an agenda for further research on public engagement for public education, closing with some final thoughts on the challenges to and possibilities for realizing robust public engagement in the current political and economic environment.

References

Akiba, Motoko, Gerald LeTendre, and Jay Scribner. 2007. Teacher Quality, Opportunity Gap, and Achievement Gap in 47 Countries. *Educational Researcher* 36 (7): 369–387.

American Political Science Association. 2004. "American Democracy in an Age of Rising Inequality," Task Force on Inequality and American Democracy. Washington, DC: Author.

Anyon, Jean. 2005. *Radical Possibilities: Public Policy, Urban Education, and a New Social Movement*. New York: Routledge.

Arias, M. Beatrice, and Milagros Morillo-Campbell. 2008. *Promoting ELL Parental Involvement: Challenges in Contested Times*. Boulder: Education and the Public Interest, University of Colorado–Boulder. Accessed at http://epsl.asu.edu/epru/documents/EPSL-0801-250-EPRU.pdf.

Boyte, Harry C. 2004. *Everyday Politics*. Philadelphia: University of Pennsylvania Press.

Buckley, Jack, and Mark Schneider. 2007. *Charter Schools: Hope or Hype?* Princeton, NJ: Princeton University Press.

Calabrese-Barton, Angela, Corey Drake, Jose Perez, Kathleen St. Louis, and Magnia George. 2004. Ecologies of Parental Engagement in Urban Education. *Educational Researcher* 33 (4): 3–12.

Campbell, Angus, Philip E. Converse, Warren E. Miller, and Donald E. Stokes. 1960. *The American Voter*. Chicago: University of Chicago Press.

Carvalho, Maria Eulina P. de. 2000. *Rethinking Family-School Relations: A Critique of Parental Involvement in Schools*. Mahwah, NJ: Lawrence Erlbaum.

Cohen, Cathy. 1999. *The Boundaries of Blackness*. Chicago: University of Chicago Press.

Cortes, Ernesto. 1996. Community Organization and Social Capital. *National Civic Review* 85 (3): 49–54.

Crawford, Susan, and Peggy Levitt. 1999. Social Change and Civic Engagement: The Case of the PTA. In *Civic Engagement in American Democracy*, ed. Theda Skocpol and Morris Fiorina, 249–296. Washington, DC: Brookings Institution Press.

Darling-Hammond, Linda. 2007. The Flat Earth and Education: How America's Commitment to Equity Will Determine Our Future. *Educational Researcher* 36 (6): 318–334.

Dillon, Sam. 2007. Alabama Plan Brings Out Cry of Resegregation. *New York Times*, September 17.

Dreier, Peter, John Mollenkopf, and Todd Swanstrom. 2005. *Place Matters: Metropolitics for the Twenty-first Century.* Lawrence: University Press of Kansas.

Ganz, Marshall. 2002. What Is Organizing? *Social Policy* 33 (1): 16–18.

Hancock, Ange-Marie. 2007. *The Politics of Disgust: The Public Identity of the Welfare Queen.* New York: New York University Press.

Hochschild Jennifer, and Nathan Scovronick. 2003. *The American Dream and the Public Schools.* New York: Oxford University Press.

Horvat, Erin, Elliot Weininger, and Annette Lareau. 2003. From Social Ties to Social Capital: Class Differences in the Relation Between School and Parent Networks. *American Educational Research Journal* 4 (2): 319–351.

Jeynes, William. 2003. A Meta-Analysis: The Effects of Parental Involvement on Minority Children's Academic Achievement. *Education and Urban Society* 35 (2): 202–218.

Kozol, Jonathan. 1992. *Savage Inequalities.* New York: Vintage Press.

Ladson-Billings, Gloria. 2006. From the Achievement Gap to the Education Debt: Understanding Achievement in U.S. Schools. *Educational Researcher* 35 (7): 3–12.

Lareau, Annette. 2003. *Unequal Childhoods: Class, Race, and Family Life.* Berkeley: University of California Press.

Lareau, Annette, and Erin Horvat. 1999. Moments of Inclusions, Class, Cultural Capital in Family-School Relationships. *Sociology of Education* 72 (1): 37–53.

Lareau, Annette, and Elliot Weininger. 2003. Cultural Capital in Educational Research: A Critical Assessment. *Theory and Society* 32 (5–6): 567–606.

Levy, Frank, and Richard Murnane. 2004. *The New Division of Labor: How Computers Are Changing the Way We Work.* New York: Russell Sage Foundation Press.

Lightfoot, Sara Lawrence. 1981. Toward Conflict and Resolution: Relationships Between Families and Schools. *Theory into Practice* 20 (2): 97–104.

———. 2003. *The Essential Conversation: What Parents and Teachers Can Learn from Each Other.* New York: Random House.

Macedo, Stephen, Yvette Alex-Assensoh, Jeffrey M. Berry, Michael Brintnall, David E. Cambell, Luis Ricardo Fraga, William A. Galston, Christopher F. Karpowitz, Margaret Levi, Meira Levinson, Keena Lipsitz, Richard G. Niemi, Robert D. Putnam, Wendy M. Rahn, Bob Reich, Robert R. Rodgers, Todd Swanstrom, and Katherine Cramer Walsh. 2005. *Democracy at Risk: How Political Choices Undermine Political Participation and What We Can Do About It.* Washington, DC: Brookings Institution Press.

Massey, Douglas S., and Nancy A. Denton. 1993. *American Apartheid: Segregation and the Making of the Underclass.* Cambridge, MA: Harvard University Press.

McAdams, Don. 2005. *Fighting for Our Schools and Winning.* New York: Teachers College Press.

Medirata, Kavitha, and Jessica Karp. 2003. "Parent Power and Urban School Reform: The Story of Mothers on the Move." New York: Institute for Education and Social Policy, New York University.

Mettler, Suzanne. 2002. Bring the State Back in to Civic Engagement: Policy Feedback Effects of the G.I. Bill for World War II Veterans. *American Political Science Review* 96 (2): 351–365.

Morris, Aldon. 1984. *The Origins of the Civil Rights Movement.* New York: Free Press.

Oakes, Jeannie. 2005. *Keeping Track: How Schools Structure Inequality.* New Haven, CT: Yale University Press.

Oakes, Jeannie, and John Rogers. 2006. *Learning Power: Organizing for Education and Justice.* New York: Teachers College Press.

Orr, Marion. 2007. Community Organizing and the Changing Ecology of Civic Engagement. In *Transforming the City: Community Organizing and the Challenge of Political Change*, ed. Marion Orr, 1–27. Lawrence: University of Kansas Press.

Payne, Charles M. 1995. *I've the Light of Freedom: Organizing Traditions and the Mississippi Freedom Struggle.* Berkeley: University of California Press.

Peterson, Paul. 1981. *City Limits.* Chicago: University of Chicago Press.

Pierson, Paul. 1993. When Effect Becomes Cause: Policy Feedback and Political Change. *World Politics* 45: 595–628.

Putnam, Robert. 2000. *Bowling Alone: The Collapse and Revival of American Community.* New York: Simon & Schuster.

Ramirez, A. Y. 2003. Dismay and Disappointment. Parental Involvement for Immigrant Parents. *Urban Review* 35 (2): 93–110.

Reay, Diane. 1998. *Class Work: Mothers' Involvement in Children's Schooling.* London: University College Press.

Rogers, John. 2004. Creating a Public Accountability for California's Schools. *Teachers College Record* 106 (11): 2171–2192.

———. 2006. Forces of Accountability? The Power of Poor Parents in NCLB. *Harvard Educational Review* 76 (4): 611–641.

Schattsneider, E. E. 1960. *Semisovereign People: A Realist View of Democracy in America.* New York: Holt, Rinehart and Winston.

Schrag, Peter. 2003. *Final Test: The Battle for Adequacy in America's Schools.* New York: The New Press.

Smock, Kristina. 2004. *Democracy in Action: Community Organizing and Urban Change.* New York: Columbia University Press.

Smrekar, Claire, and Lora Cohen-Vogel. 2001. The Voices of Parents: Rethinking the Intersection of Family and School. *Peabody Journal of Education* 76 (2): 75–101.

Soss, Joe, and Sanford F. Schram. 2007. A Public Transformed? Welfare Reform as Policy Feedback. *American Political Science Review* 101 (1): 111–127.

Stall, Susan, and Randy Stocker. 1998. Community Organizing or Organizing Community: Gender and the Crafts of Empowerment. *Gender and Society* 12 (6): 729–756.

Strolovitch, Dara Z. 2006. Do Interest Groups Represent the Disadvantaged? Advocacy at the Intersections of Race, Class and Gender. *Journal of Politics* 68 (4): 897–910.

———. 2007. *Affirmative Advocacy: Race, Class, and Gender in Interest Group Politics.* Chicago: University of Chicago Press.

Tarrow, Sidney. 1994. *Power in Movement: Social Movements, Collective Action and Mass Politics in the Modern State.* Cambridge: Cambridge University Press.

Tyack, David. 2003. Seeking Common Ground: Public Schools in a Diverse Society. Cambridge, MA: Harvard University Press.

U.S. Census Bureau. 2006–2008. American Community Survey Summary Tables, generated by John Rogers using American FactFinder. Accessed at http://factfinder .census.gov.

Verba, Sidney, Kay Lehman Schlozman, and Henry E. Brady. 1995a. *Voice and Equality: Civic Voluntarism in American Politics.* Cambridge, MA: Harvard University Press.

———. 1995b. Beyond SES: A Resource Model of Political Participation. *British Journal of Political Science* 89 (4): 271–294.

Warren, Mark R. 2005. Communities and Schools: A New View of Urban Education Reform. *Harvard Educational Review* 75 (2): 133–173.

Wells, Amy Stuart, and Robert L. Crain. 1997. *Stepping Over the Color Line: African-American Students in White Suburban Schools.* New Haven, CT: Yale University Press.

Wilson, William J. 1987. *The Truly Disadvantaged.* Chicago: University of Chicago Press.

———. 1996. *When Work Disappears.* New York: Knopf.

The Context of Public Engagement
for Public Education

2 A Brief History of Public Engagement in American Public Education

Dennis Shirley

THE HISTORICAL ORIGINS OF THE "ENGAGEMENT GAP" in public education in the United States extend back centuries. Ever since the U.S. Constitution was ratified, different groups have been excluded from formal definitions of the public or have had their citizenship so qualified that they have been compelled to create "counter-publics" for themselves. Thus, we are now confronted with the irony that the very term *public*—from the Latin *publius*, "of or pertaining to the people"—always has included some of the people and excluded others in American history.

This contradictory meaning of *public* was evident in the origins of public schools. Thomas Jefferson commonly is credited with proposing the first tax-funded, democratically governed public school system in the United States. His 1779 "Bill for the More General Diffusion of Knowledge" in Virginia proposed a unified system of common schools and grammar schools that would prepare top students for scholarships to attend the College of William and Mary in Williamsburg. The purpose of the schools was to inculcate a strict republican credo. "Every government degenerates when trusted to the rulers of the people alone," Jefferson wrote in his *Notes on the State of Virginia*. "The people themselves therefore are its only safe depositories. And to render even them safe their minds must be improved to a certain degree" (Jefferson 1787/1982, 148).

Jefferson's proposal entailed dividing each of Virginia's counties into "wards" or "hundreds" that would hold elections for school committee members or "aldermen," who would hire teachers, construct and maintain school buildings, and appoint school inspectors. "My partiality for that division," wrote Jefferson, "is not founded in views of education solely, but infinitely more as the means of a better administration of our government, and the eternal preservation of its republican principles." Jefferson was intent on establishing school governance by those parents and community members who had the greatest stake in their success. "If it is believed that these elementary schools will be better managed by the governor and council than by the parents within each ward," he argued, "it is a belief against all experience" (Jefferson, quoted in Pangle and Pangle 1993, 119).

Jefferson's proposal excluded Virginia's African American population, both free and enslaved, from consideration, and white girls were to receive an education only at the elementary school level. Only propertied white men would be permitted to vote for the aldermen, a provision governing all Virginia franchise laws at the time. Hence, the proposal divided the public into a formal, franchised set of electors and an informal public excluded from democratic participation. Although the bill was too radical for the Virginia planter elite who made up the state legislature and defeated it in 1779 and again (in a modified form) in 1817, Jefferson's efforts left an important political legacy that differed from the first public school systems in Europe, which arose in the monarchical states of Sweden and Prussia. U.S. public schools were founded not only for education of the young, but, in Jefferson's words, "infinitely more" for the practice of public engagement.

By the 1830s the momentum for educational change had shifted from the South to New England, where reformers such as Horace Mann and Henry Barnard battled for tax-supported, democratically controlled schools for all children (MacMullen 1991; Messerli 1971). Like Jefferson, the New England reformers wanted to overcome the haphazard arrangement of schooling in which children's education depended on their parents' ability to pay for a teacher, on proximity to a school house, or on the proof that they were paupers and needed charity schooling. In contrast to Jefferson, Mann was an outspoken abolitionist, hating slavery not only for its physical exploitation, but also for denying education to enslaved people. For Mann, equal access to education was crucial to achieve a basic level of social justice in American society: education could be "the great equalizer of the conditions of men—the balance-wheel of the social machinery" (Mann, cited in Cremin 1957, 87).

In spite of widespread opposition to common school reform, Mann, Barnard, and their allies made headway, and by 1870 every state had at least the beginnings of a public school system. Yet, over the past century and a half,

American public schools have not realized Mann's goal of social and educational equality. Slavery was abolished, but racism endured with enormous consequences for black children's access to schooling. Other groups of children similarly experienced limits to education. Beginning in the late nineteenth century and continuing well into the twentieth, Native American children were removed from their families and communities and sent to distant boarding schools (Adams 1995). In the Southwest, Hispanic students were also segregated. Cities like Houston, Texas, had tripartite, caste-like systems of public schooling with separate schools for whites, blacks, and Hispanics (San Miguel 1987). As industrialization and urbanization advanced, separate tracks were established in schools largely based on parents' social class backgrounds. Even after the struggles for social justice in the 1960s, public schools remain internally and externally stratified by race, class, and ethnicity. While public schools now have expanded their reach to serve all groups of students, there remains a division, albeit more nuanced than in Jefferson's time, between the formal and enfranchised public and the counter-public or informal public of the disenfranchised.

This enduring legacy of inequality has had as one of its consequences a persistent uneven distribution of public engagement for public education (although some important exceptions are documented in this volume). Analysts have offered a host of factors that foster inequalities of engagement. These include intimidation by school authorities, bureaucratic constraints, the rise of complex new accountability regimes, and teachers' wariness if not animosity toward parents. Yet beyond diagnosing the problem, an affiliated question emerges: how can we overcome these multiple factors and foster a more inclusive public engagement that will revitalize public schools and American democracy (Nagel 1987; Verba and Nie 1972)?

We can identify times in the past when Americans struggled to build an inclusive public engagement for public education and, reminiscent of Jefferson's quest, have made educational and public gains. Here, I identify five "conjunctures"—discrete historical periods in which new kinds of political, social, and educational changes occurred concurrently—selected because they illustrate how public engagement for public schools has been enacted and contested in the past. The concept of "conjunctures," as an organizing strategy, draws on (but is not limited to) the historiography of Karl Marx, who used it in studying regime changes in eighteenth- and nineteenth-century Europe (Marx 1852/1972, 1887/1967; see also Skocpol 1979). Each of these conjunctures in turn has been linked to the five forms of public engagement that Marion Orr and John Rogers identified in the Introduction to this volume. The conjunctures are as follows:

- The ex-slaves' *co-construction* of public education in the aftermath of the Civil War in the South
- Struggles for *democratic governance* of public schools in the Progressive Era at the close of the nineteenth and beginning of the twentieth century
- The emergence of *youth as participants in social movements* and their impact on public education in the 1960s
- The evolution of a new political ecology in which the complexities of developing *educational alliances and coalitions* grew in significance in the 1970s and 1980s
- The growth of *community organizing* for educational change from the 1990s to the present

The varieties of public engagement often coexisted, and the examples presented here must be viewed chiefly as heuristic devices. For example, the theme of democratic governance in the Progressive Era went hand in glove with the rise of the labor movement, various forms of co-constructed vacation schools and after-school activities, and the rise of new educational alliances that linked middle-class women's groups, socialist and populist parties, and ethnically based voluntary associations. The goal of this chapter is to identify recurrent themes that have emerged when different social groups have sought to expand public engagement for public education. With this historical context in mind, subsequent chapters in this volume explore the manner in which the forms of public engagement continue to be manifested and challenged in contemporary American education.

Co-Construction: African American Education in the South After the Civil War

Co-construction refers to the ability of a variety of actors—teachers, parents' associations, civil servants, and members of intermediary associations—to improve public education through shared voluntary action. To a certain extent, such "co-construction" was prevalent in American education before the creation of the American public school system in the decades between 1830 and 1870, but not in any systematic way.

The antebellum common school reform movement in the North and West sought to expand educational opportunity, but the movement failed to penetrate into the South before the Civil War. The southern planter class viewed public education as contrary to its self-interest and scuttled virtually every effort to create public schools. The same planter elite enforced laws that prohibited teaching literacy to blacks in any setting, such as churches or private residences. Horace Mann's association with abolitionism reinforced white southern antipathy to common schools. This antipathy was so strong that public schools were not even created to serve southern white children. Only in North Carolina and a few seaport cities, such as Mobile, Charleston, Savannah, and New Orleans, did a few early manifestations of common school reform appear. In effect, the political opportunity structure of the antebellum South was a closed system with no mechanisms for including the four million slaves in the shared creation of public life (Newman 1990; Williams 2005).

A number of social and political transformations needed to occur to establish the conditions necessary for public engagement for universal public education in the South. First, an abolitionist social movement had to be created and sustained over decades that would compel white Americans to confront the brutality and injustice of slavery. Second, given a complete breakdown in the political process, a bloody Civil War needed to be waged that would lead to the emancipation of the slaves and bring them into the body politic through the Fourteenth Amendment to the Constitution. Third, the freed people would need to mobilize themselves to co-construct with their allies a more inclusive public for public education in the South.

In recent decades, a new body of scholarship has emerged that describes just how radically newly emancipated blacks engaged themselves in educational activities after the Civil War. Scholars such as Leon Litwack (1979), Herbert Gutman (1987), James Anderson (1988), and Heather Andrea Williams (2005) have shown that significant as were the contributions of the Freedmen's Bureau, northern philanthropic societies, and hundreds of northern "schoolmarms" who volunteered to go south to instruct the ex-slaves, it was the freed people themselves who undertook the most challenging work associated with their education. Evidence comes from the correspondence of the chief inspector of schools for the Freedman's Bureau, John Alvord, who described what he called "native schools" spread throughout the South that were unattached to sources of support beyond the immediate community (Alvord quoted in Gutman 1987, 269) In these native schools parents hired teachers from their own communities who had acquired literacy surreptitiously under slavery, boarded the teachers in their homes, paid them through supply (often farm products they had grown), and pooled their resources to build schools. They defended their schools from the Ku Klux Klan and other white militias. This community-based leadership was informed by what James Anderson described as core "values of self-help and self-determination" (Anderson 1988, 5). It was a dramatic revolutionary invention of a new kind of public education characterized by the dual "quest for freedom *and* literacy" (Stepto 1991, 196).

Hence, the major players in the co-construction of the ex-slaves' education in the South were the freedpeople themselves: artisans who contributed their labor to build new schools out of brick and lumber; parents who contributed to the sustenance of teachers, largely based on their ability to pay; ministers who donated church space for classroom instruction; and adults who flooded into the new schools after a hard day of labor in the fields. It was the former slaves themselves who drove the shaping of a new political opportunity structure and a new public engagement for public schools.

A host of secondary actors also played important roles. The American Missionary Association sent hundreds of black and white northern "schoolmarms" south whose prior access to formal educations were a welcome supplement to the native schools. These women had to cope with outraged southern whites, who considered their familiarity and friendship with the ex-slaves to be an affront to their traditional customs and mores. The Freedmen's Bureau built hundreds of new schools in the South, and federal troops played crucial roles in preventing terrorist attacks both on isolated rural schools and on traveling "schoolmarms" en route to their southern destinations. Finally, southern white Republicans united with the ex-slaves in Reconstruction-era state congresses to pass legislation beginning the first southern public school systems five years after the Civil War (Faulkner 2004; Morris 1976).

The result of these multifarious forms of co-construction was an explosion of teaching and learning, as well as a new kind of public engagement in public education. The military defeat of the Confederacy; the blossoming of local, grassroots initiatives among former slaves; the contribution of outside assistance in the form of northern philanthropic support; and the empowerment under congressional Reconstruction of southern Republicans who had been suppressed by the Confederacy opened a new political ecology for public schools. Previously disconnected constituencies found new ways to combine their efforts to extend the common school reform program south, forever changing the history of American education in the process.

The new public space for public education was quickly challenged. The Freedmen's Bureau ended its educational activities in 1870 with the emergence of state systems. This withdrawal signaled a weakening of federal support for educating the freedpeople. Accommodating themselves to postwar economic realities while strategically examining ways to regain political control, white supremacist "redeemer" politicians slowly gained power throughout the South in the 1870s, and they used a variety of tactics to withhold revenues from black public schools. Reconstruction formally drew to a close in 1877 with the withdrawal of federal troops from the South, leaving the former slaves once again on their own in regard to white southern hegemony. The painstaking efforts of the freedpeople and their allies to establish political power during Reconstruction were systematically eroded in the following decades. Finally, in 1896 the U.S. Supreme Court ruled in *Plessy v. Ferguson* that the provision of "separate but equal" public facilities to blacks and whites was constitutional, providing white southerners with a pretext for excluding blacks from any meaningful participation in the public sphere and sharply curtailing their possibilities for improving their children's schools. The brief moment of euphoria and zeal for education experienced by the freedpeople with the end of slavery was suppressed, demonstrating just how fragile the conditions were in the South for creating a more inclusive public sphere for public education.

Democratic Governance: The Progressive Era

Early New Englanders were the first to organize local public schools into state systems. As rural areas evolved into townships and townships expanded into cities, school districts were formed and then divided into different wards with their own representatives that served on the larger district-wide school committees. As districts grew, the number of school committee members multiplied. The participatory character of educational governance reflected the widely held belief that school committee members would prove responsive to their local constituencies and would become practiced in the arts of self-governance. Few school superintendents were appointed in the nineteenth century, with the result that enormous power was consolidated in the hands of those elected through the ward system.

In spite of its democratic foundations, the ward system had many political problems. Enterprising journalists and middle-class women's groups repeatedly uncovered graft and favoritism, including unqualified teacher applicants who bribed school committee members; textbook companies that rewarded school committees with favors, including parties and prostitutes; and construction bids awarded to friends and family members. In many cases committees ignored the needs of teachers and children and instead became mired in elaborate payback schemes that undermined public confidence in the schools.

Starting in the 1960s, some historians questioned the prevalence of graft and corruption in school wards, arguing that this depiction was used by elites to narrow school board service to just a few individuals selected through city-wide elections. These historians contended that school wards were important venues for immigrants to obtain a voice in urban politics and that a new group of "good government" advocates wanted to constrain democratic participation to advance their own class interests. Subsequent research by William Reese has shown, however, that school committee members chosen through the ward system almost exclusively consisted of white, propertied professionals. It appears to be the case that the old ward systems were brought down not just by a new managerial elite, but also by a wide array of voluntary associations, including middle-class women's associations that assailed the ward leaders for misdirecting public resources away from the children who were the original intended beneficiaries (Reese 2002; Tyack 1974).

As a result of abuses in the ward system, a new group of professionalizing reformers, described by David Tyack (1974) as "administrative progressives," were able to push through a wide range of centralizing agendas intended to give public schools the same efficiency and outcomes they associated with the nation's largest and most successful corporations. The administrative progressives wanted smaller school boards elected from throughout the city rather than from wards or neighborhoods. They wanted to concentrate power in the hands of a full-time professional school superintendent rather than distributing it among school committee members. They had no patience with the normal give-and-take of the political process and instead favored the streamlined "principles of scientific management" espoused by Frederick Taylor. The administrative progressives argued that a school system could be more effective if run by individuals whose public service interests were not politically partisan or shaped by local or personal interests.

From one point of view, the defeat of the old ward system diminished public engagement for public education. Fewer school committee members meant fewer political and educational interactions among friends and neighbors.

These face-to-face relationships had been ordinary citizens' pipeline into the political process and could be a first step in running for higher offices. Having fewer school committee members made it more difficult for parents to ask a local leader for help for a struggling pupil or get information about school district policies or informal school practices. This separation of school politics from everyday local interactions was problematic at the time and remains so today.

Although the above critique is accurate in many regards, it does not account for other avenues of local participation in education. For example, a proliferation of grassroots advocacy groups during the Progressive Era kept democratic participation strong. During centralization, an expansive coalition of socialist, populist, and feminist advocates sponsored a school health movement for poor and working-class children to receive vaccinations and some dental care. Similar alliances, sometimes with the support of middle-class and business allies, developed the nation's first reduced-price breakfasts and lunches for children in cities like Milwaukee, Toledo, Rochester, and Kansas City. Teachers' unions and trade unions during this time advocated successfully for vacation schools, playgrounds, and educational extension activities for working-class adults in all cities (Reese 2002).

In a curious, perhaps counterintuitive way, centralization seems to have gone hand-in-hand with a number of politically progressive reforms. It appears that the new, more centralized political ecology made favoritism and the cutting of special deals at the ward level more difficult and compelled individuals to cast their particular problems as larger collective challenges. In Jean Anyon's (1997) account of struggles related to democratic governance in Newark, New Jersey, state legislation enabled mayors to dissolve boards of education, and the election of a reformist mayor broke a vicious circle of patronage and graft that characterized both that city's ward system *and* its smaller and centralized successor. Like Anyon, contemporary advocates of "empowered participatory governance" have argued that a measure of top-down control and oversight is often crucial to break up corrupt patronage systems and to protect sectors of the "informal public," such as children, from systems like school bureaucracies. That trade union organizing was expanding rapidly during the Progressive Era and that a trust-busting president—Teddy Roosevelt—dominated national politics for two terms in the midst of this era indicated that strong leaders at the state and national level could play crucial roles in protecting the poor and disenfranchised. An important lesson from the

Progressive Era is that public engagement for public education may be conditioned less by the exact mechanics of how individuals are elected or appointed to school committees or by the kind of procedures used to appoint superintendents and other officials and may be influenced more by the ability of grassroots groups to mobilize continually to compel elected officials to advance politically progressive agendas (Anyon 1997; Fung and Wright 2003).

The Emergence of Youth in the Social Movements in the 1960s

Following the Progressive Era, the 1920s was generally a period of economic and political conservatism. The 1930s brought a dramatic expansion of federal executive leadership along with a network of agencies such as the Works Progress Administration and the National Youth Administration, which were more concerned about serving and empowering the most socially disenfranchised young Americans than their local school districts ever were. In many ways World War II slowed the social reforms associated with the New Deal while the nation focused its attention on the military campaigns. It was not until the 1954 *Brown v. Board of Education* Supreme Court decision that a new educational conjuncture emerged, although one year later the tentative language of the *Brown II* decision, permitting school integration with "all deliberate speed," essentially endorsed the continuation of segregation for an undefined period of time (Kluger 1975; Tyack, Hansot, and Lowe 1984).

Court-based litigation was enormously important in providing a political opening for integration. Nonetheless, to translate a court order into everyday practice in the nation's schools, a particular kind of public engagement for public education would need to evolve. Significantly, much of the leadership in this terrain came from youth of color, who employed a variety of tactics in pursuit of social justice.

In 1957 African American youth who constituted the "Little Rock Nine" drew national attention as they courageously withstood the violence and jeers of white mobs that threatened them on a daily basis while they integrated that city's major public high school. Three years later, in February 1960, four African American freshmen from the North Carolina Agricultural and Technical College launched the first "sit-in" at an F. W. Woolworth's lunch counter in Greensboro, North Carolina, and provided another moral example of how young people who could not yet vote (at the time the voting age was twenty-one) could dramatize social injustice and agitate for change. Within less than three months, another fifty thousand black high school and college students in the South had engaged in similar sit-in actions, presenting a dramatic challenge to the entire social caste system that still persisted years after the *Brown* ruling rendered illegal the provision of separate but equal public facilities to blacks and whites (Carson 1981; Flacks 1971).

The spontaneous spread of the sit-ins by young people caught virtually everyone by surprise, including the leaders of the civil rights movement; never before had any social group of American high school and college students so rapidly seized on a social issue and thrust it into the forefront of public debate. The sit-ins galvanized not only black high school and college students in the South but also white and black students in the North, who began sympathy boycotts of F. W. Woolworth's stores and other national chains with segregated facilities in the South. "The sit-ins and the black student movement seemed to be part of a general historical process in which students, *acting in their role as students*, had become effective agents of social change," Richard Flacks later wrote (1971, 75). "Instead of waiting for leadership from other elements in the society and to promote social reform, students themselves could actually have historical effects."

Nowhere was this latent leadership capacity of young people themselves more evident than in Birmingham, Alabama, in spring 1963. After a year-long struggle in Albany, Georgia, failed to integrate public facilities, including schools, Martin Luther King Jr. decided to make Birmingham the focus of a far-reaching campaign of nonviolent civil disobedience. In many ways pervasive problems had stalled the civil rights movement. Key movement leaders, including King, were spending increasing amounts of time in jail, dramatizing the injustice of segregation but simultaneously depriving the movement of talent and direction. Obstacles included the southern white clergy whom King had addressed in his "Letter from Birmingham Jail" as well as conservative black business leaders who had made their peace with Jim Crow and argued for prudence and restraint. The movement could ill afford another debacle like Albany.

The impetus for revitalizing the movement came from hundreds of black Birmingham youths who had attended workshops on nonviolent civil disobedience held by the Southern Christian Leadership Conference (SCLC) in Birmingham churches. They pressured the movement's leaders for the opportunity to advance the freedom struggle. The turning point came when SCLC activist Reverend James Bevel approached King with the idea of organizing a "children's crusade" to march for integrated public facilities, including schools, in the city of Birmingham.

King approved of the idea, and on May 2, 1963, more than one thousand young people participated in a march for integration, with more than nine hundred arrested and imprisoned by the end of the day. The next day another twenty-five hundred appeared for a similar march, and the police released German shepherds on the crowd and blasted the young demonstrators with high-pressure fire hoses to disperse them. Newspaper and electronic media carried the atrocities in Birmingham to the farthest corners of the globe. By May 6 more than three thousand protestors filled the jails and more than four thousand were still picketing and marching. Feeling the mounting pressure, the city's business leaders worked out a deal with King on May 10 to desegregate many public and private facilities in the city. Although public schools were not an official part of that agreement, they were subsequently integrated under the leadership of mayor-elect Albert Boutwell (Branch 1988; Oates 1982).

The flagrant injustices suffered by the young civil rights activists in Birmingham, more than any other single force, led President John F. Kennedy to overcome his initial recalcitrance and to propose new civil rights legislation to Congress in June 1963. Although Kennedy's untimely death in November did not allow him to see the legislation passed, his understanding of its moral imperative, expressed to the nation in a television address on June 11, demonstrated the power of young people to get results that years of court decisions and dispersed policy initiatives had not achieved. The lesson was clear: young people who did not even possess the vote or the ability to sit on a jury could be major social activists who could change the contours of American history. Young people could create altogether new forms of public engagement for public education through sit-ins, picket lines, Freedom Rides, and demonstrations.

The newly discovered possibilities entailed in youth activism shaped the rest of the 1960s. From fall 1963 to spring 1964, hundreds of thousands of K–12 public school students participated in one-day boycotts of segregated schooling not in the South, but in northern cities such as Boston, Chicago, and Cleveland. The largest of these entailed more than 464,000 New Yorkers in February 1964, followed by another boycott by 268,000 in March. In the summer of 1964 the Congress on Racial Equality, the Student Non-violent Coordinating Committee, and the National Association for the Advancement of Colored People launched thirty "Freedom Schools" in Mississippi. These schools educated more than three thousand African American youth with a new style of emancipatory pedagogy that linked literacy acquisition to social activism and provided "an electric experience for teachers and students alike" (Payne, 1995, 303) through a "Citizenship Curriculum" that was popular with students because it affirmed their longing for social justice and gave them political tools to pursue it (Perlstein 2004).

Exasperated with the slow pace of change, including that of Democratic Party leaders at the party's national convention in 1964, young people increasingly took educational matters into their own hands. Students for a Democratic Society (SDS), a fledgling organization with just twenty-five hundred members, expanded fourfold within one year by organizing "teach-ins" on college and high school campuses against the rapidly expanding war in Vietnam. A new generation of teachers, shocked at the injustices of urban education, started "free schools" modeled on the Freedom Schools. Underground newspapers, radio stations, and "schools without walls" blossomed, offering counter-narratives to mainstream public discourse and creating new venues for young people to question and challenge established social mores.

As the decade progressed, the spirit of social protest spread. In 1968, college students in California organizing through the United Mexican American Students coordinated a massive student "blowout," or boycott, in the Los Angeles Unified School District. Calling for classes on Mexican American culture and history and the hiring of more Chicano teachers and administrators, the Los Angeles blowout inspired similar student protests in Denver, Phoenix, and San Antonio. The protests continued into 1969, reaching even into smaller rural communities in the Lower Rio Grande Valley in Texas (Acuna 2000; Navarro 1995; Shirley 2002).

The various manifestations of youth activism in the 1960s combined to change American society forever. Without the thousands of sit-ins, teach-ins, and raw courage exhibited by demonstrators such as the protestors in Birmingham in 1963, it is hard to imagine how long federal civil rights legislation might have been delayed and how much longer the war in Vietnam might have continued. Yet youth activism showed certain limitations. Most youth activists in the 1960s lacked the vote, a crucial lever for determining local, state, and federal political leaders. Their tactics of mass demonstrations, sit-ins, and boycotts were effective at raising public awareness of issues but favored a certain kind of expressive politics over the nitty-gritty, boiler-room work entailed in proposing, passing, and implementing progressive legislation. Finally, youth is by definition a transient life stage, and a preoccupation with the politics of a generational cohort could lead to an accompanying myopia regarding the need to learn patiently from "local people" with more years of experience and to organize across generations (Dittmer 1994; Payne 1995).

Coalitions and Advocacy in the 1970s and 1980s

Following the 1960s, three trends combined both to benefit and to thwart public engagement for public education. In general terms, these were demographic shifts, legislation to benefit underserved groups, and a federal- and state-level push for higher academic standards.

First, demographic and political changes brought multiethnic political leadership in many of the nation's largest cities and challenged the existing white hegemony. The shifting demographics led to new possibilities for creativity and inclusion but also for conflict and paralysis as many cities, confronted with a declining industrial base and the exodus of the middle class to the suburbs, found it hard to achieve the civic capacity needed to improve schools.

Second, girls, English learners, and students with disabilities benefited from progressive legislation and court rulings that emerged out of the social movements of the 1960s. These included important education equity gains. Regretfully, these very real gains were not linked to any broad and politically powerful strategy for increasing public engagement for public education, and their adjudication often occurred in courtrooms in a technical discourse that did not invite the public engagement of poor and working-class Americans.

Finally, growing public concern that the improvement of American education was stalled led even traditional Republican Party skeptics—like President Ronald Reagan, who had always been opposed to even the existence of a federal Department of Education—to switch course and to endorse far-reaching changes to improve American schools. At the heart of Reagan's reform approach lay the pursuit and attainment of more rigorous academic standards, the setting of which was subsequently contracted out to different professional organizations and likewise did not entail any particular strategy for increasing public engagement.

Hence, in spite of a great deal of school reform activity in the 1970s and 1980s, one finds little enthusiasm for expanding public engagement to include those most marginalized from public influence and most affected by inadequate and unequal schooling opportunities. Several factors contributed to stalling the development of powerful, progressive grassroots constituencies and networks, including economic shifts, diminished civic capacity as capital relocated away from cities, and internal divisions and factions among communities themselves.

Just as minority populations showed signs of growing in political power, the economy was shifting from an industrial to a service economy—entailing weakened labor unions, the loss of workers' benefits, and fragmentation of the working class. Simultaneously, the growing mobility of capital weakened the affinities that older ruling elites felt for a particular city and its prosperity and culture. Middle-class populations, white and black, relocated to suburbs, depriving urban centers of tax revenues and further weakening urban public school systems. These phenomena diminished "civic capacity" for educational improvement—understood here as "concerted efforts to address major community problems" (Stone 2005, 209) by multiple actors or stakeholders in an activity setting (Wilson 1987).

Further, the 1960s social movements exposed fault lines cutting through multiracial and cross-class organizations capable of uniting the poor, the working class, and sectors of the middle class such as teachers and school principals into cohesive and powerful political coalitions. The most notable example was New York City's conflict between the largely white teachers' union and the predominantly black populations of Ocean Hill-Brownsville. The black community's struggle for control of the community's schools left a lasting legacy of animosity and mistrust that fractured what in many ways had been part of the backbone of previous liberal urban coalitions. Court-ordered busing in the 1970s and 1980s ignored the deeper structures and norms that supported segregated housing patterns, provoked a backlash among white voters, and confirmed blacks' skepticism about whites' commitment to integration. Established civil rights activists lost influence and capacity to lead. Leaders such as A. Philip Randolph and Bayard Rustin, who argued for the continued merit of multiracial class-based organizing, found themselves marginalized and discredited in the black community for minimizing the extent of racism among white teachers. Finally, fault lines deepened with the dramatic growth of two social groups, which complicated the black/white framing of equity and integration. Hispanics and Asian Americans created new political constituencies with unique histories, needs, and considerations, often related to linguistic and cultural issues in schools (Clarke et al. 2006; Podair 2002)

Broadly speaking, Americans showed decreasing civic engagement across the political spectrum during the 1970s and 1980s. Americans turned to marketplace solutions to social problems that were previously seen as collective or public, including education, policing, and recreation. Even when Americans expressed political preferences, they increasingly did so through professionally managed associations in which they "participated" by writing a check once a year, never meeting another "member" of the given organization (Putnam 2000; Skocpol 2003).

In the absence of a broad social movement for full educational inclusion, a variety of advocacy groups focused on the particular needs of populations. Some of these groups advocated for equal educational rights for girls and women, bilingual education, and the education of pupils with learning disabilities. In each of these cases, decades of organizing had achieved breakthroughs in securing greater educational access, which was backed by federal law.

In the case of girls' and women's education, the passage of Title IX of the Education Amendment of 1972 to the Civil Rights Act of 1964 prohibited any educational institution receiving federal funds from discriminating against individuals on the basis of their sex. Many of the most famous Title IX lawsuits have pertained to unequal college and university athletics, but the law has had broader and deeper effects than that. Title IX pressured schools to give girls equal opportunities to take advanced placement courses in math and science and provided leverage for reducing sexual stereotypes in textbooks and affiliated curricular materials. Title IX mandated that schools may no longer advise pregnant girls to leave schools, and schools were to encourage girls to explore career opportunities in fields that traditionally had been dominated by men. When schools ignored the law, parents had leverage to sue districts and diminish funding disparities based on gender differences (American Association of University Women Educational Foundation 1995).

Second, in 1968 Senator Ralph Yarborough of Texas sponsored the nation's first Bilingual Education Act, which provided federal funds for pupils who were English language learners. At this time, there was little funding for the act and compliance by districts was strictly voluntary. Then, in a landmark Supreme Court case in 1974 (*Lau v. Nichols*), the Court ruled that it was not sufficient for a school district simply to provide identical instructional materials to children whose home language was not English. Failing to acknowledge and address different language backgrounds, according to the Court, effectively violated Title VI of the Civil Rights Act of 1964, which prohibited discrimination on the basis of national origin. Hence, the Court supported the arguments of the Chinese American plaintiffs on behalf of eighteen hundred children in the San Francisco Unified School District. This finding was especially significant because the Court ruled that equity did not mean providing students with the same materials but, rather, with the same opportunity to succeed. This much more vigorous definition of equity empowered parent activists of English language learners across the nation to push for, and receive, adequate instructional support (Brisk, Burgos, and Hamerla 2004).

Third, the Education for All Handicapped Children Act (Public Law 94–142), passed by Congress in 1975, gave children and youth with special needs, whether physical or mental, the right to a full public education and special accommodations for their disabilities. As with *Lau v. Nichols*, districts could no longer contend that they provided one set of similar conditions to all children (Giordano 2007; Heward and Cavanaugh 2005).

These advances in legislation and law expanded the Civil Rights Act of 1964 beyond race to gender, language, and learning disabilities. The laws represented major historical achievements, but each new law revealed new limits to federal legislation and Supreme Court rulings as well. Without a consistent mobilization of public will, laws designed to promote equity failed to be implemented in meaningful ways.

Perhaps the greatest educational paradox of the 1980s was that Ronald Reagan, who had campaigned for the presidency on a platform of terminating federal activity in schools, became an advocate for sweeping school reform during his first term in office. Reagan had appointed Terrell Bell as secretary of education, expecting him to dismantle the Department of Education (created just a few years earlier during the Carter presidency). Instead, Bell persuaded Reagan to convene a National Commission on Excellence in Education chaired by David Gardner, president of the University of Utah, to conduct a thorough study of American education.

Contrary to expectations, the Commission recommended a strong federal role in its report, *A Nation at Risk: The Imperative for Educational Reform*. The report used dramatic language to argue that "a rising tide of mediocrity . . . threatens our very future as a Nation and a people. . . . If an unfriendly foreign power had attempted to impose on America the mediocre educational performance that exists today," the authors contended, "we might well have viewed it as an act of war. As it stands, we have allowed this to happen to ourselves. . . . We have, in effect, been committing an act of unthinking, unilateral disarmament" (National Commission on Excellence in Education 1983, 5).

In retrospect, the *Nation at Risk* report began a transformation of the Republican Party's view of government responsibilities for education. Whereas voters gave Reagan's education policies a 28 percent approval rating in 1981, 46 percent approved the policies in 1983, after the report was issued. Reagan's successor, George Herbert Walker Bush, extended the new rhetoric of standards and accountability and convened a governors' summit in 1989 to create a new set of (recommended) national standards and assessments. Meanwhile a host of southern Democratic and Republican governors—such as Mark White of Texas, Lamar Alexander of Tennessee, Bill Clinton of Arkansas, and Bill Riley of South Carolina—discovered that they could win votes by persuading educators to agree to more accountability mechanisms in return for additional revenues (Cross 2004).

During the 1970s and 1980s, a new national consensus emerged that education was too important to be left to localities and that state and federal leadership were required to enhance pupil achievement. Bush's 1989 education summit aimed for all states to develop mechanisms to set and approve standards and then for all children to achieve standards set at high levels of proficiency by 2000. The intention was to create a new definition of public engagement in which all parents would receive information about pupil achievement in their children's schools and could use that information to gain a more objective perspective on their children's learning than would be available through a report card or simply by talking with teachers and administrators.

A number of assumptions were built into the new accountability movement. One was that Americans (and especially teachers) could agree on academic standards. A second was that children's progress could be measured objectively. A third was that the public would be able to understand testing data and would enter into meaningful conversations with educators about testing results and their implications. Finally, educators would be able to use the data to inform instruction in order to improve pupil achievement. Each of these assumptions was to be tested in the new political opportunity structure.

Community Organizing

All of the different forms of public engagement discussed thus far have limitations. Co-construction succeeded in the case of African American education in the first years after the Civil War, but co-construction by definition requires multiple parties to develop civic capacity, and with the collapse of federal support for Reconstruction in 1876, southern blacks were largely thrown back on their own resources. Democratic governance can be a vehicle for public engagement, but state-backed sanctions and guidelines must ensure that school systems focus on teaching and learning rather than opening doors to majoritarian advantage or patronage and graft. Youth activism promoted dramatic social changes in the 1960s, but the very strengths of youth movements—their spontaneous, dramatic, and subversive flair—can become weaknesses when issues are complex and need extended deliberation and compromise. Finally, although some previously excluded groups achieved legislative victories and favorable court rulings in the 1970s and 1980s, there did not develop a broad-based, multiracial, and cross-class coalition for school reform. Add to this mixture the increasing popularity of marketplace models of school reform such as charter schools, the use of educational vouchers, and the contracting out of public school funds to educational management organizations, and solutions to the engagement gap seemed elusive.

In light of these problems, one of the most intriguing recent public engagement strategies has been the emergence of community organizing for school reform. For decades community organizers tended to avoid school improvement activities, fearing that the complexities of large school systems would undermine the kinds of pragmatic, fast-paced, and highly visible "actions" that could produce highly visible victories to enable their organizations to build continued power. This reluctance appeared when the Woodlawn Organization in Chicago in the late 1960s attempted to launch new experimental schools with the district. An enormous outpouring of energy to start the schools failed due to a general lack of district capacity to depart from long-established norms and routines—a failure that confirmed organizers' beliefs that large urban districts were essentially organized against the communities that they were supposed to serve (Fish 1973).

In the mid-1980s, however, the Allied Communities of Tarrant (ACT) in Fort Worth, Texas, attempted another round of education organizing. Working with predominantly African American urban congregations, ACT targeted for improvement Morningside Middle School, the lowest-performing of twenty middle schools in Fort Worth with a history of high levels of gang violence. ACT's comprehensive neighborhood campaign included home visits, house meetings, and school assemblies. Within two years, ACT was able to reorganize the school and community, instruction was focused, the school environment was calm, and pupil achievement was the third highest of the middle schools in the district (Shirley 1997; Warren 2001).

Out of this first education organizing effort, community organizations like ACT that were affiliated with the Texas Industrial Areas Foundation (IAF) began to develop momentum for a network of "Alliance Schools" to build civic capacity and improve pupil achievement in other Texas cities such as Houston, San Antonio, Austin, and El Paso. Continuing a multifaceted organizing repertoire of "one-on-one" conversations, home visits, house meetings, research actions, and "accountability sessions," the Texas IAF piloted a model of school improvement that drew on parents as collective advocates for all of the children in their school and community, rather than individual advocates for their own children.

Community organizing during this period sought to overcome the dramatic but sporadic nature of social movements of the 1960s as well as the limitations of the litigation and legislation of the 1970s and 1980s. Social movements had difficulties sustaining themselves when key victories were accomplished and new challenges emerged in new contexts. Legislation and litigation could prove barriers to working-class populations unversed in the technical jargon of the law or the fine points of moving a bill through subcommittees and onto the floor of Congress. Furthermore, from the vantage point of community organizing, the theme of developing indigenous community leadership is generally viewed as far more important than winning a new program or electing the right candidate.

This insistence of community organizers on the priority of the local has not led to parochialism because organizers have made a point of conducting workshops and training sessions on the impact of globalization on local jobs and the necessity of improving education in the light of an emerging knowledge economy. Community organizing has been important in urban education because it provides a theory of action that develops "relational power" to reconnect families, schools, and secondary associations beyond the state or the marketplace. Some of the leading exemplars of the power of this approach include the Oakland Community Organization, which has successfully promoted small schools in collaboration with the school district; the Chicago chapter of the Association of Community Organizations for Reform Now and the Logan Square Neighborhood Association, which have united with other groups to create an innovative "pipeline" program preparing adults in a largely immigrant community to become teachers in the public schools; and the Community Collaborative for District 9 in the South Bronx, which developed a teacher support program in collaboration with New York City Public Schools that reduced teacher attrition from 28 percent to 16 percent in targeted schools in the space of a single year (Gold, Brown, and Simon 2002; Mediratta, Fruchter, and Lewis 2002).

It is still too early to judge the full potential for a nexus of community organizing, community engagement, and schooling for marginalized publics. Schools are already under tremendous external pressures, quite independent of some of the core issues important to communities. For example, organizers today must persuade school principals and superintendents that empowerment strategies for teachers and parents will not distract a school from the push for "adequate yearly progress" required by the No Child Left Behind Act (NCLB; P.L. 107–110) of 2002. Further, once they arrive at a point where they are included in decision-making forums, communities are not uniform in what they advocate. For example, some community organizations, such as People Acting for Community Together (PACT) in Miami, endorsed testing as an objective way of gauging pupil learning, while others, such as the Texas IAF, contended that the tests narrowed the curriculum and reduced instruction to low-level activities focused on memorization and recitation (Shirley and Evans, 2007).

Further, it is not clear that most community organizers actually understand the complexities of teaching and learning that make up the day-to-day pacing of instruction and curriculum development in schools. As Jean Anyon has observed (2005, 185), "School reformers and community organizers, in fact, rarely talk to each other; they typically operate in different social circles." My own research on community organizing in South Texas indicated that while some schools are able to build powerful and enduring relationships with community organizations, in others oppositional teachers can easily scuttle such relationships, arguing that alliances with community groups vitiate their professional autonomy and that groups involved in congregationally based community organizing are especially inappropriate allies given the First Amendment's disestablishment clause on the separation of church and state (Anyon 2005; Shirley 2002).

Conclusion

What conclusions might one draw from this brief history of public engagement for public education? The most important lesson might well be the necessity of perpetual struggle and acknowledgment of the fragility of social justice. Ex-slaves began to co-construct a new public school system for themselves in the South, but white "redeemer" governments came to power in the 1870s, and with the Supreme Court ruling on *Plessy v. Ferguson* in 1896, African Americans could expect little redress from the legal system when battling for integrated public facilities. Gains were made in democratic governance in the Progressive Era but only because centralizing reforms enabled grassroots groups to develop citywide strategies to hold elected officials accountable for implementing reforms that would serve poor and working-class children in the public schools. Youth activism in the social movements of the 1960s was of enormous significance in leading to the Civil Rights Act of 1964, but the subsequent deflection of much of the direct action and spontaneous features of youth organizing into litigation and legislation had the unintended effect of marginalizing public engagement and enhancing the rise of a professional managerial class of political advocates. Community organizing, a promising strategy for promoting the potential of ordinary people to engage in the public arena to improve their schools, entails many strengths but has to navigate carefully between the desires of educators for professional autonomy and the intricacies of new state testing and accountability systems.

It would appear, then, that creating effective participatory mechanisms and a lived, vibrant culture of public engagement for public education is extraordinarily demanding. Public engagement for those excluded on the basis of race, ethnicity, or class is not accomplished simply with the passage of progressive legislation. It requires robust public will and cultural understanding of civic responsibilities and individual rights. We do not know enough at this moment in time about achieving a system and culture of education that would expedite this high level of public engagement. We do, however, have a number of cases of schools and school systems that have overcome the inchoate and often fractured systems of educational politics to create newly empowered and inclusive publics that have improved public education. Yet to understand even those cases sufficiently, additional attention must be directed to the complexities of the newly emerging educational grid, a theme to which Jeff Henig will now turn.

References

Acuna, Rodolfo. 2000. *Occupied America: A History of Chicanos.* New York: Longman.

Adams, David Wallace. 1995. *Education for Extinction: American Indians and the Boarding School Experience 1875–1928.* Lawrence: University Press of Kansas.

American Association of University Women Educational Foundation. 1995. *How Schools Shortchange Girls.* New York: Marlowe & Company.

Anderson, James D. 1988. *The Education of Blacks in the South, 1860–1935*. Chapel Hill: University of North Carolina Press.

Anyon, Jean. 1997. *Ghetto Schooling: A Political Economy of Urban Educational Reform*. New York: Teachers College Press.

———. 2005. *Radical Possibilities: Public Policy, Urban Education, and a New Social Movement*. New York: Routledge.

Branch, Taylor. 1988. *Parting the Waters: America in the King Years, 1954–63*. New York: Touchstone.

Brisk, Maria Estela, Angela Burgos, and Sara Ruth Hamerla. 2004. *Situational Context of Education: A Window into the World of Bilingual Learners*. Mahwah, NJ: Lawrence Erlbaum.

Carson, Clayborne. 1981. *In Struggle: SNCC and the Black Awakening of the 1960s*. Cambridge, MA: Harvard University Press.

Clarke, Susan, Bari Anhalt Erlichson, Luis Fraga, Rodney Hero, and Mara Sidney. 2006. *Multiethnic Moments: The Politics of Urban Education Reform*. Philadelphia: Temple University Press.

Cremin, Lawrence A. 1957. *The Republic and the School: Horace Mann on the Education of Free Men*. New York: Teachers College Press.

Cross, Christopher T. 2004. *Political Education: National Policy Comes of Age*. New York: Teachers College Press.

Dittmer, John. 1994. *Local People: The Struggle for Civil Rights in Mississippi*. Urbana: University of Illinois Press.

Faulkner, Carol. 2004. *Women's Radical Reconstruction: The Freedmen's Aid Movement*. Philadelphia: University of Pennsylvania Press.

Fish, John Hall. 1973. *Black Power, White Control: The Struggle of the Woodlawn Organization in Chicago*. Princeton, NJ: Princeton University Press.

Flacks, Richard. 1971. *Youth and Social Change*. Chicago: Markham.

Fung, Archon, and Erik Olin Wright. 2003. *Deepening Democracy: Institutional Innovations in Empowered Participatory Governance*. New York: Verso.

Giordano, Gerard. 2007. *American Special Education: A History of Early Political Advocacy*. New York: Peter Lang Publishing.

Gold, Eva, Chris Brown, and Elaine Simon. 2002. *Strong Neighborhoods, Strong Schools: Successful Community Organizing for School Reform*. Chicago: Cross City Campaign for Urban School Reform.

Gutman, Herbert George. 1987. *Power and Culture: Essays on the American Working Class*. New York: New Press.

Heward, W., and R. Cavanaugh. 2005. Educational Equality for Students with Disabilities. In *Multicultural Education: Issues and Perspectives*, ed. J. A. Banks and C. A. McGee, 315–349. San Francisco: Jossey-Bass.

Jefferson, Thomas. 1787/1982. *Notes on the State of Virginia*. New York: Norton.

Kluger, Richard. 1975. *Simple Justice: The History of* Brown v. Board of Education *and Black America's Struggle for Equality.* New York: Vintage Books.

Litwack, Leon F. 1979. *Been in the Storm So Long: The Aftermath of Slavery.* New York: Vintage Books.

MacMullen, Edith Nye. 1991. *In the Cause of True Education: Henry Barnard and Nineteenth-Century Reform.* New Haven, CT: Yale University Press.

Marx, Karl. 1852/1972. The Eighteenth Brumaire of Louis Napoleon. In *The Marx-Engels Reader,* ed. R. C. Tucker, 594–617. New York: Norton.

———. 1887/1967. *Capital: A Critique of Political Economy, Volume 1.* New York: International Publishers.

Mediratta, Kavitha, Norm Fruchter, and Anne C. Lewis. 2002. *Organizing for School Reform: How Communities Are Finding Their Voice and Reclaiming Their Public Schools.* New York: New York University Institute for Education and Social Policy.

Messerli, Jonathan. 1971. *Horace Mann: A Biography.* New York: Knopf.

Morris, Robert C. 1976. *Reading, 'Riting, and Reconstruction: The Education of Freedmen in the South, 1861–1870.* Chicago: University of Chicago Press.

Nagel, Jack H. 1987. *Participation.* New York: Prentice Hall.

National Commission on Excellence in Education. 1983. *A Nation at Risk: The Imperative for Educational Reform.* Washington, DC: U.S. Government Printing Office.

Navarro, Armando. 1995. *Mexican American Youth Organization: Avant-garde of the Chicano Movement in Texas.* Austin: University of Texas Press.

Newman, Joseph. 1990. Antebellum School Reform in the Port Cities of the Deep South. In *Southern Cities, Southern Schools: Public Education in the Urban South,* ed. David Plank and Rick Ginsberg, 17–36. Westport, CT: Greenwood.

Oates, Stephen B. 1982. *Let the Trumpet Sound: The Life of Martin Luther King, Jr.* New York: Plume.

Pangle, Lorraine Smith, and Thomas L. Pangle. 1993. *The Learning of Liberty: The Educational Ideas of the American Founders.* Lawrence: University Press of Kansas.

Payne, Charles M. 1995. *I've Got the Light of Freedom: The Organizing Tradition and the Mississippi Freedom Struggle.* Berkeley: University of California.

Perlstein, Daniel H. 2004. *Justice, Justice: School Politics and the Eclipse of Liberalism.* New York: Peter Lang Publishing.

Podair, Jerald E. 2002. *The Strike That Changed New York: Blacks, Whites, and the Ocean Hill-Brownsville Crisis.* New Haven, CT: Yale University Press.

Putnam, Robert D. 2000. *Bowling Alone: The Collapse and Revival of American Community.* New York: Simon & Schuster.

Ravitch, Diane. 1974. *The Great School Wars: New York City, 1805–1973.* New York: Basic.

Reese, William J. 2002. *Power and the Promise of School Reform: Grassroots Movements During the Progressive Era.* New York: Teachers College Press.

Rieder, Jonathan. 1985. *Canarsie: The Jews and Italians of Brooklyn Against Liberalism.* Cambridge, MA: Harvard University Press.

San Miguel, Guadalupe. 1987. *"Let All of Them Take Heed": Mexican Americans and the Campaign for Education Equality in Texas, 1910–1981 (Reville Book).* Austin: University of Texas Press.

Shirley, Dennis. 1997. *Community Organizing for Urban School Reform.* Austin: University of Texas Press.

———. 2002. *Valley Interfaith and School Reform: Organizing for Power in South Texas.* Austin: University of Texas Press.

Shirley, Dennis, and Michael Evans. 2007. Community Organizing and No Child Left Behind. In *Transforming the City: Community Organizing and the Challenge of Political Change*, ed. Marion Orr, 109–133. Lawrence: University Press of Kansas.

Skocpol, Theda. 1979. *States and Social Revolutions: A Comparative Analysis of France, Russia, and China.* Cambridge: Cambridge University Press.

———. 2003. *Diminished Democracy: From Membership to Management in American Civic Life.* Norman: University of Oklahoma.

Stepto, Robert B. 1991. *From Behind the Veil: A Study of Afro-American Narrative.* Urbana: University of Illinois Press.

Stone, Clarence. 2005. Civic Capacity: What, Why, and from Whence. In *The Public Schools*, ed. Susan Fuhrman and Marvin Lazerson, 209–234. New York: Oxford University Press.

Tyack, David. 1974. *The One Best System: A History of American Urban Education.* Cambridge, MA: Harvard University Press.

Tyack, David, Elisabeth Hansot, and Robert Lowe. 1984. *Public Schools in Hard Times: The Great Depression and Recent Years.* Cambridge, MA: Harvard University Press.

Verba, Sidney, and Norman H. Nie. 1972. *Participation in America: Political Democracy and Social Equality.* New York: Harper & Row.

Warren, Mark R. 2001. *Dry Bones Rattling: Community Building to Revitalize American Democracy.* Princeton, NJ: Princeton University Press.

Williams, Heather Andrea. 2005. *Self-Taught: African American Education in Slavery and Freedom.* Chapel Hill: University of North Carolina Press.

Wilson, William J. 1987. *The Truly Disadvantaged: The Inner City, the Underclass and Public Policy.* Chicago: University of Chicago Press.

3 The Contemporary Context of Public Engagement

The New Political Grid

Jeffrey R. Henig

THE LANDSCAPE OF THE AMERICAN SYSTEM of education has been changing. Some of these changes have been steady and incremental—like the changing demands for education in a globalizing economy or inroads by minorities into positions of formal decision-making within school boards and local education bureaucracies. Others have burst forth more recently and sharply. The ratcheting up of corporate involvement in public education delivery falls in this category, as does the qualitatively different involvement of the national government via No Child Left Behind or the movement in favor of mayoral control.

Changes such as these alter the grid on which groups plan their political strategies. Organizations seeking to use or increase community engagement in education are constantly facing choices. Should they pursue their objectives through the courts or electoral politics? Should they focus at the local level, the states, or Congress? Who will make the most compatible and most effective allies? Which opponents should they appease and which should they challenge head-on? As formal and informal power and authority are reconfigured, access and veto points also change. Some political resources may become more important; others less so. Tactics that worked in an earlier era may need to be reassessed. Options once closed may now open.

This chapter introduces the concept of a changing political grid, discusses some of the major elements, and considers how these shifts in the landscape provide either new opportunities or new obstacles to public engagement.[1] I have attempted to touch on most of the broad forces that make the politics of education today different from that confronting reform-oriented supporters of public education three or four decades ago. The changing political grid, I will argue, poses serious challenges to traditional grassroots organizing strategies. The new politics for public engagement needs to be tactically more flexible, equipped to compete in multiple political venues, and built around loosely coupled relationships among distinct interests that allow them freedom to pursue specific interests while maintaining relationships that facilitate *ad hoc* coalitions.

The Concept of the Political Grid

Chess players compete on a fixed board comprising sixty-four squares, each competitor starting with sixteen pieces with a limit set of pre-programmed moves. Even so, the number of options players face is mind-boggling. The first player has twenty possible opening moves, but each of these offers the opponent a distinct array of possible and advantageous countermoves. As summarized by one online chess site:

> There are $20 * 20 = 400$ possible moves for black, depending on what white does. Then there are $400 * 20 = 8,000$ for white. Then there are $8,000 * 20 = 160,000$ for black, and so on. If you were to fully develop the entire tree for all possible chess moves, the total number of board positions is about 1,000,000,000,000,000,000, 000,000,000,000,000,000,000,000,000,000,000,000,000,000,000,000,000, 000,000,000,000,000,000,000,000,000,000,000,000,000,000,000,000,000, 000, . . . give or take a few.[2]

Now consider, for example, the options facing parents who may feel that schools are inadequate within their neighborhood. First, they must weigh the option of public engagement against simple resignation or more individualized strategies of response. Individualized responses could include residential relocation to another school district; a move to a private school, charter schools, or other public school option; or contact with any of a number of school officials in pursuit of some special accommodation designed to benefit their own child. In contrast to a personalized response, public engagement involves working collectively with others to find common ground and structure joint solutions. Such engagement can be channeled through civil society—for example, volunteering to clean up a school playground, making contributions to help teachers purchase extra supplies, or organizing parents to provide tutoring or classroom support—or they can be channeled through government via political or legal action. In this chapter (and generally throughout this volume), it is the latter—the more political forms of collective engagement—that is the particular focus.

Once parents decide to politically engage to improve schooling, they are faced with many additional choices. Broadly, these involve *level of engagement* (classroom, school, district, state, and national levels); *institutional venue* (electoral politics, courts, or bureaucracy); *issue framing* (Is there a need for more funding? Is there a need for better teachers? Is there a need for stronger leadership? Is there a need for school-level decision making? Or is the problem one of low test scores? Are there poor graduation rates? Is there a lack of focus on academic or is the focus too exclusively on academics? Is there too much tracking or too little? Is there a civil rights issue? Is there too little equity?); *selection of allies* (Will they work with the teachers union? Can they trust the business community as a reliable partner? Will they ally with multi-issue organizations? Can they build partnerships based on race and ethnicity? Will they align with a particular political party?); *tactics for influence* (How can they use the media? Can they lobby via quiet contacts? Will they testify at a school board hearing? Are they willing to engage in protest?).

As in chess, each decision generates responses, which in turn require new calculations. But unlike chess, the shape of the board and rules of engagement are in flux. Like chess players, citizens considering public engagement need to weigh costs and benefits, assess risks and probabilities. Like chess players, they must do so with imperfect information. Even the greatest chess masters cannot work through all of the available options, and the most powerful chess-playing computers that can generate and evaluate millions of board positions per second cannot see inside the mind of the opponent. But unlike chess players, the capacity of individual citizens to learn is constrained by the fact that the parameters of the game are not fixed. An opening move that works at one time—say, in the mid-1900s when the norms of localism dominated education policy making—can easily backfire in another time—such as in the contemporary era in which states and the national government are primed to intercede.

Sources of Structural Change

The political landscape is always changing. Although in some cases we can see precipitating events that signal shifts in direction or the acceleration of change, the accumulated changes are gradual; they take place over decades, and their full implications for public engagement and public education easily escape attention. There is little if any empirical literature that directly tests the proposition that these changes alter the effectiveness of particular public engagement strategies, and in almost every case there are reasonable yet competing hypotheses about whether the changes will work in favor of or undermine a more expansive role for the public.

In the remainder of this chapter, I consider a number of changes shaping the political grid: demographic shifts; reconfigured relationships among the levels and branches of government; new frameworks for standards, testing, and accountability; and growing interest in choice and privatization strategies. In each case I review reasons why these changes might provide opportunities, why they might represent challenges or threats, and how they might alter the payoff and relative effectiveness of differing strategies for public involvement. The chapter concludes with a general argument about how some traditional mobilizing strategies may need to be reconfigured to maximize impact on the new political grid.

Population Change

Shifting demographics are an important and familiar part of the story of American education. Major population transformations of the twentieth century include the massive relocation of African Americans from the South to the North and from rural areas to central cities, the steady suburbanization of the United States accelerated by "white flight" associated with court-ordered desegregation and the emergence of Hispanics as the largest minority population (Clotfelter 2004). The age configuration of the population—including the size, timing, and spatial concentration of baby booms, the aging of the American population and the way the elderly are concentrated across districts and regions—is also important, as is the way the age factors align with racial and ethnic differences.

For the most part, attention to these population shifts has centered on the consequences generated within schools and classrooms, particularly on how they affect the racial, ethnic, and economic composition, peer effects, and schools' strategies for dealing with diverse populations and either growing or shrinking enrollments. Population shifts, though, are important for political options as well. Our political system is spatially structured; boundaries drawn for school districts, legislative districts, and, in ward-based systems, for the election of school board members determine the composition of local electorates, representation at higher levels of government, and range of likely allies.

The Growing Number of "Majority-Minority" and Multiethnic School Districts

Almost fifty years ago, when the Supreme Court issued its groundbreaking decision in *Brown v. Board of Education,* 88 percent of the nation's population was white, about 10 percent was African American, and about 1.5 percent Hispanic (Clotfelter 2004). Non-Hispanic whites had not yet lost their majority status in any of the large central city school districts that we, today, associate with predominantly African American enrollment and leadership—places like Detroit; Washington, DC; Atlanta; or Baltimore (Henig et al. 1999). By 2004 the situation had dramatically changed. Nationwide, the non-Hispanic white proportion of the population had fallen to about 67 percent; just over 12 percent were African American, and the two minority populations experiencing the most rapid growth, Hispanic and Asian, had increased to 14.1 percent and 4.2 percent, respectively.[3] By 2000–2001, less than half of the student population in sixty-one of the country's hundred largest school districts were white non-Hispanic students; these populations averaged 32.5 percent Hispanic, 28.7 percent black, 31.3 percent non-Hispanic white, and 7 percent Asian/Pacific Islanders. The majority of the population in sixteen districts was black, in another sixteen districts the majority of students were Hispanic, and in thirty-two districts the majority of students were white. In the rest of the districts, the populations were so heterogeneous that no racial/ethic group could claim majority status.[4]

The political consequences of this racial transition have proven to be more complicated than anticipated. Some had imagined that the racial transition from white control to black and Hispanic control might provide the seeds for a new, progressive education regime, in which black and Hispanic educators and policy makers, linked by common experiences as marginalized outsiders, would form common bonds and redirect educational systems in ways that would more deeply and effectively build human and social capital within central city communities (Henig et al. 1999). But racial transition has not made it easier to form sustainable coalitions to support school reform. In multiethnic cities, blacks and Hispanics are as likely to see themselves as competitors as to find a common purpose (Clarke et al. 2006; Henig et al. 1999; Meier, Stewart, and England 1989; Rocha 2007). Dorothy Shipps, for example, finds evidence in Chicago of a growing fissure between blacks and Latinos, with the Latinos resenting what they see as the domination of the school system by an African American elite holding tightly to control of the jobs and resources at stake: "Latinos felt they had much to gain by engaging in 'guerilla warfare' against middle-class Blacks who ran the school system and who, they believed, withheld from Latinos the favors and resources of categorical programs and affirmative action" (Shipps 2004, 84). Race continues to be a complicating factor in local politics, even in overwhelmingly African American districts, where racial symbolism and race-based rhetoric is prevalent even in debates pitting blacks against blacks; those who favor certain reform positions associated with the business community or perceived to threaten neighborhood schools, teachers jobs, or union dominance are sometimes attacked for supporting "plantation-style politics" or being "not really black" (Henig et al. 1999, 239, 205).

Although the growing minority population in central city schools may not have radically altered the inside game of local school politics, it alters the grid in at least one important sense. Increasingly, on the state and national stage, "urban education" is interpreted as "black and Hispanic education." Research outside of the education arena has shown that policies identified in racial terms have less support in public opinion polls and are more politically vulnerable (Gilens 1995; Lieberman 1998; Soss et al. 2001). If state and national opinion about urban school reform is shaped by sentiments about race, parents and other activists at the local level might encounter a more reticent audience when they present their demands at those higher levels of decision making. In addition, the need to operate at those higher levels on the ladder of federalism is increasing.

Immigration

Immigrants from Mexico, Central America, and the Caribbean are a major factor in the racial transition just discussed. According to Randolph Capps et al. (2005), "Immigration flows in the 1990s far exceeded those in any decade in the nation's history," with about fifteen million immigrants entering the country during the 1990s compared to about ten million in the 1980s and seven million the decade before that (Capps et al. 2005, 5). Estimates for 2005 put the foreign-born population at 35,769,603, which was 12.4 percent of the total population (Pew Hispanic Center 2006, table 1).

Immigration, however, adds some dimensions beyond those related to diversity and the challenges that diversity poses to coalition building. Immigrant families tend to have more children than native-born families of the same race and ethnicity, with the result that they constitute a larger portion of the school-age population (Capps et al. 2005). The ability to speak English is increasing rapidly among U.S. Hispanics, the largest group of immigrants, but urban schools continue to face the challenge of educating large numbers of children who are non-native speakers, and from a political standpoint the obstacles to communicating with and among parents are substantial. Fewer than one in four Latino immigrants reports being able to speak English very well (Hakimzadeh and Cohn 2007). Latinos in general are also less likely than whites or blacks to go online. According to Susannah Fox and Gretchen Livingston (2007, 2), this gap is especially severe for immigrants: "76% of U.S.-born Latinos go online, compared with 43% of those born outside the U.S."

Further complicating the challenge of political mobilization in communities with large immigrant populations are the legal barriers to noncitizen voting and the wariness of taking public and potentially controversial stances among those who are in the country illegally or have family members who are so. The share of all immigrants who are undocumented has been rising; Randolph Capps et al. (2005) estimate that the share who are undocumented reached 28 percent in 2003.

Suburbanization and State Politics

Attention to suburbanization has focused on white flight and the fact that city school systems, as a result, can end up in the double bind of a higher-need population combined with fewer resources. But suburbanization has also altered the formal power of central cities in state politics. Until the 1960s, many states failed to redraw legislative districts as populations changed. During most of U.S. history, that led to a distinct bias in representation that worked against central cities; they were growing and rural areas were shrinking, but the number of legislators representing the cities did not change in pace. The U.S. Supreme Court changed that in the mid-1960s with its decisions in *Baker v. Carr* and *Reynolds v. Sims*, but ironically this mandate to make representation proportional to population happened at the very time that central cities were shrinking. Margaret Weir, Harold Wolman, and Todd Swanstrom (2005) have examined population shifts and explored how these have affected the prospects for city-suburb coalitions. Their findings show that from 1960 to 2000, central city population declined as a share of the state population in

37 states and the overall percentage of the population in large cities (>250,000) declined from 12.9 percent to 11.8 percent. In some states this decline was much more severe. In Ohio, the proportion in large cities declined from 28 to 16.2 percent; in Missouri from 28.4 to 14.1 percent; in Minnesota, from 23.3 to 13.6 percent; in Pennsylvania, from 23.0 to 15.1 percent; and in Maryland, from 30.3 to 12.3 percent. Some argue that cities can build coalitions, around education and other issues, with inner-ring suburbs that are becoming more urban in character or with rural areas that, like central cities, may be suffering from disinvestment (Orfield 1976). But Weir, Wolman, and Swanstrom are less sanguine: "To create majorities in state legislatures, large cities have always needed to add votes from representatives of other geographic areas. . . . The reduction in city representation since the 1960s has made efforts to construct majority coalitions even more challenging" (2005, 734).

The "Grey Peril"

In the year 2000, 21.7 percent of the nation's population was age sixty-five or older; by 2050 this is projected to be 41.2 percent.[5] Michael Berkman and Eric Plutzer (2005) use the term "grey peril" to refer to the aging of the American population and the threat it might pose to public education. "There is no more enduring political cleavage in America than the generation gap concerning school funding. National polls spanning nearly forty years show that older Americans are more likely to endorse lower spending on public schools and less likely to support spending increases" (p. 38).

Because older citizens no longer have children in the schools, and because many of them are on fixed incomes and worried about their exposure to higher tax rates, an older population may be one in which public school advocates face growing problems building support. Berkman and Plutzer's analysis suggests that this situation can play out differently in different areas, though. They separately analyze support for school spending in communities to which the elderly have recently migrated and communities where the population has been aging in place and find that in the latter communities, the elderly tend to be quite supportive of investing in public education—perhaps because they have family in the area or because they remain loyal to the institutions that nurtured them and their own children—but that elderly who have migrated recently are a resistant population.

The Dynamics of Federalism

The shifting of populations across district boundaries takes place against a backdrop in which the levers of power are being rearranged within the federal system. *Federalism* refers to the allocation of authority across the vertical levels of government. It incorporates formal legal aspects, having to do with such things as the wording in the U.S. Constitution, and informal sources of power and capacity that may derive from the power of the purse, public opinion and political culture, the mobilization of power, and the strength and ambition of elected officials. Formally, the strongest claim to authority lies with state government, based on the so-called "reserved powers" clause in the Tenth Amendment of the Constitution. Historically, though, local school districts have had substantial discretion due to strong traditions of localism and, for many years, limited state capacity or interest in taking a more direct role. Over the last twenty-five years or so, there have been major shifts in the tectonic plates of educational federalism. First states, and then the national government, have become much more aggressively involved, and key decisions affecting schools are increasingly made in places more distant from parent and community leaders and subjected to political pressures from a different set of constituencies.

Growing Involvement of the States

Some date the growing state role in education to the 1970s, when the U.S. Supreme Court decision in *San Antonio School District v. Rodriguez* made it clear that those challenging inequalities in school funding between wealthy and poor districts would have to fight their battles in state rather than federal courts (Manna 2006). Under both legal and political pressure to reduce reliance on local property taxes, states began to take on more of the responsibility for funding education. And, as state leaders found themselves paying more of the bills, they also began to pay more attention to how the money was actually being used. At least as important, though, were changes in the 1980s, led in part by a handful of governors who came to see public education as a critical component in their economic development strategies. The 1989 Charlottesville Summit, called for by President George H. W. Bush and attended by the nation's governors, marked both a culmination of the gradually expanding state role and an early sign of a growing nationalization of education politics which would see Presidents George H. W. Bush, Bill Clinton, and George W. Bush getting much more directly involved than had almost any of their predecessors (Manna 2006; McGuinn 2006).

Nationalization of Education Politics

Since 2001, No Child Left Behind (NCLB) has been the gorilla in the room of education politics in the United States; any discussion of school reform and American educational organization and achievement comes around to NCLB before much time has passed at all. NCLB, and particularly its provisions holding schools and districts accountable for yearly progress that reaches 100 percent proficiency by 2014, have reshaped the stage on which local education policy is set. Principals, school boards, and school superintendents must pay special attention to math and reading scores and to ensuring that progress is made within various subgroups. Looming in the background is the risk that schools or districts will be subject to sanctions, potentially culminating in reconstitution. Although most states have been slow to adopt such extreme measures, reconstitution could include states taking over schools or districts, mandating conversion to charter schools, or contracting out to private providers.

More recently, the Supreme Court decision in two school diversity cases— *Meredith v. Jefferson County Board of Education* (Louisville, Kentucky) and *Parents Involved in Community Schools v. Seattle School District*—also can be read as a sharp constraint on traditions of education localism. That ruling severely limited local districts that would consider racial balance in maintaining diverse schools, even when local plans are the result of broad political compromises, worked out over decades, and with the support of a wide range of local community stakeholders.

Implications at the Local Level

It is important not to overstate the case: localism is not dead, and the growing role of Congress and the White House does not mean that state and local officials are being rendered irrelevant. The national government cannot put its policies into effect without "borrowing strength" from the states (Manna 2006), and the states, in their turn, lack the site-specific knowledge and bureaucratic resources to pursue their goals without relying on the more developed district agencies that operate at the level where education is actually delivered. States still have considerable legal and political leverage with which to protect their zone of discretion regarding education. Local districts do not have constitutional claims on which to fall back; but in addition to the bureaucratic muscle needed to get anything accomplished, they have deep reservoirs of popular support to mobilize if state or national intervention becomes too heavy-handed. The notion of "local obsolescence" is overblown (Henig 2007).

But the relative attenuation of local power means that locally based citizen groups need to be prepared to operate in a bigger pond. Almost fifty years ago, political scientist E. E. Schattschneider noted that for groups that have generally been on the losing end in a localized political arena, expanding "the scope of conflict" can sometimes be beneficial (Schattschneider 1960, 2). A racially or ethnically distinct group in a homogenous and unwelcoming local district, for example, could benefit from shifting a battle to the state level, where it might find powerful allies who were previously uninvolved. One of the important components of NCLB, for example, the requirement that schools and district test scores must be publicly disseminated in a form disaggregated by race, income, and students' special needs, would have been politically difficult to enact locally, where officials have an incentive to mask politically volatile information about gaps. Many civil rights leaders now argue that access to this information helps them monitor and push for equity on the local agenda. But expanding the scope of conflict can be costly and demand skills and tactics that differ from those that are productive in local politics.

The most immediate and obvious costs of having to work at multiple levels of decision making involve negotiating the obstacles imposed by distance. Face-to-face contact is still a major part of effective lobbying, even in the age of Internet and email. City Hall or the school board offices may be a bus ride away; the state capital and Washington, DC, may require a plane trip. But the costs of transportation are really a small part of the story. Each level of government is characterized by a different political ecology—made of a different mix of interest groups, with access mediated through distinct institutions with their own rules of doing business, informed by different norms and with different histories and traditions. In the new landscape of federalism, not only do locally based groups of school reformers need to be able to *understand* the state and federal role; they also need to engage in what is sometimes referred to as "venue-shopping" (Baumgartner and Jones 1993, 36), tactically redirecting their political efforts to the level of government most likely to be responsive to their particular cause at a particular time. Finally, they need to be able to know the rules of the political game within that arena and have the savvy and capacity to compete.

Local groups aspiring to have a state or national effect must recruit new allies, and working with other groups can be challenging. Members of new coalitions must work through suspicions and negotiate boundaries of independence, autonomy, and leadership. Issues may have to be reframed to align with multiple groups' sense of what is fair and appropriate. Such realignments can require trade-offs—balancing the needs and interests of different core constituencies. For example, in the area of school politics, parents in a large central city might feel that reform of state finance mechanisms ought to redress long-standing inequities, but parent groups in smaller cities and rural areas might attend first to different, yet equally legitimate, claims. Successful local efforts at mobilizing engagement based on appeals to racial or ethnic identities may be counter-productive at the state and national level; conceivably, appeals based on economic equality would be more effective than those based on race.

Standards, Testing, and Accountability

From the standpoint of governance and politics, the shift of educational decision making up the ladder of federalism makes it more important for parent and community groups to understand multiple venues, to be flexible in venue shopping, and to build links to allies beyond the local district. But there is another set of implications for public engagement that flows less from the general change in the political environment than from a particular reform strategy that has been associated with growing state and federal involvement. That has to do with the marked increase in the importance of standards, testing, and accountability. A growing state and national role did not necessarily have to take this form. During the 1960s, for example, the national government's expansion of involvement focused on issues like desegregation and efforts to increase resources in low-income communities. An expanded state role in principle could be limited to attention to reducing funding inequalities, expanding choice, or shaping the required curriculum. But for various reasons the contemporary manifestation of state and national government involvement has incorporated a shift in emphasis from school *inputs* (funding, school demographics, formal curriculum) to school *outputs,* with the latter primarily measured in terms of student gains and education gaps on standardized test scores in reading and math.[6] This shift represents more than an adjustment of metrics: it redefines what constitutes equity and forces community actors to augment their claims on a fair share of jobs and resources with evidence that these have independent and causally isolatable effects.

The notion of measuring student performance according to state standards predates NCLB. The passage of the first federal Elementary and Secondary

Education Act in 1965 gave an initial kick to the movement, because Congress mandated the collection of some student outcome data to assess the impact of the program. During the 1970s and 1980s, as already noted, some states on their own initiative began instituting clearer standards and putting into place assessment regimes. But NCLB pushed all of this into a higher drive. The requirement that states test student math and reading achievement in grades three through eight and in one high school grade required the yearly administration of about forty-five million standardized tests (Toch 2006). In the three years between academic years 2004–5 and 2007–8, state spending on standardized tests increased by about $113 million, almost 25 percent (Toch 2006).

How might the growing importance of standards and testing influence the degree of public engagement, the forms it is most likely to take, and the prospects for its success? One possibility is that the standards and testing movement could facilitate parent engagement by making it easier for citizens to find out how well schools are performing. On its website discussion of testing provisions of NCLB, the U.S. Department of Education argues that testing can make parent and citizen involvement more effective: "The new law," it says, "will empower parents, citizens, educators, administrators and policymakers with data from those annual assessments."[7] Information asymmetries—in which professional educators use their inside knowledge to mask problems, to authoritatively rebut criticisms, to discredit opponents— are part of the historic environment that has made grassroots challenges to local school districts so difficult to mount and sustain. Public and specific information that lets citizens know that their schools are not doing as well as others—even if the teachers seem earnest and the children seem content— can make it easier for local leaders to broaden their base of support. And disaggregated test scores that show some groups lagging—minorities or low-income students or English language learners or those with disabilities— can expose problems that *average* test scores might previously have masked. Such disaggregation has been critical in winning the allegiance of a number of existing minority and civil rights organizations in spite of these groups' opposition to other elements of NCLB, including emphasis on school choice, opposition from unions, potential to blame low-income schools and districts for failures rooted in broader social inequalities, a narrow focus on math and reading, and the program's identification with President George W. Bush.

The high-stakes testing environment can work against some familiar attractions for citizen engagement. For example, if the goals of a reform are narrowly construed by law or other official policy, community participation or decision making becomes less relevant. The public may become skeptical of off-the shelf standardized tests; schools may lose parents' enthusiasm once held for their children learning the arts and humanities, or parents might miss the schools' attention to physical and emotional health of children or for the development of children's citizenship skills. Accountability regimes also can snuff out some promising innovative community-oriented schools that are labeled as failing based on low test scores during their vulnerable start-up years.

For example, Wells and Holme found that the rise of standardized testing has led to a narrowing of people's interpretation of what constitutes a good school, rather than stimulating public discussion of the goals of education. Racially mixed high schools with strong reputations (for strong parental involvement, a good music or theater program, student spirit, or a healthy interracial community), gradually came to be judged solely based on test scores. Because those test scores were not adjusted for student family and community background, racially and economically diverse schools tended to have lower scores. As "good school" came to mean "high score school," white and more affluent parents felt more pressure to find alternatives, creating a self-fulfilling spiral of decline (Wells and Holme 2006).

The new emphases on standards, accountability, and testing change the kinds of arguments community leaders may need to make and the kinds of skills and resources they may need to nurture. Communities that want to argue for broader subject area coverage, for example, or a richer set of assessments, cannot ignore test outcomes, and local leaders seeking to broaden public engagement will have to devote more attention to developing the independent capacity to generate, interpret, and analyze data. At the very least, this will require some additional flexibility and some capacity to analyze the available public data. But if state and local assessment regimes are focusing narrowly on a small range of indicators, serious efforts to reframe local debate would also require identifying indicators and collecting original data on other variables that more closely reflect community values. That may mean building and sustaining an in-house data analysis capacity or building partnerships with universities or research organizations that already have the requisite skills. In either case, it likely will require diverting some resources that could otherwise have been focused on grassroots organizing, media campaigns, legal support, or other strategies for engagement.

School Choice

An array of school choice options has been breaking down the historical link between the place one lives and the schools one's children attend. The most controversial of these takes students out of the public school system completely. This includes publicly funded school vouchers that families can apply toward tuition at private religious or nonreligious schools. It also includes home schooling, once a very marginal phenomenon but now expanding in both the numbers of students involved and the breadth of the types of families adopting this option. Some school choice options, though, are wholly incorporated within the traditional framework of public school districts; this includes magnet schools,[8] interdistrict public choice,[9] and more liberalized transfer options. Charter schools generally are designed to straddle the line that traditionally distinguishes public schools from private. They are officially public schools, but the charter concept envisions them to be largely independent of government regulation in their management. It has been almost twenty years since the first charter school opened in Minnesota; there are now nearly four thousand nationwide, serving an estimated 1.1 million students (Center for Education Reform 2007).

As a result of these options, the percentage of students enrolled in their assigned public school decreased from 80 percent to 74 percent between 1993 and 2003. During this time, enrollment in church-related private schools remained roughly stable at 8 percent and enrollment in non church-related private schools increased from 1.6 to 2.4 percent. Even when parents send their children to assigned public schools, more of them do so after first considering other opportunities. In about half of all cases, parents indicate that public school choice was available in their community and about one in four of the families whose children were in public schools considered enrolling them elsewhere (National Center for Education Statistics 2006).

School choice options might complicate efforts to build public engagement, especially broad-based engagement that extends beyond a particular classroom or schools. In a classic treatise, economist Albert O. Hirschman outlined ways in which the option to leave an unsatisfactory situation (exit) can be an alternative to political mobilization (voice). When personal exit becomes easier, collective engagement becomes relatively less attractive. A rational self-interested actor will recognize that public engagement is hard work and requires a continual investment of effort, while exit is often a one-time affair with the prospect of solving a problem permanently. Accordingly, Hirschman argued that there may be "an important bias in favor of exit when both options are present" (Hirschman 1970, 43).

Although some worry that the exit threat may deflate the impulse and capacity for public engagement, there is a counterargument. Literature on social capital suggests that enhanced feelings of interpersonal trust and reciprocity can lead to effective political engagement and policy (Putnam 1993) and to better functioning school communities (Bryk, Lee, and Holland 1993; Bryk and Schneider 2002; Coleman and Hoffer 1987). If school choice, as some argue, allows families to opt into communities marked by value consensus, greater responsiveness to parental input, and more intimate arrangements for cooperation, it is possible that the schools can foster social capital. It is even possible that norms and habits of involvement generated within these schools will spill over into broader realms of public engagement, making parents not only more active supporters of their children's teachers and principals but better democratic citizens overall (Buckley and Schneider 2007).

At this point, the empirical evidence one way or the other is limited and somewhat mixed. Scott Franklin Abernathy examined evidence from Milwaukee's voucher program and from the 1996 National Household Education Survey (NHES) and found some indication that parents who opt to exit from their neighborhood public schools become more active at the schools they select, but they were also among the more active at the schools they left, possibly weakening the leadership cadre at the schools from which they exit (Abernathy 2005). Using the 2003 NHES data, Jack Buckley concludes that once one controls for important background variables, parents who exercise public school choice are more likely to volunteer at their children's school but are no more involved in school activities and meetings. He also finds that parents who select private secular schools volunteer more but go to meetings and activities less, and those attending private religious schools participate less than public school parents in both volunteering and meetings (Buckley 2007). Looking at charter school families in Washington, DC, Jack Buckley and Mark Schneider find some evidence that charter schools promote attitudes associated with participation and the formation of social capital, but that difference is relatively small, does not seem to grow over time, and does not spill over into broader realms of political participation (Buckley and Schneider 2007).

Supporters of public education often are wary of school choice, seeing it as a stalking horse for a privatization movement that would weaken investment in the system and attenuate institutions designed to ensure democratic input and oversight. This concern is not unfounded (Henig 2005). Charter schools and other public school choice arrangements, however, are likely to be a fixture on the new political grid, and it is worthwhile both intellectually and tactically to recognize meaningful distinctions among different forms of choice. When done well and when incorporated into a healthy system of public oversight, choice can facilitate variations in style and focus that excite communities, but by definition, variations are problematic in one-size-fits-all models of education delivery that are anchored to assigned attendance zones (Rofes and Stulberg 2004). Furthermore, there are indications that some charter school networks might be aggressive grassroots organizers in their own right (Dillon 2007). Rather than resist choice arrangements vehemently and across the board, advocates of public engagement need to be cautious and discriminating, embracing those choice options that really do meet community needs and finding ways to ensure that families opting for one form of exit or another from the conventional system are still participating in the broader coalitions needed to protect public education as a valued and collective enterprise.

School Boards Under Siege

A major legacy of the early twentieth-century Progressive movement was the widespread adoption of school governance structures different from those in place for other core local services such as parks, roads, policing, and fire protection. School districts and school boards were configured as special-purpose islands deliberately buffered from the mainland of general-purpose government. The Progressives saw normal electoral politics as a breeding ground for partisanship, parochialisms, patronage, and intramural competition pitting neighborhood against neighborhood in beggar-thy-neighbor competition. School board elections would be formally nonpartisan, often conducted at a different time of year from other elections, boards would be expected to hire superintendents with strong in-field credentials, and districts would often have dedicated revenue streams that did not have to go through city council scrutiny.

The walls separating school districts from general-purpose governance and politics are under scrutiny and beginning to erode. The most dramatic manifestation of this process is the adoption of mayoral control. Although the particulars can vary, mayoral control gives mayors direct roles in selecting all or some school board members (or in some instances doing away with school boards entirely), a stronger role in the selection of the superintendent (often modeled on the selection of other department or agency heads), and a more direct role in budget decisions (Henig and Rich 2004; Kirst and Bulkley 2000; Viteritti 2009). Boston and Chicago are two of the earliest and most prominent examples, but other cities that have followed suit or are seriously contemplating doing so include Cleveland; Detroit;[10] Harrisburg, Pennsylvania; Oakland; Albuquerque;[11] Los Angeles; Providence, Rhode Island; New York City; and Washington, DC.

There are arguments for and against mayoral control, and there is not yet clear evidence that it has the desired impact on classroom learning. In some communities the existing governance structures are too cherished or too politically entrenched to make mayoral control a viable option. But the traditionally buffered status of school politics is under assault, and it seems probable that decisions about urban schools increasingly will involve a broader array of actors and institutions for which education is not the exclusive or primary focus. In addition, even when the process does not lead to a change in formal power, some of the same forces driving mayoral control are leading to a general increase in mayoral involvement in education, as mayors can use their considerable well of informal powers to articulate goals and standards, back school board candidates, support (or oppose) bond referenda, encourage municipal agencies to cooperate with the schools, and speak out about candidates for superintendent or the performance of the sitting occupants of that position (Grady and Hutchinson 2007; Kirst and Edelstein 2006).

The increased role for mayors is partly due to disappointment with the current formulation of school boards (Howell 2005) and is part of a backlash against educational bureaucracies and teacher unions—both portrayed as rigid, oriented more to the needs of adults than children, and adept at shifting blame in a way that impedes public accountability (Lieberman 2000). But the arguments also reflect a more expansive vision of education as both a tool for economic development and an enterprise that needs to mobilize the full range of governmental power and public support. Linking education to economic growth and human capital investment legitimates greater involvement by the business sector and by nonschool public officials who have these concerns within their normal portfolios. Governors and mayors, state legislators and city council members may be more able to ensure coordination between schools and other organs of government such as social service agencies, recreation and parks departments, community health facilities, job training programs, planning and economic development, and community colleges and public universities. And because they typically run in elections with higher participation and rely on electoral coalitions that incorporate a broader segment of the public, they may be in a better position than school board members to rally support for public investment in education and to protect schools from competing demands on revenues or antitax movements.

If general-purpose governments are becoming relatively more important, and school districts as discrete special-purpose entities somewhat less so, there are both opportunities and threats to those hoping to build public engagement in support of public schools. As already noted, mayors may be in a better position than school boards to highlight the importance of education and mobilize a broad coalition of support. But the benefits of mayoral involvement depend on the mayor's commitment to education and willingness to support education in the face of demands from other interests, including those looking to limit taxes and spending overall.

Because turnout in school board elections tends to be very low, small but intense groups—including parents and teachers—can have substantial impact. A candidate running for a ward-based seat on a school board cannot afford to stay distant from concerned parents; even a dedicated group from a single school is likely to be able to get in the door. Mayors who run citywide and in elections with high profiles and a broad and diverse electorate have other interests vying for their attention and are better positioned to provide campaign and post-election support. In sum, advocates for schools must be prepared to fight their battles on a bigger field, competing against more diverse political interests. Households without school-age children; businesses that draw their workers from a metropolitan-wide labor pool; and organizations and voters more immediately concerned about crime, or health care, or higher education, or historic preservation, or the arts: these segments of a mayor's constituency are not necessarily hostile to public schools, but neither are they as willing as teachers and parents of public school children to take it for granted that increased education funding is critically important. In addition, the corporate management style that has been associated with several of the high-profile mayoral control regimes has been criticized for leading to a closed and somewhat hierarchical process of decision making that leaves community groups on the margins and submerges debates and disagreements about values in the interest of maintaining a unified front (Chambers 2006).

Rather than rely on arguments designed to energize a constituency that is intrinsically pro-school because its children or jobs are directly at stake, those seeking public engagement under mayoral control will have to convince a more skeptical audience. That may require them to address waste, inefficiency, and other putative advantages of corporate, hierarchical, management-oriented governance without losing the professional perspectives of educators. It may be partly a question of providing evidence that the collective benefits *presumed* to follow from a good education system—better workers, the ability to attract and hold business, a richer social and cultural community—are more than just wishful thinking. And it may also require a greater readiness to work as part of multi-issue organizations, groups for which education-specific demands are just part of a progressive and social-justice-oriented agenda.

Privatization

For-profit companies in recent years have made substantial inroads into the K–12 education sphere. One component of privatization involves Educational Management Organizations (EMOs), for-profit companies that manage charter schools or public schools under contract arrangements. The fifty-one EMOs identified by the Arizona State Education Policy Studies laboratory in school year 2005–6 managed 521 schools in 28 states and the District of Columbia (Molnar et al. 2006). Six of the largest EMOs are allied through the National Council of Education Providers; in 2003 they claimed to employ more than 14,000 people, projecting employment growth of 24 percent the following year.[12] In addition, NCLB gave momentum to the for-profit sector providing Supplemental Education Services (SES), tutoring programs that provide services outside of the normal academic day (Henig 2007). A private-sector testing and publishing industry also was growing robustly before NCLB, but the federal law ensured that the state-initiated standards and accountability movement would continue to grow and to spread. Total spending for developing, publishing, and reporting required tests appears to be in the range of $500 to $750 million. Large textbook publishing firms like Pearson, Houghton Mifflin, McGraw-Hill, and Harcourt Assessment are, as Tom Toch notes, "'full-service' companies that create tests; align them with state standards; ensure they are technically sound; publish, distribute, and score them; and analyze results" (Toch 2006, 6).

There are, in principle, at least three ways in which the growing private sector role could complement the goal of expanding public engagement. The first is somewhat paradoxical: private companies could serve as useful targets to mobilize against. For organizers trying to energize generally disengaged publics, corporate entities have appeal as symbolic threats. Some of the most intense spurts of school-related organizing in inner cities, for instance, have involved campaigns against private companies. Baltimore Mayor Kurt Schmoke's decision to contract with a private firm (Education Alternatives Incorporated) to run some of its schools stirred a hornet's nest of protest that unraveled his support and derailed his plans to be "the education mayor" who would revive a failing school system (Orr 2000). In 2000 and 2001, Chancellor Harold Levy and Mayor Rudolph Giuliani invited private companies to bid on taking over some of New York City's worst schools. In response, community-based organizations rallied opposition, first getting proposals that suggested drastically cutting the number of schools from about fifty to five and then defeating a specific proposal to contract with Edison Schools in a very high-profile vote. Quite apart from any evidence about the effectiveness of Edison and other EMOs, and quite apart from the question of whether they are indeed even making money, the specter of "making profits off the children" is a potent one in some communities.

There are also more positive ways in which privatization conceivably could support broader engagement. One of these involves information. Proponents of privatization argue that a combination of market incentives and the dictates of contracting arrangements will make it much easier for citizens to get good information about schooling costs and outcomes, better arming them for collective action when that is appropriate (LaFaive 2007). Market pressure would come from families as consumers, who would want more information about the alternatives presented to them and from the felt need by private education sector firms to release information about themselves and their competitors as a form of marketing. Contracting arrangements, according to privatization advocates like Savas (2000), would enable public authorities to specify outcome indicators and directly monitor public costs and would create a more transparent information regime, accessible to citizens, than exists when public bureaucracies have a monopoly on provision and an organizational incentive to shield themselves from scrutiny.

There is a chance, too, that privatization could add political muscle to engagement efforts by pro-school coalitions. When parents and educators call for greater investment in education, they are often put on the defensive by those who question whether, in fact, money matters. This is especially the case when the parents and educators making the call come from central city and lower-income minority communities whose demand for more resources represents an implicit call for redistributory policies that would pinch middle- and upper-income suburbanites.

Although some proponents of privatization have championed it as a route to greater efficiency and lower overall costs, some of the corporate providers are arguing that good education cannot be provided on the cheap. For-profit EMOs, for example, have tended to steer away from some states or local contracting arrangements where per-pupil investment is low. They have highlighted the fact that some high-need populations are much more expensive to educate, that longer school days and school years are desirable and cost more, and that hiring and retaining truly qualified educators means raising salaries in competitive labor markets. Edison Schools, for example, has run full-page advertisements in publications such as *Education Week* with messages that often translate into a call for more public investment in education. "Solve the Following Problem: $240,000–$80,000" reads the text of one, comparing the salary of a typical commercial jet pilot to that of a principal of a public school. "We would never suggest that airline captains be paid less. But shouldn't our best principals have the opportunity to earn comparable incomes, particularly if they create an environment in which all children can achieve their full potential?" the ad concludes.[13] When corporations make these arguments, it adds legitimacy to the claims that, when made by the traditional pro-school lobby, they are seen as self-serving.

But privatization also presents serious risks. Elsewhere, I have discussed the ways in which pragmatic efforts to harness market forces might set the stage for a more substantial and self-reinforcing shrinkage of government scope, responsibility, and capacity (Henig 2005). This could come about through a systemic *power shift* (if, for example, an increased reliance on private modes of delivery weakened teachers unions and other interest groups that currently provide important support for public investment in schools or strengthened groups that currently oppose such investment); a *perceptual shift* (if, for example, an increased reliance on private modes of delivery led to a broad devaluation of the collective goods aspects of education, undermining existing beliefs in the connection between public education and collective economic, social, and civic well-being); or an *institutional shift* (if, for example, an increased reliance on private modes of delivery systematically reduced the capacity of government to carry out core functions, including the ability to design and enforce contracts).

Courts

Groups that lack large numbers and political muscle often look to the courts as an alternative to electoral politics as a venue in which to protect and advance their interests. This makes sense because both the design of courts as institutions[14] and the norms and decision rules with which courts are imbued are established deliberately to elevate constitutional provisions, even when they come into conflict with pragmatic issues of political and financial feasibility. During the 1950s, southern blacks turned to the federal courts as a venue for advancing their goals of ending segregated schooling. Faced with weakened electoral power—due to, for example, the demographic factors and shifts in federalism mentioned earlier—some families in central city (and declining rural) school districts similarly have turned to judicial action. But with the federal courts consistently unreceptive to appeals based on school financing inequities,[15] and increasingly inhospitable to cases relating to race,[16] the center of the action has shifted to state courts and appeals based on state constitutional provisions.

Unlike their federal counterparts, state courts have proven receptive to plaintiffs who argue that existing funding mechanisms have failed to provide sufficient resources to adequately fund public education as defined in state constitutions. During the 1970s and 1980s, lawyers frequently argued these cases in terms of equity claims, and despite some high-profile victories, they often lost. Since 1989, however, cases have more often been offered based on adequacy claims. Courts in about half the states have ruled on school finance decisions, and plaintiffs have won in 75 percent of these cases (Rebell 2007).

In principle, pursuit of remedies via judicial action can complement other forms of advocacy, including efforts to broaden public engagement. The articulation of a clear legal claim based on citizens' rights can stimulate public attention and convince a jaded or cynical citizenry that there are genuine prospects for positive change. At the same time, mobilization of an engaged citizenry can increase the effectiveness of a judicial approach, in particular, making it less likely that a recalcitrant legislature will stall judicial orders for funding reform. "Although the lawyers must win the battle for school improvement, in the court of law" one advisory guide suggests, "community groups can win in the court of public opinion" and make it more likely that legal victories will lead to real changes at the classroom level (Public Education Network 2005, 11).

In practice, though, there are risks to court involvement. Failed lawsuits can foster fatalism that makes it difficult to rouse citizen interest in pursuing reforms through other routes. During the early to mid-1970s, some communities were spawning progressive coalitions to build support for integrated public schools, in some cases including voluntary transporting students across city-suburb lines (Eaton 2001). The Supreme Court's decision in *Milliken v. Bradley* took mandatory court-ordered cross-district busing off the table. This need not have ended voluntary efforts or even legislatively imposed cross-district integration plans, but the court's ruling seemed in some ways to deflate other efforts as well.

Even when courts make decisions that please progressive forces in the community, long-term reliance on the courts as a venue for reform can undermine public engagement. Ross Sandler and David Schoenbrod's analysis of judicial consent decrees concludes that they do not take politics out of the process so much as they shift the politics into a less visible decision-making arena, in which electorally accountable officials are marginalized in favor of lawyers, mid-level bureaucrats, and court-appointed functionaries: "The winners are the powerful and knowledgeable" (Sandler and Schoenbrod 2003, 7). Luis Ricardo Fraga, Nick Rodriguez, and Bari Anhalt Erlichson (2005) analyze San Francisco's efforts to deal with school desegregation after a failed NAACP lawsuit and subsequent (1983) comprehensive consent decree. Over twenty years, spanning the administrations of four school superintendents, the extent to which desegregation efforts were maintained ebbed. Counter Sandler and Schoenbrod, Fraga, Rodriguez, and Erlichson see the problem as lying not in the marginalization of traditional school board politics but in the way that fragmented local politics enabled a still-influential school board to take the energy out of the court's enforcement efforts (Fraga, Rodriguez, and Erlichson 2005). Because they see the courts as a key defender of an important set of values, Fraga, Rodriguez, and Erlichson are not willing to leave the courts out of the equation (as Sandler and Schoenbrod are more willing to do). They see the courts as a valuable ally but insufficient without good political alignments to back them up.

It is likely that supporters of strong public education will need to pursue judicial, electoral, and coalition-building strategies simultaneously to maximize their impact on the new political grid. Indeed, one possible implication of the accumulated shifts discussed in this chapter is that such groups increasingly will have to be flexible, nimble, and multi-pronged. But suggesting that reformers prepare to do everything presents problems of its own.

Globalization

All of the structural changes discussed thus far take place against a backdrop of globalization: the growing interconnectness among nations associated with the greatly facilitated movement of people, jobs, capital, and ideas. Globalization can be an all-purpose explanation that is so broad and malleable that it simultaneously explains everything and nothing much at all. The literature on globalization is huge, and some of these studies demonstrate how cities' economies and populations are affected by events occurring far way; however, much more is known about the economic consequences than the political ones and more, in turn, about the political consequences for nations than for subnational governments.[17]

This is not the place to undertake a detailed tracing of the links between globalization and the choices faced by community actors in urban school districts, but suffice it to say that globalization acts as both a cause and accelerator of most of the factors already discussed. Globalization plays a role in the rising number of immigrants coming in search of jobs. It increases both the real and perceived competitiveness between the United States and other countries, raising stakes in terms of the need for high-quality schools. This heightened attention to the role of schools in producing a well-educated workforce has added fuel to the fire of the standards and accountability movement and has served to catalyze corporate interest in schooling. The choice, privatization, and mayoral control initiatives in American education have been promoted, in large measure, as necessary responses to international competition and rationalized in terms of an overarching "market metaphor" that permeates public discourse about how and why schools should change (Henig 1994; Henig and Rich 2004). Globalization also feeds privatization by expanding the market for private-educator providers; some of the largest firms working in the growing corporate education sector are also selling services in other countries, and some of the companies active in the United States are owned by, or draw substantial capital from, foreign companies and investors. Globalization means that parents and communities are increasingly scrambling to get "their child" into one of the few "high-quality" schools so that "their child" can be in a position to the land one of the highly valued "knowledge jobs" and not one of the low-wage service jobs—the extremes of the bifurcated nature of American economy brought on in part by globalization (Oakes and Rogers 2006).

With imagination, we can conjure up some ways in which globalization could facilitate advocacy and political engagement. Sassen, for example, suggests the possibility of a "new kind of transnational politics" in which nations are weaker and workers often invisible, but in which a more concrete set of encounters with the forces of global economics makes global cities a "space of empowerment for the disadvantaged" (Sassen 2004). Immigrants can generate new energy and ideas, for example, and the broadly acknowledged competitive pressure can give groups a way to frame their desire for better education in a manner that taps into the anxieties of business and middle-class families, possibly broadening the scope of their potential allies. Overall, however, it seems likely the dominant impact, at least in the near term, is to increase the distance between communities and the levers that most influence their fate and to raise the importance of being mobile, able to rapidly shift among political avenues, and to amass constituencies and resources on a larger scale.

Strategic Options on the New Political Grid

The changing political grid poses serious challenges to grassroots organizing strategies. Traditional grassroots organizing strategies are often framed around highly localized issues; targeted or presented to racial/ethnic subgroups responsive to distinct symbols and particular leaders; dependent on confrontational protests or the threat of asserted power within ward-based school board electoral systems; and aimed at achieving short-term bursts of enthusiasm intended to change the cast of characters or reframe local debates. Many of these tactics were honed by mobilizing collective action in pursuit of public goods (Olson 1971) or by building power among low-income and minority groups that have been acculturated to being politically dismissed (Alinsky 1971). These tactics emerged during a period when school boards and superintendents called the shots and parents were organized naturally within spatially defined school attendance zones, in which the demarcation between courts and political advocacy and between the public and private sectors were much more sharply defined.

The new politics for public engagement does not make these earlier strategies obsolete so much as it raises the premium on tactical flexibility and range of operating modes. The new political grid is likely to reward groups equipped to compete in multiple political venues and built around loosely coupled relationships among distinct organizations with freedom to pursue specific interests while maintaining relationships that facilitate ad hoc coalitions. There is a higher premium on knowledge, about research evidence, about doing research, and about the law. Whereas the buffered nature of local education politics previously favored groups that painstakingly nurtured access to local school boards and bureaucracies, today there is increasing payoff to groups that can work across levels of government and in multi-issue coalitions able to compete in general-purpose elections.

It is possible that new technologies might make it easier or less expensive for community-based actors to compete on this grid than was once the case. Email, blogs, listservs, and text messaging provide ways for even relatively low-income groups to rapidly and inexpensively communicate with members and potential allies. The Web now puts into reasonably ready reach a range of information on demographics, public budgets, legal precedents, and student test scores that as little as a decade ago were available only to those with considerable resources to devote to data collection and management. By bringing down the effective costs of some communication and research strategies, technology, in other words, could narrow long-standing systemic disadvantages that translate into differential in power between them and the interest groups with whom they must compete. Technology, though, like most of the other factors we have considered, can cut both ways. As in a military arms race, each new weapon system can up the ante, forcing all to invest more. Rather than narrowing the gap between those that have and those that do not, the gap can increase. Technology can make it less likely to simplify the tasks than to lengthen the list of arenas in which groups are forced to compete.

But increasing the number of arenas for public engagement poses at least two problems for community groups. First, done seriously, each new arena (technology, wider coalitions, multiple levels of government, etc.) requires additional resources. Michael Lipsky, in a classic formulation, underscored the pressures put on community-based and relatively powerless organizations that try, simultaneously, to appear credible and sympathetic to potential allies while meeting the demands and expectations of their internal constituency (Lipsky 1968).

Second, some tactics can pull collective engagement in inconsistent directions. Consider the issue of venue shopping between legislatures and the courts.

Pursuing court-focused adequacy suits encourages proponents to frame their efforts around constitutional language and judicial norms and precedents particular to their own state, whereas electoral mobilization might sometimes be more successful if framed as a national issue and in terms of broader legal and human rights. Tailoring a strategy to flourish in the courts also can tie it up in legal language that makes the story more complicated and technical than is appropriate for a mass-mobilization approach. And courts tend to decide cases on absolute principles; they are not well adapted to broker compromises. Yet at least sometimes, brokered compromises provide a broader foundation on which to build sustainable reforms.

Similar tensions emerge in the other areas as discussed in the sections above. Framing issues in racial or ethnic terms may appeal to some under-mobilized groups but at the cost of sharpening cleavages and generating a backlash from others. Working with a supportive governor to impose reform efforts on a recalcitrant school board can sap legitimacy and capacity from local institutions that ultimately are required to keep reform efforts alive. Using standardized test gaps to reinforce attention to achievement gaps can marginalize efforts to make curricula more responsive to particular concerns of parents and community organizations that are not directly reflected in math or reading test scores. Building coalitions with multi-issue organizations to gain more clout in general elections and with general-purpose governments risks losing urgency and focus on school spending. And so on down the line.

In the abstract, it might be possible for reformers to press simultaneously in multiple directions, continually striking a best balance to maximize their success, but in practice the approaches may be so dissimilar, the internal proponents of each so different in outlook and background, the trade-offs so frequent and so high-stakes, the potential for appearing inconsistent or incoherent so inherent that efforts to play on all the squares of the new political grid stretch a weak movement even thinner.

Rather than expecting any one reform organization or movement to master the increasingly complex and dynamic environment, it may make sense to envision and nurture a new organizational arrangement. A federated coalition of diverse organizations, linked by a long-term vision of increased public engagement, could allow member groups the autonomy to develop expertise and focus on specific issues, venues, and tactics. At the same time, ongoing relationships can establish mechanisms and traditions for regular and coordinated ad hoc coalitions when conditions make pooling their efforts worthwhile.

One model for accommodating flexible, ad hoc coalitions might build from the Local Education Networks approach as discussed by Brenda Turnbull in this volume or the multi-issue coalitions introduced by Lauren Wells, Jean Anyon, and Jeannie Oakes. Accounting for more of the elements found in the new political grid, such an expanded model might move beyond education to address more open-ended multi-issue organizing efforts. The informal links between school-centered and multi-issue organizations would gain from participation by representatives from various organizations, some exercising an advisory status and staffed by professional organizers. A multi-issue public engagement council could be the institutional home that facilitates communication among diverse member organizations (e.g., via a newsletter and website). Finally, we might envision a network of independent organizations committed to strong public institutions (including but not limited to education) with the freedom to pursue their own missions but within a framework of formal and informal structures.

Notes

1. Marion Orr's concept of the "local ecology of civic engagement" shares some similarities with the idea of the political grid as I define it here, although his focus is more on cultural and economic processes while I concentrate more on governance institutions (Orr 2007a).

2. HowStuffWorks, Inc., "How Chess Computers Work," available at http://computer.howstuffworks.com/chess1.htm.

3. U.S. Census Bureau, "Resident Population, National Population Estimates for the 2000s," available at www.census.gov/popest/national/asrh/2004_nat_res.html and "Population Estimates," available at www.census.gov/popest/datasets.html.

4. Data reported by states to U.S. Department of Education, National Center for Education Statistics, Common Core of Data, "Public Elementary/Secondary School Universe Survey," 2001–2, Version 1a, and "Local Education Agency Universe Survey," 2001–2, Version 1a. Data is missing for three districts in Tennessee. http://nces.ed.gov/ccd/pub_100_largest.asp.

5. U.S. Census Bureau, "U.S. Interim Projections by Age, Sex, Race, and Hispanic Origin, 2000–2050," available at www.census.gov/ipc/www/usinterimproj/.

6. A full consideration of why state and national involvement has taken this form would require a lengthy investigation and might have to take into account such factors as frustration with earlier input-oriented reforms; compatibility of an output approach with accepted practices in the business community; its adaptability to a more diverse-provider system, including contracting out; and the growing political

influence of a for-profit sector anxious to provide the output measures and confident it could win greater market penetration in such an environment. For a good discussion of the background and consequences of high stakes testing, see Heubert and Hauser (1999).

7. U.S. Department of Education, "Stronger Accountability: Testing for Results: Helping Families, Schools and Communities Understand and Improve Student Achievement," available at www.ed.gov/nclb/accountability/ayp/testingforresults.html.

8. A "magnet school" is the term used to describe special programs within schools, or entire schools, that offer a special curriculum or emphasis designed to attract students from across the district. Magnets schools initially emerged as a tool for racially integrating schools without mandatory busing.

9. These are programs, usually enacted at the state level, that make it possible for students in one district to attend public schools in another district that may offer a better or more appropriate program.

10. Detroit instituted mayoral control in 1999 and reverted to a more traditional elected school board model in 2006, but talk of moving back to a mayoral control model is still prevalent.

11. Mayor Martin Chavez has pushed for more formal power but so far has not won sufficient support in the state legislature.

12. National Council of Education Providers, Home Page, available at www.edu cationproviders.org/financial.htm.

13. This ad ran on the inside page of *Education Week's* April 11, 2007 edition.

14. For example, methods of selecting judges are designed to deemphasize partisan politics, replacing it sometimes with appointed judges, with ratings of judicial candidates' legal expertise by professional societies, and with off-cycle and nonpartisan elections. The length of terms is also meant to make courts systematically out of alignment with legislative and executive political cycles.

15. *San Antonio Independent School District v. Rodriguez* 411 U.S. 1 (1973).

16. This has been most recently and dramatically evidenced in the Louisville and Seattle cases, but for analysis of this as a gradual change clearly pre-dating the Roberts Court, see Orfield and Eaton (1996).

17. See Orr (2007b) for one exception.

References

Abernathy, Scott Franklin. 2005. *School Choice and the Future of American Democracy.* Ann Arbor: University of Michigan Press.

Alinsky, Saul. 1971. *Rules for Radicals.* New York: Vintage.

Baumgartner, Frank R., and Bryan D. Jones. 1993. *Agendas and Instability in American Politics.* Chicago: University of Chicago Press.

Berkman, Michael B., and Eric Plutzer. 2005. *Ten Thousand Democracies: Politics and Public Opinion in America's School Districts.* Washington, DC: Georgetown University Press.

Bryk, Anthony S., Valerie E. Lee, and Peter B. Holland. 1993. *Catholic Schools and the Common Good.* Cambridge, MA: Harvard University Press.

Bryk, Anthony S., and Barbara Schneider. 2002. *Trust in Schools.* New York: Russell Sage Foundation Press.

Buckley, Jack. 2007. Choosing Schools, Building Communities? The Effects of Schools of Choice on Parental Involvement. Working paper #133. New York: National Center for Study of Privatization in Education.

Buckley, Jack, and Mark Schneider. 2007. *Charter Schools: Hope or Hype?* Princeton, NJ: Princeton University Press.

Capps, Randolph, Michael E. Fix, Julie Murray, Jason Ost, Jeffrey S. Passel, and Shinta Herwantoro Hernandez. 2005. The New Demography of America's Schools: Immigration and the No Child Left Behind Act. Washington, DC: Urban Institute.

Center for Education Reform. 2007. *CER Quick Facts* 2007. Available at www.edreform.com/index.cfm?fuseAction=document&documentID=2632.

Chambers, Stefanie. 2006. *Mayors and Schools: Minority Voices and Democratic Tensions in Urban Education.* Philadelphia: Temple University Press.

Clarke, Susan E., Rodney E. Hero, Mara S. Sidney, Luis R. Fraga, and Bari A. Erickson. 2006. *Multi Ethnic Moments: The Politics of Urban Education Reform.* Philadelphia: Temple University Press.

Clotfelter, Charles T. 2004. *After Brown: The Rise and Retreat of School Desegregation.* Princeton, NJ: Princeton University Press.

Coleman, James S., and Thomas Hoffer. 1987. *Public, Catholic, and Private Schools: The Importance of Community.* New York: Basic Books.

Dillon, Sam. 2007. Union-friendly Maverick Leads New Charge for Charter Schools. *New York Times,* July 24.

Eaton, Susan E. 2001. *The Other Boston Busing Story.* New Haven, CT: Yale University Press.

Fox, Susannah, and Gretchen Livingston. 2007. Latinos Online: Hispanics with Lower Levels of Education and English Proficiency Remain Largely Disconnected from the Internet. Washington, DC: Pew Hispanic Center.

Fraga, Luis Ricardo, Nick Rodriguez, and Bari Anhalt Erlichson. 2005. Desegregation and School Board Politics: The Limits of Court-imposed Policy Change. In *Besieged: School Boards and the Future of Education Politics,* ed. William. G. Howell, 102–128. Washington, DC: Brookings Institution Press.

Gilens, Martin. 1995. Racial Attitudes and Opposition to Welfare. *Journal of Politics* 57 (4): 994–1014.

Grady, Michael K., and Audrey Hutchinson. 2007. What Mayors Can Do to Help Build Smart Education Systems. In *City Schools: How Districts and Communities Can Create Smart Education Systems*, ed. Robert Rothman, 137–150. Cambridge, MA: Harvard Education Press.

Hakimzadeh, Shirin, and D'Vera Cohn. 2007. English Usage Among Hispanics in the United States. Washington, DC: Pew Hispanic Center.

Henig, Jeffrey R. 1994. *Rethinking School Choice: Limits of the Market Metaphor*. Princeton, NJ: Princeton University Press.

———. 2005. Understanding the Political Conflict over School Choice. In *How School Choice Affects Students and Families Who Do Not Choose*, ed. Julian R. Betts and Tom Loveless, 176–209. Washington, DC: Brookings Institution Press.

———. 2007. The Political Economy of Supplemental Education Services. In *No Remedy Left Behind: Lessons from a Half-Decade of NCLB*, ed. Frederick M. Hess and Chester E. Finn, 66–95. Washington, DC: AEI Press.

Henig, Jeffrey R., Richard C. Hula, Marion Orr, and Desiree S. Pedescleaux. 1999. *The Color of School Reform*. Princeton, NJ: Princeton University Press.

Henig, Jeffrey R., and Wilbur C. Rich, eds. 2004. *Mayors in the Middle: Politics, Race, and Mayoral Control of Urban Schools*. Princeton, NJ: Princeton University Press.

Heubert, Jay P., and Robert M. Hauser, eds. 1999. *High Stakes: Testing for Tracking, Promotion, and Graduation*. Washington, DC: National Academy Press.

Hirschman, Albert O. 1970. *Exit, Voice, and Loyalty*. Cambridge, MA: Harvard University Press.

Howell, William G., ed. 2005. *Besieged: School Boards and the Future of Education Politics*. Washington, DC: Brookings Institution Press.

Kirst, Michael, and Katrina Bulkley. 2000. "New, Improved" Mayors Take Over City Schools. *Phi Delta Kappan* 80: 538–540, 542–546.

Kirst, Michael W., and Fritz Edelstein. 2006. The Maturing Mayoral Role in Education. *Harvard Educational Review* 76 (6): 152–163.

LaFaive, Michael. 2007. *A School Privatization Primer: for Michigan School Officials, Media and Residents*. Midland, MI: Mackinac Center for Public Policy.

Lieberman, Myron. 2000. *The Teacher Unions: How They Sabotage Educational Reform and Why*. New York: Encounter Books.

Lieberman, Robert C. 1998. *Shifting the Color Line: Race and the American Welfare State*. Cambridge, MA: Harvard University Press.

Lipsky, Michael. 1968. Protest as a Political Resource. *American Political Science Review* 62 (4): 1144–1158.

Manna, Paul. 2006. *School's In: Federalism and the National Education Agenda*. Washington, DC: Georgetown University Press.

McGuinn, Patrick. 2006. *No Child Left Behind and the Transformation of Federal Education Policy 1965–2005*. Lawrence: University Press of Kansas.

Meier, Kenneth J., Joseph Stewart Jr., and Robert E. England. 1989. *Race, Class, and Education: The Politics of Second-Generation Discrimination.* Madison: University of Wisconsin Press.

Molnar, Alex, David Garcia, Margaret Bartlett, and Adrienne O'Neill. 2006. *Profiles of For-Profit Education Management Companies, 2005–2006.* Tempe: Arizona State University, Education Policy Studies Laboratory.

National Center for Education Statistics. 2006. *Trends in the Use of School Choice: 1993 to 2003.* Washington, DC: Author.

Oakes, Jeannie, and John Rogers. 2006. *Learning Power: Organizing for Education and Justice.* New York: Teachers College Press.

Olson, Mancur. 1971. *The Logic of Collective Action.* Cambridge, MA: Harvard University Press.

Orfield, Gary. 1976. Is Coleman Right? *Social Policy* 6 (4): 24–29.

Orfield, Gary, and Susan Eaton. 1996. *Dismantling Desegregation.* New York: The New Press.

Orr, Marion. 2000. *Black Social Capital: The Politics of School Reform in Baltimore, 1986–1998.* Lawrence: University Press of Kansas.

———. 2007a. Community Organizing and the Changing Ecology of Civic Engagement. In *Transforming the City: Community Organizing and the Challenge of Political Change*, ed. Marion Orr, 1–27. Lawrence: University Press of Kansas.

———, ed. 2007b. *Transforming the City: Community Organizing and the Challenge of Political Change.* Lawrence: University Press of Kansas.

Pew Hispanic Center. 2006. A Statistical Portrait of the Foreign-Born Population at Mid-Decade: Washington, DC: Author.

Public Education Network. 2005. A Guide to Public Engagement and School Finance Litigation. Washington, DC: Author.

Putnam, Robert. 1993. *Making Democracy Work: Civic Traditions in Modern Italy.* Princeton, NJ: Princeton University Press.

Rebell, Michael A. 2007. Professional Rigor, Public Engagement and Judicial Review. *Teacher's College Record* 109 (6): 1303–1373.

Rocha, Rene R. 2007. Black-Brown Coalitions in Local School Board Elections. *Political Research Quarterly* 60 (2): 315–328.

Rofes, Eric E., and Lisa M. Stulberg, eds. 2004. *The Emancipatory Promise of Charter Schools: Towards a Progressive Politics of School Choice.* Albany: State University of New York Press.

Sandler, Ross, and David Schoenbrod. 2003. *Democracy by Decree: What Happens When Courts Run Government.* New Haven, CT: Yale University Press.

Sassen, Saskia. 2004. The Global City: Strategic Site/New Frontier. In *Global Tensions: Challenges and Opportunities in the World Economy*, ed. Lourdes Benería and Savitri Bisnath, 259–274. New York: Routledge.

Savas, E. S. 2000. *Privatization and Public-Private Partnerships*. New York: Chatham House.

Schattschneider, E. E. 1960. *The Semi-Sovereign People*. New York: Holt, Rinehart and Winston.

Shipps, Dorothy. 2004. Chicago: The National "Model" Reexamined. In *Mayors in the Middle: Politics, Race, and Mayoral Control of Urban Schools*, ed. Jeffrey R. Henig and Wilbur C. Rich, 59–95. Princeton, NJ: Princeton University Press.

Soss, Joe, Sanford F. Schram, Thomas P. Vartanian, and Erin O'Brien. 2001. Setting the Terms of Relief: Explaining State Policy Choices in the Devolution Revolution. *American Journal of Political Science* 45 (2): 378–395.

Toch, Thomas. 2006. Margins of Error: The Education Testing Industry in the No Child Left Behind Era. Washington, DC: Education Sector.

Viteritti, J. P., ed. 2009. *When Mayors Take Charge: School Governance in the City*. Washington, DC: Brookings Institution.

Weir, Margaret, Harold Wolman, and Todd Swanstrom. 2005. The Calculus of Coalitions: Cities, Suburbs, and the Metropolitan Agenda. *Urban Affairs Review* 40: 730–760.

Wells, Amy Stuart, and Jennifer Jellison Holme. 2006. No Accountability for Diversity: Standardized Tests and the Demise of Racially Mixed Schools. In *School Resegregation: Must the South Turn Back?* ed. John Charles Boger and Gary Orfield, 187–211. Chapel Hill: University of North Carolina Press.

II Streams of Public Engagement for Public Education

4 Public Engagement and the Coproduction of Public Education

Donn Worgs

IN 2005, CHRISTY CUNNINGHAM, a Howard University law professor, brought to-gether a group of Washington, DC, churches to establish the Community Anti-Violence Project (CAVP). After discussing what strategies they should use to achieve their objective of reducing violence, the organization decided to cre-ate an after-school tutoring program. Cunningham runs the program in two churches with the help of student tutors and church members. This modest, community-supported program serves a few dozen students ranging in age from a four-year-old to a twenty-two-year-old working on a GED, with most of the children receiving one-on-one tutoring. Cunningham explains that education is a means to community empowerment, and such empowerment can help reduce violence.[1]

The Community Anti-Violence Program is not unique. Across the United States community members are pooling resources to engage in the copro-duction of education by creating after-school and weekend programs to im-prove education outcomes. Baltimore, for example, has at least seventy-five such programs operating in churches, community centers, schools, and libraries.[2]

Coproduction takes place when "citizens, clients, consumers, volunteers and/or community organizations [work together] in producing public services" (Alford 1998, 128). Implicit in the concept of coproduction is the idea that the state lacks the will or capacity to deliver services in the manner desired by residents. Coproduction assumes a productive populace, in which commu-nity members in turn have the will and the capacity to *try* to narrow the gap between what is desired and what the state has provided.

The coproduction of education may be one of the most common and vibrant (yet unappreciated) realms of civic participation. According to the Corporation for National and Community Service, more than a quarter of all Americans volunteered in some capacity during 2006. Of those who volunteered, 21 percent engaged in tutoring or teaching (Corporation for National and Community Service 2007). We do not know in what capacity these people taught or tutored, but these data suggest that millions of people volunteer to help others learn.

To date there is no systematic study of coproduction and education. This chapter will describe some of the more common manifestations of coproduction and education and raise some of its implications. Although some scholars describe coproduction as including everything from compliance to participation in governance, I focus narrowly on participation aimed at producing services, or service delivery (Levine 1984; Rosentraub and Warren 1987). In the education context this refers to participation in the delivery of educational experiences or the provision of resources that contribute to such experiences—including instruction, supplemental in-class experiences, and out-of-class experiences. Although governance issues are quite relevant to coproduction, other chapters in this volume effectively cover this dimension.

The chapter begins with an overview of coproduction and a description of various manifestations in the realm of education. I focus on two areas that are particularly relevant to educational equity—supplemental education and creating and sustaining new schools. Benefits of coproduction include improving student outcomes and generating parent and community engagement; however, there can be some risks. For example, a narrow emphasis on coproduction may distract community members from broad reform initiatives. I conclude with suggestions for future research.

Coproduction

Coproduction posits an active rather than passive citizenry. The concept gained attention among scholars during the 1970s with the recognition that citizens were more than clients of public services and that they could "play an active role in producing public goods and services of consequence to them" (Ostrom 1996, 1073). Promotion of coproduction in the United States peaked in the 1980s, as governments that had faced calls for increased citizen participation and demands for equity beginning in the late 1960s confronted the challenge of trying to maintain or improve services during the period of fiscal strain that began in the 1970s. Coproduction emerged as one response to the call for more services at less cost. Coproduction suggested "supplementing—or perhaps supplanting—the labors of paid public officials with the service directed activities" of citizens (Brudney and England 1983, 59).

Some advocates also argued that coproduction could affect citizenship. Charles Levine, for example, argued that coproduction could enhance trust of government, increase citizen efficacy, and help revitalize a "communitarian spirit" (Levine 1984, 186). Yet, coproduction remained "the road less traveled." Instead, privatization was more likely to gain attention at various levels of government in the United States and other industrialized nations (Alford 1998). Governments trusted market forces rather than citizen engagement (Ackerman 2004).

Coproduction and Public Engagement for Educational Equity

Public engagement, as it is understood in this volume, centers on individuals engaging in collective efforts to solve community problems. The volume's tighter focus is on how community members come together to solve unequal educational opportunities and outcomes for low-income and ethnic and racial minority students. Coproduction is a somewhat complicated fit. On one hand, much of what fits the definition of coproduction is clearly within the purview of public engagement as just described. Community members coming together to create and support a school or a community organization gathering resources to help provide added programs to a local school are all easy to see. On the other hand, much of what may count as coproduction may seem like mere voluntarism. Should a group of office workers tutoring students during their lunch hour or parents holding a PTA bake sale be considered engagement? Might these be productive activities without rising to the threshold of public engagement? Is there a threshold above which activities are engagement and below which they are voluntarism?

There is a threshold, but it is not based on the tasks performed (e.g., a bake sale or tutoring); rather, it is based on the extent to which the tasks are part of an effort aimed at solving community problems. Harry Boyte and Nancy Kari (1996) make this point in their discussion of "public work." For them, public work is about ordinary people working collectively to produce public goods and services and to solve common problems. They note the work of East Brooklyn Congregations (EBC) in the Nehemiah housing project. The EBC members' efforts entailed a wide variety of tasks, including mundane tasks like stuffing envelopes. The authors note, however, that what "distinguished

Nehemiah from 'voluntarism' or 'helping out' was not the specific tasks but the character of the effort as a whole: Nehemiah was about changing a whole community" (Boyte and Kari 1996, 19). In much the same manner, Professor Cunningham and the church members that produce the CAVP are engaged in public work. They are seeking to transform their community through improving educational outcomes for students.

There are many examples of people working to solve community problems through coproduction. Coproduction aimed at enhancing equity is often found in connection to other forms of engagement—in particular, social movements and community organizing. The freedom schools started during the civil rights movement are a clear example of the coproduction of education as an element of a social movement (Adickes 2005). There are many examples of community organizing efforts spawning coproduction of education. In both circumstances (social movement and community organizing) activists incorporated coproduction into their strategy for change.

Like other forms of engagement, participating in coproductive activities can further politicize individuals and lead to their participation in broader reform efforts. For example, the Baltimore Algebra Project, an affiliate of the national program founded by civil rights veteran Bob Moses, initially involved high school students serving as math tutors for middle school students. In 2003, after the school system proposed reducing the program's budget, students added an organizing component to the project. They have since participated in walkouts, protests, and an attempted citizen's arrest of the state school superintendent. Their activism has resulted in gaining access to top school officials and seats at public hearings (Yung 2007). Their agenda has evolved from tutoring to protecting the funding for their program to broader issues of school reform.

Participation in coproduction can lead to greater politicization and more expansive engagement in two ways. Most simply, a participant gains awareness of a public problem or challenge. This greater awareness may then lead them to action. Consider the new tutor who is confronted with the extent of academic distance between some disadvantaged students and mainstream students. An administrator noted that when she first began working with the youth in her program, she expected the students to be behind but was amazed by the "shockingly poor reading skills." Such a realization may motivate some individuals to expand their engagement related to education issues.

The other manner in which participation may lead to greater engagement comes from the developmental impact on the participant. Boyte and Kari claim that engaging in public work can develop an individual's sense of him- or herself as a "contributor," which in turn can build or generate strategic capacities (Boyte and Kari 1996). One may increase his or her capacity as well as his or her sense of efficacy. Beyond the potential internal transformation, there is also the social capital that develops among participants. Thus, engaging can potentially lead to increased awareness of the issues and challenges that exist, as well as an enhanced capacity and sense of efficacy, and it can create connections to networks and social capital development.

Yet there may be a potential disadvantage as well. There is the possibility that coproduction in education may drive away potential activists or cause them to limit their activities to a narrow focus. Frustrating experiences with school administrators, for example, may deter some individuals from future participation. There may also be those who view their time as better spent working directly with a particular school or set of students than to engage in efforts to move a seemingly immovable school bureaucracy.

Coproduction and Education

Across the United States there are countless examples of people contributing their efforts to enhance the educational experiences of youth in their communities. Many communities place a high value on coproduction, though not all efforts are aimed at enhancing equity. Parent groups in well-off communities, for example, are particularly adept at raising significant funds to supplement school budgets to pay for academic or recreational programs. One recent study of California schools found that more than half of the elementary and middle schools in the top quintile in terms of family income raised $25,000 or more in a given year (Brunner and Imazeki 2008). Donald McAdams observed that some parent groups in Houston have raised "up to $100,000 per year for teaching materials, computers, stage curtains, or whatever the school needed" (McAdams 2000, 61). Again, this volume is focused on engagement aimed at enhancing equity. In this regard, there are two categories of coproduction that are particularly relevant to this discussion: providing supplemental educational experiences and mobilizing resources to create and sustain new schools.

Coproduction in Supplemental Programs

It is widely believed that supplemental educational experiences can enhance achievement or even close the achievement gap (Gordon, Bridglall, and Meroe

2005). Federal policies like the 21st Century Community Learning Centers and the requirements for Supplementary Education Services (SES) in No Child Left Behind are two examples of the national discourse on supplemental programs. Some advocate supplemental education programs to equalize access to quality education within low-performing schools. Edmund Gordon, Beatrice Bridglall, and Aundra Saa Meroe (2005) argue that the achievement gap stems from a gap in exposure to learning environments outside of the school day. They claim that even good schools may not be enough and that supplemental programs are needed in low-income communities, in particular, to help construct the web of support and out-of-school experiences necessary for high academic achievement: "High academic achievement is closely associated with exposure to family and community-based activities and learning experiences that occur both in and out of school in support of academic learning." For students of color in particular, "these opportunities are generally underdeveloped" (p. ix).

Aside from academic achievement, such programs can add content that traditional schools do not cover. This is often the case with cultural and ethnic group-sponsored programs (e.g., Nelson-Brown 2005; Zhou and Kim 2006). These groups see the programs as a means for cultural promotion and preservation. Yet, these programs usually have academic components as well (Nelson-Brown 2005). Some have argued that participation in supplemental programs may account for the academic achievements of many Asian American students (Bhattacharyya 2005; Peng and Wright 1994; Zhou and Kim 2006).

Of course, supplemental programs are not necessarily provided through coproduction, nor does coproduction necessarily focus on equity. Much of the funding for Supplementary Education Services from NCLB is going to for-profit providers, and other programs like the 21st Century Community Learning Centers may be administered by the schools themselves. Further, in middle- and upper-income communities parents can afford to pay for tutoring, after-school, weekend, and summer programs provided by private-sector entities. Coproduction offers a different source of support for supplemental programs than federal funds or family wealth. Examples include large institutionalized programs such as the Higher Achievement Program in Washington, DC, funded by foundation grants, with multiple centers, hundreds of students and dozens of volunteer tutors. Other examples are like the small and informal efforts of "Club 2012," a group of African American parents in Virginia who bring their sons together for homework sessions and weekend enrichment to address the racial achievement gap (Chandler 2007).

Supplemental programs vary tremendously. To the observer, some programs might appear lifeless and bureaucratic, while others reflect heroic efforts of sacrifice, vision, and determination. Regardless, taken together they illustrate a realm in which many individuals are working together to improve the educational outcomes for children. I turn now to some specific examples of coproduction through supplemental programs in Hampton, Virginia, and Baltimore, Maryland, to illustrate some of the various forms these efforts might take and some of the implications they hold for public engagement around education.[3]

Coproduction in Supplemental Programs in Hampton, Virginia

Hampton, Virginia, has pursued coproduction enthusiastically. During the 1980s and 1990s, city officials sought to include citizens and community groups in community policing, planning, neighborhood revitalization, and education—specifically with the delivery of after-school programs (Stone and Worgs 2004). In a context of fiscal strain, Hampton administrators cultivated citizen-initiated projects and an ethos of collaboration across government and community groups. Two education examples illustrate the nature of partnership and engagement.

The Y. H. Thomas Community Center is the product of a mobilizing effort in one of Hampton's historic black neighborhoods. During the years of segregation, the facility was the city's black junior high school, but the school was closed when the school system was integrated. After years of use for recreational programs and other sundry uses, the city government decided to demolish the building. The decision outraged the community for both symbolic and practical reasons. The structure, named after a leading black educator, was the alma mater of many in the community. Beyond the symbolic, the structure was used extensively for recreational programs that served neighborhood youth. Community members and school alumni mobilized and, as a result, forged an agreement with the city government. The city would renovate the building and convert it into a community center staffed by neighborhood volunteers. The center opened in 1996, fully staffed by volunteers who administered a variety of programs, including an after-school educational program, GED preparation classes, and a computer lab. Some years later, the center gained a paid executive director and some part-time staff (Stone and

Worgs 2004). By 2003, the center had as many as fifty students attending the after-school program, which included twenty-five volunteer tutors. The center continues to operate recreation and academic programs, as well as a "Kids Café," which provides food to students after school.

Also in Hampton, the Queen Street Baptist Church, led by a minister with experience in community development, played an active role in community revitalization efforts. The church now runs a food cooperative, health education classes, adult education classes, housing programs, a credit union, and other activities. The church partners with the local government and the school system to run after-school tutorial programs and to run one of the city's neighborhood learning centers. The church staffed the programs with retired teachers and other volunteers. Church leaders view their programs as complementing the city government and accomplishing what the city government cannot (Stone and Worgs 2004).

There have of course been political challenges to much of this work. In the case of Y. H. Thomas, the city first resisted an all-volunteer community center. Yet, in this and other cases, programs that were the products of community mobilization eventually fit well with the city's needs and with city programs. Y. H. Thomas and the Newtown Learning Center (also the product of community mobilization in a historically black community) became showpieces within the city's set of community learning centers. Each benefited from the establishment of a new city program, In-SYNC (Innovations for School, Youth and families, Neighborhoods and Communities). In-SYNC is a partnership between the city's Neighborhood Office and the school system connecting schools to communities. Ultimately, the program became largely focused on operating a set of after-school programs, with the activities of Y. H. Thomas, Newtown, and the Queen Street Baptist Church as key elements of the program.

It is important to note that this alignment of community efforts and the city agenda resulted from city leaders' purposeful policy decisions to tap the value of mobilized community members. For example, leaders from both Y. H. Thomas and Newtown Learning Center were beneficiaries of such decisions—they were graduates of a city program called the Neighborhood College that helped local activists learn about the workings, resources, and limitations of the local government. Participants learned to access outside resources and, perhaps most important, had the opportunity to network and build relationships with each other and with city officials.

The broader policy context also served to support coproduction of education in Hampton. The school system faced increasing pressure under the state's high-stakes testing regime. Within that context, the school system and local government were willing to provide resources to support the efforts of community members that could support gains in achievement. This translated into political support for In-SYNC to tap the civic energy of community members to support education.

Coproduction in Supplemental Programs in Baltimore

Baltimore has a number of supplemental programs operated by residents and civic groups. A survey I conducted revealed seventy-five programs during the 2006–2007 academic year, but the survey could not account for many informal groups; also, the most important institutions surveyed, schools and churches, produced low response rates. Nevertheless, the number is useful as a baseline. Below, I describe two supplemental programs that illustrate different approaches and yield additional insights into the realm of resident-produced supplementary programs. The Child First Authority, like the Hampton example, employs a strong partnership with the local school system. The Reclaiming Our Children and Community Project is independent of the school system, although it tries to align its work with school needs.

The Child First Authority runs an after-school program with twelve sites, serving an average of twelve hundred students per day. Child First is a product of the efforts of Baltimore's affiliate of the Industrial Areas Foundation, BUILD (Baltimoreans United in Leadership Development). BUILD, comprised of Baltimore city congregations and others, has been active in community organizing since 1977 (Orr 2001).

BUILD established the Child First Authority during its work for school reform in the 1990s. The BUILD leaders' vision was for the city to have an "authority" for children, in the same way that there was a "stadium authority" that had been developed to build and manage the new stadiums for the city's professional sports teams. Like the Maryland Stadium Authority and other public-private partnerships in the city, BUILD wanted this new authority to have a dedicated funding stream. After much effort, the organization garnered the support of the city council and Mayor Kurt Schmoke. In 1996, legislation established the Child First Authority—a formal partnership between the city and BUILD. The program's board is selected by BUILD, the mayor, and the city council (Fashola 1999). The program does not have a dedicated funding stream, but it does receive regular allocations from the city government.

The program's two objectives are to provide academic and cultural enrichment experiences and to organize a base of support for schools, children, and communities. The first objective is addressed through the program content. Students spend their first hour of each session essentially preparing for standardized tests, and they spend the remaining time participating in academic or cultural enrichment activities. The program sessions are administered by paid staff with the help of parent and community volunteers.

To organize support for the schools, children, and communities, the group organizes and trains parents in leadership development to prepare them as advocates for their children and their schools. Each site is led by a planning team comprising parents, teachers, the principal and other administrators, community members, and an organizer. To be selected as a site, schools agree to provide space and access to teachers and administrators. The school also agrees to support the parent organizing component (Fashola 1999).

The organizing element is no small matter, and the schools often do not fully understand what they are agreeing to with regard to the parent organizing. BUILD organizers follow the established IAF strategies of one-on-one meetings, potluck dinners, and neighborhood walks. Ultimately, many of the parents support school improvement by volunteering during the school day, advocating for improved facilities and resources, and so forth. Beyond the specific successes of the mobilized parent activists, BUILD leaders believe that they are creating public spaces for citizen engagement. As the parents become more engaged, they become empowered, and they ultimately enhance their efficacy as citizens.

The Reclaiming Our Children and Community Project (ROCACP) stands in stark contrast to Child First. Where Child First is the product of a citywide community organization leveraging its political influence, ROCACP stems largely from one individual. The program is directed by Dante Wilson. Wilson, who has a background in social work, started the program with his own money and continues to support it personally as well as with fundraising and grants.

The program operates out of a building on a block on West Baltimore Street in one of the city's more distressed neighborhoods. Each day, Wilson walks younger children in the program to the facility. Once the children settle down, the group has a daily debriefing or a moment of reflection. In what is essentially a group counseling session, students learn positive thinking tools and ways to address challenges they face.

The after-school program serves school children aged five to twelve. In 2006 the program served more than fifty different children, with an average of twenty-five attending daily. Wilson is joined by three or four regular volunteers (including his wife) and others who come for special events and programs. During the session, the students complete their homework and participate in supplemental activities to prepare them for standardized tests, as well as arts and crafts activities. The children participate in African American cultural activities, learn aspects of African American history, and hear guest speakers. They also get a hot meal during each session.

The program has a strong mental health emphasis. Even the academic work is intended to promote emotional and mental health. Occasionally, mental health professionals meet with individual students at the site. Wilson may arrange outside therapy sessions and will often bring children to the sessions himself. ROCACP also holds weekly group sessions for teenagers. At these sessions teens discuss the challenges they face and strategies for coping with them. Their regular attendance is about twenty teens, but this can double for special events, holidays, or when a large meal is served. Wilson advocates broadly on behalf of his students. He regularly intervenes in school matters on behalf of particular students. This is no small matter as the program is known for working with difficult children, who often come from rather difficult circumstances.

In these examples, we see partnerships between school officials, local government, and community members that align community resources with the school systems' goals of supporting student achievement. Although ROCACP is independent, it also aligns its efforts with the school system's objectives; for example, it helps students prepare to pass standardized tests. Additionally, the programs' mental and emotional support can make the children's in-school experiences more productive.

Child First, coming out of a community organizing model, prioritizes mobilizing parents for power. ROCACP, with its social service orientation, facilitates students and families who need services. Although program leaders have different visions about how they can achieve their missions, they are all proactive community members attempting to enhance students' education.

When administrators of these and twelve other supplemental programs in Baltimore and Washington, DC, were interviewed, several themes emerged.

Common to all of the interviewees was a tremendous level of commitment and significant personal sacrifice. They expend tremendous resources and time. For example, when asked about the funding for their programs, three program directors mentioned work that they do; "a night job," "speaking engagements" or "workshops" were mentioned as means for funding the programs. They viewed the program as a personal financial responsibility, though they did not speak of making "donations." Individuals with full-time jobs spoke of spending ten, twenty, or thirty hours per week or more on their programs.

Two questions that emerge when considering the activities of these individuals are "Why would they make this level of commitment?" and "What is the appeal of this form of engagement?" Part of the answer to the first question seems to lie with their sense of the importance of the work. The administrators believe that they are doing critical work. As one stated, "For me this is so serious. It's about saving lives." Their perception of the critical nature of the work is reflected in an interesting way—prioritizing feeding the children. A majority of the interviewees placed a high priority on feeding the children—especially serving "hot meals." That they put so much emphasis on the food reflects their perception of the extent of what the children need.

The answer to the second question seems to be related to the administrators' sense that their efforts will have an impact. The sense of efficacy taken together with the administrators' views of the public schools also helps explain why these individuals choose this form of engagement. The respondents were consistent in their relatively low regard for what the public schools are achieving. One claimed that the schools are "setting our children up for failure." Another claimed that the teachers are trained to teach but are "not qualified to reach the youth." Although many had some success with partnering with the schools, it seems to have been difficult. Describing the process of trying to get a list of the textbooks used by children from a certain school, a respondent said it was "like pulling teeth."

Most of the administrators felt that working for system reform was futile. Child First and one other group advocated school reform, but few others had reform as a priority. One program administrator in Washington, DC, had trouble recalling her participation in any school reform activity—despite having recently worked on the successful election campaign for the Washington, DC, school board president. She found the effort had become irrelevant after the mayor took control of the school system.

It was a recurring theme that the program administrators preferred working directly with youth over working for school reform. One woman who said she thought reform was possible reported spending three hours per week on those activities and almost forty hours per week on her supplemental program, which was not her source of employment. Another respondent said he understood that his efforts would not "help all of the city's children." Ultimately, even those who reported that they did work for school reform claimed that their work with small groups of students would have a larger impact.

Interestingly, the expressed ambivalence about working for system reform is not an ambivalence about political action per se. This is evident in the program administrators' responses when asked if their projects were "political." They responded with two answers, based on their interpretation of the question. Those who interpreted the question in terms of local electoral politics said no and followed with statements about their relationship with local politicians, such as "there are a few that support the program," "Some support us but we're not in anyone's pocket," "I don't care about politics," or that relationships were useful in terms of "learning about available funding." Those who interpreted the question as being about building or wielding power all said yes. They each in turn followed with a statement about struggling for power, such as "Yes, everything we do is political," "Absolutely! . . . people don't like to talk about power," or "I guess so; because the long range goal is community empowerment of disfranchised people. To the extent that political empowerment is political, it's political."

The picture that emerges is that these individuals feel there is great need, and they have the potential to be effective and make a difference. They view "politics" as a potential distraction from more productive work. They see themselves as engaged in community building and view education as a key means for that process. What is intriguing is that they have broad goals and visions of community change—"community empowerment" as more than one said—but for the most part their actions are directed at small focused projects, serving at times only a handful of children.

Coproduction and the Formation and Support of New Schools

The supplemental programs demonstrate a desire to have a direct impact on learning. This desire is also manifest when community members organize to help create new public schools. New York City provides some excellent examples. Since the early 1990s the IAF affiliates in New York have partnered with the city to create five schools, and a sixth is currently being developed. Ross (1998) detailed how one of the affiliates, East Brooklyn Congregations, was concerned about two underperforming high schools in the area. EBC leaders eventually decided against taking over the two schools and instead sought to create two new public high schools based on the EBC's ideals. Although the city officials were reluctant partners, the EBC succeeded in establishing the schools. Most recently, another IAF affiliate, South Bronx Churches (SBC), has worked with the city to create a new $129 million high school campus that would include four new high schools, one of which will be supported by the SBC (Williams 2004; New York City Office of the Mayor 2004).

Although the IAF examples are instructive, the most common examples of communities organizing to create schools can be found among charter schools. The political process that the EBC engaged in (which required mobilizing their membership, pressure politics, and high-level negotiations) stands in contrast to the "application process" needed to gain a charter school—though politics has not been removed from the process. This development has made creating a school a viable strategy for many community organizations.

Currently, charter school policies open up opportunities for coproduction as well as the prospect of privatization or marketization of education. On one hand, parents and community groups can play a significant role in creating charter schools. On the other hand, charter supporters seek to infuse competition into the public schools by providing an exit option for those unable to choose a private school. In a sense, charter schools provide opportunities for both "voice" and "exit."

Charter schools are a diverse group with different types of organizations founding the schools. Henig et al. (2005) have noted two broad categories of charters. Market-oriented schools are founded or co-founded by for-profit education management organizations (EMOs). Mission-oriented schools are founded by educators, nonprofit or social service organizations, local businesses, and community and parent groups (Henig et al. 2005).

Mission-oriented charter schools rely heavily on outside partners. These partners tend to include public institutions and nonprofits but may include for-profit organizations (Wohlsetter et al. 2004). Partners are sought to help with a variety of issues, including curriculum development or delivery, financial resources, and management, as well as locating and providing facilities (Smith and Wohlsetter 2006). Wohlsetter, Smith, and Malloy (2005) argue that organizational features such as the voluntary creation by any interested entity, the minimal rules that constrain their operation, and the access to per pupil funding, but lack of financial support for facilities and other needs, make charter schools conducive to partnering. Although funding for charter schools is more complex than per pupil funding and charter schools often have fiscal advantages over traditional schools, many charter schools could not function without significant financial and other types of outside support from organizations, businesses, government entities, and parents.

Many charter schools promote parent involvement as a key goal. In fact, charter schools have been found to have higher levels of parent involvement—including serving as in-school volunteers and being involved in governance, budgeting, and instructional issues (Bifulco and Ladd 2005). Robert Bifulco and Helen Ladd attribute this difference to institutional arrangements (decentralization and choice), the fact that charter schools tend to be established in areas with above-normal levels of parent participation, and that more involved parents tend to select charter schools, what they refer to as "parent sorting" (Bifulco and Ladd 2005). Parent sorting, with more active parents choosing charters, could disadvantage traditional schools. The implications for student achievement are unclear, but this dynamic suggests a possible redistribution of the benefits that accrue with greater parent involvement (Bifulco and Ladd 2005).

A glance at some specific schools proves helpful to this discussion. Three Baltimore charter schools are noteworthy sites of coproduction, and an Atlanta school further illustrates some of the implications of charter school coproduction for democracy and equity. The discussion of the Baltimore schools is based on interviews, media accounts, and Web-based information. The discussion of the Atlanta school is based on Katherine Hankins's (2005) description of the founding and operation of the Neighborhood Charter School.

Baltimore Charter Schools

Although the state of Maryland was relatively late in passing charter school legislation in 2003, in 1996 Baltimore's New Schools Initiative created "innovative" schools freed from the bureaucratic requirements that were—and still are—operated by "partners" and governed by boards that included external stakeholders. The measure is said to have been the model for the state charter legislation (Baltimore City Public Schools). At present, there are thirty-one charter and new schools operating in the city.

The Baltimore schools reflect much of what has been noted by national studies in terms of what entities run the schools. Three schools in particular— the Patterson Park Public Charter School (PPPCS), New Song Academy, and the Empowerment Academy—are examples of parents and community members coproducing education. New Song Academy and Empowerment Academy were founded by churches and are each located in communities on Baltimore's West side with high rates of poverty. PPPCS is in a neighborhood that had been in decline but is now undergoing redevelopment and gentrification. The effort to establish the Patterson Park school entailed extensive organizing and meetings of parents and other community members and was led by the Patterson Park Development Corporation, the neighborhood community development corporation that has led the redevelopment effort.

The majority of students in each school qualifies for free or reduced lunch—New Song with just over 80 percent, Empowerment with 75 percent, and Patterson Park having the lowest at 66 percent (during the 2007–8 school year). Patterson Park has the most diverse student population with 65 percent, black, 24 percent Latino, and 9 percent white. The other two schools were practically all black (Maryland State Department of Education [MSDE] 2007).

The three schools have partners that include local colleges, private businesses, cultural institutions, and other community groups. Each school depends on outside funds to operate. New Song, for example, must raise $400,000 from grants and other sources in addition to its $900,000 allocation from the school system (Krupp 2007). In some years they have had to raise as much as $500,000 (Neufeld 2006). The school is housed in the New Song Community Learning Center which was built with contributions from partners like the developer Rouse & Company.

In the case of the Empowerment Academy, the church found the location (a closed former public school), contributed manpower to prepare it for occupation (cleaning, painting, moving furniture, etc.), and helped with some of the initial costs. It continues to provide significant financial support and pays for some staff. A school administrator estimated the financial contribution from the church to be about $250,000 per year. Empowerment Academy and New Song Academy use volunteers to maintain the schools and to serve as mentors, tutors, and "reading buddies."

PPPCS and Empowerment Academy promote parent and community involvement. Patterson Park's website states that "involvement of parents and other community members is integral to the vision and mission" of the school

(PPPCS). The Empowerment Academy also emphasizes parent and community participation. School officials have implemented the National Network of Partnership Schools (NNPS) model for school, family, and community partnerships and prominently display a poster with information on family involvement.[4]

Both schools also require significant parent contributions—thirty hours per family (fifteen hours for single parents) at PPPCS and fifty hours per family at the Empowerment Academy. Both have a staff position dedicated to coordinating volunteers. PPPCS recently received funding for a volunteer coordinator through Americorp, and the Empowerment Academy has a parent-community liaison paid for through the church.

Neighborhood Charter School

Atlanta's Neighborhood Charter School (NCS) is the product of extensive resource contributions by parents and community members in one of Atlanta's gentrifying neighborhoods. Much of the work put in to establishing the school was provided by a group of individuals that Katherine Hankins terms a "professionalized volunteer labor force" (Hankins 2005, 53). During the organizing process that led to the founding of the school, a group of well-educated, middle-class professionals spent from ten to sixty hours per week writing grant applications, soliciting funds, and researching curricular models, among other tasks (Hankins 2005).

The school emphasizes parent involvement and partnerships with local cultural institutions. Parent volunteers have participated in workdays (preparing, cleaning, and maintaining the physical space), and spent time in the classroom supporting instruction. Parents serve on many committees that have significant responsibilities like the personnel committee, the finance committee, and the fund-raising committee. All parents are required to contribute at least ten hours of volunteer time per year (Hankins 2005).

Fund-raising is critical for the school's existence. In fiscal year 2003, for example, the school district provided the school with $833,000 while the faculty and staff compensation alone totaled $863,000. The next year, the allocation was almost 20 percent less than expenses. Thus, the school must raise a significant amount of funds to cover its expenses. Beyond that, the actual cost of operating the school is not reflected in its budget as the additional services provided by professional volunteers are not included in the budget (Hankins 2005).

The NCS is an interesting example of civic participation and democratic citizenship—the product of broad community effort. Yet, it raises some concerns about equity. As noted, the school is located in a gentrifying neighborhood and does not reflect the demographics of Atlanta students. In 2006, 48 percent of the NCS students were white, compared to 9 percent of the public school population. Twenty percent of the NCS students qualified for free or reduced lunches, while 75 percent of the students in the school system qualified (Neighborhood Charter School 2007; Governor's Office of Student Achievement 2008). In addition to these disproportionate student enrollments, the school illustrates how some residents seem to have more opportunity to make important school decisions. Hankins is troubled by the district's charter policy that essentially expands citizenship rights for some (through the opportunity to design and run public schools) but not for others. In addition, schools like NCS benefit from the middle-class status of their parents who have the family structure, financial standing, education, and professional training that allow them to provide valuable support (Hankins 2005).

Charter school policies provide an opportunity for coproduction of public education but offer only limited inroads in terms of progress toward goals of equity—and at times even exasperate disparities between more- and less-privileged residents. Even in the case of those schools that serve disadvantaged populations—like the Baltimore schools—they offer only limited and often unequal opportunities for families to gain access. In Baltimore, charter school admission can be based on varied procedures and criteria, including geographic proximity and transportation; first-come, first-served policies; waiting lists or sibling preferences; random selection; and so forth. Regardless of the method of selection, certain parents will be advantaged in the process. Those who have greater access to information and knowledge about navigating administrative processes are much more likely to gain access to these schools.

Ultimately, these schools are largely an exit option for advantaged residents dissatisfied with the traditional public schools. Despite the implications for enhancing disparities, charter policies do create opportunities for collaborative efforts in schools that may provide educational advantages, even if they are limited in their capacity to bring about system equity. Schools like the Empowerment Academy, with the help and support of community members, provide enhanced educational experiences for a small number of children while broader system reform remains elusive.

The policy environment creates incentives and obstacles for these collaborative efforts. The nature and extent of coproduction is related to these incentive structures. As Ostrom claimed, coproduction is ultimately a function of the "incentives that encourage the active participation of others" (Ostrom 1996, 1073). These charter schools illustrate how policies can promote civic participation but also have the capacity to reinforce disparities related to race and class and perhaps create new disparities.

Discussion

The foregoing examples support Harry Boyte and Nancy Kari's contention that civic energy abounds and "that a rich array of civic work in many diverse settings is evident across the country," although its possibilities and full significance has not been widely understood (Boyte and Kari 1996, 5). These examples suggest some important insights into this realm of engagement. Two recurring characteristics of many of the collaborative efforts considered here are worth highlighting. First, a number of the projects were part of broader community development initiatives, and second, many of the projects were either led by or partnered with faith-based organizations.

Broad community development efforts generate synergies with education improvement and reform. The Patterson Park Public Charter School was one of many projects led by the Patterson Park Development Corporation. Child First was just one initiative within BUILD's agenda that has included affordable housing, a living wage campaign, and various other issues. The New Song Academy is one of the church's community-building initiatives alongside other educational programs, a chapter of Habitat for Humanity, and a health co-op (New Song Community Church 2008). This synergy comes from views that education is either a critical element of community development (e.g., BUILD) or that the existence of quality schooling is central to the stabilization of a community (a sentiment in Patterson Park). That these entities choose to bring about change by charter schools or supplemental programs suggests a lack of confidence in the state's capacity to respond to perceived needs but also suggests a willingness to contribute efforts to supplement, augment, or even supplant the efforts of the state.

Faith-based organizations, specifically churches, are ever present in this realm. Faith-based organizations are widely recognized as vehicles for civic action. There is much research and literature on faith-based organizing and community development that need not be rehashed here, but there is a point of importance that needs to be emphasized in this context. Churches need to be understood not merely as institutions or as single actors but as collections of individuals or as vehicles through which individuals are engaged in civic action. That understanding forces us to consider all of the individual decisions to engage. When a church partners with a school for a tutoring program—it is not just a minister or a program director that chooses to engage, each tutor and each volunteer chooses to participate. If these individual volunteers have an understanding of their actions similar to that of the program directors described above—then the democratic implications are striking.

Obstacles to Coproduction

Effective coproduction is not easy to achieve. Governments and government officials (including school systems and school officials) may not share the priorities of community members or want to relinquish control over resources. The providers of supplemental programs were almost unanimous in citing school principal support as a necessity and at times a major challenge. One program director, who grew hostile just thinking about having to close down a site because of the lack of cooperation and support from the principal, stated, "A number of principals are [expletives] and I'm not working with [expletives]!"

An administrator with Child First described struggles with principals over the balance of activities specifically aimed at improving test scores (the schools' preference) and a broader variety of enrichment activities (Child First's preference). The result has been a compromise—where they dedicate the first hour of the session to preparation for the state exams and the remaining time to other activities covering other academic topics or cultural enrichment.

Resources are also a major obstacle. These include facilities, food and supplies, and staff salaries. The resource strain seems to hit programs that work with the low-income communities the hardest. One program director noted that he had individuals from the community who would volunteer from time to time but often they could not stay long because they needed to work.

Implications for Democracy and Equity

Coproduction aimed at enhancing education has some important implications for equity in education and for democracy. Some of these implications appear beneficial, and others pose challenges for equity and the functioning of democracy.

Potential advantages include improved educational experiences for students with limited increased expenditures as well as an expansion of the array of relationships between students and adults who may serve as mentors and or advocates. In addition to the benefits to the youth, the coproducers who engage in these activities may reap benefits as well. Participating in these collaborations bring residents opportunities for enhancing individual efficacy and, ultimately, building civic capacity. For example, the Child First parents volunteer to help the program, which benefits their children, but their mobilization extends to other social concerns and political issues and keeps the community organized. Activists in Hampton who organized to save Y. H. Thomas were able to direct this political energy to other issues. Through coproduction, they developed an enhanced sense of their political efficacy.

Yet, there are also indications that coproduction can further disadvantage already disadvantaged communities. Coproduction assumes "a productive populace" but not necessarily an equitable one, as the players in these partnerships may press for parochial, narrow, or self-serving agendas. Middle- and upper-income communities may work to maximize their existing advantages (Brudney and England 1983). As a comparison outside education, critics have claimed that community policing has led to disparate policing—as communities that are better organized are more likely to build the relationships with police who are then more responsive to their needs (Thacher 2001). This logic seems to hold for the coproduction of education as well. Thus, policies that promote coproduction may be placing distressed communities in an even more disadvantageous position.

Coproduction can be a driving mechanism for creating charter schools and therefore becomes implicated in educational inequalities that some have associated with charter schools. For example, charters have been associated with parent and student sorting, with middle-class families having more options and capacity to maneuver through the system and gain educational advantages. Further, Joanna Smith and Priscilla Wohlsetter note that some partnering institutions avoid the "problems and limitations of partnering with a large urban school district" by working with charter schools (Smith and Wohlsetter 2006, 259). In a sense the charters may serve as an exit option for both parents and potential partners. The schools provide an option that serves the needs of parents and partners but may ultimately further disadvantage traditional schools.

Coproduction in education may also have implications for efforts aimed at system reform. One program administrator listed a number of criticisms about the public school system and expressed a desire to see system change, yet he explained that his organization does not do "advocacy work," because they "prefer to work with small groups of students." When would-be activists and partners like this individual focus on particular programs, the resources and energy behind systemic reform may be diluted. Coproduction projects—although extensive and requiring much in terms of effort and resources—are essentially narrow initiatives, as compared to system reform. Importantly, these projects may compete for the attention and resources of would-be partners and reformers. In a sense, coproduction may provide an "exit option" for would-be reformers—they can exit the frustration of education politics in favor of a project in which their efforts are more likely to have a direct, though narrow, impact.

Even a program as extensive and expansive as the Child First Authority does not contradict this notion. Although they operate in a dozen neighborhoods across the city, parents mobilize around maintaining funding for the program and around needs of their specific sites. When detailing their accomplishments, a program official noted many school-specific projects, such as renovating playgrounds, renovating locker rooms, attracting partners for a school, and the like. The model may lend itself to organizing around the twelve specific schools but has limited if any impact on the other schools in the system. The ultimate question is whether coproduction projects, given the effort, resources, and focus invested in them, serve as steps toward greater equity or as detours from broad-based reform that might impact more students.

Choosing Coproduction—Public Engagement as an Assurance Game

The interviews with program administrators revealed that most of them consciously chose to invest their time and energy in coproduction projects rather than broader system reform efforts. Considering these decisions in the context of administrators' perceptions of the realm of education politics and possibilities for education reform suggest that they and others may approach public engagement in a manner similar to what Dennis Chong described as an "Assurance Game" (Chong 1991).

In his study of the civil rights movement, Chong argues that the typical rational actor model for understanding collective action needed to be recast.

The traditional contention has been that individual rationality leads to the collective action problem of free-riders. Simply stated, individuals desire collective benefits but are reluctant to contribute to (or pay their share for) the acquisition of collective benefits. When enough people make that calculation, too few people will contribute and the collective benefit is not produced. Chong, however, points to social and psychological factors that change the structure of benefits for the individual, so that contributing to the collective good is preferable to free-riding. Thus people prefer to participate or contribute to successes, although they still prefer not to participate in unsuccessful efforts.

So Chong suggests the population is filled not with free-riders but, rather, with potential contributors. The decision to contribute depends on whether one has assurances that enough other actors (other community members, government officials, etc.) will cooperate and contribute to assure success. Individuals ultimately choose to act based on their perceptions of the probability of success—perceptions in turn based on the likely contributions of others.

Returning to public engagement around education, one would find that if there is a population of potential contributors, these potential contributors will assess the probability of the success of their engagement. If success is not viewed as complete reform of the school system, but rather as increasing the number of children who have access to quality educational experiences, then coproduction through supplemental programs or charter schools may be an attractive course of action, while engaging in attempts at system-wide reform would be less attractive—based on the perceived likely contributions of other actors.

Although coproduction may be more desirable given these calculations, over time it is possible coproducers may be more inclined to work for system reform. Chong claims that social networks increase one's confidence that others will contribute. Thus if engagement through coproduction builds social capital, as well as a sense of efficacy and even trust in government, then the threshold for participation in broader reform efforts may be lower for those who are actively engaged in coproduction.

Chong's assurance game points to some strategies for expanding the participant base for public engagement in education reform. Such a strategy would assure a critical number of collaborators in the reform process. Consider the Hampton case. City officials aligned community interests and efforts and the city's agenda. They did this by presenting a broad vision (collaborative governance with a priority on human capital development), supported by policies and practices. They provided resources and support to community actors and consciously built networks and relationships between government officials and community members (Stone and Worgs 2004).

Hampton was an exception. Baltimore, where would-be partners viewed one another as obstacles rather than opportunities, is more typical. Even so, there are some hints of potential. For example, Baltimore's Rognel Heights Cultural Center was given control of a city building. Using this tremendous resource, the center supported learning programs for dozens of city children, including preparation for standardized tests. Likewise, the City's Office of Suspension refers "difficult children" to ROCACP. These students may get help with emotional issues as well as added preparation for the standardized exams—at no cost to the school system.

Interestingly, although few of the coproducers interviewed for this study support the focus on standardized tests, most, even those who are hostile to the school system, seek to align their efforts in some way with the exam requirements because they feel it is in the students' interests to pass these exams. It is not clear how effective coproducers are, but it is notable that coproducers are consciously trying to align their efforts with those of the state.

The task for those interested in equity is to find the means to tap this latent civic energy in ways that are consistent with a reform agenda. This is the lesson of Hampton. If harnessing this energy is possible, it promises to bring additional resources to reform efforts, as well as an opportunity for civic growth and enhanced civic capacity. In the current context, this is difficult. Absent a guiding vision with which to align, potential contributors will either stay on the side awaiting assurances of cooperation or seek narrow but important successes.

Conclusion

The coproduction of education is a vibrant area of public engagement. Consideration of this phenomenon reveals many ways that ordinary residents commit their time, energy, and money to improve the education of young people. These activities have the potential to improve education outcomes, build social capital, increase awareness of political issues, enhance individual efficacy, and spark additional political and civic action. But they also have some potential drawbacks such as the disparities that may arise out of the coproduction of more-advantaged groups, and the fact that coproduction may provide an "exit option" for potential contributors. Institutions, organizations and individuals may opt away from engaging in broader systemic reform efforts in favor of a focus on one school or a supplemental program serving a small group of students.

It seems clear that many individuals find coproduction to be an appealing mode for engaging in education. The appeal and potential impact suggest that it can be an effective element of a broader reform strategy. There is much to learn about this form of engagement to better understand how to integrate coproduction into a strategy for system reform. Future study needs to assess how much of this activity is taking place and its impact on achievement and school reform. We need to learn more about the people who engage in these projects—their motivations as well as the impact these activities have on them as civic actors. Our expanded understanding of coproduction in education will contribute significantly to our understanding of public engagement in general and promises to be of great value as we continue to forge strategies to bring about equity in education outcomes.

Notes

1. Interview with C. Cunningham, July 27, 2007.

2. Based on survey and exploratory research by the author from 2006 to 2007. The number is likely more than that given the near impossibility of finding all of the more informal initiatives.

3. The descriptions of the programs in Hampton are based on previous research conducted on citywide initiatives aimed at community building. The descriptions for the programs in Baltimore are based on interviews conducted as part of an ongoing study of the coproduction education in the city.

4. The NNPS model for school, family, and community partnerships is built around four key elements: the establishment and leadership of an Action Team for Partnerships (a committee of educators, parents, and community partners charged with planning and leading the effort to engage all families and the community); a framework for six types of involvement (parenting, communicating, volunteering, learning at home, decision making, and collaborating with the community); a one-year action plan for partnerships; and program evaluation (Epstein et al. 2002).

References

Ackerman, John. 2004. Co-governance for Accountability: Beyond "Exit" and "Voice." *World Development* 32 (3): 447–463.

Adickes, Sandra. 2005. *The Legacy of a Freedom School.* New York: Palgrave MacMillan.

Alford, John. 1998. A Public Management Road Less Traveled: Clients as Coproducers of Public Services. *Australian Journal of Public Administration* 57 (4): 128–137.

Bhattacharyya, Maitrayee. 2005. Community Support for Supplementary Education. In *Supplementary Education: The Hidden Curriculum of High Academic Achievement*, ed. Gordon, Edmund, Beatrice L. Bridglall, and Aundra Saa Meroe, pp. 249–272. Lanham, MD: Rowman & Littlefield Publishers.

Bifulco, Robert, and Helen Ladd. 2005. Institutional Change and Coproduction of Public Services: The Effect of Charter Schools on Parental Involvement. *Journal of Public Administration Research and Theory* 16: 553–576.

Boyte, Harry C., and Nancy N. Kari. 1996. *Building America: The Democratic Promise of Public Work*. Philadelphia: Temple University Press.

Brudney, Jeffrey, and Robert England. 1983. Toward a Definition of the Coproduction Concept. *Public Administration Review* 43 (1): 59–65.

Brunner, Eric, and Jennifer Imazeki. 2008. Fiscal Stress and Voluntary Contributions to the Public Schools. *Education Finance and Policy* 3 (4): 402–423.

Chandler, Michael. 2007. Black Parents Seek to Raise Ambitions: Loudoun Group Works to Keep Sons Interested in Academics and Achievement. *Washington Post*, February 20.

Chong, Dennis. 1991. *Collective Action and the Civil Rights Movement*. Chicago: University of Chicago Press.

Corporation for National and Community Service. 2007. Volunteering in America: 2007 State Trends and Rankings in Civic Life. Washington, DC: Author.

Epstein, Joyce L., Mavis G. Sanders, Beth S. Simon, Karen Clark Salinas, Natalie Rodriguez Jansorn, and Frances L. Van Voorhis. 2002. *School, Family, and Community Partnerships: Your Handbook for Action*. Thousand Oaks, CA: Corwin.

Fashola, Olatokunbo. 1999. The Child First Authority After-School Program: A Descriptive Evaluation. Report No. 38. Baltimore: Center for Research on the Education of Students at Risk.

Gordon, Edmund, Beatrice L. Bridglall, and Aundra Saa Meroe. 2005. *Supplementary Education: The Hidden Curriculum of High Academic Achievement*. Lanham, MD: Rowman & Littlefield.

Governor's Office of Student Achievement. 2008. 2006–2007 Report Card—Atlanta Public Schools. http://gaosa.org/report.aspx. Downloaded January 9, 2008.

Hankins, Katherine. 2005. Practicing Citizenship in New Spaces: Rights and Realities of Charter School Activism. *Space and Polity* 9 (1): 41–60.

Henig, Jeffrey, Thomas Holyoke, Heath Brown, and Natalie Lacierno-Paquet. 2005. The Influence of Founder Type on Charter School Structures and Operations. *American Journal of Education*. 111 (4): 487–522.

Krupp, Elysha. 2007. New Song Educates the Whole Child. *Baltimore Examiner*, July 7.

Levine, Charles. 1984. Citizenship and Service Delivery: The Promise of Coproduction. *Public Administration Review* 44: 178–189.

Maryland State Department of Education. 2007. 2007 Maryland Report Card. www .mdreportcard.org/. Downloaded January 9, 2008.

McAdams, Donald. 2000. Fighting to Save Our Urban Schools—and Winning! Lessons from Houston. New York: Teachers College Press.

Neighborhood Charter School. 2007. Fact Sheet: 2006–2007 School Year. www.neighborhoodcharter.com/factsheet.html. Downloaded September 26, 2007.

Nelson-Brown, Jason. 2005. Ethnic Schools: A Historical Case Study of Ethnically Focused Supplemental Education Programs. *Education and Urban Society* 38: 35–61.

Neufeld, Sara. 2006. Successful School Fighting to Survive: New Song Academy Is Left Behind While City Funds Go to Failing Facilities. *Baltimore Sun.* March 26.

New Song Community Church. 2008. Our Ministries. www.nsc-church.org/aboutus .htm. Downloaded January 9, 2008.

New York City Office of the Mayor. 2004. Mayor Michael R. Bloomberg and Schools Chancellor Joel I. Klein Announce New Secondary School Campus in Bronx. Press Release. December 2.

Orr, Marion. 2001. BUILD: Governing Nonprofits and Relational Power. *Policy Studies Review* 18 (4): 71–90.

Ostrom, Elinor. 1996. Crossing the Great Divide: Coproduction, Synergy, and Development. *World Development* 24 (6): 1073–1087.

Patterson Park Public Charter School. 2007. Patterson Park Public Charter School. www.pppcs.org/index.htm. Downloaded January 9, 2008.

Peng, Samuel and DeeAnn Wright. 1994. Explanation of Academic Achievement of Asian American Students. *Journal of Educational Research* 87(6): 346–352.

Rosentraub, Mark, and Robert Warren. 1987. Citizen Participation in the Production of Urban Services. *Public Productivity Review* 10(3): 75–89.

Ross, Timothy. 1998. Grassroots Action in East Brooklyn: A Community Organization Takes Up School Reform. In *Changing Urban Education*, ed. Clarence Stone, pp.118–138. Lawrence: University Press of Kansas.

Smith, Joanna, and Priscilla Wohlstetter. 2006. Understanding the Different Faces of Partnering: A Typology of Public-private Partnerships. *School Leadership and Management*, 26 (3): 249–268.

Stone, Clarence, and Donn Worgs. 2004. Community Building and a Human-Capital Agenda in Hampton, Virginia: A Case Analysis of the Policy Process in a Medium-size City. George Washington Institute for Public Policy Working Paper Series, Working Paper No. 12. Washington, DC: George Washington University.

Thacher, David. 2001. Equity and Community Policing: A New View of Community Partnerships. *Criminal Justice Ethics*, Winter/Spring, pp. 3–16.

Williams, Joe. 2004. New HS Megaplex: 129M Mott Haven Plan, *New York Daily News*, December 3.

Wohlstetter, Priscilla, Courtney Malloy, Guilbert Hentschke, and Joanna Smith. 2004. Improving Service Delivery in Education Through Collaboration: An Exploratory Study of the Role of Cross-Sectoral Alliances in the Development and Support of Charter Schools. *Social Science Quarterly* 85 (5): 1078–1096.

Wohlsetter, Priscilla, Joanna Smith, and Courtney Malloy. 2005. Strategic Alliances in Action: Toward a Theory of Evolution. *Policy Studies Journal* 33 (3): 419–442.

Yung, Fiona. 2007. Community Mobilizing Around Education Reform: A Baltimore Case Study. Unpublished master's thesis. Towson, MD: Towson University.

Zhou, Min, and Susan Kim. 2006. Community Forces, Social Capital, and Educational Achievement: The Case of Supplementary Education in the Chinese and Korean Immigrant Communities. *Harvard Educational Review* 76 (1): 1–29.

5 Democratic Institutions, Public Engagement, and Latinos in American Public Schools

Luis Ricardo Fraga and Ann Frost

You would never mistake Jesse Lopez for a revolutionary. Soft-spoken, with a shy smile beneath his gray mustache, the retired school custodian and amateur mariachi hardly seems like an instigator. Yet if Latinos come to dominate California politics someday, Lopez will have helped make it happen.

Lopez was one of three plaintiffs in a lawsuit earlier this year against the Madera Unified School District aimed at greater Latino participation on the school board in the San Joaquin Valley town. An injunction in the case is forcing Madera Unified, which is 82% Latino, to change the way it elects its board. The decision has already begun to reshape school boards, city councils, and special districts throughout California. Dozens of jurisdictions have Latino majorities with few, if any, Latino elected officials—the very conditions that led to the ruling that the Madera district's electoral system had fostered "racially polarized voting" in violation of the California Voting Rights Act. "I think what we're looking at is a quiet revolution," said Robert Rubin, an attorney with the San Francisco-based Lawyer's Committee for Civil Rights, which brought the Madera case. "I think this will sort of usher in the transfer of power from the Anglo community to the Latino community . . . with fair and equitable voting procedures."

—Mitchell Landsberg, *Los Angeles Times*, January 4, 2009

THE SYSTEM OF PUBLIC EDUCATION in the United States is distinct from those of most other democracies in that the national government has very limited formal governing authority over public schools. Although in recent times the national government has played an increasing role, such as through federal court decisions regarding racial segregation and legislation like the No Child Left Behind Act, on the whole public schools are structured under the principle of American federalism; and under this principle, states and their local school districts are the primary levels of governance with consistent and immediate impact on educational policy and practice.[1] It is clear that the federal government has come to play an increasing role in education; however, states still set most standards regarding curriculum and teacher certification, as well as levels of state contributions to educational spending. In addition, it is local school districts[2] that largely determine school locations, the hiring of superintendents and principals, and most of the specific policies and practices that directly affect teachers and students.

By one recent count, there are approximately 15,014 local school systems in the United States (U.S. Census Bureau 2002a). These districts vary considerably in size of student enrollment, number of schools, budgets, and formal structures of governance. They range from the largest school system in New York City, with more than one million students, 1,400 schools, and 79,000 teachers, to one-room schoolhouses that still exist in some rural areas of the country. Of these school systems in the United States, 13,506 are independent with their own governing authority and 1,508 are operated by states, counties, municipalities, or townships.

One common characteristic of all school systems, however, is that they are centers of democratic governance (Tyack 2003; Hochschild and Scoveronick 2003; Berkman and Plutzer 2005; Clarke et al. 2006). Independent school districts are headed by elected school boards. The last time the Census of Governments included information about school board membership was in 1992. It was reported that there were 88,434 elected school board members serving at that time (U.S. Census Bureau 1992). Of these, 53,268 were elected at-large, 30,325 were elected from single-member districts, and 4,838 were elected through other mechanisms. In such school systems, campaigns, elections, and voter preferences are critical components of attempts to influence educational policy and practice by segments of the public, including parents with children enrolled in schools, teachers' unions, textbook publishers, realtors, racial-ethnic groups, neighborhood associations, taxpayer groups, and other interest groups. Although scholars such as William Howell (2005) claim that the power of school boards has declined significantly over the last few decades due to increased mandates from national and state governments, school boards are still major centers of electoral contestation among competing claims for access to decision making in educational policy. Boards have even been able to reassert their influence over educational policy despite court mandates, thus making board elections critical junctures in determining whose interests would be served in policy decision making (Fraga, Rodriguez, and Erlichson 2005). In dependent school systems, this electoral contestation is directed at mayors, city council members, county officials, and state officials who have influence over public education and similarly must appeal for support from segments of the electorate (Henig and Rich 2004).

It is this role of local school systems as centers of democratic governance subject to pressures from legitimate stakeholders that also explains why parents sometimes choose to influence educational policy makers on a more regular basis outside of the formal electoral process. This is done in two basic ways. First, parents can act as private citizens, making sure that the schools serve their own children's needs. Parents can do this by participating in traditional school activities such as parent-teacher associations and by volunteering in a child's school or through advocacy on behalf of an individual child, such as in private meetings with teachers and administrators. Second, parents and their advocates can organize as a type of interest group with collective ideas and concerns outside of the traditional structures of parent participation in schools. In so doing, parents attempt to expand their individual capacities to influence educational policy makers by building alliances with other parents and interested parties to oversee and influence school practices to attempt to better integrate their children's needs in the daily operation of schools and school systems. Through such efforts parents can also build social capital among themselves, allowing them to better collaborate with school officials to further enrich the educational experiences of their children. Whether this is done to compensate for perceived deficiencies in their capacity to influence educational policy solely through the election of board members or it is done as an appropriate complement to traditional electoral mechanisms to hold schools accountable, the school system as a center of democratic governance is apparent.

Relatedly, therefore, parent and other citizen participation in education policy decision making in school districts is yet another arena in which to examine the breadth and depth of civic engagement in the United States. Stephen Macedo et al. (2005) argue that robust civic engagement in democratic institutions has several benefits that are worth enhancing. For example, robust civic engagement can enhance the quality of democratic governance when the accumulated knowledge of involved individuals and articulated citizen preferences are included in policy decision making. Additionally, the legitimacy of government is enhanced when citizens and residents directly "participate in their own self rule." In addition, active participation in institutions of democratic governance can "enhance the quality of citizens' lives" (Macedo et al. 2005, 4) by allowing them to see themselves as part of larger communities with responsibilities and opportunities to build a larger collective good. In sum, in addition to the traditional role assigned to schools as agents of political socialization for their students (Gimpel, Lay, and Schuknecht 2003), systems of public education, as centers of democratic governance, also serve as important arenas in which adults are socialized into civic engagement in an area of direct importance to their children and families.

However, we also know that civic engagement in public school systems has not always been equally open or responsive to all parents with children in schools. Our history of inequality in public education by race, ethnicity, and class is among the most significant stains on the operation of American schools as systems of democratic governance.[3] In addition, traditional disparities in civic engagement across these social cleavages in running for office, campaigning, voting, and organizing (Verba, Schlozman, and Brady 1995) are also likely to appear in the arena of public schools.

In this chapter, we examine the challenges Latino parents face in advancing their interests and the interests of their children within systems of democratic governance in public education. We begin with a discussion of the growing presence of Latino students in school systems throughout the country and the continuing problems faced by these students. We also discuss Latino parents' consistently high expectations for their children's performance in schools, despite the barriers these parents face in effectively engaging with these schools. In the second section we explore how fundamental elements of systems of school board election, particularly the prevalent use of at-large elections, limits the opportunities that Latino parents have to affect educational policy decision making at the local level. We also discuss how the status of many Latino parents as noncitizens bars them from any chance to vote for school board members. In the third section we discuss how Latino parents, despite barriers, directly, and at times successfully, engage with school board members, school administrators, and teachers to advocate on behalf of their children's interests. In the final section, we outline the elements of a research agenda that would expand our knowledge of strategies that school officials *and* Latino parents can pursue to better collaborate in efforts to promote the successful academic achievement of Latino students in American public schools.

Latino Students and Educational Challenges

It is well known that Latinos are now the largest and one of the fastest-growing non-white ethnic-racial segments of the American population. In 2006 the American Community Survey of the U.S. Census Bureau estimated that Latinos constituted 14.8% of the U.S. population, while African Americans were 12% (U.S. Census Bureau 2006). Unlike the percentage of African Americans, however, the percentage of Latinos in the population is projected to grow. According to one projection, by 2050 Latinos will make up almost 25% of the national population. It is also projected that in that same year 52% of the population will be Caucasian, a slim majority (U.S. Census Bureau 2002b).

Given the growth in the Latino population overall, it is no surprise that Latinos are also the largest non-white ethnic-racial segment of students enrolled in public schools across the nation. In 2005–2006 there were 9,641,407 Latinos enrolled in public schools, which was 19.8% of all students (National Center for Education Statistics 2007). In addition, Latinos represent the fastest-growing racial-ethnic segment of public school enrollment. National Latino student enrollment has grown dramatically—356% since 1968 (Orfield and Lee 2004, 13). By comparison whites constituted 27.8 million (57%) of all public school students in 2005, reflecting a decline of 20% since 1968, and African Americans numbered 8.4 million (17.2%) of all students, an increase of 31% since 1968 (National Center for Education Statistics 2007).

Interestingly, a larger share of the Latino population is of school age than is the case for non-Hispanic whites. The 2004 Current Population Survey estimated that 26.8% of all Latinos were between the ages of five and nineteen while only 19% of the non-Hispanic white population was in this age range (U.S. Census Bureau 2004). A little-appreciated fact about Latino youths who are currently living in the United States is that a full 85.6% of them were born in the United States and thus are American citizens. By comparison, only 39.4% of Latinos above the age of eighteen were born in the United States (Carnevale 1999).

Just as dramatic as the national enrollment increases is the growing presence of Latinos in our public schools in all regions of the country. For example, from 1972 to 2002, Latino student enrollment in public schools doubled in the Northeast, to 12.2% of all students there; grew by more than three and a half times in the Midwest, to 7.1%; grew by just under three times in the South, to 17.4%; and doubled in the West, to 38.6% of all students. In Fall 2005, Latinos constituted 54% of students enrolled in New Mexico schools, the largest ethnic-racial segment enrolled there. They were also the largest plurality of students in California, at 48.5%, and in Texas, at 45.3%. In addition, they represented sizeable percentages of the students enrolled in Arizona, 39.0%; Nevada, 33.6%; Colorado, 27.1%; Florida, 23.9%; New York, 20.1%; Illinois, 19.0%; and New Jersey, 18.2% (National Center for Education Statistics 2007).

Most Latino students attend schools in larger cities. For example, the Los Angeles Unified School District (LAUSD) included 516,357 Latino students in 2006–2007; Latinos are 73.3% of all students in the LAUSD. In that same school year, Latinos also constituted a sizeable percentage of students in Miami-Dade County, at 67.1%; Houston, at 59.3%; New York City, at 45.2%; and Chicago, at 38.3%.

Researchers at the Harvard University Civil Rights Project found that many Latino students also attend highly segregated schools. It is estimated that in 2005, 39% of all Latino students attended schools where 90 to 100% of the students were either Latino or African American. Just as significantly, these researchers found that 49% of all Latino students attended schools where more than 75% of all students came from families whose incomes qualified them for free or reduced lunch (Orfield and Lee 2005, 2006).

It is also the case that a very substantial percentage of Latino students are classified as English language learners (ELLs). Although state standards used to determine if a student is an English leaner vary across the country, Gandara and Contreras estimate that 40 to 45% of all Latino students nationally are ELLs. In California, the state with the largest number of ELL students, the state Department of Education estimated that 46% of all Latino students enrolled in its public schools in 2006 were English Language Learners (Gándara and Contreras 2009, 361, fn. 8).

Unfortunately, it is equally well known that this fast-growing group, a group whose success in American society will undoubtedly have a direct impact on the well-being of the country as a whole, has one of the lowest levels of formal education attainment of any segment of the American population (Valdés 1996; Valenzuela 1999). Whether one looks at scores on standardized tests (Carnevale 1999; Garcia 2001), English language acquisition among English language learners (Macias 1998; Riley and Pompa 1998; Hakuta and Beatty 2000), dropout and graduation rates (Secada et al. 1998; Greene and Winters 2006), or propensity to enroll in college (Olivas 1986), Latinos lag well behind almost every other major segment of the American population.

Quirocho and Daoud (2006) report that among the reasons that Latino students do not perform better in elementary and secondary education—which has direct implications for the likelihood that they will attain post-secondary training and college attendance—is that Latino parents are not effectively and consistently engaged in their children's school system and especially in their children's public schools. Issues related to limited formal education, values, language, cultural literacy, citizenship status, and income are often cited as among the primary reasons that Latino parents are unwilling and unable to be supporters and leaders of their children's attempts to succeed in school.

Claims are consistently made that Latino parents have little interest and capacity to participate in their children's schools. Researchers note comments such as following:

- "Well, you can't expect anything from these children. Their parents don't care and they come from transient families." Carlos F. Diaz (2001), as quoted in Quirocho and Daoud (2006, 255).
- "They don't come to school to help in the classroom. We try, but we just can't get them here" (Quirocho and Daoud 2006, 260).
- "They don't and can't help in the classrooms" (p. 260).
- "They don't help their children with homework" (p. 260).
- "They just don't care as much as the other parents do" (p. 260).

A study of two schools in southern California found that Latino parents agreed that some families do not do enough to help their children with their homework and that some parents often let their children watch too much television (Quirocho and Daoud 2006, 263).

As is the case with subsets of all parents, the above characterizations likely apply to some portion of Latino parents. However, findings from a number of surveys indicate that the above characterization is not accurate for large portions, and at times clear majorities, of Latino adults in the United States.

A national survey of Latino public opinion conducted by Bendixen and Associates in 2004 found that in response to the question, "What do you think is the most important issue to you and your family today—education, jobs and the economy, health care, terrorism, or immigration?" just over a quarter (26%) of Latinos listed education as *the* most important issue. Education ranked second only to jobs and the economy, which was ranked first by 30% of respondents. However, education was well ahead of the other issues: 20% of respondents listed health care, 15% immigration, and 6% terrorism (New California Media 2004). The Pew Hispanic Center (2004) reported that in their survey of Latino registered voters, education received the highest ranking as an issue that would be extremely important in determining the presidential votes of 54% of respondents. By comparison, the economy and jobs were ranked as extremely important by 51%, health care and Medicaid by 51%, and the war in Iraq by 40%.[4] In the Latino National Survey,[5] 9% of respondents forced to choose "the most important problem facing the Latino community today" ranked education third, behind illegal immigration at 30% and unemployment/jobs at 12% (Fraga et al. 2006). This is a significant change from the relatively low ranking of education as the most important "national" or "local" problem as revealed by the Latino National Political Survey in 1989, in which only 3% of respondents listed education, well behind social problems cited by more than 60% of respondents (de la Garza et al. 1992, 88–89). As reflected in these polls, education is one of the most important policy issues to Latino adults.

In 2003 the Pew Hispanic Center (PHC) conducted a national survey that focused exclusively on issues related to education. Interestingly, they report that despite continuing low test scores on achievement tests, relatively high dropout rates, and low rates of college completion, "Hispanics do not emerge from this survey as a disgruntled population that views itself as greatly disadvantaged or victimized" (Pew Hispanic Center 2004, 2). The PHC also reports that Latinos, especially those who are immigrants, are more "positive" and "optimistic" about public schools than are whites or African Americans. They continue, however, that "a sizeable minority of Latinos takes a negative view of the state of public education" (Pew Hispanic Center 2004, 3). Approximately 29% of Latino respondents would give the public schools in their "community" a grade of C, D, or F, and a full 38% would give these grades to the public schools in "the nation as a whole" (Pew Hispanic Center 2004, 4). The Latino National Survey also reveals this favorable view of American public education: 32% of all respondents to the survey gave their "community's public schools" the grade of A and another 38.1% gave them a B. Only 19% gave them a C and very small percentages gave them a D, 5.3%, or an F, 5.5%. Despite consistent evidence that Latinos struggle to take full advantage of the opportunities made available in education, they are predisposed to view schools favorably.

Findings from the Latino National Survey (LNS) also reveal that the overwhelming majority of Latino parents have both high aspirations and high expectations of how their children will perform in schools. Substantial percentages of these parents also report high levels of participation in their children's schools. This is the case even among Latino parents in the first generation, that is, Latinos who are immigrants to the United States.

When Latino parents are asked how far they "would like" to see their child go in school and how far they expect their child "to actually go in school," they express very high aspirations and expectations (Fraga et al. 2006). Interestingly, this largely holds across generations. Nationally, 38.6% of all respondents would like to see their child graduate from college and 55.4% would like to see the child attain a graduate or advanced professional degree. A smaller percentage of first-generation respondents, 35.9%, would like to see their child graduate from college compared to other generations. Interestingly, respondents in the fourth generation represent the smallest percentage, 39.9%, of those who would like to see their child go to graduate school or receive an advanced professional degree.

Similarly, 41.7% of all respondents expect their child to graduate from college and 40.3% expect them to attain a graduate or advanced professional degree. Only 23.7% of the respondents in the fourth generation expect their child to obtain a graduate or advanced professional degree. These data reveal that a very small percentage of respondents nationally and across generations would like or expect their child to graduate only from high school or obtain only vocational training after high school.

Further data from the Latino National Survey reveal that reported contact with school officials—including meeting with a teacher, attending a parent teacher association (PTA) meeting, and volunteering in the school—is of great importance to Latino parents. A large percentage, 90.2%, of all respondents reported meeting with teachers, and there is no significant variation by generation. A full 74% of all respondents indicated having attended a PTA meeting. Interestingly, the highest percentage, 77.5%, was reported by first-generation parents and the smallest response, 64.3%, was reported by fourth-generation parents. Just over half of all respondents, 52.4%, reported volunteering in the schools. This rate was noticeably lower in the first generation, 47.8%, and highest in the third generation at 73.1%. These responses indicate that large percentages of Latino parents meet teachers, attend PTA meetings, and just over half even volunteer in their children's school.

These survey results suggest that Latino parents—even those in the first generation—have high aspirations and expectations for their children in schools. They also reveal that Latinos report participating at very high rates in their children's schools. Perceptions and statements that Latino parents lack interest to engage with their children's schools may be accurate for a subset of Latino parents but are clearly inaccurate in characterizing sizeable majorities of these parents.

A longitudinal study of eighty-one Latino students and their parents over a seven-year period from kindergarten to sixth grade found that Latino parents' educational aspirations for their children were high throughout the elementary years, but expectations for achievement fluctuated. They also found that immigrant Latino parents attributed high instrumental value to formal schooling, and neither time lived in the United States nor perceived experiences of discrimination diminished this view (Goldenberg et al. 2001).

Although Latino parents do want their children to excel in school, some do not have the knowledge of what is required to achieve academic success in schools in the United States. In one study, thirty-six Mexican immigrant families with children in the third, fifth, and seventh grades were interviewed regarding goals for their children. Most of the parents wanted their children to become lawyers and doctors, but did not understand that a college degree is required to enter these professions. Those who understood that college is important lacked the ability to help their children with applications or financial aid. Thus, although these parents made a priority of helping their children with homework, they lacked the knowledge and ability to help children succeed at higher levels of education (Cooper, Denner, and Lopez 1999).

One major barrier to more consistent Latino parent participation is that their views of what constitutes effective engagement with the school differ from teachers' views. Teachers report that parents should participate in formal activities, while Latino parents say that informal at-home activities constitute involvement. There are also differences in the perceived roles of teachers and parents. Latino parents believe there is a clear line between the roles of parent and teacher and that parents should nurture and teach morals, respect, and good behavior, while the school and teachers should instill knowledge. They respect teachers and do not want to interfere in the teachers' efforts to educate their children. This desire to avoid interfering often causes teachers to believe that the parents do not care about their children's education (Tinkler 2002).

Not surprisingly, some Latino parents point to language barriers as a major obstacle to their further participating in their children's schools. Latino parents often cannot communicate with teachers, particularly when the school does not employ interpreters. Language also becomes a barrier to the parents' ability to help children with homework (Tinkler 2002).

Some scholars argue that the misperceptions on the part of teachers in regard to Latino parents and children has led to the unfortunate consequence of Latino children being tracked by teachers and administrators to classes where they receive lower-level instruction and related curriculum (Villenas and Deyhle 1999). When teachers place Spanish-speaking students in low-level classes in English and math, they can set the students on a course for remedial-level classes throughout their academic careers (Cooper, Denner, and Lopez 1999).

There are a number of other barriers to Latino parental involvement in schools. The first is the school environment, where Latino parents often feel unwelcome and intimidated and where teachers do not have the skills to deal with parents. Cultural differences, which appear with the different work styles practiced by the schools and Latino families, can also be a barrier to participation. Another barrier is presented by the parents' level of education, which may mean that parents do not have the skills to help their children with homework and which contributes to parents feeling intimidated by teachers. Psychological issues can also pose a barrier to parental involvement because parents may have had previous negative experiences with education that prevent them from getting involved now. A final barrier can be logistical issues, such as lack of time due to working long hours, the need for child care, and a lack of transportation (Tinkler 2002).

Latino Parents and School Board Elections

The most formal way that Latino parents can engage with their public schools is through voting for school board members to elect representatives who will advocate for and effectively serve their children's interests. As previously stated, the vast majority of school districts elect their school board members. Although board members do not receive a salary and have no personal staff, and as a result are often dependent on district administrators for much policy analysis, they do authorize and oversee important aspects of education policy, including school locations, teacher assignments, student disciplinary policy, curriculum design, and budgetary allocations. Most significantly, it is the school board that hires and fires the school superintendent, arguably the most important educational policy maker in every district. How successful are Latinos in using school board elections as a means to ensure that their children's needs are effectively represented on a school board and thus addressed by school systems?

Although there is no systematic study of Latino voting rates in school board elections, a wide body of research has found that that variation in the ways that school board members are elected can directly determine how representative a school district is likely to be of Latino communities. The two primary ways that school board members are elected is either at-large or from single-member districts. In at-large election, all qualified voters in an entire district vote for school board members. In some school systems, all candidates compete with one another, each voter is able to cast an individual vote for separate candidates consistent with the number of contested seats, and the top vote getters are elected. In other at-large systems, voters similarly can cast a vote for individual candidates consistent with the number of contested seats; however, candidates file for specific places on the ballot (these places do not refer to geographical areas), and a candidate only competes with those who filed for the same place. By contrast, in single-member district systems, the school district is divided into geographically defined representational units and voters cast only one vote for their preferred candidate, who is running in the area where the voter lives.

The literature has consistently documented the way that at-large elections can limit the success of Latinos to serve on school boards (Fraga, Meier, and England 1986; Meier and Stewart 1991; Meier and Juenke 2005; see Fraga and Elis 2008 for the distinct experiences of Latinos in California).[6] At-large elections make it much more difficult for Latino communities concentrated in specific geographical parts of a school district to build citywide coalitions to support their first-choice candidates for office. Systems of single-member district elections make the selection of first-choice candidates by Latino voters much more likely when district lines are drawn to build on distinct geographical areas of Latino population concentration. Levels of Latino representation on school boards is higher in single-member district systems than it is in at-large election systems, controlling for population size, political resources, and other relevant sociodemographic characteristics and whatever variations exist in overall voter participation across districts.

Just as important, this same research finds that higher levels of Latino representation on school boards are associated with the appointment of more Latino administrators. Having more administrators is then associated with the hiring of more Latino teachers, even after controlling for a variety of contextual factors, including the size of the Latino population. Most significantly, this literature finds that larger numbers of Latino teachers are associated with more successful experiences for Latino students in schools, including performance on standardized tests and graduation rates, again controlling for relevant group and contextual factors. What this research reveals is that school boards that are designed to be more representative of their diverse communities not only have board members who are more diverse, but educational outcomes for all students improve as board representativeness is translated into more responsiveness to diverse students through greater representativeness in administrative and teaching ranks.

Very few cities allow authorized noncitizens to vote in local elections. Ron Hayduck (2006) reports that noncitizen voting is allowed in only six small towns in Maryland. It is unclear as to whether this right extends to voting in school elections in these communities as well. What is very clear is that the exclusion of noncitizen parents from voting in school elections, even when they have a child in the school, sends a very clear signal that these parents have little capacity to influence the selection of the most powerful decision makers who oversee educational policies. Given high immigration rates among some Latino subgroups, and given the especially high propensity of immigrants from Mexico and Central America to enter the United States without proper documents, these Latino parents have virtually no capacity to affect electoral outcomes. One recent study estimates that of the 1.5 million children of immigrants ages twelve to seventeen in California, approximately 80% of them are U.S. born (Grantmakers Concerned with Immigrants and Refugees 2008, 7). It is likely that a sizeable number of the parents of these children have not become U.S. citizens. These children, therefore, have parents who are formally excluded from participating in the selection of school board members.

One study showed that Latinos in positions of power in schools sent cues to Latino parents that changed their attitudes about participation and increased their school involvement. Paru Shah (2007), the study's author, develops a conceptual model of parental involvement in education with an emphasis on how descriptive representation plays a role for involvement on the part of Latino parents and tests the model using data from 324 Latino parents with children in the Chicago Public Schools. Shah finds that Latino representation does motivate Latino parents to participate in schools. Latino parents are more likely to participate in their children's schools when those schools have more Latino teachers and more Latinos on Local School Councils (LSCs). Although LSCs do not have the same authority as most system-wide school boards, they do represent an additional layer of school governance that can allow for noncitizen voting and can therefore formally engage noncitizen parents directly in selecting school leaders.

Overall, this research suggests that single-member district systems do lead to greater opportunities for Latino voters to elect their first-choice candidates to public office, with related benefits in bureaucratic representation and student outcomes. In such cases, Latinos are provided clear incentives to participate fully and engage in school board elections with the motivation that their engagement has a high probability of leading to the election of school board members who will work to benefit their children and their communities. As centers of democratic governance, school boards provide legitimacy to the overall education system. A school board that is more reflective of the diversity of its population is much more likely to be informed by the variety of perspectives of its community and have more of its decisions accepted as legitimate by its students, teachers, parents, and voters. Barriers to Latino voter success in electing first-choice candidates, whether by representational structure or by disenfranchisement of noncitizens, is likely to lead to less-representative school board members and other important school officials. The overall consequence of such a system of school governance is that it is less inclusive of the diversity of interests among its students and parents and characterized by student outcomes that remain problematic.

Latino Parent Influence on School Officials

As stated earlier, it is this role of local school systems as centers of democratic governance subject to pressures from stakeholders through a variety of mechanisms that also explains why some parents choose to influence educational leaders outside of the formal electoral process. Whether acting as private citizens ensuring that the schools serve their individual children's needs, participating in traditional school activities such as parent teacher associations, or organizing as a type of interest group with group ideas and resources, parents can attempt to increase their opportunities to influence educational policy makers.

The discussion in Chapter 2 is an example of such efforts as is the discussion in Chapter 6. Here we offer the example of a Latino parent organizing a project at a public middle school in California, called La Familia Initiative, to demonstrate how parents and students can become effective advocates on their own behalf (Jasis and Ordóñez-Jasis 2004–2005). The project was created by a group of Latino parents and supported by a local nonprofit agency. The purpose was to help create a better learning environment for Latino children, to ensure that they had more rewarding high school experiences, and to create a system for increased parental involvement with the school.

At its inception the project's core principles were to improve achievement for all students and particularly for the lowest-performing students and to create an organization that would meet independently of the school but that would work toward a partnership with the school, conducting all meetings in Spanish and allowing school staff to attend meetings only on invitation. The group would elect a few parents to be leaders. They would serve terms of just three months to maximize participation and encourage new leadership. Parents were asked to reach out to and invite other parents to attend meetings. The creation of this group and the ongoing impact of its meetings generated a sense of growing empowerment among Latino parents (Jasis and Ordóñez-Jasis 2004–2005).

The efforts of the project to engage with the school showed school officials that Latino parents were articulate, organized, and involved in their children's education. Among the results of their well-thought-out requests for school improvement were the approval and adoption by school officials of a number of recommendations, including some that dealt specifically with official school policies. These early successes encouraged the parents to increase their efforts and to expand them to district-wide issues. The success achieved by the project is attributed to the parents' commitment to close cooperation and participation with the school and to their effort to get the school officials to recognize the parents as the most important influence in their children's schooling. The components of the successful partnership between the parents and the school included the parents' engagement through *convivencia* (moments of collective creation, solidarity, and bonding), the teachers' commitment to improving academic performance, the project's focus on student achievement, the institutionalization of leadership, the joint process of discovery among all stakeholders in the school community, the commitment to open school symbolic spaces to emerging communities, the commitment to organizing work with feasible and visible results, and the sensitivity and openness to other communities (Jasis and Ordóñez-Jasis 2004–2005). Through this enriched civic engagement, the system of school governance was clearly more responsive to the needs of its Latino community and was able to partner with Latino parents in an attempt to sustain this engagement.

This example and others in this volume demonstrate that effective engagement of Latino parents with their schools is possible and can be a catalyst to forging new and collaborative relationships with schools and school systems. The identification of shared community interests, culturally sensitive methods of community organizing, and clear strategies for institutional change are common in each of these efforts.

Increasing the Public Engagement of Latino Parents

Our examination of existing research on how Latinos engage with public school systems reveals that barriers persist in making it difficult, although not impossible, for these parents to become effective contributors to their children's educational success. The high interest that Latino parents consistently report in their children's education, in combination with the dramatically high aspirations and expectations that they have of how their children will do in school, suggests that there is a rich foundation of social capital on which schools can build. When it can be shown that systems of school board election and qualifications for voting inhibit the capacity of Latino parents to influence school policy, these should be changed if parent engagement is desired by school officials. Similarly, schools and school systems should work with community organizations and groups of parents to devise innovative strategies as to how best to engage Latino parents in their children's education. Although it is unlikely that one best system of parental engagement will be found, there are sufficient examples across diverse Latino communities to serve as useful guides to communities of school officials and parents who want to work toward long-term school reform that better serves the needs of this growing segment of the population. Efforts that include a great deal of relationship building and training of parents *and* school officials to structure collaborative relationships between these two groups are likely to lead to greater civic engagement by parents in schools. Latino parents can effectively partner with school officials to work for change in both their own communities and their children's schools. Contestation over cultural differences between communities and schools need not lead to perpetual tension and division.

Our review of existing studies also indicates that there are some significant gaps where research can provide greater guidance to more informed policy and practice to expand Latino engagement in public schools. Following are some areas where research would greatly help parents, school officials, grant makers, and other relevant stakeholders better understand how to further empower Latino parents to become direct contributors to their children's academic success:

- Under what conditions do election structures limit the capacity of Latinos to elect their first-choice candidates to school boards? How significant are regional differences in the relationship between election structures, population concentration, and board representation? How significant are differences between urban and rural areas?

- What conditions best predict whether or not a school system and community have the *will* and *capacity* to attempt a major new initiative to increase parental involvement in educational policy? As stated earlier, there are a number of recommendations as to what should be done to improve Latino parental involvement in schools. We know very little about the conditions that determine how communities come to decide that greater engagement is a goal worth pursuing.

- What are the unique challenges to greater Latino engagement with public schools in new-arrival emerging communities such as those in areas of the Midwest and South? What best predicts a welcoming as compared to a hostile reception by community leaders and school officials to significant growth in Latino student enrollment over a short period of time?

- What is the best balance between school/district initiated efforts and community-based efforts to increase Latino parental involvement in schools? The research is unclear on this point. Should that balance be negotiated by relevant stakeholders prior to an initiative or should the balance develop organically from the push and pull of a contentious politics?

- What are the barriers to sustaining a commitment by all stakeholders to greater engagement by Latino parents with their public schools? We have research that suggests barriers to change and proposals for what should be done to increase parental participation. We know very little about effective strategies to sustain an initial effort for increased parental involvement.

The current presence and continued growth in the Latino population and especially in Latino public school enrollment makes unquestionably clear that in the future these communities' experiences with schools will have long-lasting consequences for American public education and American society generally. Patterns of economic growth, upward mobility, and meaningful expansions in the realization of the American dream will be driven by Latino experiences in fundamental ways. It will be unfortunate if current and future education reform efforts do not fully integrate the unique resources present in Latino communities to directly engage with formal institutions of school governance and community-based efforts to complement these formal structures and hold their leaders accountable and simultaneously raise expectations of Latino parents as to what they can do to improve the educational opportunities for their children.

Notes

1. For a general discussion of schools in the United States, see Wirt and Kirst 2005, especially chapter 2, "Overview of the Education Political System."

2. The state of Hawaii is an exception. It has a statewide system of public education and no local school districts.

3. See, for example, Myrdal (1944), Hochschild (1984), and Gándara and Contreras (2009).

4. Respondents were allowed to cite as many issues as they wanted as extremely important.

5. The Latino National Survey, which was conducted between November 2005 and July 2006, was a forty-minute telephone survey of all Latinos living in the United States. A total of 8,624 respondents were interviewed from fifteen states and the DC metro area. State representative samples of Latinos were drawn from Arizona; Arkansas; California; Colorado; the DC Metro area, including portions of Virginia and Maryland; Florida; Georgia; Illinois; Iowa; Nevada; New Jersey; New Mexico; New York; North Carolina; Texas; and Washington. Each state had a minimum of 400 respondents. The number of respondents in California was 1,200; in Texas, New York, and Florida, it was 800 each; and in Illinois, it was 600. This sampling design captured approximately 87.5% of all Latinos living in the United States. The principal investigators of the LNS were Luis R. Fraga, John A. Garcia, Rodney E. Hero, Michael Jones-Correa, Valerie Martinez-Ebers, and Gary M. Segura. Only parents with at least one child currently enrolled in school were asked the questions regarding education. Because of the large sample, the LNS was able to generate data for respondents who were in the first, second, third, and fourth generations. Copies of the tables with responses by generation can be secured from the authors.

6. The same relationship between school board representation and educational outcomes is found for African Americans (Meier and England 1984; Meier, Stewart, and England 1989).

References

Berkman, Michael B., and Eric Plutzer. 2005. *Ten Thousand Democracies: Politics and Public Opinion in America's School Districts.* Washington, DC: Georgetown University Press.

Bositis, David A. 2002. *Black Elected Officials: A Statistical Summary 2000*. Washington, DC: Joint Center for Political and Economic Studies.

Carnevale, Anthony P. 1999. *Education = Success: Empowering Hispanic Youth and Adults*. Princeton, NJ: Educational Testing Service.

Clarke, Susan E., Rodney E. Hero, Mara S. Sidney, Luis R. Fraga, and Bari A. Erlichson. 2006. *Multiethnic Moments: The Politics of Urban Education Reform*. Philadelphia: Temple University Press.

Cooper, Catherine K., Jill Denner, and Edward M. Lopez. 1999. Cultural Brokers: Helping Latino Children on Pathways Toward Success. *Future of Children* 9 (2): 51–57.

de la Garza, Rodolfo, Louis DeSipio, F. Chris Garcia, and Angelo Falcon. 1992. *Latino Voices: Mexican, Puerto Rican, and Cuban Perspectives on American Politics*. Boulder, CO: Westview Press.

Fraga, Luis R., and Roy Elis. 2008. Interests and Representation: Ethnic Advocacy on California School Boards. *Teachers College Record* (forthcoming).

Fraga, Luis R., John A. Garcia, Rodney Hero, Michael Jones-Correa, Valerie Martinez-Ebers, and Gary M. Segura. 2006. Latino National Survey (LNS) computer file ICPSR20862-v3. Ann Arbor, MI: Inter-university Consortium for Political and Social Research (distributor), March 26, 2010. doi:10.3886/ICPSR20862.

Fraga, Luis R., Kenneth J. Meier, and Robert E. England. 1986. "Hispanic Americans and Educational Policy: Limits to Equal Access." *Journal of Politics* 48 (4): 850–876.

Fraga, Luis Ricardo, Nick Rodriguez, and Bari Anhalt Erlichson. 2005. Desegregation and School Board Politics: The Limits of Court-Imposed Policy Change. In *Besieged: School Boards and the Future of Education Politics*, ed. William G. Howell, 102–128. Washington, DC: Brookings Institution Press.

Gándara, Patricia, and Frances Contreras. 2009. *The Latino Education Crisis: The Consequences of Failed Social Policies*. Cambridge, MA: Harvard University Press.

Garcia, Eugene E. 2001. *Hispanic Education in the United States: Raices y Alas*. Lanham, MD: Rowman and Littlefield.

Gimpel, James G., J. Celeste Lay, and Jason E. Schuknecht. 2003. *Cultivating Democracy: Civic Environments and Political Socialization in America*. Washington, DC: Brookings Institution Press.

Goldenberg, Claude, Ronald Gallimore, Leslie Reese, and Helen Garnier. 2001. Cause or Effect? A Longitudinal Study of Immigrant Latino Parents' Aspirations and Expectations, and Their Children's School Performance. *American Educational Research Journal* 39 (3): 547–582.

Grantmakers Concerned with Immigrants and Refugees. 2008. Integration Potential of California's Immigrants and Their Children. http://gcir.org.

Greene, Jay P., and Marcus A. Winters. 2006. Leaving Boys Behind: Public High School Graduation Rates. www.uark.edu/ua/der/EWPA/Research/Accountability/1779.html.

Hakuta, Kenji, and Alexandra Beatty, eds. 2000. *Testing English-language Learners in U.S. Schools*. Washington, DC: National Academy Press.

Hayduk, Ron. 2006. *Democracy for All: Restoring Immigrant Voting Rights in the United Sates*. New York: Routledge.

Henig, Jeffrey R., and Wilbur C. Rich, eds. 2004. *Mayors in the Middle: Politics, Race, and Mayoral Control of Urban Schools*. Princeton, NJ: Princeton University Press.

Hochschild, Jennifer. 1984. *The New American Dilemma: Liberal Democracy and School Desegregation*. New Haven, CT: Yale University Press.

Hochschild, Jennifer, and Nathan Scoveronick. 2003. *The American Dream and the Public Schools*. New York: Oxford University Press.

Howell, William G. 2005. Introduction. In *Besieged: School Boards and the Future of Education Politics*, ed. William G. Howell, 1–23. Washington, DC: Brookings Institution Press.

Jasis, Pablo, and Rosario Ordóñez-Jasis. 2004–2005. Convivencia to Empowerment: Latino Parent Organizing at La Familia. *High School Journal* (December–January): 32–42.

Landsberg, Mitchell. 2009. Madera Unified Case Is Changing Elections Throughout California. *Los Angeles Times,* January 4. http://articles.latimes.com/2009/jan/04/local/me-madera4.

Macedo, Stephen, Yvette Alex-Assensoh, Jeffrey M. Berry, Michael Brintnall, David E. Campbell, Luis Ricardo Fraga, Archon Fund, William A. Galston, Christopher F. Karpowitz, Margaret Levi, Meira Levinson, Keena Lipsitz, Richard G. Niemi, Robert D. Putnam, Wendy M. Rahn, Rob Reich, Robert R. Rodgers, Todd Swanstrom, and Katherine Cramer Walsh. 2005. *Democracy at Risk: How Political Choices Undermine Citizen Participation, and What We Can Do About It*. Washington, DC: Brookings Institution Press.

Macias, Reynaldo F. 1998. *Summary Report of the Survey of the States' Limited English Proficient Students and Available Educational Programs and Services, 1996–97*. Washington DC: National Clearinghouse for Bilingual Education.

Meier, Kenneth J., and Robert E. England. 1984. Black Representation and Education Policy: Are They Related? *American Political Science Review* 78 (June): 392–403.

Meier, Kenneth J., and Eric Gonzalez Juenke. 2005. Electoral Structure and the Quality of Representation on School Boards. In *Besieged: School Boards and the Future of Education Politics*, ed. William G. Howell, 199–227. Washington, DC: Brookings Institution Press.

Meier, Kenneth J., and Joseph Stewart Jr. 1991. *The Politics of Hispanic Education: Un paso pa'lante y dos pa'tras*. Albany: State University of New York Press.

Meier, Kenneth J., Joseph Stewart Jr., and Robert E. England. 1989. *Race, Class, and Education: The Politics of Second Generation Discrimination*. Madison: University of Wisconsin Press.

Myrdal, Gunnar. 1944. *An American Dilemma: The Negro Problem and Modern Democracy.* New York: Harper & Row.

National Center for Education Statistics. 2007. Digest of Education Statistics Tables and Figures. Accessed December 16, 2007 at http://nces.ed.gov/pubs2007/pesenroll06/tables/table_2.asp.

New California Media. 2004. Survey of Latinos. San Francisco.

Olivas, Michael A., ed. 1986. *Latino College Students.* New York: Teachers College Press.

Orfield, Gary, and Chungmei Lee. 2004. *Brown* at 50: King's Dream or *Plessy's* Nightmare? Cambridge, MA: The Civil Rights Project, Harvard University. www.civilrightsproject.ucla.edu/research/reseg04/resegregation04.php.

———. 2005. *Why Segregation Matters: Poverty and Educational Inequality.* Cambridge, MA: The Civil Rights Project, Harvard University. http://bsdweb.bsdvt.org/district/EquityExcellence/Research/Why_Segreg_Matters.pdf.

———. 2006. *Racial Transformation and the Changing Nature of Segregation.* Cambridge, MA: The Civil Rights Project, Harvard University. www.civilrightsproject.ucla.edu/research/deseg/Racial_Transformation.pdf.

Pew Hispanic Center. 2004. National Survey of Latinos: Education. Washington, DC.

Quirocho, Alice M. L., and Annette M. Daoud. 2006. Dispelling Myths About Latino Parent Participation in Schools. *Educational Forum* 70 (Spring): 255–267.

Riley, Richard W., and Delia Pompa. February 1998. *Improving Opportunities: Strategies from the Secretary of Education for Hispanic and Limited English Proficient Students.* Washington, DC: U.S. Department of Education, Office of Bilingual Education and Minority Language Affairs.

Secada, Walter G., Rudolfo Chavez-Chavez, Eugene Garcia, Ciprano Munoz, Jeannie Oakes, Isaura Santiago-Santiago, Robert Slavin. 1998. *No More Excuses: The Final Report of the Hispanic Dropout* Project. Washington, DC: U.S. Department of Education.

Shah, Paru. 2007. Motivating Participation: The Symbolic Effects of Latino Representation on Parental Involvement in Schools. Unpublished manuscript available from the author.

Tinkler, Barry. 2002. A Review of the Literature on Hispanic/Latino Parent Involvement in K–12 Education. Denver: Assets for Colorado Youth.

Tyack, David. 2003. *Seeking Common Ground: Public Schools in a Diverse Society.* Cambridge, MA: Harvard University Press.

U.S. Census Bureau. 1992. *Census of Governments.* Government Organization. Washington, DC: U.S. Department of Commerce.

———. 2002a. *Census of Governments.* Government Organization. 1, no. 1. Washington, DC: U.S. Department of Commerce.

———. 2002b. National Population Projections. I. Summary Files, Total Population by Age, Sex, Race, and Hispanic Origin. Population Division, Population Projections Branch. Aug. 2. www.census.gov/population/www/projections/natsum-T3.html.

———. 2004. *Current Population Survey.* Washington, DC: Department of Commerce.

———. 2006. *American Communities Survey.* Washington, DC: U.S. Department of Commerce.

Valdés, Guadalupe. 1996. *Con Respeto, Bridging the Distances Between Culturally Diverse Families and Schools: An Ethnographic Portrait.* New York: Teachers College Press.

Valenzuela, Angela. 1999. *Subtractive Schooling: U.S. Mexican Youth and the Politics of Caring.* Albany: State University of New York Press.

Verba, Sidney, Kay Lehman Schlozman, and Henry E. Brady. 1995. *Voice and Equality: Civic Voluntarism and American Politics.* Cambridge, MA: Harvard University Press.

Villenas, Sofia, and Donna Deyhle. 1999. Critical Race Theory and Ethnographies Challenging the Stereotypes: Latino Families, Schooling, Resilience, and Resistance. *Curriculum Inquiry* 29 (4): 413–445.

Wirt, Frederick M., and Michael W. Kirst. 2005. *The Political Dynamics of American Education.* 3rd ed. Richmond, CA: McCutchan Publishing Corporation.

6 Community Organizing for Education Reform

Mark R. Warren

OVER THE PAST TWENTY YEARS community organizing has emerged as a powerful new form of public engagement for education reform across the country. In California, the Oakland Communities Organization organized primarily through its base in local churches to prompt the Oakland School District to open forty small schools as a solution to overcrowded and failing schools in the city's "flatlands." In Chicago, the Logan Square Neighborhood Association has trained more than one thousand parent mentor leaders across eight schools who used their newly acquired skills to work with educators to open community learning centers, conduct home visitation programs, and launch a "grow your own" teacher program. In New York, community organizations in the Community Collaborative for District 9 gathered ten thousand signatures and worked with the United Federation of Teachers (UFT) union to convince the school district to launch a lead teacher program, providing experienced teachers with additional pay and release time to mentor new teachers. In one of the earliest and the largest single set of community-based reform efforts, the Industrial Areas Foundation network launched an Alliance School initiative with more than one hundred schools across Texas, spawning a wide variety of reform initiatives at the school level. Meanwhile, in Denver, Padres and Jovenes Unidos brought hundreds of students at predominantly Latino North High School together with adult organizers to press the district into a thorough redesign of the low-performing school. The group now collaborates with the district on implementing the reform, while continuing to organize to change zero-tolerance disciplinary procedures that feed a "school-to-prison pipeline." In Mississippi, local organizations in the rural Delta region allied with Southern

Echo to win passage of the Mississippi Adequate Education Program, which provided an increase of $650 million in state funding for some of the poorest school districts in the country. Local affiliates continue to organize to elect school board members accountable to the predominantly poor, African American families in the counties.[1]

These are but a few examples of a new field of activity in public education reform that has been growing in localities throughout the country. Community organizing is beginning to make a significant impact of reform efforts in public education, yet it has remained largely under the radar screen of school reformers. In this chapter, I bring this emerging field to light and provide an analytical overview of community organizing as a form of public engagement.

Community Organizing as a Form of Public Engagement

The publication of this book indicates a growing appreciation for the importance of public participation in education reform, particularly in our nation's cities. The book's introduction identifies an "engagement gap." Large numbers of residents, particularly in low-income communities of color, do not have opportunities to shape the development of education policy and practice for their children. Public engagement efforts often take the form of the kinds of civic alliances discussed in Chapter 7 by Lauren Wells, Jean Anyon, and Jeannie Oakes. These alliances build the civic capacity that can help districts develop and implement effective reforms. They also generate the political capacity that helps districts sustain reform efforts, while holding public officials accountable to improved practice.

Important as they are, however, these alliances are typically represented by relationships that are "top heavy" with the perspectives and leadership of business, philanthropic, and civic elites. Clarence Stone and his associates (Stone et al. 2001) studied eleven alliances across the country. Although some included representatives from community-based organizations and citywide parent groups, even these showed a weak base of community participation. Stone et al. reported "urban parents are scarcely visible as *active* stakeholders in the current school improvement movement. Among our eleven cities, the most likely source of a parent voice is the middle-class remnant that remains" (p. 83, emphasis in original). Jeffrey Henig and his associates (Henig et al. 1999, 189) also found the lack of a broad community and parent-based movement in the eleven urban districts they studied, calling this critical absence "the dog that hasn't barked."

Low-income parents typically work long hours and find themselves beset by a range of challenges that make participating in political action difficult, from finding adequate housing and health care to dealing with drugs and violence in their neighborhoods. It is important to remember, though, that low-income parents are not uniquely disengaged; direct participation in organized civic and political action has declined across the board in the United States (Putnam 2000). However, low-income communities lack the resources of their more affluent counterparts and exhibit greater needs. The main problem may not lie in the individual, passive parent, but rather in the lack of opportunity for participation. Studies consistently show that parents of all race and class backgrounds care deeply about their children's education (Valenzuela and Black 2002). However, as Theda Skocpol (2003) has shown, the civic landscape is now skewed toward advocacy organizations that speak for people, rather than involve them directly in civic and political life. Most civic organizations either provide services to, or advocate for, low-income families; few serve as vehicles for their active participation. The result is a widening inequality in political participation (Schlozman et al. 2005) and the increasing power of elites in public policy (Hacker, Mettler, and Pinderhughes 2005). The civic alliances that represent public engagement in our urban districts are therefore typical of the kinds of advocacy coalitions that operate in other realms of public policy at the state and national level.

We face a situation where the people with the strongest self-interest in education reform—that is, low-income parents of color whose children attend urban public schools—find themselves missing at the table. The danger with the term *public engagement* is that it can hide race and class differences. The failure of our urban schools represents a systemic question of social injustice and reflects the lack of power of low-income communities of color (Anyon 1997). Fully half of all black and Latino youth continue to fail to graduate high school with their peers, with the proportions even greater in large, urban districts (Orfield et al. 2004). In more affluent communities where parents are well organized and politically influential, such poor performance is not normally tolerated nor allowed to persist. Yet parents in low-income communities often do not have the political clout to effect change. We aspire to be a public, but constructing an inclusive, democratic public requires confronting the current reality of division and exclusion. It requires creating opportunities and vehicles for marginalized communities to enter public life in powerful and effective ways.

Community organizing has emerged as an important vehicle for generating strong and sustained forms of public engagement in low-income communities. Organizing constitutes a distinct tradition that differs in focus from the better-known form of advocacy group politics. Rather than advocating "for" people, the organizing approach focuses on the active engagement of grassroots people themselves in the politics of creating social change, on developing the capacity of people to lead change efforts, and on building power to address inequalities and failure in public policy and institutions (Warren 2005). There are now hundreds of community organizing groups working across the country to affect school reform at the neighborhood and district level; increasingly, groups are working together to address state policy. Although they have yet to attain much of a public profile beyond their immediate localities, organizing efforts are engaging thousands of parents and community residents and, sometimes, youth. They work to create the political will for change, to support school reform efforts, and to hold public officials accountable for real improvements in the quality of life of their children.

The Community Organizing Tradition

Organizing has a long tradition in American democratic life. In fact, some scholars (Skocpol, Ganz, and Munson 2000) suggest that nineteenth- and early twentieth-century America constituted "a nation of organizers" who built a rich network of voluntary associations that connected Americans across lines drawn by class, if not race and gender, generating broad influence in public life. Organizers built the populist movement, settlement houses, and unions; African American organizers built a rich network of fraternal associations (Skocpol, Liazos, and Ganz 2006), while women organizers formed the National Congress of Mothers, which became the PTA (Skocpol 1992). Unfortunately, many of these early membership associations have declined (Skocpol 2003), leaving the less well-off in particular with little effective power (Verba, Schlozman, and Brady 1995). Contemporary community organizing represents a modern form of the country's rich democratic organizing tradition, a promising strategy for revitalizing participation in civic and political life (Warren 2001).

The roots of community organizing can be traced to these earlier populist and settlement house movements (Fisher 1994). But community organizing began to be formally established as a distinct practice through the work of Saul Alinsky in Chicago in the 1930s (Alinsky 1971; Horwitt 1989). Alinsky sought to work with institutions that structured community life, like religious congregations, to build leadership and power for working-class people. Just as the Congress of Industrial Organizations (CIO) was organizing workers in industry, Alinsky sought to create organizations through which working people could create change in their neighborhoods. Alinsky became famous for his brash tactics; he once claimed to have fed baked beans to a group of community residents and led them to a "fart-in" at Rochester symphony hall to protest Eastman Kodak's discriminatory hiring practices. Alinsky worked hard to professionalize the field of organizing. In addition to founding the Industrial Areas Foundation (IAF), which has grown to become one of the largest organizing networks in the United States, Alinsky lectured widely and wrote two books that profoundly influenced the generation coming to political activism in the 1960s (Reitzes and Reitzes 1987).

The social movements of the 1960s also shaped the emerging field of community organizing in a variety of ways. The civil rights movement had roots in a long tradition of local organizing, often led by women. Leaders like Ella Baker, Fannie Lou Hamer, and Septima Clark worked closely with local people, developing political consciousness and action from the ground up, tying local organizing efforts to the national movement (Payne 1995; Robnett 1997). Baker emphasized training local people, and she mentored the young organizers who conducted the early lunch counter sit-ins and joined the Student Nonviolent Coordinating Committee. Clark worked with the Highlander Folk School to form the Citizen Education Program, which combined literacy teaching with personal growth and collective activism. The Highlander Center helped connect organizing to the practice of critical social inquiry developed by Paulo Freire (Freire 2000; Horton and Freire 1990).[2]

Historically, the struggle for education and the struggle for liberation have been fundamentally interconnected in the African American community (Perry 2003). African American community mobilization in the 1960s and early 1970s often focused on the struggle for a good quality public education, whether that took the form of desegregation, community control, or other avenues (Ture and Hamilton 1992[1967]). As the social movements of the 1960s demobilized, however, community organizing as a field of action persisted and, in fact, began to grow. However, organizing groups came to focus less on education and more on community development issues, like affordable housing, economic development, and the quality of neighborhood life. In part, this direction followed a broader trend where public funding became available to support "bricks and mortar" development projects like housing construction and job training programs (Vidal 1992). Philanthropies, like the Ford Foundation, which had supported community action in the 1960s, also moved to fund community development corporations and other efforts at concrete and tangible neighborhood improvements (Howard Samuels Center 2006). By the 1990s, however, the pendulum began to swing back toward public education, as I discuss below; and today, efforts at education reform find themselves shaped by the structure of the field of community organizing.

The Contemporary Field of Community Organizing

The largest community organizing networks in existence today, as well as a large variety of independent efforts, draw explicitly from Alinsky's tradition, although they have revised his strategies in a variety of ways. The largest set of these networks, including the IAF, the Pacific Institute for Community Organization (PICO), the Direct Action and Research Training Center (DART) and the Gamaliel Foundation, have continued Alinsky's focus on institutions, turning to base themselves largely in religious congregations (Warren and Wood 2001). The members of local organizations in these networks are mostly congregations joined typically by smaller numbers of unions, community associations, and sometimes public schools. They are sometimes called *faith-based* networks, although the IAF prefers the term *broad-based* to signal the variety of organizations involved. Organizers engage community residents and leaders by forging connections to these institutions. Institutions provide a stable base of finances and pre-connected networks of people, and they contain values—such as religious commitments to caring and social justice—that motivate and sustain participation in organizing (Warren 2001; Wood 2002).

By contrast, other organizing efforts have individual, not institutional, members.[3] The Association of Community Organizations for Reform Now (ACORN) network constitutes the largest representative of this approach (Beam and Irani 2003; Delgado 1986; Fisher 2009), but many organizing groups recruit members and raise dues income through individuals.[4] These projects typically organize people in their neighborhoods or across a locality, mobilizing them to address an issue of common concern. Organizers seek to mobilize members and the networks in which community leaders participate. However, rather than being institutionally based, these networks are more informal and perhaps more fluid.

Many institutional and individual models of community organizing seek to build multiracial organizations. Nevertheless, these efforts tend to focus on issues of particular concern to communities of color. Indeed, a majority of their members are people of color. However, they do not center their organizing explicitly on race (Warren 2001; Wood 2002; Wood and Warren 2002). Other organizing efforts do place race in the forefront (Delgado 1997). These projects often draw explicitly from the tradition of the civil rights movement or the Chicano movement. Although white participants often participate as allies, these organizing efforts center their work in communities of color. Here organizers engage local people through their connection to a common racial experience and identity. Moreover, they design their action campaigns to target issues of racial discrimination. There are no formalized national networks of these groups, but many affiliate to state or regional networks like Southern Echo in Mississippi and Californians for Justice. A number of independent groups also fall within this tradition, like Padres y Jovenes Unidos in Denver and the Los Angeles Community Coalition. Intermediaries like the Center for Third World Organizing (CTWO) and the ERASE Racism project provide connections and support for some of these independents (Wood 2002).

Although groups inspired by Alinsky tend to focus on adults, the more race-based groups typically include youth as well, continuing the civil rights movement tradition of intergenerational organizing. Youth organizing efforts draw from the traditions of youth participation in the civil rights movement (Carson 1981) and the Chicano movement (Munoz 1989), among others. In fact, the field of youth organizing appears to be rapidly growing, even among the traditionally adult-oriented groups, and becoming particularly important in the work of high school reform (Mediratta 2006; Warren, Mira, and Nikundiwe 2008). By the early years of this decade, there were hundreds of youth organizing efforts across the country, and one study estimated that 75 percent of them addressed education reform in some way (Endo 2002). Many of these efforts have expanded to district-level significance. In Philadelphia, for example, Youth United for Change and the Philadelphia Student Union led a movement to transform secondary education by establishing small, theme-based high schools (see this book's Chapter 11, written by Elaine Simon, Eva Gold, and Maia Cucchiara). In Boston, the Hyde Square Task Force won the city's approval to pilot its new civics curriculum for high schools, while in Baltimore, the Algebra Project has been organizing to pressure the state of Maryland to comply with court orders to provide $800 million in additional funding to city schools (Warren, Mira, and Nikundiwe 2008). In Los Angeles, South Central Youth Empowered thru Action allied with InnerCity Struggle and other groups to gain college prep level courses at all district high schools (see Chapter 9 in this book, written by John Rogers and Ernest Morrell). Meanwhile Californians for Justice, a statewide alliance of youth organizations, won a two-year delay in the implementation of the state's mandatory high school exit exams (Californians for Justice Education Fund 2004).

Youth organizing exhibits some distinguishing characteristics compared to adult community organizing. While Alinsky and his adult followers have been stubbornly pragmatic (Fisher 1994), youth organizers stress developing political consciousness (Ginwright and James 2002; HoSang 2003). Although many adult community organizing groups tend to avoid framing their work in racial terms (Amulya et al. 2004; Warren 2001), youth organizing efforts typically talk openly about racial identity and structural racism (Quiroz-Martinez, HoSang, and Villarosa 2004). Youth organizing groups also place a strong emphasis on cognitive and other developmental benefits to young people (Ginwright 2003). Although youth organizing itself largely takes place in local groups, these efforts often link young people nationally and encourage them to see themselves as part of a national, or even international, movement. At times, youth organizing around school reform has grown out of adult-based efforts, while in other cases youth have taken the lead in education organizing, bringing in parents and adults (Warren, Mira, and Nikundiwe 2008). Despite the growing importance of youth organizing, the focus of this chapter will remain on organizing groups that are primarily adult-focused, which continue to constitute the large majority of the field.

The Turn of Community Organizing to Education Reform

As noted above, when the field of community organizing grew in the 1970s and 1980s, groups concentrated their work mainly on pressing local community needs like affordable housing, economic development and neighborhood safety. They seldom targeted schooling. In fact, twenty years ago one would have been hard pressed to find an organizing group addressing public education reform.[5] Starting in the late eighties, however, organizing groups began to appreciate the need to tackle school reform again. Organizers began to see that it made less and less sense to try to revitalize communities when the neighborhood schools continued to fail. First of all, success in school was becoming increasingly critical to the life chances of the children in the families participating in the organizations. In addition, as families began to improve their circumstances, often through the economic development and job training projects won through organizing campaigns, they would likely move out of their neighborhoods if good schools were not available.

Consequently, beginning in the early 1990s, organizing groups across the country began to turn their attention to the crisis in public education in their communities (Warren 2005). Initially, many organizing groups took the approach of marshalling their base to build the political will to get educational institutions to meet community demands. This approach followed standard organizing practice as had been applied to community development issues. In other words, most organizing groups had honed their skills in efforts to compel city housing authorities to enforce codes and banks to end redlining and lend in inner city neighborhoods and to get a variety of services improved (Briggs, Mueller, and Sullivan 1997). I have elsewhere called this a "unilateral" approach to power, where power is understood to be the force to make others do your bidding (Warren 2005).

It soon became apparent, however, that "banging on the door" from the outside of public schools was too limited a strategy, and groups searched for ways to collaborate with educators at the school or district level. Collaboration became necessary for several reasons that remain valid today. First of all, the institutions of public schooling are weak. Urban schools in low-income communities lack resources. They often have less-qualified teachers, overcrowded classrooms, older buildings in need of serious repair and upgrading, inadequate textbooks, and outdated facilities. Second, the social infrastructure of public schooling is also weak. At the building level, educators rarely form strong, trusting communities ready to work together to improve education (Bryk and Schneider 2002). Rather, schools in low-income communities are rent by internal divisions, often along racial lines (Payne 2008), while teachers are often isolated and atomized (Johnson 2004). In other words, groups could not simply demand that schools improve and expect the institutions of public schooling to have the financial or social capacity necessary to respond.

Organizing groups found they needed to build relationships with educators and contribute directly to reform efforts. Conceptually, this shift can be understood as moving from unilateral to relational power (Warren 2005). If unilateral power involves power "over" others, relational power emphasizes power "with" others, or building the power "to" accomplish common aims. In other words, organizing groups build power to influence education reform, but they are looking to build power with educational institutions whenever possible. The dynamic tension between conflict and collaboration in organizing is an enduring one (Warren 1998).[6] At the beginning of their efforts, groups often have to marshal enough power to be recognized and to gain a seat at the table. And they may need to mobilize their supporters at various times to push their campaigns along. However, in the end, groups will need to find some ways to collaborate with educators if they want to reform institutions.[7]

Partly because the institutions of public education are so weak, improving public education is enormously difficult. Changing individual schools takes tremendous time and energy (Beam and Irani 2003; see also Shirley 1997), and most organizing groups have only one or two organizers dedicated to this work. Getting significant and lasting results is slow. Although organizing can prompt some quicker gains, such as fixing buildings and changing policies, gains in student achievement take much more time and energy. Moreover, improved education and better learning are not so easy to demonstrate concretely to participants. Test scores are useful, but remain limited as a full measure of the impact of organizing efforts on school communities. An organizing group can point to housing units built in the neighborhood because of a specific action campaign. However, it will take many years and more subtle measures to demonstrate the effects of organizing on school reform.[8] Finally, poor schooling outcomes by low-income students of color are often maintained by deeply held values, including racial and class prejudice that leads some teachers to believe that such students cannot achieve at high levels (Oakes and Rogers 2005; Perry 2003). Organizing to change structures and practices, then, may not be sufficient. Organizing groups also have to build new kinds of relationships between educators and families to challenge stereotypes and transform values (Oakes and Rogers 2005; Warren et al. 2009). Consequently, education reform may well represent the hardest thing community organizers have ever tried to achieve. Yet they appear to remain deeply committed to the effort.

Organizing as a Cycle

How does organizing actually work? First of all, organizing styles and strategies vary across the field (Smock 2004). In this section, I have tried to create a composite picture of the features of organizing that appear to be broadly shared. Any one group, however, may emphasize one aspect more than another. In particular, there is some evidence that institutionally based groups, like the IAF and others, emphasize relationship building and leadership development more than individually based groups like ACORN, which may excel at quick mobilizations around issues (Speer et al. 1995; Swarts 2002). However, even some of the "mobilizers" have come to appreciate the particular importance of long-term relationship building and investments in the knowledge and skills of parent leaders that is necessary to make an impact in the field of education work (Simon, Pickron-Davis, and Brown 2002; see also this volume's Chapter 8 by Sara McAlister, Kavitha Mediratta, and Seema Shah).

Figure 6.1[9] presents organizing as a cyclical process oriented toward building power. Organizing starts with relationships. Organizers seek to connect people to each other for the purposes of taking public action. They build what scholars have called *social capital*. *Social capital* refers to the resources inherent in the relationships between people that help them achieve collective aims (Coleman 1988; Putnam 2000). Where financial capital and human capital are in short supply, as they are in many low-income communities, social capital can provide a critical resource (Warren, Thompson, and Saegert 2001). In fact, it provides the key source of power for community organizing groups.

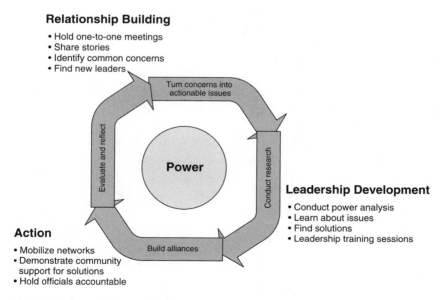

Relationship Building
- Hold one-to-one meetings
- Share stories
- Identify common concerns
- Find new leaders

Turn concerns into actionable issues

Evaluate and reflect

Power

Conduct research

Leadership Development
- Conduct power analysis
- Learn about issues
- Find solutions
- Leadership training sessions

Action
- Mobilize networks
- Demonstrate community support for solutions
- Hold officials accountable

Build alliances

Figure 6.1 Organizing as a Cycle

Some organizing networks have formalized strategies for building relationships, centered on holding a one-to-one meeting between participants
(Chambers 2003). However, all organizing groups work to build relationships
in one way or another. Community residents hold a series of conversations,
often in small groups as in house meetings, in which they share stories and
identify common concerns. Out of these conversations, leaders begin to identify actionable issues. We can conceive of this "coming together" as the beginning formation of a public ready to engage in action around education
reform.

Leadership development also plays a central role in most organizing efforts.
As issue campaigns develop, organizing groups provide training to emerging
community leaders. Leaders learn how to conduct research to investigate the
issue at hand and find solutions to propose. They analyze power relations to
identify possible allies and identify ways to influence decision makers. More
broadly, organizers help teach local leaders the skills and knowledge they
need to become public leaders in their community.

At some point, the group takes action around its campaign. These actions
can take the form of large assemblies at which public officials are asked to support the group's agenda. Alternatively, they can be smaller, collaborative actions
where leaders work with teachers, for example, to start a community-learning
center at a school. Organizing groups have a reputation for close attention to
evaluating the results of every action. Reflection on practice is perhaps organizing's paradigmatic learning process, the primary method of leadership
training.

Relationship building and leadership development are key to effective
public engagement, as these may scaffold low-income parents (many with
important knowledge and abilities to bring to schools) who lack the confidence and the education to feel they can participate as equals (Horvat,
Weininger, and Lareau 2003; Lareau and Horvat 1999). Standing alone, these
parents are even less likely to engage in civic matters outside the school. Coming together in community organizing efforts, people can find mutual support
among people like themselves who have similar experiences and face similar
challenges (Delgado-Gaitan 2001). They build what scholars have called *bonding social capital* (Putnam 2000). With a foundation of bonding social capital,
parents and community residents are more likely to build "bridging" ties to
educators and other actors in the civic arena (Warren, Thompson, and Saegert
2001).

Meanwhile, leadership development includes opportunities to learn the knowledge and skills to collaborate as equals with educators or civic actors who have more formal education and specialized knowledge. Leaders learn how to chair meetings, they learn how to analyze educational policy, and they learn how to conduct a "power analysis" and other techniques that help them become strategic political actors.

Community building and training helps participants become efficacious and confident. This can be a transformative experience for parents and other leaders who move from a position of isolation and powerlessness to one of connectedness and power—from individual concern for their own child to an interdependent sense of public interest (Delgado-Gaitan 2001; Warren et al. 2009). They can enter the broader world of public engagement—such as in civic alliances—in larger numbers, from a position of strength and with the ability to play a meaningful role.

The Field of Community Organizing for Education Reform

I have suggested that organizing can be an effective way to bring low-income parents and community residents into the process of public engagement. What evidence do we have that organizing processes actually engage large numbers of participants and develop strong leaders? A growing body of research presents case studies of individual education organizing efforts.[10] This research gives us a qualitative sense of how organizing works to build broad and deep participation and develop leaders. It documents how organizing groups, in many cases, have brought hundreds of residents into action around school reform issues.

We also have one source of quantitative data: the results of a national survey of institutionally based organizing groups conducted by Interfaith Funders in 1999 (Warren and Wood 2001). The survey included groups in the IAF, the Pacific Institute for Community Organization (PICO), the Direct Action and Research Training Center (DART), and Gamaliel Foundation networks as well as other organizations that similarly follow the faith-based, institutional model. All 133 organizing groups identified as active at the time were surveyed; the groups covered 33 states and the District of Columbia. The report concluded that the field had built wide and deep local roots in American congregations and communities over the past twenty-five years. About 3,500 religious congregations participated in these groups and reached between one and three million Americans through their organizing work.

The survey also found that this form of organizing generates large numbers of local leaders. Nearly 24,000 core leaders participated actively in these groups, an average of 178 in each, while at least 100,000 participants attended public actions of these groups on a regular basis, around 750 per organization. The groups in this survey may be somewhat larger on average than the typical community-organizing group. Nevertheless, this survey is our best quantitative evidence of the extent to which organizing engages the public.

It is not known what proportion of community organizing groups engage in education reform. However, in the survey just mentioned, the majority of groups reported that they had addressed education issues within the past two years. Just over 60 percent of groups who answered the question on the survey listed some kind of education organizing work. I think this 60 percent figure is a reasonable estimate for the field of community organizing as a whole.

How many groups actually conduct community organizing? We have no census of the number of community organizing groups. However, we can count those that are part of national networks. There are approximately 274 organizing groups that are affiliates of national networks. About 182 are in the networks following the institutional model. The IAF and PICO each have about 55 local affiliates across the country, while the Gamaliel Foundation has 50 and DART has 22 local affiliates concentrated in Florida and the Midwest. Meanwhile, ACORN, the only national network following the individual model, had 92 affiliated organizations in 2007.[11]

We can estimate that perhaps another hundred or so local organizations are part of smaller networks at the state or regional level. Southern Echo, for example, is a regional network with about a dozen affiliated groups in Mississippi. Other networks include the Virginia Organizing Project, Californians for Justice, the InterValley Project in New England, and the Regional Congregations and Neighborhood Organizations Training Center based in Los Angeles.

It is very difficult to estimate the number of independent community organizing groups. No survey has done so, and there are problems of establishing precise criteria for inclusion.[12] However, we know that big cities like Chicago, New York, and Los Angeles are home to a wide range of independent organizing groups. Anecdotal evidence suggests that virtually every U.S. city has an organizing group of some sort. The U.S. Census Bureau counts 363 metropolitan areas. If we exclude rural areas and conservatively estimate ten groups for each of the ten largest cities, two groups for each of the next fifty, and one group for each of the rest, we would have about five hundred groups.[13]

Adding up the independent and networked groups, I would therefore estimate that there are perhaps eight hundred community-organizing groups active in the urban United States. If 60 percent of them are engaging in school reform work, that makes about five hundred groups. This estimate is substantially higher than the one given by experts in the field in 2001 but I believe it to be a reasonable current figure. A team at NYU (Mediratta and Fruchter 2001) and at Research for Action (Gold, Simon, and Brown 2002b) combined the results of their independent efforts to identify education organizing groups and estimated that there were somewhat more than two hundred community organizing groups actively working on public education in 1999. That is probably a low estimate for the current period. Some groups may not have been included in that count, perhaps because their public education work was new or small, and the field has likely grown substantially since 1999.

This raises a final consideration. We do not know how many of the organizing groups that work on education issues do so in a sustained manner. Particularly because education work has been so challenging to community organizing groups, some groups may take on one specific education issue and then move on to other concerns (Stone, Orr, and Worgs 2006). Others, most notably the Southwest IAF network, have made a long-term commitment to work on public education. The Texas IAF's Alliance Schools project is now nearly twenty years old. Thus, it may be best to consider the estimate of five hundred education-organizing groups to be a high-end figure. The number of groups that do substantial and sustained education organizing probably lies between two hundred and five hundred.

Goals of Education Reform Organizing

I have so far considered the methods used by community organizing to engage low-income parents and community residents in education reform and considered some evidence that these methods do engage people broadly in active forms of participation. I have also estimated the size of the field to show that it represents a significant force. Now I turn to a consideration of the various ways that groups have sought to address education reform.

First of all, it is important to recognize that the paradigm for organizing is decidedly different from typical school reform thinking. The organizing process starts with the concerns, interests, and energy of participants, not a program developed by experts. When groups first begin to organize parents and community residents, they often focus on immediate concerns around safety issues or facilities. Parents can tell if their children are in danger, if their classrooms are overcrowded, or if their schools are in need of serious repair. As parents start to take action around these kinds of issues, they begin to build their leadership capacity. They get to know how the system works. They become exposed to schooling processes and sometimes start to build relationships and trust with educators. As a result, they build the capacity to take on education policy issues that are more complex.

A second distinctive aspect of the education work of community organizing groups is that they connect school reform to efforts to address the broader needs of families and children. Organizing groups are multi-issue because they take a holistic approach to child and family development. When Austin Interfaith began organizing at Zavala Elementary School in East Austin, parents expressed concern over the lack of healthcare for their children (Shirley 1997). If children lack adequate healthcare, they cannot learn well. So Austin Interfaith's first campaign was to get the school board to open a health clinic at the school. Through the knowledge and relationships built in that campaign, the group went on to organize a Young Scientists pilot project providing advanced science training at the school. Meanwhile, as schools in Austin became involved in Austin Interfaith, they helped support the group's campaign for job training programs for the children's parents.

As the Austin example shows, most education organizing efforts eventually develop some focus on improving instructional practice, even if an organizing campaign starts with safety or climate issues (Beam and Irani 2003; Mediratta, Shah, and McAlister 2009). This is a development that school reformers would likely appreciate, and for good reason. In the end, improving academic achievement rests fundamentally on what happens in the classroom (Elmore 2004). However, this view is too narrow if it excludes other crucial factors that affect children's learning—in the home, school, and community. Organizing groups work on a variety of issues that shape the education and development of children. The IAF affiliate in Los Angeles called One LA worked with a principal to organize at his school in a highly transient neighborhood. One LA leaders found that the school had a 40 percent turnover rate every year. They conducted a series of house meetings with parents and developed a campaign to address housing needs surrounding the school. Both educators and parents who became leaders through this organizing effort reasoned that any improvement in instructional practice would be meaningless if the school community could not be stabilized.

In the end, community organizers and leaders are not primarily educational policy or practice experts. They address teaching and learning issues as part of a broader agenda facing families and communities; indeed, that is one of their strengths. In this way, organizing groups take the community into schools but they also take schools out into the community.

Within the context of work specifically around education, organizing groups work on a wide variety of issues that all matter to improving learning. The National Center for Schools and Communities (2002a) surveyed forty organizing groups in 1999. Table 6.1 outlines the issues that were addressed.

Many organizing groups work to increase the resources available to public schools, working to construct new schools or provide more textbooks. They

Table 6.1 Priority Issues for Educational Organizing

Accountability	Environment/Safety/ Materials	Equity/Equal Opportunity
Accountability: System-wide	Physical Plant	Tracking/Student Equity
Accountability: Teachers	Crowding/School Construction	Special Education for Discipline
Accountability: Leadership	Materials/Textbooks	Bilingual Education
Hiring of Superintendent	Class Size	Racial Discrimination
Training of District Leadership	Safety/Drugs	Budget Allocation Equity
Misuse of Title I Funds	Environmental Hazards	Suspensions
Parent Involvement	Bus Travel Time	Access to College Prep
Student Involvement	Corporal Punishment Truancy Police in Schools	More Counselors Special Needs Students
Standards and Performance	*Special Programs*	*Quality of Instruction*
Reading Scores	Small Schools	Professional Development: Teachers
Math Scores	School-to-Work Connection	Substitute Teachers
Other Scores	Alliance Schools	Direct Instruction
Quality of Curriculum	After-School Academic	Tutoring
Homework	After-School Recreational	
Academic Standards		
Dropout Rates		

Source: National Center for Schools and Communities (2002a, 14).

also address school climate issues, improving safety and physical plant. Some groups work to change policy concerning special education or access to college prep courses. Many have worked to open after-school programs. As noted above, an increasing number are addressing issues related to instruction, including improving the professional development of teachers. Some have sought to help open new schools with a social justice orientation and/or a strong relational culture that, for example, gives priority to family and community engagement. Organizing groups seek greater accountability of public schools. They seek to increase the participation of parents, young people, and community residents in the work of school reform and sometimes in school governance structures. Finally, many groups work to improve relationships between educators and parent/community leaders in schools and at the district level.

There have been several attempts to document ways in which the work of organizing groups has improved schools. The Cross City Campaign for Urban School Reform elaborated an "indicators framework" that outlined eight areas in which organizing makes a significant contribution (Gold, Simon, and Brown 2002b). Some were more directly education-centered, including equity, school/community connection, school climate, and high-quality curriculum and instruction. Other areas were broader, including leadership development, community power, social capital, and public accountability. The Community Involvement Program at the Annenberg Institute for School Reform has developed a conceptual framework to document how organizing groups work to achieve school reform goals by increasing school capacity in a number of domains (Mediratta 2004); the institute has collected data to show that high-capacity organizing efforts in several districts are associated with increased student attendance, improved test scores, and higher graduation rates (Mediratta, Shah, and McAlister 2009).

In short, organizing groups impact public education reform in many ways. This impact cannot be reduced to a simple and linear theory of change with only a few factors and outcomes (see also Baum 2003). Nevertheless, it might be helpful to summarize in three broad ways how organizing efforts work to affect education reform. Community organizing groups (1) organize a political constituency to build the political will for change; (2) contribute to increasing the capacity of schools to change; and (3) hold systems accountable to improve the education provided to children in low-income communities.

Community organizers and parents cannot directly transform instruction; that is the province of professional educators. However, organizing can influence instructional practice in a number of important ways. It can help generate an internal consensus and will to improve on the part of educators. It can build trust and social capital throughout the whole school community to expand schools' capacity to change (Bryk and Schneider 2002; Shirley 1997). It can help develop leaders, including educators at the school, who can lead change processes (Shirley 1997). Organizing can also increase face-to-face relational accountability in the school (Mediratta and Fruchter 2003), leading to a more immediate accountability for school improvement to an organized and educated parent force in the school. When communities of color are strong and well organized, they can begin to change stereotypes teachers hold of low-income children of color and their families (Oakes and Rogers 2005; Warren et al. 2009), which can foster change in practice.

The wide scope of participation in community organizing broadens the agenda for public education reform. Many parents and community leaders resist the reduction of education to academic achievement, at least as measured by test scores. They want their schools to produce citizens and future leaders capable of creating healthier communities and a more vibrant democracy. For example, the Texas IAF Network's "Vision for Public Schools" paper (Texas Interfaith Education Fund 1990, 3–4) declares, "Public schools in the American tradition have never been institutions of merely technical preparation, but were conceived from the beginning as institutions of a democratic culture . . . the tradition of the democratic 'common school' remains essential to our conception of public schools to this day." Community organizing efforts challenge public schools to be centers of community life. Meanwhile, they also connect education reform to a broad agenda for policy changes in housing, economic opportunity, health care, and other issues (Anyon 2005; see also Chapter 7 in this book).

Expanding the Scale of Community Organizing

As community organizing has expanded, organizers and leaders from affiliates in the larger networks have begun to share their work on a regular basis. The Texas IAF network has expanded such meetings across the Southwest (Warren 2001). PICO, with an active state network in California for many years, has more recently promoted connections at the national level (Wood 2007). ACORN has a national education office to connect local organizations (Beam and Irani 2003). Southern Echo coordinates the work of local organizations across Mississippi. Increasingly, venues bring organizing groups together from different networks and include unaffiliated groups as well. Intermediaries like the Cross City Campaign for Urban School Reform, Communities for Public Education Reform, and the Center for Community Change, and private foundations that fund this work, like the Ford and Charles Stewart Mott Foundations, have sponsored such meetings (see, for example, Corbin 2002).

Over time, groups have also developed relationships with school reform experts and organizations. The Oakland Communities Organization worked closely with the Bay Area Coalition for Equitable Schools in its campaign to open small smalls (Gold, Simon, and Brown 2002a). The Community Support Program at the Annenberg Institute, formerly at the Institute for Education and Social Policy of New York University, has provided technical assistance and leadership training to parents and other members in New York ACORN, Mothers on the Move, the Community Collaborative for District 9, and other organizing groups in New York City.

Through these collaborations (within network and cross-group and with professional intermediaries), the field of organizing has increased its knowledge and capacity to participate in school reform. Consequently, in a survey of twenty-six organizing groups, Leigh Dingerson, John Beam, and Chris Brown (2004) found that groups now often start by tackling issues concerning instructional practice. These are more typically the better-resourced groups with connections to networks or intermediaries that can provide or support the quick development of expertise on instructional issues. In the end, though, networks and groups have to be careful not to impose a particular issue or approach if there has not been a sufficient base of local leaders who claim it enthusiastically as their own.

Although most organizing groups work at the neighborhood, school, or district level, increasingly, many want to affect state policy. There are two routes to expanding capacity. Some local organizations in national or regional networks collaborate with each other to build the power to address state-level policy, often piloting model initiatives locally. For example, the Sacramento PICO affiliate developed a model program for teachers to visit their students' homes. The PICO California network lobbied the state legislature to fund the program statewide (Wood 2007). Alternatively, organizers build alliances across groups within different networks or with unaffiliated independents, advancing a common cause. For example, LSNA, ACORN, and other organizations worked together to push the Illinois legislature to fund a "grow your own teacher" program modeled on the *Nueva Generacion* initiative piloted by LSNA (see Chapter 8 by Sara McAlister, Kavitha Mediratta, and Seema Shah in this book).

There is some tension between the way organizing groups operate and the demands of reform coalitions. The distinctive contribution of organizing groups lies in participation from residents of low-income communities. This is accomplished by responding to the concerns, interests, talents, and energies of these residents and the immediate relevance of local issues (Warren 2001). It is at that level where people, in face-to-face relationships, can establish the bonding social capital necessary for effective civic engagement. As organizing groups participate in alliances to get to the scale necessary to affect reform at the district or state level, they risk losing the relationships that are the foundation of their base.

In light of all these concerns, community organizing groups can best contribute to public engagement when they have the capacity to combine active organizing in schools and neighborhoods with collaborative, district-level (and sometimes state-level) reform initiatives. Groups with the highest capacity often combine issues and types of activity to create synergies of social capital, leadership, expertise, and resources.

Challenges Facing the Field

There are tremendous challenges facing the field of community organizing for school reform. Precious few organizing groups have the capacity to operate at the multi-level and multi-issue scale just suggested. Small, localized organizing groups can make contributions around specific issues. But the number of larger networks or coalitions with the sophistication and capacity to act at a significant scale in any district remains limited. Multi-level work is a challenge, especially when the resources available to organizing remain quite small.

Funding for education organizing is meager compared to the undertaking at hand. The survey of faith-based organizing groups cited above found that the median annual budget of these groups was about $150,000 (Warren and Wood 2001). Another survey put the amount closer to $250,000 (Mediratta and Fruchter 2001). Meanwhile, a typical multi-issue organizing group spends only a portion of its budget on education work. Most groups have only one or two organizers devoted to education organizing.

Organizing groups raise their funds from a mix of member dues, private foundations, and local fundraising, but the role of private philanthropy is significant. More than half of the groups in one study received 80 percent of their funding from private foundations (Mediratta and Fruchter 2001, 66). Most groups refuse government funds to protect political independence. The role and influence of private foundations on education organizing and community organizing more broadly has not been systematically studied. After eschewing the funding of community activism in the 1970s and 1980s, however, many of the large private foundations, like the Ford Foundation, returned to funding organizing in the early 1990s (Howard Samuels Center 2006). I have argued elsewhere (Warren 2001) that the willingness of private foundations to provide extra funding specifically for education organizing was critical to the ability of the Texas IAF to launch its Alliance Schools initiative in the early 1990s. More recently, private funders have encouraged organizing groups to collaborate and have supported intermediaries to provide technical assistance to organizing efforts (Howard Samuels Center 2006). Nevertheless, the total amount of financial resources available to organizing efforts remains small by any standard.

A second challenge facing the field of education organizing comes from the No Child Left Behind Act (NCLB) and high-stakes testing regimes that sometimes threaten to cut off the room for experimentation necessary for organizing efforts at the school level. Even the Texas IAF, one of the strongest organizing networks, has struggled to maintain momentum in this new environment (Shirley and Evans 2007). Of course, implementation of testing regimes varies by state and locality. Texas is home to some of the harshest implementation, where some district officials give principals a set number of years to raise test scores and threaten them with dismissal if they fail. In such a climate, calls for creating portfolio assessment, as tried by the Austin IAF affiliate, have fallen on deaf ears in school administration.[14]

Groups have struggled to advance in the face of other changes in what Jeffrey Henig (in Chapter 3 of this book) refers to as the *new political grid*. Mayoral control of school districts may limit opportunities for organizing groups to exert influence with local school board members. Privatization of schooling pulls education out of the public domain, again potentially limiting the influence of organizing groups (see Chapter 11 of this book).

Organizing groups have also struggled to find common ground with teacher unions. Many of the more prominent organizing networks, like the Texas Alliance Schools, have operated in areas with weak unions. Others, like the Logan Square Neighborhood Association in Chicago or the Oakland Communities Organization, work directly with teachers on initiatives that do not require official endorsements by teacher unions. However, many reform proposals require union approval, and many organizing groups would like to expand their power by forming alliances with teacher unions. There have been some recent examples of such alliances. The Community Collaborative for District 9 gained the cooperation of the UFT in New York for a lead teacher program, an alliance that proved critical to the success of the initiative (Fabricant 2010). For years, the New York UFT, the largest American Federation of Teachers (AFT) local in the country, has allied with many organizing groups in the Alliance for Quality Education. Still, strong and active alliances between teacher unions and community organizing groups remain rare.

The community organizing field is also highly fragmented. Its strength lies in its local base and sometimes in its state-level reach. But there are few networks that operate at the national level. Some networks have begun to experiment with national-level work but not around education issues (Whitman 2006; Wood 2007).[15] ACORN had a national education office, but it mainly supported the local or state-level campaigns of its affiliates and tried to spread successful programs it developed in one place to its other affiliates (Beam and Irani 2003). In other words, regional- and national-level connections serve more to stimulate and support local work than to be venues for federal action.

Locally based collaborations across different organizations, while becoming a bit more common as in the South Bronx and Chicago, are still rare, as groups often compete with each other for turf. Yet collaborations seem important to building the capacity of groups to influence deeply the core processes of teaching and learning at the school level over a sustained period of time. The Grow Your Own Teacher program in Chicago and the lead teacher program in the Bronx show the potential for addressing this issue; both are collaborations among organizing groups and intermediaries. The Texas IAF is more ambitious—taking organizing right into schools with the weight of a large and sophisticated network behind it. The results are impressive (Shirley 1997), but it is unclear how deep and broad the internal reform work will go and how long it can be sustained.

Conclusion

The challenges facing urban school reform are great. Community organizing is not a "silver bullet" to solve these problems. However, particularly when they ally with other reform agents, organizing groups have begun to show the potential to make a real impact on public education in low-income communities.

There is now wide appreciation among educators for the importance of engaging families and communities as partners in the education of children (Henderson et al. 2007); there is also growing appreciation for the role of family-school partnerships in individual school improvement (Bryk, et al. 2010). As we have seen, community organizing is an effective vehicle to build these partnerships. Meanwhile, organizing efforts have a broader and more explicitly political mission as well, as they work to engage families and communities in political actions aimed at school reform. Community organizing builds the voice of people with the greatest direct stake in improving the education of children in low-income communities. Unlike conventional partnerships, organizing builds power for parents and other residents as independent and powerful actors.

The discourse of public engagement can sometimes neglect the centrality of power to school reform. Yet inequalities in resource distribution and power lie at the heart of the failure of public education for low-income children of color. Community organizing explicitly seeks to build power for parents and communities who have been left out of the American Dream. It brings the organized voice of those with the strongest self-interest into debates over the course of public schooling. However, school reform cannot stand alone as the answer to poverty, racism, and social injustice. The call to increase public engagement must extend broadly to American social and urban policy. Changing schools must be linked to efforts to change broader social structures, which requires political mobilization to connect schools to community revitalization at the local level (Warren 2005) and to government policy at the national level (Anyon 2005). Community organizing represents an important vehicle for making these kinds of connections.

The people with the fewest resources and those who have been excluded most often in our society may not be the first to answer a call for public engagement. However, they can emerge as leaders to play a critical role in education reform. The power of organizing takes time to develop and comes through patient, base-building work in schools and communities. By building power, organizing works to create a truly inclusive public and transform schools into institutions that extend and strengthen democracy.

Notes

1. For further discussion of these examples, see the following studies: Oakland (Gold, Simon, and Brown 2002a; Mediratta, Shah, and McAlister 2009); Chicago (Blanc et al. 2002; Hong 2009; Warren 2005); New York (Fabricant 2010); Texas (Shirley 1997; Shirley 2002; Warren 2001); Denver (Padres and Jovenes Unidos 2007); and Mississippi (Margueritte Casey Foundation 2005).

2. For a further discussion of these issues and of the role of critical social inquiry in organizing, see Oakes and Rogers (2005). The women's movement broadly, and the organizing efforts of women of color in particular, also influenced the field as it emerged in the 1970s, bringing to the field a stronger appreciation of the importance of relationships and connections between personal and political life, among other things (Morgen and Bookman 1988; Naples 1998; Stall and Stoecker 1998).

3. For a related, but different, typology of the field of community organizing, see Swarts (2008).

4. At the time of this writing, ACORN was in the process of disbanding while its local affiliates and state federations reorganized in different ways to continue their work.

5. Of sixty-six organizing groups surveyed in 2000, only six had been doing education work prior to 1990 (Mediratta and Fruchter 2001, 12)

6. There are some groups that have abandoned confrontation entirely, calling their work "consensus organizing." For a discussion, see Gittell and Vidal (1998). Meanwhile, Clarence Stone et al. (1999) call this kind of collaborative approach to power a social reproduction model and argue that it is critical to establishing civic capacity to effect district-level reform.

7. Half of forty organizing groups surveyed in 1999 reported collaborations at the district level (National Center for Schools and Communities 2002b).

8. In an important recent study, researchers at the Annenberg Institute for School Reform (Mediratta, Shah, and McAlister 2009) were able to show that community organizing, when pursued in a district over time with intensity and at sufficient scale, is positively related to improvements in student outcomes. They found that schools engaged with community organizing groups had higher student educational outcomes, including higher attendance, test score performance, high school completion, and college-going aspirations.

9. This figure was inspired by the organizing cycle diagram created by the PICO affiliate in San Jose, California, People Acting in Community Together (PACT), but I have significantly revised it. Some other networks, like the IAF, also describe their organizing process as a cycle, although they highlight different aspects. For PACT, see www.pactsj.org/about_pact/building_social_capital.html; for the IAF affiliate One LA's description of the organizing cycle, see http://onela-iaf.org/aboutus/cycle.php.

10. Dennis Shirley (1997, 2002) presents case studies of a number of local organizing efforts involved with the Texas Industrial Areas Foundation and its Alliance Schools (see also Warren 2001; Warren 2005). The Cross City Campaign for Urban School Reform and Research for Action conducted five case studies (Gold, Simon, and Brown 2002b), including the Logan Square Neighborhood Association (Blanc et al. 2002; see also Hong 2009), Oakland Communities Organization (Gold, Simon, and Brown 2002a), New York ACORN (Simon, Pickron-Davis, and Brown 2002), Austin Interfaith (Simon and Gold 2002), and the Alliance Organizing Project in Philadelphia (Gold, Pickron-Davis, and Brown 2002). On organizing in Philadelphia, see also Mediratta et al. (2001). John Beam and Sharmeen Irani (2003) examine ACORN's work across the country. The Community Involvement Program now at the Annenberg Institute has sponsored a number of case studies, including Mothers on the Move (Mediratta and Karp 2003) and New Settlement Apartments in the Bronx (Zachary and Olatoye 2001), as well as several broader overviews of the field (Mediratta 2004; Mediratta and Fruchter 2001). Celina Su (2009) has recently published a study of four education organizing groups in the Bronx, while Michael Fabricant (2010) has analyzed reform efforts in the South Bronx. Marion Orr (1999) has examined organizing efforts in Baltimore in the 1990s, while Howell Baum (2003) has studied a different set of efforts in that metropolitan area more recently. Concha Delgado-Gaitan (2001) has examined Latino community organizing in a town in California. Jeannie Oakes and John Rogers (2005) have studied Parent U-Turn in Los Angeles as well as youth organizing and collaborative efforts (see also Rogers 2006). See also Gold et al. (2001) and Rhodes and Gold (2002).

11. These numbers are based on the self-reports of the various networks. Some of the groups may be just forming or now defunct. Alternatively, groups in the largest cities can be very big and often function as alliances of somewhat distinct individual groups. I have not included the National Training and Information Center as a national network because local groups affiliate more loosely to this network, which provides training, technical assistance, and research; see Heathcott (2005). The count of ACORN affiliates was made by Swarts (2007) just before the crisis in 2008 that led to the national network's demise. I maintain the count for my purposes, as the majority of these groups seem to be reconstituting themselves to remain active at the local level in some form.

12. In one effort, Michelle Renee (2006) identified sixty-four equity focused education organizations in California, but many of them appear to be professional advocacy groups. It is difficult to determine what proportion conduct direct organizing.

13. Organizing groups are active in many rural areas. We have no reliable estimate of the numbers of these groups, so I have excluded them from the count here.

14. There is important variation in how organizing groups have responded to NCLB with some finding its provisions useful in their local contexts (Shirley and Evans 2007; see also Rogers 2006).

15. The National Training and Information Center did once bring together local groups for a coordinated national campaign on school facilities (Mediratta and Fruchter 2001, 12).

References

Alinsky, Saul D. 1971. *Rules for Radicals: A Practical Primer for Realistic Radicals.* New York: Random House.

Amulya, Joy, Christie O'Campbell, Ryan Allen, and Ceasar McDowell. 2004. "Vital Difference: The Role of Race in Community Building." Cambridge, MA: Center for Reflective Practice, Massachusetts Institute of Technology.

Anyon, Jean. 1997. *Ghetto Schooling: A Political Economy of Urban Educational Reform.* New York: Teachers College Press.

———. 2005. *Radical Possibilities: Public Policy, Urban Education, and a New Social Movement.* New York: Routledge.

Baum, Howell S. 2003. *Community Action for School Reform.* Albany: State University of New York Press.

Beam, John M., and Sharmeen Irani. 2003. "ACORN Education Reform Organizing: Evolution of a Model." New York: National Center for Schools and Communities, Fordham University.

Blanc, Suzanne, Joanna Brown, Aida Nevarez-La Torre, and Chris Brown. 2002. "Case Study: Logan Square Neighborhood Association." In *Strong Neighborhoods, Strong Schools, The Indicators Project on Education Organizing.* Chicago: Cross City Campaign for Urban School Reform.

Briggs, Xavier de Souza, Elizabeth J. Mueller, and Mercer Sullivan. 1997. "From Neighborhood to Community: Evidence on the Social Effects of Community Development." New York: Community Development Research Center, New School for Social Research.

Bryk, Anthony, and Barbara Schneider. 2002. *Trust in Schools: A Core Resource for Improvement.* New York: Russell Sage Foundation Press.

Bryk, Anthony S., Penny Bender Sebring, Elaine Allensworth, Stuart Luppescu, and John Q. Easton. 2010. *Organizing Schools for Improvement: Lessons from Chicago.* Chicago: University of Chicago Press.

Californians for Justice Education Fund. 2004. "The ABC's of Justice: Students and Parents Fighting for Racial Justice in California Schools." Oakland, CA: Californians for Justice.

Carson, Clayborne. 1981. *In Struggle: SNCC and the Black Awakening of the 1960s.* Cambridge, MA: Harvard University Press.

Chambers, Edward T. 2003. *Roots for Radicals: Organizing for Power, Action, and Justice.* New York: Continuum.

Coleman, James S. 1988. "Social Capital in the Creation of Human Capital." *American Journal of Sociology* 94 (Supplement): S95–S120.

Corbin, Gene. 2002. "Overcoming Obstacles to School Reform: A Report on the 2002 Organizing for Educational Excellence Institute." Philadelphia: Research for Democracy, Temple University Center for Public Policy and the Eastern Pennsylvania Organizing Project.

Delgado, Gary. 1986. *Organizing the Movement: The Roots and Growth of ACORN.* Philadelphia: Temple University Press.

———. 1997. *Beyond the Politics of Place: New Directions in Community Organizing in the 1990s* Oakland, CA: Applied Research Center.

Delgado-Gaitan, Concha. 2001. *The Power of Community: Mobilizing for Family and Schooling.* Lanham, MD: Rowman & Littlefield.

Dingerson, Leigh, John M. Beam, and Chris Brown. 2004. "Twenty-six Conversations About Organizing, School Reform, and No Child Left Behind." Washington, DC: Center for Community Change.

Elmore, Richard F. 2004. *School Reform from the Inside Out: Policy, Practice, and Performance.* Cambridge, MA: Harvard Education Press.

Endo, Traci. 2002. "Youth Engagement in Community-Driven School Reform." Oakland, CA: Social Policy Research Associates.

Fabricant, Michael. 2010. *Organizing for Educational Justice: The Campaign for Public School Reform in the South Bronx.* Minneapolis: University of Minnesota Press.

Fisher, Robert. 1994. *Let the People Decide: Neighborhood Organizing in America.* New York: Twayne Publishers.

———. 2009. *The People Shall Rule: ACORN, Community Organizing, and the Struggle for Economic Justice.* Nashville: Vanderbilt University Press.

Freire, Paulo. 2000. *Pedagogy of the Oppressed.* New York: Continuum.

Ginwright, Shawn. 2003. "Youth Organizing: Expanding Possibilities for Youth Development." In *Occasional Papers Series No. 3.* New York: Funders Collaborative on Youth Organizing.

Ginwright, Shawn, and Taj James. 2002. "From Assets to Agents of Change: Social Justice, Organizing, and Youth Development." *New Directions for Youth Development* 96: 27–46.

Gittell, Ross, and Avis Vidal. 1998. *Community Organizing: Building Social Capital as a Development Strategy.* Thousand Oaks, CA: Sage.

Gold, Eva, Marcine Pickron-Davis, and Chris Brown. 2002. "Case Study: Alliance Organizing Project." In *Strong Neighborhoods, Strong Schools: The Indicators Project on Education Organizing.* Chicago: Cross City Campaign for Urban School Reform.

Gold, Eva, Amy Rhodes, Shirley Brown, Susan Lytle, and Diane Waff. 2001. "Clients, Consumers, or Collaborators?: Parents and Their Roles in School Reform During

Children Achieving, 1995–2000." Philadelphia: Consortium for Policy Research in Education.

Gold, Eva, Elaine Simon, and Chris Brown. 2002a. "Case Study: Oakland Community Organizations." In *Strong Neighborhoods, Strong Schools: The Indicators Project on Education Organizing.* Chicago: Cross City Campaign for Urban School Reform.

———. 2002b. "Successful Community Organizing for School Reform." In *Strong Neighborhoods, Strong Schools: The Indicators Project on Education Organizing.* Chicago: Cross City Campaign for Urban School Reform.

Hacker, Jacob, Suzanne Mettler, and Dianne Pinderhughes. 2005. "Inequality and Public Policy." In *Inequality and American Democracy: What We Know and What We Need to Learn,* ed. Lawrence R. Jacobs and Theda Skocpol, 156–213. New York: Russell Sage Foundation Press.

Heathcott, Joseph. 2005. "Urban Activism in a Downsizing World: Neighborhood Organizing in Postindustrial Chicago." *City and Community* 4: 277–294.

Henderson, Anne T., Karen L. Mapp, Vivian R. Johnson, and Don Davies. 2007. *Beyond the Bake Sale: The Essential Guide to Family-School Partnerships.* New York: The New Press.

Henig, Jeffrey R., Richard C. Hula, Marion Orr, and Desiree S. Pedelescleaux. 1999. *The Color of School Reform: Race, Politics and the Challenge of Urban Education.* Princeton, NJ: Princeton University Press.

Hong, Soo. 2009. *A Cord of Three Strands: Organizing Parents, Schools and Communities for Educational Change.* Unpublished Dissertation, Harvard University, Cambridge.

Horton, Myles, and Paulo Freire. 1990. *We Make the Road by Walking: Conversations on Education and Social Change.* Philadelphia: Temple University Press.

Horvat, Erin McNamara, Elliot B. Weininger, and Annette Lareau. 2003. "From Social Ties to Social Capital: Class Differences in the Relations Between Schools and Parent Networks." *American Educational Research Journal* 40: 319–351.

Horwitt, Sanford D. 1989. *Let Them Call Me Rebel: Saul Alinsky, His Life and Legacy.* New York: Knopf.

HoSang, Daniel. 2003. "Youth and Community Organizing Today." In *Occasional Papers Series on Youth Organizing.* New York: Funders Collaborative on Youth Organizing.

Howard Samuels Center. 2006. "Assessing Community Change: An Evaluation of the Ford Foundation's Community Organizing Initiative 2000–2004." New York: CUNY Graduate Center.

Johnson, Susan Moore. 2004. *Finders and Keepers: Helping New Teachers Survive and Thrive in Our Schools.* San Francisco: Jossey-Bass.

Lareau, Annette, and Erin McNamara Horvat. 1999. "Moments of Social Inclusion and Exclusion: Race, Class, and Cultural Capital in Family-School Relationships." *Sociology of Education* 72: 37–53.

Marguerite Casey Foundation. 2005. "A Case Study: Southern Echo." Seattle: Marguerite Casey Foundation.

Mediratta, Kavitha. 2004. "Constituents of Change: Community Organizations and Public Education Reform." New York: Institute for Education and Social Policy, New York University.

———. 2006. "A Rising Movement." *National Civic Review* 95: 15–22.

Mediratta, Kavitha, and Norm Fruchter. 2001. "Mapping the Field of Organizing for School Improvement." New York: Institute for Education and Social Policy, New York University.

———. 2003. "From Governance to Accountability: Building Relationships That Make Schools Work." New York: Institute for Education and Social Policy, New York University.

Mediratta, Kavitha, Norm Fruchter, Barbara Gross, Christine Donis Keller, and Mili Bonilla. 2001. "Community Organizing for School Reform in Philadelphia." New York: Institute for Education and Social Policy, New York University.

Mediratta, Kavitha, and Jessica Karp. 2003. *Parent Power and Urban School Reform: The Story of Mothers on the Move.* New York: Institute for Education and Social Policy, New York University.

Mediratta, Kavitha, Seema Shah, and Sara McAlister. 2009. *Community Organizing for Stronger Schools: Strategies and Successes.* Cambridge, MA: Harvard Education Press.

Morgen, Sandra, and Ann Bookman. 1988. *Women and the Politics of Empowerment.* Philadelphia: Temple University Press.

Munoz, Carlos Jr. 1989. *Youth, Identity, Power: The Chicano Movement.* New York: Verso.

Naples, Nancy A. 1998. *Community Activism and Feminist Politics: Organizing Across Race, Class and Gender.* New York: Routledge.

National Center for Schools and Communities. 2002a. "From Schoolhouse to Statehouse: Community Organizing for Public School Reform." New York: National Center for Schools and Communities, Fordham University.

———. 2002b. "Unlocking the Schoolhouse Door: The Community Struggle for a Say in Our Children's Education." New York: National Center for Schools and Communities, Fordham University.

Oakes, Jeannie, and John Rogers. 2005. *Learning Power: Organizing for Education and Justice.* New York: Teachers College Press.

Orfield, Gary, Daniel Losen, Johanna Wald, and Christopher B. Swanson. 2004. *Losing Our Future: How Minority Youth Are Being Left Behind by the Graduation Rate Crisis.* Cambridge, MA: The Civil Rights Project at Harvard University.

Orr, Marion. 1999. *Black Social Capital: The Politics of School Reform in Baltimore, 1986–1998.* Lawrence: University Press of Kansas.

Padres and Jovenes Unidos. 2007. "The Long Journey to Reform North High School." *Education Organizing* 26: 8–10.

Payne, Charles M. 1995. *I've Got the Light of Freedom: The Organizing Tradition and the Mississippi Freedom Struggle.* Berkeley: University of California Press.

———. 2008. *So Much Reform, So Little Change: The Persistence of Failure in Urban Schools.* Cambridge, MA: Harvard Education Press.

Perry, Theresa. 2003. "Up from the Parched Earth: Toward a Theory of African-American Achievement." In *Young, Gifted and Black: Promoting High Achievement Among African-American Students*, ed. Theresa Perry, Claude Steele, and Asa Hilliard III, 1–10. Boston: Beacon Press.

Putnam, Robert D. 2000. *Bowling Alone: The Collapse and Revival of American Community.* New York: Simon & Schuster.

Quiroz-Martinez, Julie, Daniel HoSang, and Lori Villarosa. 2004. "Changing the Rules of the Game: Youth Development & Structural Racism." Washington, DC: Philanthropic Initiative for Racial Equity.

Reitzes, Donald C., and Dietrich C. Reitzes. 1987. *The Alinsky Legacy: Alive and Kicking.* Greenwood, CT: JAI Press.

Renee, Michelle. 2006. *Knowledge, Power and Education Justice: How Social Movement Organizations Use Research to Influence Education Policy.* Unpublished dissertation. Los Angeles: University of California–Los Angeles.

Rhodes, Amy, and Eva Gold. 2002. "Lessons Learned About Parent Organizing: A Case Study." Chicago: Research for Action and The Philadelphia Education Fund.

Robnett, Belinda. 1997. *How Long? How Long? African-American Women in the Struggle for Civil Rights.* New York: Oxford University Press.

Rogers, John. 2006. Forces of Accountability? The Power of Poor Parents in NCLB. *Harvard Educational Review* 76(4): 611–641.

Schlozman, Kay Lehman, Benjamin I. Page, Sidney Verba, and Morris P. Fiorina. 2005. "Inequalities of Political Voice." In *Inequality and American Democracy: What We Know and What We Need to Learn*, ed. Lawrence R. Jacobs and Theda Skocpol, 19–87. New York: Russell Sage Foundation Press.

Shirley, Dennis. 1997. *Community Organizing for Urban School Reform.* Austin: University of Texas Press.

———. 2002. *Valley Interfaith and School Reform.* Austin: University of Texas Press.

Shirley, Dennis, and Michael Evans. 2007. "Community Organizing and No Child Left Behind." In *Transforming the City: Community Organizing and the Challenge of Political Change*, ed. Marion Orr, 109–133. Lawrence: University Press of Kansas.

Simon, Elaine, and Eva Gold. 2002. "Case Study: Austin Interfaith." Chicago: Cross City Campaign for Urban School Reform.

Simon, Elaine, Marcine Pickron-Davis, and Chris Brown. 2002. "Case Study: New York ACORN." In *Strong Neighborhoods, Strong Schools: The Indicators Project on Education Organizing*. Chicago: Cross City Campaign for Urban School Reform.

Skocpol, Theda. 1992. *Protecting Soldiers and Mothers: The Political Origins of Social Policy in the United States*. Cambridge, MA: Harvard University Press.

———. 2003. *Diminished Democracy: From Membership to Management in American Civic Life*. Norman: University of Oklahoma Press.

Skocpol, Theda, Marshall Ganz, and Ziad Munson. 2000. "A Nation of Organizers: The Institutional Origins of Civic Voluntarism in the United States." *American Political Science Review* 94: 527–546.

Skocpol, Theda, Ariane Liazos, and Marshall Ganz. 2006. *What a Mighty Power We Can Be: African American Fraternal Groups and the Struggle for Racial Equality*. Princeton, NJ: Princeton University Press.

Smock, Kristina. 2004. *Democracy in Action: Community Organizing and Urban Change*. New York: Columbia University Press.

Speer, Paul W., Joseph Hughey, Leah K. Gensheimer, and Warren Adams-Leavitt. 1995. Organizing for Power: A Comparative Case Study. *Journal of Community Psychology* 23: 57–73.

Stall, Susan, and Randy Stoecker. 1998. "Community Organizing or Organizing Community? Gender and the Crafts of Empowerment." *Gender and Society* 12: 729–756.

Stone, Clarence, Kathryn Doherty, Cheryl Jones, and Timothy Ross. 1999. "Schools and Disadvantaged Neighborhoods: The Community Development Challenge." In *Urban Problems and Community Development*, ed. Ronald F. Ferguson and William T. Dickens, 339–380. Washington DC: Brookings Institution Press.

Stone, Clarence N., Jeffrey R. Henig, Bryan D. Jones, and Carol Pierannunzi. 2001. *Building Civic Capacity: The Politics of Reforming Urban Schools*. Lawrence: University Press of Kansas.

Stone, Clarence, Marion Orr, and Donn Worgs. 2006. The Flight of the Bumblebee: Why Reform Is Difficult but Not Impossible. *Perspectives on Politics* 4: 529–546.

Su, Celina. 2009. *Streetwise for Book Smarts: Grassroots Organizing and Education Reform in the Bronx*. Ithaca, NY: Cornell University Press.

Swarts, Heidi. 2002. "Shut Out from the Economic Boom: Comparing Community Organizations' Success in the Neighborhoods Left Behind." In *Nonprofit Sector Research Fund Working Paper Series*. Washington, DC: The Aspen Institute.

———. 2007. "Political Opportunity, Venue Shopping, and Strategic Innovation: ACORN's National Organizing." In *Transforming the City: Community Organizing and the Challenge of Political Change*, ed. Marion Orr, 134–161. Lawrence: University Press of Kansas.

————. 2008. *Organizing Urban America: Secular and Faith-based Progressive Movements*. Minneapolis: University of Minnesota Press.

Texas Interfaith Education Fund. 1990. *The Texas I.A.F. Vision for Public Schools: Communities of Learners*. Austin: Texas Interfaith Education Fund.

Ture, Kwame, and Charles V. Hamilton. 1992[1967]. *Black Power: The Politics of Liberation*. New York: Vintage Books.

Valenzuela, Richard R., and Black, Mary S. 2002. "'Mexican Americans Don't Value Education.' On the Basis of the Myth, Mythmaking and Debunking." *Journal of Latinos and Education* 1 (2): 81–103.

Verba, Sidney, Kay Lehman Schlozman, and Henry E. Brady. 1995. *Voice and Equality: Civic Voluntarism in American Politics*. Cambridge, MA: Harvard University Press.

Vidal, Avis C. 1992. "Rebuilding Communities: A National Study of Urban Community Development Corporations." New York: Community Development Research Center, New School for Social Research.

Warren, Mark R. 1998. "Community Building and Political Power: A Community Organizing Approach to Democratic Renewal." *American Behavioral Scientist* 41: 78–92.

————. 2001. *Dry Bones Rattling: Community Building to Revitalize American Democracy*. Princeton, NJ: Princeton University Press.

————. 2005. "Communities and Schools: A New View of Urban Education Reform." *Harvard Educational Review* 75: 133–173.

Warren, Mark R., Soo Hong, Carolyn Heang Rubin, and Phitsamay Sychitkokhong Uy. 2009. "Beyond the Bake Sale: A Community-Based, Relational Approach to Engaging Parents in Schools." *Teachers College Record* 111 (9): 2209–2254.

Warren, Mark R., Meredith Mira, and Thomas Nikundiwe. 2008. "Youth Organizing: From Youth Development to School Reform." *New Directions in Youth Development* 117 (Spring): 27–42.

Warren, Mark R., J. Phillip Thompson, and Susan Saegert. 2001. "The Role of Social Capital in Combating Poverty." In *Social Capital and Poor Communities*, ed. Susan Saegert, J. Phillip Thompson, and Mark R. Warren, 1–28. New York: Russell Sage Foundation Press.

Warren, Mark R., and Richard L. Wood. 2001. "Faith-Based Community Organizing: The State of the Field." Jericho, NY: Interfaith Funders.

Whitman, Gordon. 2006. "Beyond Advocacy: The History & Vision of the PICO Network." *Social Policy* 37: 50–59.

Wood, Richard L. 2002. *Faith in Action: Religion, Race and Democratic Organizing in America*. Chicago: University of Chicago Press.

————. 2007. "Higher Power: Strategic Capacity for State and National Organizing." In *Transforming the City: Community Organizing and the Challenge of Political Change*, ed. Marion Orr, 162–192. Lawrence: University Press of Kansas.

Wood, Richard L., and Mark R. Warren. 2002. "A Different Face of Faith-Based Politics: Social Capital and Community Organizing in the Public Arena." *International Journal of Sociology and Social Policy* 22: 6–54.

Zachary, Eric, and Shola Olatoye. 2001. "Community Organizing for School Improvement in the South Bronx." New York: Institute for Education and Social Policy, NYU School of Education.

7
Broad-based Public Engagement
Alliances and Social Movements
Lauren Wells, Jean Anyon, and Jeannie Oakes

ALLIANCES CONNECT ACTIVIST INDIVIDUALS and groups across neighborhoods, cities, regions, and states to address social problems. Alliances create synergies of interests, power, and experience among grassroots and advocacy organizations whose members include progressive educators, parents, and youth who live and/or work in the communities most burdened by inequality and educational failure. Some groups joining such alliances already focus on educational issues; others have deep activist roots in other social policy arenas such as housing, public safety, or welfare. Activist alliances may also draw in groups outside their communities to add complementary knowledge, expertise, and influence. These might include research centers, intermediary organizations, and other civic groups, education professionals, business partners, and philanthropy.

Not all alliances are composed of so many different groups; an alliance can be two groups that stay together only until they accomplish a short-term goal. The Educational Justice Collaborative in California (EJC) is an example of an extensive, multidimensional, diverse network that includes affiliates of membership-based grassroots organizations, such as Association of Community Organizations for Reform Now (ACORN) and Pacific Institute for Community Organization (PICO); local grassroots organizing groups, like Parent-U-Turn and the Community Coalition of South Los Angeles; youth organizing groups, such as Inner City Struggle and Californians for Justice; legal advocacy groups, including the ACLU and Public Advocates; policy advocates, such as the Advancement Project and PolicyLink; research centers, including the Institute for Democracy, Education, and Access at the University of California–Los Angeles (UCLA); and regional and state organizations, including the United Way of Greater Los Angeles and the California League of Women Voters.

The broad spectrum of organizations joining such alliances makes clear not only that a wide range of Americans believe that high-quality public education is essential to a well-functioning democracy and to young people's life chances, but also that many see it as worth fighting for. The growing presence of these activist alliances also reflects huge disappointment with the continuing failure of urban school systems to provide poor Black and Latino students with the learning opportunities that lead to high academic achievement.

Education reform alliances, like the individual activist organizations of which they are composed, aim to build public knowledge about the inequitable conditions under which many low-income children of color attend school, increase their own membership's grasp of effective education policy and practices, and create robust networks prepared to act locally and nationally to make significant improvements. By combining forces with others, individual groups seek to increase their geographic reach, legitimacy, power, resources, and technical expertise in order to maximize their chances of shaping education policy and practice.

Additionally, to the extent that these public engagement alliances advance the participation of politically and economically marginalized communities, they contribute to what is or may become a broader movement for social and economic justice. They challenge the historical patterns that keep some groups on the margins of public policy creation. They also make it far more likely that attention will be drawn to the underlying *structural* political and economic arrangements that impact equity in schools. As such, they have the potential to influence and be part of broader movements for social and economic justice.

This chapter explores public engagement alliances seeking to improve the quality of education afforded to low-income students and students of color. We describe some broad characteristics of groups that make up different alliances and differences in the alliances thus formed; we argue that these characteristics, in turn, may be useful analytic tools for further study. For example, we identify alliances that are national, statewide, and local in scope; alliances that benefit from philanthropic funding; alliances in which intermediaries offer services that extend the reach of community groups across constituencies or lines of power and influence; and others. These types of groups coalesce in ways that are unique to time, place, target issues, resources, and relationships; thus they account for the tremendous diversity among alliances.

We also explore what research says about the impact of these alliances on public education and public engagement, and raise questions about their meaning and consequences for democracy. Finally, we link alliances for educational justice to the prospects for a broad-based movement for social and economic justice. Although the coming together of diverse organizations to pursue collective goals is not sufficient to fuel a social movement, it may be a necessary element. Alliance building prepares organizations and individuals to respond to opportunities for movement activism that cut across schooling and extend into other political and economic arenas. And, like social movements, alliances for education reform connect what may feel like personal, individual exclusion or subordination to social structure and political causes. However, alliances are just one component of a full set of dynamics that characterize social movements, including cross-sector thinking and action; national scope; and the quest for fundamental cultural, social, and economic transformation.

Alliances: Theory and Action

Unallied community-based activist groups lack capacity for comprehensive campaigns needed to win fundamental reforms—particularly at the regional or state level. Community groups that focus on specific and local issues directly affecting their members (e.g., local school crowding, teacher vacancies) have limited numbers and small geographic reach, lack familiarity and legitimacy among influential sectors, and are limited in resources and technical expertise may still make progress if their goals are modest and they stick to taking action on problems school by school. However, many local groups find that their initial and limited wins cannot be sustained; or they realize that they have only touched on a small piece of a larger systemic problem that influences the issues they have addressed. In such cases they may seek out alliances. Issues-based groups (e.g., rights for immigrant or special education students) rarely change their primary focus. As a result, the work of different groups (with different primary issues) can be disjointed and uncoordinated— perhaps competitive—thus diminishing their impact.

However, as different issues-based groups scale up their efforts to address district and state-level problems, they may find common ground in the people who are exposed to multiple social inequalities. For example, a group concerned primarily with immigrant rights might have an affinity with advocates for bilingual education. Most groups are likely to see advantages in being able to call on the many other grassroots constituencies when they try to apply public pressure on policy makers and raise the general level of awareness about particular problems and equitable solutions.

Alliances are formed to effect change at particular levels of influence or governance, as illustrated by the following school district-, state-, and national-level focus of organizations. At the *district level*, New York City's Transforming Education for New York's Newest (TENYN) seeks higher-quality education for immigrant students and English language learners (ELLs) in New York City's public schools. It foregrounds problems with implementing Regent's learning standards for ELLs, teacher and instructional quality, parental access to multilingual communication, appropriate assessment and student placement, and the inclusion of immigrant special interests in education policy making (Bezahler, Cahn, and Schwerner 2004).

New York's *state-level* Alliance for Quality Education (AQE) was formed to demand policy solutions to systemic education problems. AQE focuses on adequate funding to create quality schools for all of New York public school children and public participation and transparency in school funding issues. (See the Alliance for Quality Education website, listed at the end of this chapter.)

At the *national level*, the Cross Cities Campaign for Urban School Reform (Cross Cities) united groups in urban areas across the nation to share information and strategies. Cross Cities formed a network of groups in Baltimore, Denver, Chicago, Houston, Los Angeles, New York, Oakland, Philadelphia, and Seattle that sought decentralized authority at the school level, small schools, heterogeneous student grouping, school cultures that are supportive of teachers, and accountability focused on student achievement.

Although they differ in the scope of their policy efforts and the education problems they address, these three types of alliance link constituency building, policy work, and grassroots engagement in education reform. They address commonly held interests, and draw on existing organizational resources while building new organizational capacity. In each case, their collaboration recognizes that broad-based coalitions and multiple capacities are needed to effect and sustain change.

In Chapter 3 of this book, Jeffrey Henig suggests that a number of changing social and political dynamics require public engagement strategies that have "tactical flexibility and a range of operating modes." Henig argues that the "new political grid" is more suited to groups capable of working at multiple levels of government and in multi-issue coalitions. These alliances produce the flexibility needed to adapt to rapidly changing policy environments and increase the venues in which different organizations can be politically active around a specific issue (see Chapter 3). Accordingly, TENYN, AQE, and Cross Cities pursue civic capacity that enables tactical flexibility by aligning groups with different strengths and strategies to make concerted efforts across communities, regions, or states. Diverse groups use their "weak ties" to enhance their power, producing a new capacity that includes the organizational equivalent of social capital (Granovetter 1973). These alliances work toward three ends: (1) enhancing the quality of education immediately in schools serving low-income urban students and thereby improve student outcomes; (2) institutionalizing the participation of low-income communities of color as an essential element of sustainable school reform; and (3) altering the underlying *structural* political and economic arrangements that impact equity in schools by locating the interests of low-income communities of color at the center of policy making and reform.

TENYN, for example, brought together the New York Immigrant Coalition (NYIC) and Advocates for Children (AFC). NYIC is a coalition of more than two hundred groups in New York State advocating for the rights of immigrant communities; AFC is a New York City advocacy and legal group that focuses on the education needs of the city's poor children. This alliance advanced an education policy agenda around the needs of immigrant and ELL students. The alliance of NYIC and AFC cross-fertilized both organizations' expertise and increased their visibility and capacity in new areas—NYIC with education and AFC with immigrant rights. Importantly, many of the organizations belonging to NYIC are grassroots community organizations, while others include academic institutions and human service organizations with policy expertise. Ultimately, TENYN's alliance with NYIC and AFC added resources and technical capacity to grassroots efforts through the support of intermediary organizations, nonprofits, and philanthropy that focus on education issues.

Importantly, each organization typically maintains its identity, its own agenda, and its own forms of engagement. Community organizations in alliances continue to build their membership in order to respond effectively to local issues. Advocacy alliances bring research and policy analyses to broad audiences and convene stakeholders around critical education issues. At their best, alliances allow the organizations to complement the identities, goals, and capacities of each organization as they collectively pursue a common interest.

Public engagement by alliances of grassroots and advocacy groups representing low-income communities is grounded in theories of change that assume that collective power is required to propel decision makers to act on the behalf of children who experience such inequities. Further, the alliances are guided by the strong presumption that those who best understand students and what they experience are parents and members of their communities. Whereas people who already possess power are likely to frame their participation as apolitical (that is, as *not* exercising power), alliances are explicit in their goal to acquire and use political power to correct fundamental inequalities. They offer a forum for collaboration to develop community power to attempt to alter the political and social arrangements that prop up inequity, exclusion, and subordination.

Alliances that join grassroots organizing efforts with advocacy groups and intermediary organizations can be expected to advance the interests of their member groups to the extent that they do all of the following:

- Bring to the surface common interests and collective solutions. Raise awareness that many of the school problems different communities face also exist in other schools, helping people understand the systemic nature of educational inequities and diminishing community members' sense of isolation.
- Increase membership and geographic reach.
- Leverage resources and technical expertise. Alongside nonprofit organizations, alliances increase the activist and community groups' research tools and technical knowledge.
- Employ an effective ecology of civic infrastructure that promotes differentiated participation across venues and builds on the different strengths and strategies that each group brings.
- Extend legitimacy and power—for example, when grassroots community groups partner with those in more powerful positions, such as mainstream organizations, policy advocates, elected officials, and professional educators.

The examples in this chapter demonstrate that it takes a lot of work to establish the common values, structures, and practices around which organizations can align themselves. Groups and organizations can be territorial, tied to their institutional views and strategies, unaware of their organizational limitations, or preoccupied with getting credit for "wins." In other words, they can be settled in their own ways. In order to create effective alliances, organizations and individuals must overcome historical legacies of distrust between people of color and whites, and between low-income and middle-class communities; they must value and incorporate different configurations of race, class, gender, citizenship, and age interests as they go about their work.

Alliances: An Engagement Menu

The "new political grid" Henig envisions calls for organizations to be flexible in their press for public engagement. This flexibility implies more than groups being strategic in their actions and choice of partners. Rather, it suggests that groups should identify their strengths and assess the potential for alliances that can reinforce and add to them. Likewise, policy makers might consider these when looking for appropriate entry points for public support of public engagement. Alliances may be characterized by one or more of the following:

Based on issues
Pursuing a broad education justice agenda
Building enduring institutional structures to support public engagement
Nonprofit status that builds capacity
Intermediary status
Resource-generating philanthropic status

Issue-Based Alliances

Increasingly, groups that do not normally work together are forming alliances around particular issues. For example, the Alliance for Quality Education (AQE), founded in 2000 (described above), unites 230 organizations of parents, children's advocates, schools, teachers, clergy, labor unions, business leaders, and others across the state of New York to address school finance reform. This alliance grew out of local efforts—in this case, The Campaign for Fiscal Equity's (CFE) work to equalize state education spending for New York and other large cities in the state. Realizing that the CFE strategy needed allies state-wide, AQE established base chapters in New York City and Albany (Schwerner 2005). AQE draws on traditional organizing strategies like leadership development and direct action, as well as dissemination of research, extensive media relations, electronic activism, and policy work and lobbying. The alliance has also added star power with AQE spokespersons Cynthia Nixon, a New York City public school parent and actress from the popular HBO series, *Sex in the City*, and hip-hop artist and entrepreneur Russell Simmons. These strategies and resources enable

AQE to make highly visible, rapid responses to the changing policy environment and to play a role in local and state budget processes (Schwerner 2005).

Alliances Pursuing a Broad Education Justice Agenda

Beyond specific issues or policy goals, alliances sometimes share visions of what public education can and should be. Chicago's Logan Square Neighborhood Association (LSNA) envisions strong schools as the center of community life and parents as vital participants in both the educational process and school governance. LSNA frequently joins with other organizations to lead programs and press for reform. Partnering with the Chicago Public Schools (CPS), LSNA's Parent Mentor Program trains parents and then places them in classrooms in ten Chicago elementary schools as teachers' aides for up to a year. LSNA works with Chicago State University on the Nueva Generacion Project and the Grow Your Own Teacher Program, both of which train parents and community members to be competent, culturally responsive teachers. LSNA is not only an alliance in the sense that it brings together different organizations; it also builds unity among the multiethnic communities and institutions of the Logan Square and Lathrop/Hamlin neighborhoods around a vision of a shared "place to live, work, play, raise children, run a business and worship" (Logan Square Neighborhood Association website).

Building Enduring Institutional Structures to
Support Public Engagement

Often organizations with similar issues and strategies come together to increase their power to affect decision makers and to gain visibility for their agendas. They seek a strong social- and political-capital infrastructure to sustain wins and support future agendas generally, rather than rely on ad hoc organizing to identify and solve particular education problems as they arise. Some of these alliances function more like chapters of a single organization than like separate organizations.

Two examples of this type of alliance are the Kentucky-based Prichard Committee (the Committee) for Academic Excellence in Kentucky, which was founded in 1990, and Good Schools Pennsylvania (GSPA), which was founded in 2001 by former Philadelphia superintendent David Hornbeck. Like AQE, GSPA has offices and organizers located strategically throughout the state to mobilize parents, students, teachers, and other community members— forming a network of fourteen thousand adults and youth who support equitable funding and school reform for low-income rural and urban schools. Each local office builds community engagement, develops strategic alliances with other organizations, and monitors local legislators and school districts (Good Schools Pennsylvania website). Using traditional organizing methods and legislative meetings, GSPA's local offices deliver the message that a sound school funding formula should be based on equity, adequacy, efficiency, predictability, and accountability. The alliance's work has led to greater funding from the legislature and Pennsylvania governor Edward Rendell.

The Committee, now a private nonpartisan citizen advocacy group that spans the state of Kentucky, began in 1980 as a thirty-member citizen panel that sought reforms in higher education. In 1982 it established itself as an independent nonprofit and increased its membership to a hundred citizens from across the state. Their early work included town forums and citizen action workshops on leadership and organizing skills. The Kentucky Education Reform Act (KERA) of 1990 introduced systemic reform that reduced funding inequities, established a school-based governance model and implemented statewide assessment, incorporated many of the Committee's recommendations, and provided a platform to advocate for all Kentucky students. Like the other alliances discussed, the Committee works to build an informed public. They produce various publications using various media outlets, and have established a toll-free telephone line and a blog to respond to questions and get public input (Prichard Committee for Academic Excellence website). In 1997 the Committee developed the Commonwealth Institute for Parent Leadership (CIPL), which consists of three two-day parent training sessions that emphasize broad local engagement through increased understanding of KERA and data-based information about the school system. CIPL trains cadres of parents to be decision makers alongside teachers and administrators. Participants design and implement a parent involvement project that focuses on student achievement; and they commit to be part of a parent leadership network that involves other parents in the schools. Many have become school council and board members; a few sit on state commissions. Prichard's training model has been nationally recognized and adopted in fourteen states (Prichard Committee for Academic Excellence website).

Capacity-building Alliances with Nonprofits

In many cases, nonprofit organizations work either with a single organization or with alliances. The nonprofits may include independent organizations with social- or educational-justice agendas and philanthropic organizations with specific issue, policy, or strategy interests. These nonprofits use their resources and/or their technical expertise to strengthen membership-based or activist organizations.

There are many examples of such nonprofits, including the National Center for Schools and Communities (NCSC) at Fordham University in New York City; the Applied Research Center (ARC) in Oakland, California; the Center for Third World Organizing (CTWO), also in Oakland; and the Center for Community Change (CCC) in Washington, DC. Some like NCSC, support organizations that work through school and community partnerships (National Center for Schools & Communities website). Others, including ARC, CTWO, and CCC support organizations emphasize using research on racial inequality to influence public policy, advocacy, organizing, and networking. They form extensive collaborations with other organizations, including teachers unions, universities, and social service agencies (Applied Research Center website; Center for Community Change website; Center for Third World Organizing website).

Research nonprofits support grassroots organizing, advocacy groups, and alliances; they provide high-quality data about schools and school districts, as well as research-based strategies for supporting school improvement. The Annenberg Institute for School Reform (AISR), affiliated with Brown University; the Institute for Democracy, Education, and Access (IDEA) at UCLA; and Research for Action (RFA), a nonprofit research organization located in Philadelphia, are three leading research nonprofits (Research for Action website). AISR's work is national in scope. IDEA projects are based in California, with many focused on the Los Angeles Unified School District (LAUSD). RFA works within the Philadelphia School District. Each of these research organizations houses projects that span the spectrum of education reform.

All three organizations develop and share information that points to critical areas of need in public schooling, is accessible to the general public, and is easily useful to equity-minded reform groups. They generate data and policy analyses to support community groups working on problems in their local schools. They develop relationships across the district and maintain long-standing relationships with many community-based organizations, advocacy groups, and parent and youth organizing groups, political leaders, and legislative bodies. Through its Educational Justice Collaborative (EJC), UCLA's IDEA convenes seminars for parents and students about education access and equity, provides training on research methods and analysis of data, and supports campaign-focused action-research projects in California. AISR coordinates the New York City Coalition for Education Justice (NYCEJ), which informs and mobilizes stakeholders to advocate for middle school reform in New York City. In 2007, the AISR released a research report, *New York City's Middle-Grade Schools: Platforms for Success or Pathways for Failure?* These organizations, and others like them, use research to propel community engagement in education reform in three primary ways: (1) carrying out research for the public about education issues in general, as well as about local schools; (2) training parents and other community members to design and implement action-research projects in their schools; and (3) investigating the role that education organizing is playing in school change.

Intermediaries

Other capacity-building organizations are primarily interested in roles at the interstices of different groups; they connect, convene, facilitate, build bridges between powerful groups and those that have little power, and, in a multitude of other ways, support alliances. Intermediaries are more inclined to see themselves as catalysts than as principle actors in reform activities. A key role of intermediaries is to transmit information and research, keeping local groups apprised of developing education policy issues. Equally important, intermediaries can be conduits to the halls of power—helping constituencies gain access to policy-formulating venues. Meredith Honig (2004, 67) offers this generic definition of intermediaries:

> Intermediaries are organizations that occupy space *in between* at least two other parties. Intermediary organizations primarily function *to mediate* or to manage change in both of those parties. Intermediary organizations operate independently of these two parties and provide distinct value beyond what the parties alone would be able to develop or amass by themselves. At the same time, intermediary organizations depend on those parties to perform their essential functions.

The Public Education Network (PEN), the Center for Education Policy (CEP), the National Council of La Raza (NCLR), and the Education Law Center (ELC) are examples of intermediary organizations that link different sectors of the community at large and advocate for school reform at local, state, and national levels. PEN, CEP, and NCLR are national independent intermediaries that work at all levels of education policy. PEN is a national association of local education foundations (LEF) that themselves may act as intermediaries between constituent groups, schools/districts, and community residents—engaging broad publics, and leveraging existing community assets (Public Education Network website). CEP is a national independent advocacy group that engages public input through forums and symposiums across the country and provides information on education issues through publications and research reports; it, too, convenes meetings and provides expert advice (Center on Education Policy website). NCLR, the largest civil rights and advocacy organization committed to advancing the needs of the Latino community, supports communities with resources and networks; NCLR advocates for educational policies to make public education include the needs of Latino students across the nation (National Council of La Raza website). ELC is a state-level legal advocacy organization that provides technical assistance, information, and support to attorneys, school districts, and local organizations seeking to achieve full implementation of the reforms and programs mandated in New Jersey's landmark school funding case *Abbott v. Burke* (Education Law Center website).

These organizations' intermediary position between "the public" and decision makers—including district and state education administrators, legislators, and the courts—allows them to produce information that evaluates local, state, and national education policies in light of the needs of school districts and their schools. Intermediary organizations are seen to know something about both "the public" and decision makers that neither group could know without intermediaries acting somewhat as reliable informants. This role requires these organizations to establish legitimacy with stakeholders from both sides and to be viewed as entities that can accurately present the interests of each group and facilitate change.

Resource-generating Funder Alliances

Donors' collaboratives entail collaboration among philanthropic foundations and add to community and advocacy organizations' resources; they work independently or they may form alliances. The Donors' Education Collaborative and the Ford Consortium on Constituency Building for School Reform, both begun in 1995, and Communities for Public Education Reform, formed in 2007, are three examples of foundations pooling their resources to support public engagement. The objectives of these alliances are threefold: (1) to increase the financial and organizational capacity of groups to build stakeholder engagement in education reform; (2) to raise the visibility of education organizing among national and local funders in order to increase the legitimacy of education organizing as a strategy to elevate the conditions and outcomes of public schools, particularly those in historically marginalized communities; and (3) to facilitate collaboration among grantmakers (Communities for Public Education Reform website; Hirota and Jacobs 2003). The Ford Consortium supported individual organizations in three core areas of work: policy and evaluation, public information, and constituency building (Hirota and Jacobs 2003). Donors' Education Collaborative, working on the belief that coordinated work between multiple organizations maximizes financial resources and builds the capacity and reach of their efforts, supports the work of four alliances across New York City (Hirota, Jacobowitz, and Brown 2000, 2004). Communities for Public Education Reform also supports alliances for education reform. However, the scope of the alliance's efforts is national, with four current project sites: Chicago, Denver, Philadelphia, and New Jersey (Communities for Public Education Reform website).

Donors' collaboratives aim to create long-term alliances between organizations and individuals, build knowledge, public will, strategic effectiveness, and multi-year foundation support needed for systemic changes. Donors' collaboratives organize convenings of grantees to exchange ideas, learn from research, develop knowledge skills for reform, build relationships, and share strategic approaches. Communities for Public Education Reform provides additional support for organizations to receive technical assistance, travel for cross-site visits, and more (Communities for Public Education Reform website).

Each of the types of alliances discussed augments the existing resources of the activist public engagement organizations. The alliance typology we have presented here demonstrates that organizations of all varieties are finding it useful, if not necessary, to join with others to increase awareness of and support for addressing particular education problems. The many configurations of alliances expand access to the political venues and increase the flexibility with which groups can respond to and anticipate rapidly changing political environments. As alliances build new capacities, increase knowledge about issues, add to their membership bases, establish relationships with policy makers, marshal data, and create new narratives about the sources and solutions to educational inequities, they are in effect preparing themselves for the sort of prolonged public engagement that can lead to social movements.

The Challenges of Building Alliances Among Diverse Organizations

A discussion of the social and organizational barriers facing diverse organizations that represent diverse interests and come together to forge alliances is beyond the scope of this chapter. However, because the success of alliances that seek to bring about education policy reform with systemic impacts hinges on their ability to navigate barriers that can affect the ability of different organizations to work together well, we call attention to some of these obstacles here.

It is tough work keeping any organization focused and cooperative. When two or more organizations join for a common venture—especially when the stakes are high—the obstacles can be overwhelming. And yet, remarkably, this is the starting point for many alliances that are making productive strides toward socially just education within and across communities. Alliances among diverse organizations must also face other challenges that are more unique to their *counter*cultural missions.

Middle-class, college-educated people tend to have more experience with civic and city-wide organizations than people from historically marginalized communities—especially with organizations that focus on education, such as the parent-teacher association (PTA). This involvement brings them experiences, confidence, contacts, and other capital that supports their inclination to engage in collective action. Among this middle-class population are education and other professionals who participate in these organizations in ways that are sometimes supportive—sometimes oppositional—and often dominant.

Due to patterns of historical exclusion and discrimination, low-income communities of color generally have less positive experiences with addressing programmatic or policy issues. Often their only school dealings have been to resolve conflicts and to solve immediate and particular concerns.[1] Also, PTAs and other traditional groups in urban schools do not have the capacity and clout that these groups have in suburban communities. Communities that have experienced disenfranchisement thus stand to benefit from capacity-building that focuses on participation with diverse partners including civic elites. This is a long-term and labor-intensive process and may be in tension with organizational or coalitional needs for short-term policy results. For example, foundations, as funders, may signal their intentions to "build capacity" but still insist on "measurable results" determined by short-run benchmarks to accompany leadership development and sustainable relationships.

Cross-race coalitions bring additional complications, not only in creating alliances between whites and communities of color, but also among marginalized groups that perceive that they are competitors for schooling resources and opportunities. These alliances must build understanding between groups with competing interests and realign traditional power relations and dynamics (Wells 2009). This is often easier for alliances that are issue-based. In fact, recurring themes, such as structural racism, immigrant rights, ideological differences, and access to political power, present ongoing challenges to alliance formation (Applied Research Center website). Recent reports suggest that building meaningful multiracial coalitions requires putting racial justice at the center of collaborative efforts and that all groups involved: (1) recognize their interests, (2) believe they will benefit from the coalition, (3) have an independent power base and control decision making, and (4) understand that the coalition is formed with specific goals (Applied Research Center website).

Schools can feel particularly unapproachable to people who are not familiar with them and who do not have organized support to back them up. On the surface, coalitions and alliances are less institutional—less formal—but they can still present barriers to would-be members, new members, or anyone in the community who is not in a leadership position. Alliance intermediaries or even organizational leadership may not always speak well, accurately, or understandably on behalf of the entire membership (Applied Research Center website). On the other hand, people who are accustomed to being disempowered and disregarded are inclined to distrust large, formal organizations, even those that they may be supporting or funding. They may also lack a sense of entitlement, which is an essential element of personal and collective power (Wells 2009). Even such well-regarded intermediaries as the Center for Community Change may be seen as the voice of the elite, not ordinary people.

Where Do Alliances Fit in Building Social Movements?

One comprehensive definition of social movements, summarizing several decades of sociological research, asserts that social movements exist when individuals and organizations are involved in "collective conflictual relations with clearly identified opponents" (Della Porta and Diani 2006, 20). The conflict involves "an oppositional relationship between actors who seek control of the same stake—be it political, economic or cultural power—and in the process make . . . claims on each other which, if realized, would damage the interests of the other actors" (Tilly 1978, in Della Porta and Diani 2006, 21). Thus, the conflict can be cultural and/or political-economic. The conflict has as a goal to promote (or, in the case of most conservative movements, to oppose) progressive social change.

Many of the alliances we have described exhibit characteristics seen in social movements: networks of individuals and organizations in many cities; learning, relationships, and actions that generate social and cultural capital; building common purpose, and so forth. Key to alliances and movements are dense informal networks of organizations and individuals. By relying heavily on the leadership and participation of those who are most affected by the injustice or objects of campaigns, actors share a deep collective identity, sense of common purpose, and commitment (Touraine 1981; Della Porta and Diani 2006).

Although actions by alliances do not, in themselves, constitute a social movement, public engagement alliances are potential building blocks of social movements. The relationships, knowledge, skills, and other capacities that alliances develop are partly unspent in any particular issue campaign. The residue—saved or even latent social capital—can be used at strategic moments that arise unpredictably and uniquely, depending on the local and national contexts. The civil rights movement is an example. As black churches in the South began to publicly confront Jim Crow segregation, the networks among women and families in congregations became vital links between communities; these networks allowed news of activities to spread and encouraged participation in protest. Similarly, the alliances that arose between the Student Non-violent Coordinating Committee, the Southern Christian Leadership Conference, the Congress on Racial Equality, and other civil rights organizations were important spurs to growth of regional and then national planning. With collaboration, a joint vision, and a fortuitous catalyst, public education organizing and alliance building could develop into a national social movement.

Social Movements: Cross-sector Thinking

Social movements respond to the links among social, political, and economic sectors. Even though it may not seem to be the case when one is in the classrooms and corridors of a high-poverty urban school, very few educational problems originate in local schools or neighborhoods. Macroeconomic decisions made by federal bodies and organizations (for example, decisions about

minimum wages and corporate taxes), arrangements made among metro-
area developers and other power brokers (for example, to locate public transit,
routes and job centers), and public policies promulgated by state and city politicians (regarding, for example, housing, health facilities, and law enforcement) create conditions in poor neighborhoods that severely constrain high-
quality public schooling (see Anyon 2005a for other examples of such policies).
Local remedies that do not act on the links between social, economic, and political factors rarely suffice—at least not in the long run.

In addition, holding two low-wage jobs to make ends meet can sap the
energy of a parent and make it more difficult for her to negotiate the public
systems and advocate for her children. Being poor in a rich country can lead
to ill-placed shame, pervasive despair, and anger. Living in poverty means
experiencing daily crises of food, finding a place to live, and keeping your
children safe. All this can be debilitating and can certainly dampen the enthusiasm, effort, and outlook with which urban children and their families approach K–12 education. The low social status and perceived lack of clout often
ascribed to those who are poor and black or Latino may prevent staff in institutions like schools, government agencies, and hospitals from offering respect
and proper treatment. It often leads to a lack of accountability on the part of
the public institutions themselves—a situation that is rarely, if ever, allowed to
occur in affluent communities and districts.

At the same time, more is at stake in school reform than raised test scores.
Educational opportunity is at stake; democratic public voice and engagement
is at stake. And, ultimately, we would argue that social justice is at stake. In
our view, educational opportunity and even public engagement for school reform have not made the social changes that constitute a just environment for
low-income students and their families. In *Radical Possibilities* (Anyon 2005a;
see also 2005b), Jean Anyon makes the case that educational opportunity is
a necessary, but not sufficient, condition of social justice, that educational opportunity without economic opportunity carries a false promise. Economic
reforms would bring jobs with high wages, health care, and decent housing to
poor people and poor neighborhoods that would be crucial to sustainable,
systemic school reform.

Social Movements: Cross-sector Action

In some metropolitan areas, community organizations have joined labor, religious, and political groups to confront foundations, governments, and banks

on regional and statewide levels. These coalitions challenge metropolitan and federal policies that affect local problems. These groups demand that governments at varying levels carry out their responsibilities to residents, as in more affluent municipalities.

One example is the Campaign for Sustainable Milwaukee, a long-term, broad-based advocacy coalition composed of more than two hundred community, religious, labor, and business organizations. The coalition was formed to address a number of interrelated issues affecting the city and region that were beyond the capacity of any one organization to address. The campaign's success stems from its strategy of campaigning for specific issues that were identified by members as meaningful to a broad base of people. The issues also had to address the quality of life of the entire region, especially Milwaukee's inner city. Since 1996, Sustainable Milwaukee has focused on higher wages in area jobs, workforce training, and transit reform for job access. Sustainable Milwaukee was instrumental in pressing for the passage of the city's Living Wage Ordinance (which mandated that employers pay workers at a higher rate than the federal minimum wage). During the effort, the Living Wage Campaign task force found that just over 50 percent of the local jobs paid less than $20,000 annually. The ordinance was approved by both the city and county of Milwaukee as well as the school district, stipulating a 1996 minimum wage of $7.70 per hour plus benefits.

Just as with the work of activist education alliances described earlier, the efforts of regional and state coalitions around these other social and economic issues have not solved the problems of low-income urban residents in Milwaukee, Buffalo, or Massachusetts. Much more needs to be accomplished. The existing coalitions are fragile, are not connected to one other, and, nationally, are few in number. But their collaborations across social sectors have won wage, transportation, and labor union victories that demand our attention. Their collaborative, region-wide methods might be usefully employed by those concerned with urban educational reform. Indeed, these campaigns did not include as targets state or district education policy or policy makers. If school reform and public engagement for school reform were to ramp up to include long-term collaborations with groups involved in multi-issue campaigns like those described here, it could constitute important social movement building.

These alliances have made important local and metro area gains, but are too few in number and too limited in geographical scope to have made national,

fundamental changes. Despite these weaknesses, their cross sector collaborations remain significant models of allying networks and groups and in this
sense constitute important models for education reform groups.

Indeed, joining with education organizers and education reform groups
would strengthen these groups. Although the groups we describe (like others
not mentioned) collaborate across political or economic sectors, they ignore
education. For example, the 2005 national immigrant bus rides to Washington, DC, focused on immigrant rights to decent jobs. Participants were working class/low income men and women of color living in urban neighborhoods
and whose children most likely attended stressed, financially strapped public
schools. Had the immigrant groups included education reform in their campaign for civil rights, it might have strengthened their case. In addition, it
could have gained them allies from education organizing groups, networks,
and alliances.

Social Movements: Seeking Fundamental Transformation

Social movements generally try to transform, rather than work within, the
political grid Henig describes. In contrast, alliances often aim to address specific rights or improvements *within* the grid. For example, many of the education alliances described above focused on school improvement in low-income
districts. Housing groups are focused on the availability of affordable homes
and apartments, and living wage campaigns focus on raising the minimum
wage. One could argue that these groups seek fundamental changes to the
social order, and indeed, in some cases, they may constitute "small social
movements" (Anyon 2005a). But when compared say, to the civil rights movement of the 1950s or the labor movement of the 1930s, these campaigns have
narrower goals.

Elevating the public conversation to one that frames educational inequities as a violation of fundamental constitutional rights might create opportunities for education reformers, community organizers and advocates, and
community members to explicitly relate the relationship between educational
quality and education achievement to struggles for living wages, decent jobs,
health care and housing, and immigrant rights. In addition, establishing this
link could also provide opportunities for those working to achieve educational
equity to collaborate with groups already working in these other arenas,
broadening their efforts in ways that could lead to social movement building.
Although "education as a constitutional right" remains very much contested,

framing the public engagement discussion with this *goal* provides a larger conceptual umbrella that might help "name" and thus elevate educational injustice so that it achieves parity with previous inequities social movements have challenged, such as women's suffrage, abolition, and civil rights.

Clearly, efforts across sectors of the political economy would be important to solving the problems of education in low-income areas. In *Radical Possibilities* (2005a), Jean Anyon describes several regional alliances across the country. Although limited in scope and effect, and certainly not always successful, urban low-income youth, progressive unions like SEIU, living wage campaigns, and immigrant groups are examples of what might be called fledgling social movements. These campaigns could be coordinated and linked to the work of activist education alliances. The synergy that might result would be important in catalyzing the power of a national social movement. There are many examples of city- and region-wide collaborations that could provide a model for the transformation of educational reform and public engagement efforts into collaborative efforts at social movement building.

Social Movements: A National Focus

Social movements are typically national. As the examples of the U.S. civil rights movement and the labor movement suggest, full-blown social movements engage the whole nation. This national scope and agenda are part of what gives the movements power to demand fundamental political or economic change. It may be that the important challenge of globalization for public engagement efforts—from community organizing, to alliances, to social movement building—is that campaigns need to *transcend neighborhoods*. The issues around which public engagement groups develop campaigns need to be those that affect people in most or all of the neighborhoods of a city and in most or all of the cities of the state and nation. And the analysis that informs public engagement work needs to make the link to global causes. In this regard, analyses ought to transcend local power sources as causes and be supplemented by the identification of national and global developments and policies that affect neighborhoods. For instance, a local campaign against an underfunded urban school or district might connect the lack of public monies available for education to lowered state and federal tax rates on corporations or to the huge federal spending on foreign wars. And, as we have suggested above, we could expect synergy if we connected this local effort for increased education funding to alliances across sectors and indeed across the nation—in this case by joining education funding struggles to national anti-war alliances.

According to scholar David Horton Smith, the United States has 7.5 million grassroots associations and 2 million nonprofits with paid staff (cited in Bothwell 2003, 3). Poor urban neighborhoods are home to many of these associations. Researchers in one lower-income Chicago neighborhood, for example, found more than 150 associations. Among these were such groups as the Dickens Block Club, Act Now, Amistad Spanish Speaking Youth, and Damen Ave. Revitalization Effort (Kretzmann and McNight 1993). Urban housing projects are not devoid of citizen associations, either. In the Cabrini-Green public housing project in Chicago, for example—which journalists and politicians had long described as devoid of community—researchers identified extensive social networks and neighborhood institutions, many organized and run by residents. A selected list of community-based groups included four religious congregations, a legal services group, youth sports organizations, tutoring and college preparation, a pre-school, a day care, a newspaper, counseling, and job training. The existence of active resident organizations in poverty-stricken neighborhoods belies the stereotype of a passive, unconcerned population. Citizen engagement in organizations is present; what is missing, however, is the coordination of these groups across neighborhoods of the city, the region, the state, and the nation.

In the last twenty-five years, activist alliances for school reform may have prepared the ground for substantial change. And the year 2000 brought with it twenty-five years of legal battles at the state level to remove urban educational inequities, such as that facilitated by the AQE in New York. More than 70 percent of these court cases have been successful, and many new state mandates have been written by the courts; more than a few await the public political pressure that might force full funding. These cases and the years of education organizing that are behind us and that continue may provide the legitimation and leverage needed for national movement building.

It is unlikely that public engagement in the form of community organizing or collaborative alliances that are local and not connected nationally, and that are not aimed at fundamental changes, would produce the constitutional and other legal transformations wrought by these social movements. All this suggests that community organizing and activist alliances are necessary but not sufficient to building social movements.

The Potential Impact of Social Movements on Schools, Districts, and U.S. Democracy

Progressive social movements have not always been successful, but throughout U.S. history, social movements from the political Left have often had profound results. They have led to passage of a number of social policies that have increased the rights of working people, women, and minorities (e.g., the Populist movement of the late 1800s, Socialist movement of the early 1900s, the 1930s labor movement, the civil rights movement, and both women's movements of the twentieth century). These social movements led to important policy accommodations on the part of governments and social institutions.

Previous social movements have impacted education. Although in many ways education remains much the same as in 1900, there have been progressive changes wrought by the concerted protest: immigrants' struggles for education in the early 1900s yielded adult worker education and Catholic schools for children; the civil rights movement led to national Head Start programs as well as increased recognition and educational opportunities nationwide; Latino struggles produced bilingual education; the 1970s women's movement yielded curricular change as well as increased entitlements in schools and districts; disability rights organizing also has prompted federal protections and entitlements. Along with continuing and coalescing the work described earlier in this chapter, activist education alliances could seize on opportunities that could develop into a social movement. There is also evidence that past social movements have raised economic opportunities for parents and thereby increased the school achievement of their children.

Although not the only source of new resources or opportunities in low-income educational settings, social movements have made substantial gains in providing these to schools and districts in need. Head Start, for instance, was a product of the civil rights movement, designed by activists in rural Mississippi as a way to support families whose children they were teaching. These movement activists made sufficient contributions to the education of the children that their program was picked up by the federal government. Head Start moved to center stage in the Johnson administration and has remained a major source of opportunity for the education of young children.

Although *Brown v. Board of Education* did not initially bring about education integration in the South, it did renew and strengthen activist organizing toward that end; ultimately, the decision de-legitimated separate but equal accommodations in the civil sphere. As a consequence of the national social movement for political rights of black Americans, this decision and others following it produced vastly increased opportunities in education for people of color—in admissions decisions, in administrative openings, in curricula, and in expanded programs. The women's movement of the 1960s and 1970s also was responsible for increased opportunities in education, specifically for female students. It provided the legal mechanisms that yielded women's sports programs and increased admissions to higher education and job opportunities. Curricular resources also flowed from the women's movement's concerns. A final example of increases in opportunities and resources *via* social movement pressure is bilingual education. Bilingual programs were implemented in most parts of the nation as a result of the bilingual education movement that evolved out of the civil rights movement (San Miguel and San Miguel 2004). Federally mandated bilingual programs created new educational opportunities for non-English speaking children to learn the dominant language and culture of the United States.

Educational resources and opportunities are often increased as a result of other forms of public engagement, such as community organizing and group alliances as well, but these improvements tend to be local or restricted to districts (and, in a few cases, to entire states) and do not have national effects, as was the case with the effects of the social movements noted above. When social movements successfully apply national pressure, they often result in legal or constitutional changes that increase the pool of persons who can participate in U.S. democratic institutions.

Conclusion

In the Preface to this book, Marion Orr and John Rogers ask,

> What is public engagement? . . . Public engagement cannot be reduced to individual acts such as voting, speaking with a teacher, or choosing a school. Public engagement emerges as parents, community members, and youth identify common educational problems and work together to address them. Public engagement both builds on and seeks to foster interdependence. . . . In the words of Martin Luther King Jr.: "We are caught in an inescapable network of mutuality, tied in a single garment of destiny."

Although there are differences between alliances and social movement building and other forms of public engagement described in this book, this definition of public engagement captures important elements common to them all. Those common elements are efforts to respond to a shared concern, interdependence among individuals, and collective struggle.

Perhaps a next step in public engagement efforts would be to build on the networks public engagement has created so far and utilize and extend nationwide the existing alliances among groups. To strengthen these networks and collaborations, development of an agenda that is national and agreed on, and that incorporates into the platform the effects of political economic policies and arrangements on all levels that constrain efforts to make education equitable, would be an important step.

Notes

1. Although not a book on education, Kristina Smock's *Democracy in action: Community organizing and urban change*, published by Columbia University Press in 2004, shows the tension surrounding efforts to organize around big issues and the implications for movement building.

References

Anyon, Jean. 2005a. *Radical possibilities: Public policy, urban education, and a new social movement.* New York: Routledge.

———. 2005b. What "counts" as education policy? Notes toward a new paradigm. *Harvard Educational Review,* 75th anniversary issue. March: 65–88.

Bezahler, Lori, Susan Cahn, and Cassie Schwerner. 2004. Lessons learned: collaborative mobilizing for educational reform. *Responsive Philanthropy.* Winter 2003/2004. www.ncrp.org/files/rp-articles/RP-Winter2003-2004-Collaborative_Mobilizing_for_Education_Reform.pdf.

Bothwell, Robert O. 2003. The decline of progressive policy and the new philanthropy. Retrieved from COMM-ORG Papers 2003. http://comm-org.wisc.edu/papers2003/bothwell/ (accessed March 4, 2010).

Della Porta, Donatella, and Mario Diani. 2006. *Social movements: An introduction.* Oxford, UK: Blackwell.

Granovetter, Mark. 1973. The strength of weak ties. *American Journal of Sociology* 78 (6): 1360–1380.

Hirota, Janice M., Robin Jacobowitz, and Prudence Brown. 2000. *The Donors' Education Collaborative: Strategies for systemic school reform.* Chicago: Chappin Hall Center for Children, University of Chicago.

———. 2004. *Pathways to school reform: Integrating constituency building and policy work.* Chicago: Chappin Hall Center for Children, University of Chicago.

Hirota, Janice M., and Lauren E. Jacobs. 2003. *Vital voices: Building constituencies for public shool reform: A report of the Ford Constituency Building Study.* Chicago: The Academy for Educational Development and Chapin Hall Center for Children University of Chicago.

Honig, Meredith. 2004. The new middle management: Intermediary organizations in education policy implementation. *Educational Evaluation and Policy Analysis* 26: 65–87.

Kretzmann, John, and John McNight. 1993. *Building communities from the inside out: A path toward finding and mobilizing a community's assets.* Chicago: Acta Publications.

San Miguel, Guadalupe, and Guadalupe San Miguel Jr. 2004. *Contested policy: The rise and fall of federal bilingual education in the United States, 1960–2001.* Denton: University of North Texas Press.

Schwerner, Cassie. 2005. Building the Movement for Education Equity. In *Rhyming hope and history—Activists, academics and social movement scholarship,* ed. D. Croteau, W. Hoynes and C. Ryan, 157–175. Minneapolis: University of Minnesota Press.

Tilly, Charles. 1978. *From mobilization to revolution.* Reading, MA: Addison-Wesley.

———. 2004. *Social movements, 1768–2004.* Boulder, CO: Paradigm, 2004.

Touraine, Alaine. 1981. *The voice and the eye: An analysis of social movements.* Cambridge: Cambridge University Press.

Wells, L. 2009. *At the front of the bus: A community-based perspective of the community, issues, and organizing efforts to improve public schooling in Newark, New Jersey.* PhD diss., University of California–Los Angeles.

Websites

Alliance for Quality Education (AQE). www.aqeny.org (accessed March 4, 2010).

Applied Research Center (ARC). www.arc.org (accessed March 4, 2010).

Center for Community Change (CCC). www.communitychange.org (accessed March 4, 2010).

Center for Third World Organizing. http://ctwo.org (accessed March 4, 2010).

Center on Education Policy (CEP). www.cep-dc.org/ (accessed March 4, 2010).

Communities for Public Education Reform (CPER). www.communitiesforpubliceducationreform.org (accessed March 4, 2010).

Education Law Center (ELC). www.edlawcenter.org (accessed March 4, 2010).

Good Schools Pennsylvania. www.goodschoolspa.org (accessed March 4, 2010).

Institute for Responsive Education (IRE). www.dac.neu.edu/ire/home.html (accessed October 22, 2007).

Logan Square Neighborhood Association. www.lsna.net/home.aspx (accessed March 4, 2010).

National Center for Schools & Communities (NCSC). www.ncscatfordham.org/pages/home.cfm (accessed March 4, 2010).

National Council of La Raza (NCLR). www.nclr.org/ (accessed October 20, 2007).

Prichard Committee for Academic Excellence. www.prichardcommittee.org (accessed March 4, 2010).

Public Education Network (PEN). www.publiceducation.org (accessed March 4, 2010).

Research for Action. www.researchforaction.org/index.html (accessed March 4, 2010).

III

Sites of Public Engagement
for Public Education

8 Improving Teacher Quality Through Public Engagement in Chicago

Sara McAlister, Kavitha Mediratta, and Seema Shah

IN CHAPTER 6 OF THIS BOOK, Mark Warren discusses community organizing and the engagement of low-income communities and communities of color in public education reform. In this chapter, we explore how such organizing is transforming community engagement in urban public education by defining and winning support for reforms targeted at improving the core instructional capacities of schools. These new engagement efforts are designed to support successful student learning and to develop culturally responsive relationships with the communities that urban public schools serve.

In Chicago, despite a long history of powerful community organizations and a schooling context of decentralized governance, public involvement in public education has often been relegated to school-support activities, particularly volunteerism and fund-raising. Although the creation of Local School Councils in 1988 substantially increased parent and community representation and provided a platform for expanded public engagement in educational decision making, efforts to improve public schooling's human capital—teacher quality—have been monopolized by education professionals.

Efforts in Chicago to use public engagement to improve teacher quality emerged through a convergence of two distinct parent organizing efforts within the larger political context of the No Child Left Behind Act. In Logan Square, a neighborhood on the West Side of Chicago, a group of Latina mothers working as mentors in their children's schools focused on teaching as a way to expand the cultural knowledge and competencies of their children's teachers. Supported by the Logan Square Neighborhood Association (LSNA), these

neighborhood women entered into a "grow-your-own" teacher-training program, which LSNA developed in collaboration with a local university (Blanc
et al. 2002). At the same time, on the West Side of Chicago, a group of African
American community residents and parents concerned about poor student
outcomes in North Lawndale schools launched an effort to recruit more qualified teachers. Supported by the Illinois Association of Community Organizations for Reform Now (ACORN), they attended job fairs to identify and recruit
qualified candidates to their schools. But the annual exodus of these recruits,
mostly new and inexperienced white teachers, led the group to look for a pool
of teachers from within their community who might be more likely to stay in
North Lawndale schools.

   This convergence of interest in a new teacher pipeline led to an alliance
between the two organizations—LSNA and Illinois ACORN—that ultimately
produced a statewide initiative to bring 1,000 new teachers of color to schools
serving low-income communities and communities of color. Working with
other influential organizations, the two groups built a broad coalition of education stakeholders that skillfully used No Child Left Behind's teacher quality
mandates, and the growing national attention to the issue of teacher recruitment and retention, to win state legislation and supporting budget appropriations for a teacher pipeline program. As of December 2007, the Illinois state
legislature had appropriated $7 million to support 545 teacher candidates pro-
gressing through 16 local consortia of universities and community groups
(Grow Your Own Illinois 2008).

   The teacher pipeline campaign provided a platform from which community leaders and organizers could promote public engagement locally and
across the state. It linked community organizing groups with institutions of
higher education, teachers' unions, and school system officials to develop new
local teacher pipeline programs. Although LSNA and other organizations
were deeply involved at all levels of the campaign, in this case study we focus
on the unique role that Illinois ACORN played in the construction of new
teacher pipelines.[1] We examine the schooling problems that propelled parents, community members, and ACORN staff to organize to improve teacher
quality, and we explore how local concerns and actions grew to a statewide
teacher quality campaign that produced the Grow Your Own program that is
in place today.[2]

   Reflecting on Illinois ACORN's work on this education campaign, we discuss how other community organizing groups—particularly those of color

from low-income communities—might engage in education reform. We argue that community organizing helps parents and community members draw on community knowledge, values, and expertise to help schools develop the core capacities they need for teaching and learning. We find that organizing groups can use their extensive political relationships and expertise to build consensus among education stakeholders as a first step to improving education for children whose schools need improvement the most.

Illinois ACORN's Model of Organizing

Illinois ACORN, now known as Action Now, has a twenty-five-year history of organizing in the working-class and predominantly African American and Latino South Side and West Side Chicago neighborhoods of Englewood, West Englewood, Little Village, and North Lawndale. Illinois ACORN has led successful campaigns to expand affordable housing, challenge predatory lending, improve access to health care, remove barriers to citizenship, and improve education in neighborhoods where its members live. The organization currently has thousands of dues-paying members and a full-time staff of seven organizers and two research staff.

ACORN's mission is to build power among low- and moderate-income community residents so the residents can hold government and the private sector accountable for meeting neighborhood needs. The organization posits that power develops when large numbers of community members mobilize to challenge imbalances in political power. Like other community organizing groups, ACORN activists generally believe that the people who are directly affected by societal inequities should participate in developing solutions that address their needs.

Illinois ACORN works from a *direct membership* model of organizing. Individuals are recruited into the organization through door-knocking and other one-on-one outreach strategies and are supported in developing their leadership capacities by participating in campaign activities and through leadership training (Beam and Irani 2003; Delgado 1986; Mediratta 2004; Swarts 2007). The organization is structured to ensure member representation and control at each level of decision making. As one ACORN leader explains: "We [members] do everything. We all have our [local membership] meetings on the South Side, the West Side, Little Village. . . . [And then], once a month we get together at a board meeting and we decide collectively what we're going to do."

Local neighborhood chapters hold meetings, choose campaign issues, and develop and implement local campaign actions. These local chapters send representatives to city- and statewide decision-making bodies, which discuss and help implement campaign strategy and organizational development. The organizer's role in this process is "to build the organization, to mobilize people into action around issues they're concerned about, to develop leaders, and to move people into campaigns" (Talbott 2003a).

Though the organization works extensively on school reform, it generally does not carry out school-based parent recruitment. Instead, parents and community residents who become involved in ACORN neighborhood chapters work on education issues as well as other community concerns. The neighborhood chapter structure encourages residents, parents, grandparents, and other caregivers to participate on education-related issues.

Entering the School Reform Arena

ACORN's entry into education organizing was facilitated by a series of opportunities within the city's schooling landscape. During the 1980s, the organization had sporadically mobilized members to protest school closures and other specific incidents. The Illinois state legislature's passage of the Chicago School Reform Act of 1988 provided what Kingdon (2003) has termed a "policy window" for ACORN to pursue its mission of public participation, government accountability, and neighborhood improvement. The centerpiece of the 1988 reform legislation was a shift in power from centralized control to new school-based teams, called Local School Councils (LSCs), which included the school principal and six parents, two community members, and two teachers elected to two-year terms.[3] LSCs were given the authority to hire and fire school principals, to develop school improvement plans, and to control roughly half of schools' budgets. (For a detailed discussion of the Chicago School Reform Act, the movement leading to its creation, and its implications for reform, see Chambers 2006; Fung 2006; Hess 1991; and O'Connell 1991.)

ACORN mobilized its members for LSC elections as a way to exert influence over the performance of local schools. In the first year of the reforms, eighty-seven ACORN members won seats on councils in South and West Side Chicago schools. Imogene Sommerville, a veteran ACORN leader and long-term LSC member, recalls that the new governance role transformed parents into key participants in the school community, and educators were forced to take them seriously:

Once it was clear to the principals that their job future was dependent on parents and community residents, schools started welcoming us all. . . . We were no longer invisible or outsiders. [The school principal] asked my idea about things going on at the school, and shared his strategies and plans. (Russo 2004, 57)

But members struggled with the complexity of the problems facing schools. Madeline Talbott, head organizer of Illinois ACORN, recalls,

Once we put people on the LSCs, it created much more interest in the part of the membership about what the heck do we do about the schools. How does a community organization engage with classroom education? We didn't have an answer to that question. (Talbott, 2003a)

Shortly after the law's passage, local foundations began supporting parent and community leadership on LSCs by funding community organizations to train LSC members (McKersie 1992). In 1993 the Annenberg Challenge significantly expanded these resources through a grant to build the capacity of LSCs to lead meaningful reform and to support networks of schools in partnering with universities, community organizations, and school reform groups (Shipps, Sconzert, and Swyers 1999). ACORN used these funds to access education reform experts to inform the work of LSC members and to grapple with the underlying question of how a community-led organization might facilitate school improvement.

Teacher Quality as a Lever for Systemic Reform

The partnership between ACORN and influential school reform organizations—most notably the Small Schools Workshop, the Cross City Campaign for Urban School Reform, and Designs for Change—became a crucial source of access to data, research, and expertise for parents and community members that led to the organization's focus on teacher quality. During a training session on education in 1999, a group of ACORN members in the West Side chapters of Englewood, West Englewood, and North Lawndale began to look carefully at teaching and learning in their schools. Members examined the math and reading curricula being used, observed classes in local schools, and reviewed data assessing and comparing school performance across different Chicago neighborhoods. As differences in classroom instruction and student achievement across schools became clear, ACORN leaders became convinced that the key to improving their schools was recruiting more experienced and effective teachers. Talbott recalls, "During a workshop with Michael Klonsky [of the Small Schools Workshop] and ACORN leaders one Saturday afternoon, parents asked, 'How do we impact the classroom?' And Klonsky said, 'It's all about the teachers...you need to get good people into the classroom'" (2003a).

In spring 2000, twenty-five West Side ACORN leaders launched a drive to recruit highly qualified teachers to their schools. With logistical support from ACORN organizers, the ACORN leaders placed ads in local and citywide media, collected resumes, screened applicants, and met with principals to discuss promising candidates. Though principals were supportive, the experience proved a frustrating introduction to the challenge of recruiting qualified teachers to work in high-poverty schools. Talbott explains, "It was very hard to get people who sent resumes to come to the West Side for an interview, and many of them who [took jobs] did not stay. Because they wanted a job, they went in, [and] then they left" (2003a). Few teachers saw the West Side schools as platforms to build a career.

From this experience, ACORN staff and leaders began to understand that the problem of finding and keeping qualified teachers could not be solved only though local recruitment efforts. The difficulties ACORN encountered in recruiting qualified candidates stemmed from limitations in the pool of candidates, as well as from a lack of district attention to teacher quality in West Side schools. As part of their research on teacher quality months later, ACORN members and organizers attended an Annenberg Foundation-sponsored forum on urban teaching during which the director of Human Resources for the Chicago Public Schools (CPS) described his efforts to recruit teachers to high-poverty schools. The district had intensified recruitment from major universities and had begun recruiting internationally for teachers for high-shortage areas with offers of stipends and other incentives. Still, CPS faced massive vacancies every year. The district's struggles with recruitment captivated ACORN. "Here's a guy who's recruiting thousands of teachers every year, because he has to—that's his job," Talbott explained. "But we knew that recruiting a few teachers who come in and run out again wasn't working. And then we got it. We realized we needed to climb in and become part of the process" (2003a).

In fall 2000, ACORN leaders convened to discuss developing a broad campaign to improve teacher quality across all the schools in ACORN neighborhoods, rather than targeting specific schools. The West Side chapter presented the issue to Illinois ACORN's board, which approved the decision to take the campaign organization-wide. The school district had just announced a major campaign of school capital improvements, and the promise of an infusion of school facilities funds provided an opening for ACORN leaders to meet with principals of schools in ACORN neighborhoods about their resource needs. ACORN organizers trained leaders to interview the principals, coaching them on how to talk with principals in a supportive way and how to frame questions about teacher quality in terms of advocating for greater resources for the school.

After the interviews, ACORN organizers compiled the leaders' data to create an inventory of the resource needs of each neighborhood school. They discovered that although the principals dearly wanted *qualified* teachers, they were desperate, annually, for *any* teachers, because vacancies were so widespread that schools were forced to rely on long-term substitutes to fill classrooms. In the neighborhoods where ACORN organized, the data showed that North Lawndale had the most severe shortage of qualified teachers.

This discovery led ACORN to initiate a more extensive analysis of teacher resources in Chicago schools. ACORN hired a senior research analyst, who began collecting public administrative data on teacher qualifications in neighborhood schools. Because the district would not provide data on teacher qualifications, ACORN filed a Freedom of Information Act request with the state to obtain teacher certification records. These data revealed large numbers of teachers in ACORN neighborhoods who were teaching without proper certification in their subject area; in some schools, more than half of the regular classrooms were staffed by teachers who lacked elementary teacher certification.

To force the district to prioritize teacher quality in North Lawndale schools, ACORN released a public report showing disparities in teacher quality between North Lawndale schools and higher-performing schools across the city. Initially, ACORN leaders planned to present their report at the city-wide school board's monthly public meeting, but the meeting was moved a week forward and the ACORN report was incomplete. A group of fifty ACORN leaders attended the board meeting to insist that the district address the inequitable distribution of qualified teachers. Denise Dixon, the mother of four children in CPS schools and then president of Illinois ACORN, demanded: "You were able to open Northside College Prep and Payton College Prep [two new selective-enrollment high schools] with full complements of teachers. Why should they get teachers with masters and doctorates when we can't even get teachers with credentials?" (Rossi 2001a).

Without their report, ACORN leaders could only present the evidence of vacancies and uncertified teachers they had gathered through their school visits. But when reporters asked the district's human resources director to respond to ACORN's demands, he confirmed that the situation was dire— halfway through the school year, more than thirteen hundred positions remained unfilled (Rossi 2001a).

After the school board meeting, Chicago Schools CEO Paul Vallas invited ACORN to meet with him to discuss their demands. Vallas had led the school district since the legislature had approved mayoral control in 1995, and he had a reputation for being responsive to organizing. "Vallas could count," Talbott has written. "If he felt you had no community or parent base, he ignored you. But he cared about organizations with a base" (Russo 2004, 54). ACORN leaders presented Vallas with the inventory of schools' needs they had assembled during the fall. He responded immediately to the requests for capital improvements, but he seemed uncertain about how to address the teacher vacancies and ultimately agreed to work with the group to improve new teacher recruitment.

The following week, ACORN completed and released its report, *Leave No School Behind: Instructional Inequality and its Impact on ACORN Neighborhood High Schools* (Association of Community Organizations for Reform

Table 8.1 Chicago ACORN Schools Research, May 2002: North Lawndale (Region 3) Elementary Schools

Number of Schools	Special Education Students	Special Education Teachers Without Special Education Teaching Certificate	Regular Classroom Teachers Without Regular Classroom Teaching Certificate	One-Year Teacher Turnover, 1998–99
North Lawndale Elementary Schools				
21	16% (1,757 of 11,155)	41% (35 of 86)	37% (207 of 565)	12% (79 of 651)
North Lawndale High Schools				
2	19% (279 of 1,445)	42% (5 of 12)	24% (21 of 89)	13% (13 of 101)

Source: Revised from Association of Community Organizations for Reform Now (ACORN).

Now, 2001a). The report examined disparities in the distribution of qualified teachers in the Chicago Public Schools and argued that schools in ACORN neighborhoods were staffed by teachers with fewer educational credentials, years of overall teaching experience, and years teaching at their current school, compared to high-performing schools in the city. It also argued that these differences contributed to lower achievement scores, higher dropout rates, and fewer students taking the college entrance exams.

The analysis established ACORN as a key resource for data on teacher quality; ACORN staff and leaders were extensively quoted in the media. Dixon explained,

> We were so forward about what we wanted for our children, what we needed, that press picked up on it. It was pretty cool to be heard, to actually have a solution to the problem, and not like we're just complaining. We're saying, this is wrong, and this is how you fix it. It's pretty amazing. (Dixon 2003)

Although Vallas was angered by the public criticism that resulted from ACORN's report, he could not ignore it. Talbott described their interaction:

> Here we come with a study criticizing CPS and he was furious. He had just agreed to meet monthly with us, and in the next meeting he brought in maps and charts to prove that everything we had said was wrong. . . . But he was engaged; he was very engaged. (Talbott 2003a)

ACORN organizers understood that without sustained, vocal demands for change, it was unlikely that CPS would respond to their concerns. But they also understood the reluctance of education officials to work with groups viewed as narrowly oppositional. Pressure without access was unlikely to yield much change. A group of ACORN leaders and organizers began meeting regularly with CPS's human resources staff to explore how the district hired and retained teachers. Behind closed doors, district officials acknowledged that although they had never looked systematically at variations in teacher qualifications across the district, rates of teacher retention and experience in North Lawndale seemed to be among the lowest in the city.

That summer, ACORN leaders and organizers returned to the North Lawndale schools to obtain data on teacher vacancies and certified teachers needed. They passed the data they collected to the district. When schools opened in the fall, ACORN leaders conducted follow-up meetings with principals. These visits revealed that although there were continuing vacancies in the areas of library, counseling, and special education, every classroom in North Lawndale had a teacher. ACORN credited the dramatic reduction in teacher vacancies to CPS's decision to move a strong recruiter to North Lawndale, as well as to the energy and focus that CPS's Human Resources director brought to teacher recruitment across the system.

Just before the beginning of the school year, Mayor Daley replaced Vallas with Arne Duncan, who had served for two years as the CEO's deputy chief of staff. Because Duncan had employed a much more collaborative style of working, the Chicago school reform community anticipated that Duncan's appointment would usher in a new wave of reforms focused specifically on improving instruction in CPS schools. The new leadership seemed to offer another "policy window" focused on issues of teacher recruitment and quality (Lenz 2004; Russo 2004).

In fall 2001, with guidance from ACORN staff, the *Chicago Sun-Times* produced its own analysis of teacher certification data in Chicago schools and ran a lengthy series on the district's problems with recruiting and retaining certified teachers. Each article referenced ACORN's work on teacher quality and included quotes from ACORN leaders (Fuller 2001; Rossi, 2001b; Rossi and Grossman 2001; Rossi, Beaupre, and Grossman 2001). Shortly after, ACORN produced a follow-up to its March 2001 analysis of teacher qualifications, in a report that analyzed district-wide high school teacher certification data (Association of Community Organizations for Reform Now, 2001b). ACORN's analysis again revealed pervasive inequities in teacher quality across CPS. Schools serving low-income communities of color had much higher percentages of unqualified teachers than more affluent schools had. ACORN's report received considerable press coverage, and, together with the *Sun-Times* series, the coverage solidified ACORN's reputation as a knowledgeable and forceful advocate for improved teacher quality.

Unpacking the Problem of Teacher Turnover

For the next several years, ACORN continued its focus on improving teacher quality in North Lawndale, while expanding its campaign to include other ACORN neighborhoods. These teacher quality campaigns coincided with the enactment of the federal No Child Left Behind (NCLB) Act, which required states to formalize teacher qualification standards and to ensure that all classes were taught by highly qualified teachers. The law also required states and districts to inform parents when their children were not taught by qualified teachers and to report annually data on the distribution of qualified teachers among high- and low-poverty schools.

NCLB brought new urgency to the issue of teacher quality. The requirement that districts inform parents when their children were taught by less-than-qualified teachers opened another avenue for ACORN's teacher quality demands. The act also added flexibility about who to target. NCLB gave new power to the Illinois State Board of Education to determine criteria for highly qualified teachers in the state. By focusing its organizing pressure on the Illinois State Board of Education, ACORN gained more room to maneuver in the delicate push-and-pull negotiations with CPS. Leaders carried out street actions against the Illinois State Board of Education when it failed to distribute letters informing parents of teacher qualifications as NCLB required, while politely requesting that CPS release the results of an audit of teacher qualifications required by the law. In addition to providing data for ACORN's campaign, the teacher quality letters and audit results helped energize ACORN members and recruit them into the campaign. (See Shirley and Evans [2007] for an analysis of ACORN's response to NCLB nationally.)

Increased attention to recruiting qualified teachers brought more certified teachers and fewer vacancies to local schools in ACORN neighborhoods. Although recruitment improved, retention did not. As the parents on the West Side had discovered, getting teachers to accept jobs in their schools was only the beginning of the struggle. Many teachers transferred as quickly as they could to wealthier schools or suburban districts. Indeed, the district's improved recruitment strategies and intensified focus on attracting certified teachers actually exacerbated the teacher turnover problem—young, white, suburban teachers entered West Side and South Side schools with little intention of staying any longer than they had to.

ACORN leaders and school principals initially believed that the new teachers were vulnerable because of their unfamiliarity, and perhaps discomfort, with the neighborhood. Gwen Stewart, an ACORN leader in North Lawndale, explained, "Part of the problem is that new teachers only stay for a short while. They're young, Caucasian, recently came to Chicago. It's culture shock when they walk outside the building" (2003). A North Lawndale principal observed that although the new teachers were well prepared in content knowledge, many had difficulty relating to the neighborhood children: "I felt they were committed, they wanted to help the children, but just didn't know what to do."

Through the North Lawndale Learning Community, a consortium of schools, universities, social service agencies, and community organizations, ACORN began a program of home visits for new teachers as part of an induction program run by the Steans Family Foundation. Drawing on a strategy used by the Pacific Institute for Community Organization (PICO) National Network in California, the home visits were intended to introduce teachers to local families and help them feel more connected to the neighborhoods. Principals and ACORN leaders hoped that developing relationships between teachers and residents could begin to counter teachers' stereotypes and reduce the "culture shock" that drove them out of local schools.

Though the home visits were immensely popular with teachers, principals, and leaders, ACORN found little evidence that they stemmed the flow of new teachers out of neighborhood schools. ACORN released two more reports in 2002 and 2003, but these reports focused on teacher turnover rather than teacher recruitment. Schools in North Lawndale, Englewood, and Little Village were losing more than 20 percent of teachers each year on average, with a few schools turning over nearly half their staff. Worse, many teachers left after just one year, creating substantial recruitment and induction costs for the district. As before, ACORN balanced public demands for change with a collaborative approach to the district, meeting with CPS staff in the weeks before the report came out. Al Bertani, CPS's chief officer of professional development, noted,

> They were politically smart enough to kind of position their work in such a way that they could say, "We know that this is a problem. We know you're working on this problem. We're trying to bring more of a spotlight on it in relation to the neighborhoods that we serve." (Bertani 2004)

The Grow Your Own Campaign

By 2003, after three years focusing on teacher quality, ACORN's leaders had come to understand that teacher turnover was a problem across low-income urban districts and that the scale of the problem required a more comprehensive solution than teacher home visits or whatever induction programs the district could design. ACORN located the source of the problem in the system of teacher preparation, which was "churning out people who are staying one or two years and no more" (Talbott 2003b). ACORN's data analyses revealed that retention was better among non-white teachers in

North Lawndale, yet graduates of teacher preparation programs were increasingly young, white, and suburban and seemed largely unprepared or unwilling to teach in low-income, urban communities of color.[4] Until there was an increase in the number of qualified teachers with the cultural preparation to understand and the commitment to teaching in communities like North Lawndale, trying to keep new teachers in ACORN schools seemed a futile exercise.

With funding from the Ford Foundation, ACORN convened LSNA and two other school reform organizations—the Cross City Campaign for School Reform and Designs for Change. Together, these groups formed the Chicago Learning Campaign (CLC) to focus on a systemic strategy for improving teacher quality. LSNA had begun a "grow-your-own" teacher-training program in partnership with Chicago State University. The program, called Nueva Generación, provided a bachelor's degree in education leading to full bilingual certification for a group of thirty women who Logan Square had trained as school-based parent mentors (Blanc et al. 2002). ACORN staff and leaders saw in Nueva Generación a workable solution for creating a pipeline of qualified teachers who would stay in neighborhood schools. Research on similar "grow-your-own" teacher pipeline programs from across the nation showed encouraging results in terms of program completion, retention, and teacher quality (DeWitt Wallace-Reader's Digest Fund 1997; Clewell and Villegas 2001).

In addition, the Nueva Generación model had the potential to solve several problems underlying the teacher quality issue. Parents from the neighborhood, who had already spent time working in schools, would begin their teaching careers with deep commitments to their neighborhood schools and extensive relationships with neighborhood families. Such teachers would not face the culture shock that traditionally recruited teachers experienced. When ACORN spoke to members and neighborhood residents about who they would like to see teaching in local schools, respondents spoke of wanting the kind of teachers coming out of this program. "The more I talk [to people], the more I see people would rather have the parent who lives across the street from them come to the school, but [they're] just not certified," noted an ACORN organizer.

The Nueva Generación model also offered a new approach to teacher preparation. It required a commitment on the part of the university to train a cohort of teachers specifically for "hard-to-staff" schools, as well as a commitment to improve access to teacher preparation programs for people of color from low-income neighborhoods. Chicago State University, which had partnered with LSNA in developing Nueva Generación, invested in developmental classes and other supports that neighborhood participants needed to complete their training. The model incorporated many of the best educational practices for nontraditional students, including child care, tutoring, and counseling. In addition, the program's cohort system allowed participants to form close relationships and provide mutual support throughout their training. In this way, the teacher pipeline program promised a strategy of coproduction, linking university and community. Community members would play a central role in recruiting and designing the supports for cohort members and in defining the qualities of an effective teacher. These effective teachers would be members of the local community, with a commitment to neighborhood schools and a special understanding of students' needs (see this book's Chapter 4, written by Donn Worgs).

With help from its allies in the CLC, ACORN assembled its own grow-your-own program based on LSNA's model. ACORN members and organizers recruited paraprofessionals and community members from North Lawndale schools to form a cohort of teacher candidates, reaching out to local universities and community colleges to provide the necessary preparation.

Within the CLC, ACORN advocated for institutionalizing the LSNA model on a broad scale by developing state legislation to establish a reliable funding stream and lend legitimacy to the model as a viable way to prepare teachers. Rather than replicating the pipeline program in a handful of Chicago neighborhoods, ACORN pushed CLC members to view the grow-your-own programs as a lever to reinvent teacher recruitment and preparation. Talbott argued:

> If we can do research on this issue in other cities and find out if teacher turnover is as high, and we can organize all teacher aides and paraprofessionals in all our cities, and demand [grow-your-own], we can transform teacher preparation. (Talbott 2003b)

For ACORN, a statewide campaign would give local chapters a concrete way to impact teacher quality while recruiting large numbers of new members—principally teacher paraprofessionals—into the organization.

ACORN and its CLC allies pushed the teacher quality campaign forward. The coalition reached out to CPS because the limitations of the school system's traditional strategies to recruit and retain teachers in neighborhoods like North Lawndale were becoming clear. CPS had already identified a set of hard-to-staff schools that needed more intensive supports for new teachers, and the school system recognized that even teachers who were committed to teaching in low-income schools were unprepared by their university programs for the realities of those schools. District officials thus saw the CLC's proposal to scale up the Nueva Generación model as a targeted solution to a problem of mutual concern. CPS's director of mentoring and induction, Amanda Rivera, who had served as a principal in Logan Square, became an early ally. Her experience with the LSNA parent mentors had demonstrated to her "the kind of relationship they developed with the students, the comfort level, the knowledge of that school community that new teachers often lack" (Rivera 2004).

The CLC began meeting with university and community college officials, the teachers' and principals' unions, and local and national foundations to consider how to scale up LSNA's model. CLC members understood that to advance their demands at the state level, they would have to build and demonstrate the commitment of a broad array of supportive organizations and institutions across the state (see both the Foreword and Chapter 3 of this book). Universities and colleges were interested in the work because they knew that they were failing to produce enough teachers of color and saw in the grow-your-own model the potential for "new resources for things that in their hearts they know they should be doing" (Talbott 2005). But many university educators had reservations that paraprofessionals and parents without college degrees could complete a college program and become skilled teachers if the certification requirements were kept the same as for traditional teachers. Chicago State University, LSNA's partner in Nueva Generación, became a crucial ally in building support among higher education institutions, as did the dean of education of the University of Illinois at Chicago, which had run a paraprofessional-to-teacher program in several Chicago neighborhoods.

By the end of 2003, the Chicago Learning Campaign had expanded its effort to draft state legislation by gaining support from community organizations, universities and community colleges, district officials, and local and state legislators. Participants in the new Grow Your Own (GYO) Task Force identify ACORN, and particularly Talbott, as facilitating consensus around the draft legislation. Amanda Rivera, a senior CPS official, observed,

ACORN was able to recruit all the key stakeholders and to hold very amicable planning sessions. We were able to move rather quickly and get consensus, which is not easy when you have all those institutions and some personalities that can be challenging. (Rivera 2004)

Like most sophisticated organizing groups, ACORN and LSNA had gained the attention of local legislators, who responded to the groups' ability to mobilize large numbers of voters and act publicly on their members' demands. The organizing groups' influence on elected representatives impressed higher education leaders, who had spent the past legislative session fending off cuts to their institutions designed to resolve a state budget crisis. ACORN and LSNA members traveled to Springfield to meet with legislative leaders and explain the grow-your-own programs. Three other Chicago organizing groups—Target Area Development Group, the Kenwood-Oakland Community Organization, and the Southwest Organizing Project—were recruited into the task force; these organizations brought the governor's office and additional legislators into the campaign.

In late January 2004 the new GYO Task Force convened a Grow Your Own Summit to solidify constituency and legislative commitments to the draft legislation. District staff, higher education officials, and legislators spoke to an audience of almost a hundred community leaders and other allies. A delegation from North Carolina presented retention data from a grow-your-own program in that state. Nueva Generación participants described their experiences, and ACORN leaders described their teacher turnover study. An official from the University of Illinois at Chicago distributed maps showing where the university's teacher preparation graduates were placed to make the case for a grow-your-own program in Chicago's black and Latino neighborhoods. The summit served as a public accountability session in the tradition of grassroots organizing, in which officials were asked to "sign on" to the legislation. Arne Duncan's chief deputy for education, Barbara Eason-Watkins, publicly committed the Chicago school district's support, as did the chair of the state senate's education committee and representatives of the Chicago Teachers Union and the Service Employees International Union (SEIU) 73, which represented some paraprofessionals. Two senators agreed to sponsor the bill in the state legislature. Following the summit, the task force expanded its membership to include representatives from other Illinois school districts struggling with teacher turnover, which strengthened support for the bill among legislators across the state. Talbott recalls:

By getting [all of the institutional players] to the table, we were in a position where nobody was opposing the legislation . . . nobody that regularly operates in Springfield and cares about these issues. And then with the summits we developed . . . players that were aware of the legislation even if they were not supporting it, they made a decision not to oppose it when they got a feel for who was at the table and what kind of support it had. (Talbott 2006)

The Grow Your Own Teachers Act was passed during the 2004 legislative session. The law sought to "increase the diversity of teachers by race, ethnicity, and disability, and prepare them for hard to staff positions and hard to staff schools in areas serving a substantial percentage of low-income students" (Grow Your Own Illinois 2006b). It also set a goal to produce a thousand new teachers, with an average retention period of seven years, by 2016. Districts with low performance and persistent teacher turnover could join a local consortium that included a university or a community college, and either a community organization or a union, and apply for grants to provide teacher training to paraprofessionals or community residents. Community organizations were defined as nonprofits having the "demonstrated capacity to train, develop, and organize parents and community leaders into a constituency that will hold school and school district accountable for achieving high academic standards" (Grow Your Own Illinois 2006b).

A state budget crisis prevented an appropriation from accompanying the bill that year, but the governor's support for the bill encouraged task force members to believe that an appropriation would follow in the next year. The Illinois State Board of Education solicited contract proposals to administer the program and award grants on behalf of the state. Though a consortium of universities also applied for the contract, the contract went to the GYO Task Force, which renamed itself Grow Your Own Illinois to reflect an expanding statewide membership (Grow Your Own Illinois 2006a).

Task force members worked the next year to solidify support for a legislative appropriation and to assist the state board in developing program rules. There was broad consensus among task force members about the overarching vision of the Grow Your Own program. However, some members, particularly from the university and colleges, thought that local constituencies with few resources would not be able to build the academic skills of GYO candidates. These members pushed for university-based teacher preparation programs and for their own role as "lead partners" in implementing local GYO programs.

But the organizing groups argued against entrusting the new program to the entrenched bureaucracies of higher education that might recreate "what they've been doing all along" (Talbott 2005), rather than build new programs that fully anticipated the needs of GYO candidates and prioritized the community connections at the core of the GYO vision.

With outreach and recruitment by task force members, local consortia formed across the state and began recruiting candidates, which raised the profile of the Grow Your Own Teachers Act among downstate legislators and helped build a statewide constituency for legislative funding. In 2005, following a second GYO summit—again attended by community leaders, university officials, district representatives and legislators—the state legislature authorized a $1.5 million appropriation for GYO, providing planning grants for ten consortia. The following year the legislature passed an additional $3 million appropriation for implementation grants. To date, GYO has received over $14 million in total appropriations and has continued to expand the program to meet the goal of 1,000 teachers by 2016.

GYO Illinois now provides a variety of supports to local GYO projects across the state. Staffed by organizers from various community organizing groups and led by Anne Hallett, former director of the Cross City Campaign for School Reform, GYO Illinois has amassed considerable expertise and political clout. The organization helps districts analyze their teacher turnover and teacher diversity data to assess their eligibility for GYO funding and helps build local consortia, recruit teacher candidates, and design teacher preparation programs based on best practices (Grow Your Own Illinois 2006a).

To date, 545 candidates supported by twelve consortia across the state are enrolled in courses and progressing toward their certification. More than 87 percent are people of color, and 72 percent work full-time in addition to attending courses—many as paraprofessionals in local schools. The majority of the consortia include a grassroots community organizing group as the community partner; these groups recruit candidates from their own neighborhoods and help build constituencies to fight for continued funding for GYO. To date, eight of twelve public universities in Illinois belong to GYO consortia (Grow Your Own Illinois 2008).

Managing Confrontation

During the period of state-level negotiations regarding GYO, tensions erupted in Chicago over a CPS proposal dubbed Renaissance 2010, which was announced in June 2004. Renaissance 2010 aimed to create "100 new schools in neighborhoods across the city over the next six years, providing new educational options to underserved communities and relieving school over-crowding in communities experiencing rapid growth" (Chicago Public Schools 2008).

ACORN and other community organizations in Chicago demanded greater transparency. The organizations were particularly concerned about the district's plan to replace low-enrollment and low-performing schools in rapidly gentrifying neighborhoods with new schools, many run by outside partners freed from contractual regulations. ACORN viewed the strategy as an effort to reduce the influence of the teachers' union, which ACORN was cultivating as an ally on GYO. In addition, ACORN viewed Renaissance 2010 as a deliberate effort to displace low-income families from downtown Chicago neighborhoods. Talbott explains:

> [We've been] fighting on the balanced development/subsidized housing side and now education turns out to be directly related. [The city is] trying to im-prove the schools fast enough that they can attract some people to $300,000 townhomes that are starting to go up and higher. Nobody wants a lousy school. They've got to do something and [Renaissance 2010] is what they choose to do. The people in the community now realize that this is not for them and are up in arms. People in West Englewood are starting to get it that we will never see a community school that is opened for twelve hours, but [CPS is] promising that all of the midtown schools will be open for twelve hours and on and on. (Talbott 2004b)

The campaign against Renaissance 2010 campaign jeopardized ACORN's collaborative relationship with the Chicago school district. Yet the growing support for GYO across the state made it less vulnerable to shifting dynamics within the city. ACORN skillfully balanced pressure with continued collabo-ration and preserved the joint work on GYO. District officials noted that ACORN's reputation as an organization that fought tenaciously to make sure that "schools that are struggling, those schools that are more racially and eco-nomically isolated . . . have access to the additional resources they need" en-sured a level of respect for ACORN's positions, even when in opposition to the district's positions.

Implications for Public Engagement in Education Reform

What is the impact of Illinois ACORN's work on improving teacher quality? What can the organization's experiences teach us about public engagement in education reform? We argue that community organizing is shifting the domain of public engagement in school reform by focusing the improvement efforts of parents and community members on core schooling capacity questions and by challenging educator assumptions about the nature of the knowledge and relationships with the community that schools need to serve children.

ACORN's work progressed from sporadic opposition to school closings and participation on LSCs into core instructional and cultural issues. This shift responded to the urgent need for school improvement in ACORN neighborhoods and took advantage of strategic opportunities provided by district, state, and national political contexts. These opportunities included new funding, NCLB mandates, and the changing priorities of school district leadership.

Drawing on data made accessible in part by NCLB's provisions for transparency, ACORN helped parent and community leaders examine the factors that contribute to school quality. With clear, documented disparities in teacher preparation, ACORN helped its members identify a policy-relevant factor that, if addressed, would remedy a source of the persistent education disadvantages faced by low-income children of color. Thus, the organization defined a new arena for parent and community engagement in schools, even in the context of the relative and limited empowerment that the Chicago school system offered. "Until we started doing this," Talbott recalls, "people did not see teacher quality as an issue for parents. They'd relegate parents to this little area of parent involvement, not understanding that we don't want to be *involved*, we want quality education. What [ACORN members] taught us was that the natural place for parents in schools is on teacher quality" (2003a).

ACORN's legitimacy in pursuing teacher quality reforms was strengthened by the innovative analyses the organization produced, using state-level data about teacher credentials. ACORN's status was also enhanced by the organization's skill in combining these administrative data analyses with members' direct experiences of schooling conditions and problems. ACORN leaders sent their children and grandchildren to local schools; they served on LSCs; they visited principals and reviewed school report card data; they organized home visits for new teachers. Because ACORN leaders and organizers were constantly recruiting new members, they brought direct, on-the-ground knowledge about what was happening inside of schools into all their campaigns.

The iterative process of collecting and blending data from multiple sources helped ACORN organizers and leaders uniquely grasp the complexity of the problem of improving teacher quality. ACORN discovered the huge shortage of qualified teachers in its neighborhood schools—a problem that the district had struggled to resolve. ACORN realized that recruitment alone could not stem the startling turnover in North Lawndale and the other ACORN neighborhoods and understood that the problem of teacher turnover began not with recruitment but with the selection and preparation of teacher candidates.

In addition, the Grow Your Own strategy was not just a matter of adding energy and resources to solving the school staffing problems. ACORN and its allies challenged traditional assumptions about the competencies and knowledge necessary to effectively serve low-income communities of color. ACORN's strategy framed teacher preparation as an ongoing process of co-production between education organizations (universities and districts) and community constituencies (local organizations, parents, and residents). By creating a statewide Grow Your Own program, ACORN and its allies sought to institutionalize the use of local assets—parents and community residents' sense of belonging and connectedness to their communities—to provide a supply of teachers prepared to make a long-term commitment to work in historically hard-to-staff schools.

As other authors in this volume argue, public engagement depends not only on public interest and commitment, but on the existence of a platform for engagement, consensus-building, and sustained partnership. In Chicago, ACORN stimulated parent and community engagement in their own neighborhoods and across neighborhoods. ACORN's model facilitated broad neighborhood engagement among many low-income people who initially prioritized discrete concerns, such as housing, immigration, education, and so forth. Thus, the organization's representational structure kept its membership robust and ensured a sense of urgency, conviction, and accountability in its interactions with elite stakeholders.

Throughout its teacher quality campaigns, ACORN utilized an inside-outside engagement strategy, in which collaboration with system insiders was

carefully calibrated with outside pressure. Part of ACORN's success in man-
aging the inherent tensions of such a dual strategy stemmed from its capacity,
as a community organizing group, to identify and appeal to the self-interest of
individuals and organizations. But ACORN's success was also facilitated by
the unique capacities of its staff—its head organizer has amassed more than
twenty-five years of experience, and its senior data analyst had previously
worked as a university professor of public policy. These strengths aided the
CLC, and later the GYO task force, in building and maintaining effective partnerships not only with the district, but with community organizations, the
teachers union, and institutions of higher education, despite the obvious differences in organizational interests.

Conclusion

Proponents of public engagement typically argue its importance in creating
demands for reform and, more recently, in sustaining reform. But the experience of Illinois ACORN suggests at least two additional and crucial benefits
of public engagement in education. First, the group's efforts to improve
teacher quality demonstrate how an engaged public can advance school reform strategies through the introduction of community knowledge. Second,
ACORN's capacity for strategic engagement, consensus-building, and man-
aging inside-outside partnerships demonstrates that grassroots organizing
groups can ensure that the beneficiaries of reform are the communities most
in need.

The teacher pipeline program that resulted from ACORN's public engagement in Chicago schooling offers the hope of transforming the quality of instruction in high-poverty neighborhoods. This approach is consistent with
the literature on teacher preparation and retention and is supported by early
evidence from other teacher pipeline programs nationally. Though one thousand new teachers will not resolve the problems of teacher vacancies or teacher
diversity in Chicago, the scale and visibility of the effort suggests the potential to impact not only on how teacher preparation is conceptualized and
implemented, but also on how communities are engaged in the effort. Talbott
observes:

> [Grow Your Own] is not just a program for quality teachers from the commu-
> nity, but a movement where at all levels of the community, it becomes a pas-
> sion. People really want it and believe in it, and are enthusiastic about it. And

I guess I'd like to propose, at least in our view, that that movement and passion has something to do with how the schools turn out in the end. It's not just about whether you do the work, but about whether there is a movement behind it. (Talbott 2005)

Notes

Norm Fruchter conducted a portion of the fieldwork on which the chapter relies and contributed to early drafts. Wherever possible, we secured permission to attribute quotes by name. In several cases where we were unable to locate an interviewee, we have attributed their quote by role, e.g. "an ACORN leader."

1. As of January 2008, Illinois ACORN disaffiliated with ACORN and became Action Now. Because the work described in this chapter was carried out under its affiliation with ACORN, we refer to the organization using its former name.

2. This chapter draws on data collected for a larger study of community organizing for school reform. As part of that study, we conducted twenty-eight interviews with Illinois ACORN organizers and members, principals, district and state education officials, and allies. We conducted multiple interviews with ACORN staff over time to document the evolution and policy impacts of ACORN's campaigns. The balance of quotations in this chapter is not reflective of the important and ongoing roles that ACORN members played in the work.

3. During the 1980s, dissatisfaction mounted with a failing school system in which the dropout rate of some high schools approached 70 percent; student achievement was far below national norms; and a bloated, impenetrable bureaucracy and constant labor strife impeded reform. A six-week strike in September 1987, the ninth in eighteen years, catalyzed the frustrations of parents, community groups, education reformers, and business groups, which had been pushing for management reforms centered on increasing local control. Intense organizing and coalition building led to the 1988 Chicago School Reform Act, which shifted budgeting to the school level and established LSCs, among other reforms.

4. An Illinois Education Research Council report confirms ACORN's observations: CPS was recruiting increasing numbers of white teachers with master's degrees, who were the group least likely to stay in high-poverty, high-minority schools (De-Angelis and Presley 2007).

References

Association of Community Organizations for Reform Now. 2001a. *Leave no school behind: Instructional inequality and its impact on ACORN neighborhood high schools.* Chicago: Illinois ACORN.

———. 2001b. *Leave no school behind: Preliminary findings from the second report: Instructional inequality in seventy-one Chicago public high schools.* Chicago: Illinois ACORN.

Beam, John M., and Sharmeen Irani. 2003. *ACORN education reform organizing: Evolution of a model.* New York: National Center for Schools and Communities, Fordham University.

Bertani, Al. 2004. Personal interview with author, November 18.

Blanc, Suzanne, Joanna Brown, Aida Nevarez-La Torre, and Chris Brown. 2002. *Case study: LSNA, Logan Square Neighborhood Association. Strong neighborhoods, strong schools. The indicators project on education organizing.* Chicago: Cross City Campaign for Urban School Reform.

Chambers, Stefanie. 2006. *Mayors and schools: Minority voices and democratic tensions in urban education.* Philadelphia: Temple University Press.

Chicago Public Schools. 2008. Chicago Public Schools: Renaissance 2010. www.ren2010.cps.k12.il.us/ (accessed March 4, 2010).

Clewell, Beatriz Chu, and Ana Maria Villegas. 2001. *Absence unexcused: Ending teacher shortages in high-need areas.* Washington, DC: The Urban Institute.

DeAngelis, Karen J., and Jennifer B. Presley. 2007. *Leaving schools or leaving the profession: Setting Illinois' record straight on new teacher attrition.* Edwardsville: Illinois Education Research Council.

Delgado, Gary. 1986. *Organizing the movement: The roots and growth of ACORN.* Philadelphia: Temple University Press.

DeWitt Wallace-Reader's Digest Fund. 1997. *Recruiting, preparing and retaining teachers for America's schools. Progress report: Pathways to teaching careers.* Pleasantville, NY: Author.

Dixon, Denise. 2003. Personal interview with author, February 22.

Fuller, Janet Rausa. 2001. Parents' interest a key to success: Volunteer, keep tabs on children. *Chicago Sun-Times*, September 10.

Fung, Archon. 2006. *Empowered participation: Reinventing urban democracy.* Princeton, NJ: Princeton University Press.

Grow Your Own Illinois. 2006a. About Grow Your Own Illinois. www.growyourownteachers.org/AboutUs/index.htm (accessed March 4, 2010).

———. 2006b. Grow Your Own Teachers Education Act (Summary). www.growyourownteachers.org/Resources/ILStateBill.htm (accessed March 4, 2010).

———. 2008. Grow Your Own Teachers: An Illinois Initiative. www.growyourownteachers.org/BeAnAdvocate/GYO%20descriptionFeb%2008.pdf (accessed March 4, 2010).

Hess, G. Alfred Jr. 1991. *School restructuring, Chicago style.* Newbury Park, CA: Corwin Press.

Kingdon, John W. 2003. *Agendas, alternatives, and public policies*, 2nd ed. New York: Addison-Wesley Educational Publishers.

Lenz, Linda. 2004. Stars were aligned behind Daley. [Electronic version]. *Catalyst Chicago*, June. http://catalyst-chicago.org/stat/index.php?item=133&cat=0 (accessed March 4, 2010).

McKersie, Bill. 1992. *Philanthropy's paradox: Chicago school reform: The role of Chicago foundations in reform, 1987–1990*. Paper presented at the meeting of the American Educational Research Association, San Francisco. Unpublished manuscript.

Mediratta, Kavitha. 2004. *Constituents of change: Community organizations and public school reform*. New York: Institute for Education and Social Policy.

O'Connell, Mary. 1991. *School reform Chicago style: How citizens organized to change public policy*. Chicago: Center for Neighborhood Technology.

Rivera, Amanda. 2004. Personal interview with author, November 18.

Rossi, Rosalind. 2001a. End teacher shortage now, parents urge. *Chicago Sun-Times*, February 22.

———. 2001b. Teacher woes worst in poor schools. *Chicago Sun-Times*, October 10.

Rossi, Rosalind, Becky Beaupre, and Kate N. Grossman. 2001. Other states do it better. *Chicago Sun-Times*, September 9.

Rossi, Rosalind, and Kate N. Grossman. 2001. Substandard teachers under the microscope. *Chicago Sun-Times*, September 24.

Russo, Alexander. 2004. "Third wave"—or lull—in Chicago school reform. In *School reform in Chicago: Lessons in policy and practice*, ed. Alexander Russo, 1–12. Cambridge, MA: Harvard Education Press.

Shipps, Dorothy, Karin Sconzert, and Holly Swyers. 1999. *The Chicago Annenberg Challenge: The first three years*. Chicago: Consortium on Chicago School Research.

Shirley, Dennis, and Michael Evans. 2007. Community organizing and No Child Left Behind. In *Transforming the city: Community organizing and the challenge of political change*, ed. Marion Orr, 109–133. Lawrence: University Press of Kansas.

Stewart, Gwen. 2003. Personal interview with author, November 22.

Swarts, Heidi. 2007. Political opportunity, venue shopping, and strategic innovation: ACORN's national organizing. In *Transforming the city: Community organizing and the challenge of political change*, ed. Marion Orr, 134–161. Lawrence: University Press of Kansas.

Talbott, Madeline. 2003a. Personal interview with author, February 22.

———. 2003b. Personal interview with author, October 7.

———. 2004a. Parents as school reformers. In *School reform in Chicago: Lessons in policy and practice*, ed. Alexander Russo, 55–62. Cambridge, MA: Harvard Education Press.

———. 2004b. Personal interview with author, July 12.

———. 2005. Personal interview with author, November 3.

———. 2006. Personal interview with author, May 17.

9 "A Force to Be Reckoned With"

The Campaign for College Access in Los Angeles

John Rogers and Ernest Morrell

Taking Back Our Education

As she began her senior year at Roosevelt High School in East Los Angeles, Nancy Meza was struck by how few classmates remained. More than sixteen hundred students had enrolled in Roosevelt's ninth grade four years before. Fewer than six hundred joined Meza in the senior class (California Department of Education 2007). Meza knew that there were several reasons why so many young people were dropping out. Roosevelt's five thousand students—all Latino and almost all poor—often felt lost and unsafe within the dramatically overcrowded campus. Counselors responsible for nearly a thousand students each had little time to offer guidance or support. Many students felt that Roosevelt's curriculum, which featured few college preparatory courses, was not preparing them to be successful adults.

Angered and frustrated by these conditions, Meza decided to "help take back our education" (Meza 2005). She joined InnerCity Struggle (ICS), a community-based organization of students and young adults who work collaboratively to build the power of youth in East Los Angeles. Along with other ICS members, Meza distributed student surveys to document and understand the scope of Roosevelt's problems. She joined delegations of ICS members who shared their concerns and ideas for policy changes with Roosevelt's principal and local elected officials.

While winning important concessions such as three additional guidance counselors, Meza and the ICS members discovered that many of their concerns extended beyond the control of local officials. They began to meet with

227

students from other youth organizations across the city to discuss district-wide policies shaping student progress toward graduation and college. Like the members of ICS, youth in South Los Angeles' Community Coalition had been organizing to address the dropout problem in their schools. Recognizing the need for greater power to make gains at the district level, students from ICS allied with the Community Coalition and several other community and civic organizations committed to educational reform. Under the banner of Communities for Educational Equity (CEE), ICS became part of a campaign to make college preparatory courses the "default curriculum"—that is, the courses that all students would enroll in and not just a few students who are left to their own devices to make these high-stakes choices.[1] Meza was soon working with Latino and African American students across the city, education justice advocacy groups, and established civic organizations like the United Way.

During her final semester at Roosevelt, Meza played a leading role in the citywide campaign for college access. She helped organize workshops that informed youth about the uneven distribution of college preparatory courses and why this inequality mattered. Along with other members of ICS, Meza collected the signatures of thousands of East Los Angeles students and parents on petitions supporting the campaign. She joined student leaders in accountability meetings with individual school board members. The student leaders used these meetings to share their ideas, communicate their power, and (ultimately) secure endorsements for new policy. In June, Meza and hundreds of students and parents wearing red and blue "Let Me Choose My Future" T-shirts rallied outside the board of education. As the ICS members danced and chanted "Give us life prep, not a life sentence," board members overwhelmingly passed a resolution guaranteeing all Los Angeles students access to a college preparatory curriculum (Hayasaki 2005a).

What lessons does Nancy Meza's story hold for public engagement in public education? ICS Executive Director Luis Sanchez saw the campaign's success as evidence that community mobilization in the form of rallies, church meetings, and petitions could effect policy change. "Students fought to make this happen" (Hayasaki 2005a). Marqueece Harris-Dawson, the director of the Community Coalition, similarly argued that the citywide alliance constituted accountability from the bottom up. The newly empowered organizations now could engage the school district as a "service provider [that] has to deliver" (Kaplan 2005a). School board members differed in their assessment of this emerging power of organized youth and community groups. School board president Jose Huizar told a reporter, "it is great to see parents and students work together to demand these courses" (Alcala 2005). Yet, his fellow board member David Tokofsky worried that vocal youth do not necessarily have the understanding necessary to create good public policy. "The civic engagement part of what they are doing is really great," commented Tokofsky, "but I wonder about whether they are [learning to deal with] . . . the unavoidable complexities of civic and political life" (Merl 2005).

This chapter examines the recent campaign for college access against the backdrop of a long history of educational governance in Los Angeles dominated by professionals and civic elites. We look to the past to trace policies that have excluded or discouraged Latino and African American youth from participation in educational politics. By contrast, we look to ICS and its participation in the CEE alliance to explore the possibility of a dramatically different, and more inclusive, public life being created in Los Angeles. We are interested in the effects of this recent campaign on the quality of education and civic life in Los Angeles. We are also interested in Sanchez's claim that the campaign for college access represents "an opportunity to start a movement, a big one" (Kaplan 2005a).

The chapter proceeds through four sections. The first section reviews the history of educational governance in Los Angeles, highlighting the ways that elite decision making and racial politics have shaped patterns of participation as well as educational opportunities. The second section focuses on ICS as a democratic and inclusive site of civic learning and public development in East Los Angeles. Section three explores the process through which ICS became part of a larger alliance in the context of the citywide campaign for college access. The final section describes public policy and public engagement after the school board vote as a way to assess the possibilities for, and challenges to, creating more equitable schools and political life through youth organizing and reform alliances.

Racial Politics and Educational Governance in Los Angeles

The centrality of Latino and African American youth and grassroots organizing to the campaign for college access is particularly noteworthy given the history of educational governance and reform in Los Angeles. During the first half of the twentieth century, as Los Angeles grew from a small city of a hundred thousand to a metropolis of two million, white professional elites governed a predominantly white school district (Pitt and Pitt 1997). Progressive reformers ushered in this governance structure in 1903 with a city charter that replaced the old ward politics with central district administration and civil service standards for hiring and promotion. The professional managers who took over for the ward bosses explained that scientific administration, rather than public participation, held the key to more efficient management in a rapidly growing school system (Raftery 1992).

In addition to providing a guiding rationale for the emerging bureaucracy, modern science served as a vehicle to justify policies that differentially impacted the city's diverse constituencies. School leaders invoked the science of public health to impose their own cultural standards of hygiene and nutrition on immigrant populations. Educators warned against immigrant children overeating fruits and vegetables (which were thought to contain too much water) and instructed Mexican mothers to replace tortillas with bread (Raftery 1992; Sanchez 1993). Similarly, in the 1920s, Los Angeles educational leaders embraced the new science of intelligence testing as a tool for sorting students into different educational pathways or tracks. They did not recognize, or were not concerned by, the cultural specificity of the knowledge these tests assessed. District officials merely acknowledged that the vast majority of "low mentality" children came from immigrant districts as they placed disproportionate numbers of Mexican American students into vocational, as opposed to academic, programs (Gonzalez 1999).

As the African American and Latino population of Los Angeles grew between 1920 and 1960, district officials maintained an official stance of color blindness that belied racially driven policies inside and outside the schools (Smith 1982). During this period, almost all African Americans and Latinos lived in working-class neighborhoods in South and East Los Angeles. The schools in these neighborhoods generally served multiracial student bodies and often received poorer resources (worse facilities or teachers with less training) than schools to the west or north that enrolled almost exclusively white students (Gonzalez 1999; Wild 2002). One explanation for these disparities lies in the insularity of the board of education. No Latinos served on the school board until 1967 (Nava 2002). Fay Allen, the lone African American elected to the school board before 1965, served only one term (from 1939–1942), during which time she was denied access to committee meetings held at the exclusionary Jonathon Club (Turpin 1965; Raftery 1992).

Ironically, after the U.S. Supreme Court overturned legalized school segregation in *Brown v. Board of Education*, Los Angeles' multiracial schools gave way to increasingly African American enrollment in South Los Angeles and Latino enrollment in East Los Angeles (Caughey 1967). Segregated African American and Latino schools in Los Angeles grew in the post-*Brown* era for a variety of reasons. Federal housing, banking, and insurance policies facilitated the movement of whites out of working-class neighborhoods in the central city. At the same time, housing discrimination—sustained through official policy and vigilante violence—restricted the rapidly expanding African American and Latino populations to particular areas of the city (Sides 2003). Further, although the school district generally assigned students to schools based on residential proximity, it waived these rules in mixed-race areas, allowing whites to attend primarily white schools in surrounding neighborhoods (Caughey and Caughey 1973). By the early 1960s, African American and Latino students represented about 40 percent of enrollment in the Los Angeles Unified School District, and nearly all of these students attended racially segregated schools (Los Angeles City School District 1966; Caughey 1967). Overcrowded and staffed with the least experienced teachers, the segregated schools of South and East Los Angeles produced the highest dropout rates in the city (Webb 1965; Martyn and Clark 1967).

Against the backdrop of sit-ins across the southern United States, civil rights activists initiated public protests against segregated and unequal conditions in Los Angeles schools. In 1963 a coalition of Los Angeles organizations, including the NAACP, the ACLU, CORE, labor unions, and several black churches, joined under the banner of the United Civil Rights Committee (UCRC) to push for school integration and educational equity. UCRC led a freedom march in June 1963 that was, at the time, the largest civil rights protest in Los Angeles history. Unfortunately, neither this march nor CORE's subsequent hunger strike at the Los Angeles Board of Education elicited much response from the all-white school board (Sides 2003). In August of that same year, the ACLU challenged the district's discriminatory policies with *Crawford v. Board of Education of the City of Los Angeles*—a class-action lawsuit that would embroil Los Angeles for the next two decades (Ettinger 2003).

Students in East Los Angeles took note as civil rights activism created greater public awareness of the system's failure to address educational inequality. In the fall of 1967, young people in several Eastside high schools began talking with community activists about holding a student walkout to force the district to address their concerns (Munoz 1974). Lincoln High social studies teacher Sal Castro encouraged the students to write down their grievances. What emerged was a list of thirty-six demands that highlighted material deficiencies (dilapidated buildings, overcrowded classes, too few counselors) and the students' desire for a stronger community voice in shaping their education (Haney-Lopez 2003). This agenda received unprecedented attention from elite civic institutions and civic leaders when thousands of students walked out of Eastside high schools in March 1968 (Heussenstamm 1972). The *Los Angeles Times*, the superintendent, and the school board publicly acknowledged the need to remedy problems in Eastside schools even as they objected to the students' methods of direct action (School Boycotts Not the Answer 1968). Equally important, the students offered themselves and the broader public a vision of young people of color as viable political agents (Haney-Lopez 2003).

The shift from rule by elite professionals to increasingly diverse and contentious participation coincided with the withdrawal of white and middle-class students from Los Angeles public schools. In 1950, roughly seven of eight students enrolled in the Los Angeles Unified School District were white (Kerchner 2007). By 1990, whites represented one of eight students in the district (California Department of Education 2007). In 1978, a property tax revolt across California led to the passage of Proposition 13, which severely restricted the funding base for public education (Carroll et al. 2005). By the late 1980s, Los Angeles business and civic leaders rarely sent their children to Los Angeles public schools, and civic elites paid little attention to public education (Kerchner and Menefee-Libey 2003).

A resurgence of civic interest in public education emerged as Los Angeles struggled through a deep recession in the early 1990s. The decline of the aerospace industry at the end of the Cold War combined with a national economic downturn produced a loss of more than 150,000 jobs (Haydamack, Flaming, and Burns 2005). Business and civic leaders looked to education as a strategy for reestablishing Los Angeles' economic competitiveness. They joined with educational insiders and community representatives to create a far more inclusive civic leadership group than had prevailed in previous decades. The Los Angeles Educational Alliance for Restructuring Now, or LEARN, represented more than six hundred organizations, with a leadership team featuring the CEOs of ARCO, Times Mirror, and Security Pacific Bank; the heads of the Urban League and a community organizing coalition; and the president of the teachers' union and the school superintendent (Bradley 1993; Kerchner and Menefee-Libey 2003). LEARN followed prevailing insights from management studies calling for a shift from centralized bureaucracy toward greater budget and decision-making authority at the local level. In theory, this meant that principals, working with newly trained teachers as well as parents, would have greater autonomy and bear greater responsibility for educational results (Bradley 1993).

LEARN encouraged locally generated reform activity in several Los Angeles schools, but it also fostered bureaucratic backlash and elite frustration, which in turn led to community resentment. The school board advanced both a top-down and bottom-up approach to change when it adopted the LEARN reform model in 1993. It decreed that all schools should be LEARN schools within five years, but, in deference to the teachers' union, it left to each school the decision about whether and when it would join the reform. Educators in many schools remained wary of the reform, and the district's central office administration often stood in the way of efforts to decentralize resources and authority (Hendrie 1997). LEARN's business leaders quietly pressured district leadership to share power and accelerate the reform. When this strategy failed, they created a new committee (independent of LEARN) and financed the election of a slate of candidates to the school board (Blume 2000; Kerchner and Menefee-Libey 2003). In 1999 the new school board majority ousted Ruben Zacarias, the first Latino superintendent in Los Angeles. LEARN supporter Maria Casillas echoed the sentiments of many in the Latino community when she noted that Zacarias's firing exposed the contradictions of a reform that tells parents "we want them to become involved" and yet takes action without their support (A School System Is a Terrible Thing to Waste 1999).

Civic Learning and Public Development in East Los Angeles

As business elites, the teachers' union, and district leadership jockeyed for control in the wake of LEARN's demise, grassroots community groups began to mark a different path to educational reform across several Los Angeles neighborhoods. The emergence of these groups reflected a sense of educational crisis in several communities. Conditions in much of South and East Los Angeles were demonstrably worse in the early 2000s than they had been a decade before. A new wave of immigration alongside the failure of the state and district to build new classrooms added significant new enrollment to already overcrowded schools. In addition, ill-conceived state and district policies created a shortage of qualified teachers that was felt most acutely in Los Angeles' poorest communities (Oakes 2002).

Community groups also engaged in educational reform because they were frustrated with *who* was making educational decisions and *how* these decisions were being made. The school board remained an insular and largely unresponsive body in 2000, with five white members out of seven in a district that enrolled more than 70 percent Latinos and less than 10 percent whites. "Parents and students were not calling the shots," remembers one community leader, and, as a consequence, decision makers did not address problems with a sense of urgency (Melvin 2007). Wanting both to improve the desperate conditions and to have more of a say, several grassroots community groups became increasingly active in their local schools and at the district level.

One such group was ICS in East Los Angeles, led since 1999 by Luis Sanchez and Maria Brenes.[2] ICS was founded in the early 1990s to address youth violence in the Eastside housing projects and neighborhoods by arranging gang truces. Over time, the group had become more focused on the "reasons behind the violence, and a lot of that had to do with lack of opportunities"— particularly in the schools (Merl 2005). ICS has sought to remedy these problems by changing "the power relations between the people and the schools" (Brenes 2004). This has meant "build[ing] civil society in East LA" so that informed and active community members hold elected officials and educators accountable for providing quality school conditions (Sanchez 2004). Importantly, Sanchez and Brenes have imagined youth as central players in this democratic movement. "Historically," Brenes explains, "young people have been the catalyst for change. They have a lot of energy and an eye for understanding what is wrong with society, in part because they are most impacted by the problems" (Brenes 2004).

Brenes recognizes that although many young people "know what the problems are . . . they haven't been taught what they can do to change the problems that they see" (Brenes 2004). ICS has taken responsibility for bridging this gap, creating an array of civic development opportunities at local schools and in its storefront office. About three hundred students regularly participate in "United Students" clubs across four Eastside high schools and two Eastside middle schools. These clubs are officially recognized by school officials. As such, they provide ICS organizers access to youth and offer students a site inside school where they can learn about and respond to shared problems. Each United Students club meets weekly with a faculty sponsor and an ICS organizer to discuss issues of concern, identify targets of change, and plan collective actions.

ICS provides more intensive political education in its off-campus offices. It regularly offers the "Strike School Academy," a fifteen-week after-school training program for East Los Angeles youth that invokes the legacy of the 1968 student walkouts. The Academy provides young people with data about learning resources at their schools, instruction in research techniques aimed at documenting educational problems, and readings in politics and social change (Merl 2005). The workshops are based on popular education methods, encouraging youth to discuss the problems they encounter at school every day and understand these problems in relation to broad political structures. "When we talk about locked bathrooms," notes Brenes, "they are able to make the connections to the historical context" that shapes how educators treat students and how resources are distributed (Brenes 2007). As a consequence, youth participants have developed both new understanding and new civic commitments. One student reports: "I went from being used to living in these conditions and not caring, to realizing and being aware of how bad our school and community is, to wanting to do something about it. Now my passion is to help people" (What Kids Can Do.org. 2003, 5).

Since 1999, ICS has trained more than five hundred young people in skills they need to develop and lead successful campaigns for change. Communication workshops have provided youth practical advice on how to reach out to other youth and how to present their case to skeptical adults. Another set of workshops has offered young people the "basics of media activism" (Brenes 2004). "I used to read the newspapers and watch the news and think that everything was accurate," reports one participant in ICS's media collective. "Now I realize there's a lot of inaccuracy. I know not to believe everything we read or see" (What Kids Can Do.org. 2003, 7). The media collective has trained students to identify, cultivate, and communicate effectively with sympathetic reporters (Brenes 2005). In addition, the media collective has taught youth to create their own independent media (fliers, webpages, digital video, etc.) so that they can control the messages they want to share in their school and community (Garcia 2004).

Although ICS has offered an extensive curriculum in political education, its leaders believe that young people learn as well through political action. Part of this action comes in the form of outreach to fellow students or members of the broader community. Much of the school-based outreach has been conducted through the United Students clubs. The clubs often hold rallies during lunch, using hip hop or punk rock groups to attract attention before talking with students about campaign issues. ICS members also canvass door to door in their neighborhoods, informing voters about how upcoming elections can impact opportunities in the local schools.

Organizing campaigns have offered ICS members potent opportunities for civic engagement and civic development. Campaigns often begin with youth gathering data and scanning the political landscape to identify issues of interest to fellow students and opportunities to effect changes in policy. ICS members then create power maps that assess all the potential political actors who could either assist or obstruct their efforts. This analysis leads to the development of a strategic plan that includes ideas for direct outreach and media engagement. As actions are taken at each stage in the process, members and organizers assess what has been done and rethink their strategies.

ICS members have gained experience, insight, and confidence by taking on new roles in the course of campaigns. In 2002, ICS members challenged Roosevelt High School to end its punitive approach to school discipline. They conducted surveys to determine how many students had been suspended and how these suspensions had shaped students' subsequent behavior. The ICS members connected with educators and scholars around the country who had developed alternatives to the so-called zero tolerance discipline policies. The students brought this information to regular meetings of Roosevelt's discipline committee—meetings that had previously only included teachers and administrators. Eventually, they negotiated a new set of discipline policies with the school's principal (Vasquez 2004). In addition to this tangible "win," students emerged from the campaign with a deep understanding of the issues and a better sense of how to engage officials to effect change.

Similarly, in 2004, ICS students built power and confidence through their campaign for a new high school on the Eastside. This campaign was sparked when district officials failed to take action to relieve overcrowding at Garfield High School's five-thousand-student campus. The district's decision to halt plans for a new school resulted, in the words of the Los Angeles Times, "from political squabbles, public relations blunders, and a dispute over location" (DiMassa 2004). ICS responded by building insurmountable public pressure for change. The students created a petition calling for a new high school and went door to door in the community seeking signatures. They also met with local pastors who allowed the students to present their concerns at church meetings. With petitions in hand, the students held one-on-one meetings with elected officials who had a say in local land use—members of the city council, the school board, and the county board of supervisors. When these officials did not take immediate action, ICS brought scores of students to public meetings. They held a march of four hundred students and parents from the county supervisor's building to the board of education (Brenes 2004). Having honed their message in several media trainings, the ICS students presented an extremely compelling case on local television. Ultimately, the very officials who had given up on building a school in East Los Angeles came to champion the idea. A spokesman for one official noted, "If the community supports this plan, we are behind it" (DiMassa 2004).

Communities for Educational Equity

ICS's emerging power on the Eastside coincided with growing educational activism across many Los Angeles communities. *Williams v. California,* a class action lawsuit filed in May 2000 challenging educational inequity, spurred both media attention to, and foundation interest in, the decrepit conditions in many public schools (Oakes 2004; Oakes and Rogers 2006). Many broad-based community organizations such as Association of Community Organizations for Reform Now (ACORN), Pacific Institute for Community Organization (PICO), and the Community Coalition focused time and resources on educational organizing. Previously unaffiliated parents came together in vibrant organizing groups such as Community Asset Development Redefining Education (CADRE) and Parent-U-Turn to work for change in their children's schools (Oakes and Rogers 2006). Simultaneously, an influential group of Latino leaders (including the publisher of the Spanish-language daily newspaper *La Opinion* and several CEOs) founded Alliance for a Better Community (ABC) to foster support among Latino parents for educational reform. ABC's agenda was shaped by a 2000 survey that found that education was far and away the most important social issue for Latino business and civic leaders (Melvin 2007).

Seeing the many streams of activism in the early 2000s, some organizers began imagining the power of a common flow. Alberto Retana, the director of community organizing in South Los Angeles' Community Coalition, remembers: "We had been going at it alone for a long time and hadn't been getting anywhere. A coalition gives you power. You have more geographic representation. And it is more democratic. And you have a greater impact if you can show you have a citywide alliance that crosses geography and race" (Retana 2007). When Retana met ABC's executive director, Veronica Melvin, at a state-wide meeting on teacher quality, the two leaders discovered that they both had been thinking about creating a "critical mass" of groups focused on reforming Los Angeles education (Retana 2007). They convened a meeting in summer 2004. "Community Coalition invited their CBO friends and we [ABC] invited our CBO friends," and more than twenty groups talked about how to improve education across low-income communities in Los Angeles (Melvin 2007). The organizations that participated—youth groups like ICS and the Community Coalition, parent groups like the African American Parent/Community Coalition for Educational Equity, and civic groups like the United Way of Greater Los Angeles—agreed to form a new coalition that eventually became Communities for Educational Equity or CEE (Sanchez 2006).

CEE's first challenge was to forge an agenda for a common campaign. Some groups wanted to hold the district accountable for its extraordinary high dropout rate. But, as Luis Sanchez later noted, "you can't just be against something" (Kaplan 2005a). Alberto Retana (2007) recalls: "We wanted to do organizing in a way that was asking . . . the district to adopt something positive—increase the number of students who would go to university." Several of the CEE groups had been involved in an unsuccessful effort to advance this agenda through state-wide legislation in 2002. State Senator Richard Alarcon had proposed that the college preparatory curriculum (the so-called A-G course sequence) become the default curriculum for all California high schools (California State Senate 2002). Although the powerful vocational education lobby had killed the legislation at the state level, many within CEE thought that a local initiative might have a better opportunity for success (Melvin 2007).

A campaign to create the conditions necessary for college access appealed to CEE groups for several reasons. Alberto Retana (2007) reasoned that, by setting a clear goal for high schools, organizing groups would gain "a lever to push for resource reallocation." Veronica Melvin envisioned the push to implement a universal college preparatory curriculum as a strategy for advancing a broad set of reforms that would improve the high school graduation rate. The call for college access for all students also promised to shift the public conversation from a focus on student failure to a focus on student success. Members of CEE hoped that this shift would help raise expectations across the school system (Melvin 2007). It also might reengage the broader community by turning attention from narrow indicators such as test scores to broader concerns about how well Los Angeles schools were preparing students for their future (Retana 2007).

The focus on college access also resonated with deeply felt concerns of many Los Angeles families about their economic prospects. Between 1970 and 2000, the proportion of middle-class residents in Los Angeles declined as the proportion of low- and high-income residents rose. Although this "hollowing out" of the income distribution has been common across the nation's metropolitan areas, it has been felt most dramatically in Los Angeles. By 2000, Los Angeles had a smaller proportion of middle-income neighborhoods than any of the nation's one hundred largest metropolitan areas (Booza, Cutsinger, and Galster 2006). In Los Angeles' bifurcated economy shown in Figure 9.1, young people and parents alike increasingly have come to view college education as

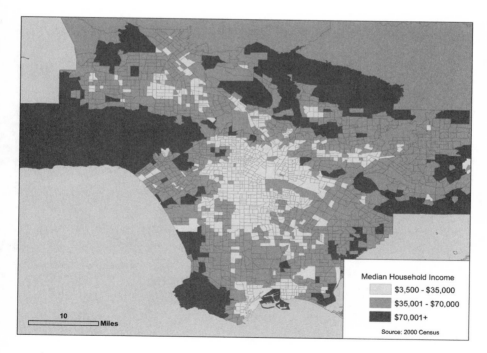

Figure 9.1 Income Inequality in Los Angeles County Neighborhoods. Created by Veronica Terriquez, UCLA's Institute for Democracy, Education, and Access.

critical to upward mobility. Recent surveys have suggested that a college degree has become a near universal goal across class, race, and immigration
status (Bendixen 2006; Affeldt et al. 2007). Yet, as of 2000, patterns of college
degree attainment differed markedly across Los Angeles' neighborhoods. (See
Figure 9.2.)

In fall 2004, the CEE groups agreed to support a campaign to make the
college preparatory (A-G) curriculum the default curriculum for all high
schools in Los Angeles. Foundation support enabled several key organizations (Community Coalition, ABC, and ICS) to dedicate staff to the campaign
(Melvin 2007). Member organizations of the CEE found that their coalition
provided them with important information and resources. At each CEE meeting, Alberto Retana led the group through a "power analysis" assessing the
political landscape shaping the campaign. Because of their diverse social networks, participants were able to contribute complementary insights about

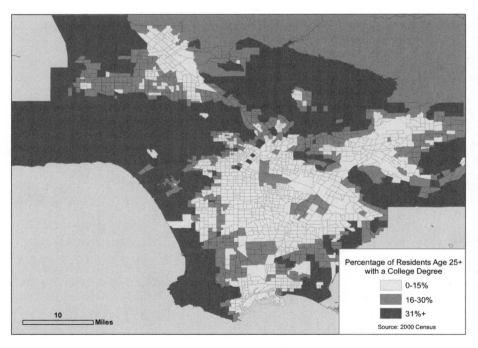

Figure 9.2 Los Angeles County Residents with a College Degree. Created by Veronica
Terriquez, UCLA's Institute for Democracy, Education, and Access.

what elected officials and other key players were thinking. These networks also proved helpful as the groups reached out to decision makers. Although the school superintendent would not return calls from ICS, he would respond to Maria Casillas, a longtime reformer and executive director of Families in Schools. Conversely, ICS had the strongest relationship to school board president Jose Huizar, who had been meeting regularly with ICS youth since 2002.

Despite its resources, the campaign faced an uphill battle. When Jose Huizar introduced the A-G resolution in April 2005—a few weeks before the scheduled vote—CEE had secured the commitments of only two of seven board members. John Perez, the president of the powerful teachers' union, seemed poised to oppose the resolution, citing the need to protect vocational coursework (Murray 2005). District leadership and several board members shared concerns about the resolution with Huizar and members of CEE. They worried that A-G would increase dropout rates and argued that many students did not want to go to college and hence should not be required to pass college preparatory courses (Sanchez 2006).

The CEE responded to these concerns with community organizing, data gathering, strategic communications, and coalition building. To counter the claim that students were not interested in college, CEE initiated a petition drive across Los Angeles. ICS members gathered eight thousand signatures in East Los Angeles alone (Sanchez 2006). The process of circulating petitions brought ICS members into churches and community groups and heightened public attention on the campaign. ICS members also collected more than three thousand responses to a student survey they conducted at Roosevelt and Garfield high schools. Almost all respondents indicated an interest in college, and three in four reported that their parents were the primary people pushing them toward this goal (Sanchez 2006).

The CEE also worked with the media to shape a persuasive narrative about why the resolution was needed. The coalition challenged the view that interested students already had a right to choose the college pathway. Rather, current policies harmed many students by denying them a meaningful chance to pursue college. The members of CEE identified and trained young people to speak with the press about their experiences. The *Los Angeles Daily News* reported the story of ICS member Jonathan Perez, who "never really had the option to take the right classes" because no one at Garfield High had explained college requirements (Radcliffe 2005). Similarly, the *Los Angeles*

Times reported on sixteen-year-old Takoura Smith of the Community Co-alition, who was forced to bring in her mother to meet with her counselor so that she could be moved into a college pathway (Hayasaki 2005b). Both students were able to draw on research done in collaboration with CEE to show that their schools offered far fewer college preparatory classes than schools in more affluent areas of the city. The self-evident unfairness of data presented a compelling story. As Luis Sanchez made clear, the power of this narrative lay in showing the relationship between unequal educational opportunities and an increasingly unequal economic system that left students with "few options other than working at McDonald's or Wal-Mart" (Sanchez 2005).

Although highlighting issues of inequality silenced many opponents, it did not, in and of itself, win over traditional advocates of vocational training. Here a different strategy was in order. Under the leadership of the United Way, the CEE built relationships with Los Angeles business and labor sectors that had influence on vocational training. Sandy Mendoza of the United Way helped the CEE groups frame a message about the A-G campaign that business and labor leaders could understand. CEE advocates began to talk about "educated youth for an educated workforce" and to describe college prep as "life prep" (Mendoza 2007). This position resonated with businesses like Southwestern Bell Communications, who recognized that all their employees needed strong math and science skills. But just as important as the message was the messenger. Mendoza brought youth from ICS and the Community Coalition to meet with United Way staff and business leaders. She remembers that the youth were extremely well informed and able to win over business leaders by speaking "from their hearts" (Mendoza 2007).

Direct engagement won support of other business leaders, including recalcitrant school board members. In fall of 2004, ICS youth began regular meetings with David Tokofsky, who represented part of the Eastside. At first thirty or forty students met with him. Then a group of four hundred ICS members confronted him at his school board office. The students felt that "he needed to hear them out, hear the inequity that they were experiencing, and the solution they were proposing" (Brenes 2007). Their persuasive force turned on both the deep roots of ICS in Tokofsky's district and on the novelty of this exchange. Elected officials, as ABC's Veronica Melvin (2007) points out, were "not accustomed to having youth say what type of education they wanted."

On June 14, 2005, the A-G resolution was adopted by a 6–1 vote (Kaplan 2005b). The resolution charged the school district with implementing "a rigorous and relevant course sequence that satisfies the A-G requirements as part of the graduation requirement" beginning with the students entering ninth grade in 2008 (Board of Education of the City of Los Angeles 2005, 50). It further called for the district to take steps over the next three years to ensure that conditions would be in place to support student success, including improvement of middle school education, a realignment of curriculum, and professional development for teachers. Finally, it directed the superintendent to create an A-G implementation committee that would collaborate with "Communities for Educational Equity and other stakeholders to incorporate community involvement in the development and implementation of the District's strategy" (Board of Education of the City of Los Angeles 2005, 52).

Although it is impossible to tease out the effect of CEE's different strategies, Veronica Melvin (2007) certainly is right that "it was huge that youth were involved." The youth provided the numbers that gave force to the campaign's claims. And, as Maria Brenes (2007) suggests, they kept "the movement accountable and relevant." It is also certainly correct that the campaign's victory required a broad-based movement. The CEE's extensive social networks provided the information and access necessary to move public opinion, vested interests, and elected officials.

Public Engagement After the Victory

How has the campaign for college access affected education and civic life in Los Angeles? Since June 2005, the district has moved forward to implement the reform but often in ways that seem more responsive to the letter than the spirit of the resolution. District administrators have encouraged middle schools and high schools to redesign their curricula so that all courses move students on a pathway to college eligibility. As a result, there was a slight increase in the proportion of A-G courses offered across the district in the first year of the reform. The district also took modest steps to improve conditions necessary for successful college preparatory programs. It placed mobile science carts in schools that did not have the laboratories necessary for college preparatory biology, physics, and chemistry. And the district encouraged high school principals to place appropriately trained teachers in college preparatory courses, though its impact in this area has been only marginal.

In its role on the A-G implementation task force, the CEE has monitored the district's progress and prodded it to be more bold, transparent, and responsive to the community. By January 2007, the CEE was sufficiently concerned with the pace of the reform that it wrote an open letter to the new superintendent (and retired Navy admiral) David Brewer. The CEE told the superintendent that its aim was not simply to implement a new graduation requirement, but rather to enact a new "vision for public education in Los Angeles that is defined by high expectations" and high quality. The letter expressed concern that the reform was "fragmented" and lacked the "depth and breadth to create the capacity needed" to make college access for all a reality. The CEE concluded, "Your ship is already in the water, and we want to see it arrive at its rightful destination. We do not want this ship to sink" (Communities for Educational Equity 2007).

Despite their concerns with the district's progress, the CEE leadership had ample reason to be hopeful about the broader impact of the campaign. Many members of the coalition noted that the campaign had changed the public conversation about education in Los Angeles. "The opposition is on the defensive," reasoned Community Coalition's Alberto Retana (2007). "We are talking about education in a new way," argued Sandy Mendoza of the United Way. Although "people previously focused on what students or parents weren't doing," they now looked at "how the district can improve" (Mendoza 2007). For Veronica Melvin (2007) of ABC, the campaign had "changed the conversation" to what "opportunities [are needed] . . . for quality local schools." This new conversation pointed to a broader cultural shift in expectations. ICS's Maria Brenes (2007) spoke of "a changing world view among students, parents, educators, and school board. . . . Before it went unchecked when school board members said not everyone should go to college. Now it is unpopular to say that."

The campaign also signaled the emergence of a new elected and civic leadership with greater connections to the grassroots. Monica Garcia, who had served as the liaison between the CEE and school board president Jose Huizar, won election to the school board with momentum from the campaign's success. One ICS organizer joined her staff in 2006 and another directed the successful school board campaign of Yolie Flores Aguilar in 2007. At the same time, Sandy Mendoza leveraged the excitement from the A-G campaign to forge a new agenda for the United Way. The United Way has established a five-year plan that directs grant money to organizing efforts aimed at school reform. Mendoza also uses the United Way's standing in the business community to bring "the grassroots message [about educational reform] to the board rooms." As Mendoza says, "We are not your grandfather's United Way anymore" (Mendoza 2007).

In addition to bringing greater funding and legitimacy to organizing, the success of the A-G campaign has shifted the power relations between education officials and grassroots groups. Because district leaders know that "parents and students are now watching . . . [they] "can't dismiss us" (Melvin 2007). Maria Brenes (2007) notes that when ICS members meet with principals or district administrators, the officials understand that the youth can attract media "attention . . . and influence policy." The organized youth have become "a force to be reckoned with" (Brenes 2007).

Looking to the future, ICS and the members of CEE hope to develop new strategies for using their newfound power to produce the tangible changes in schools that they care about. They recognize the importance of serving as watchdogs over the district, as in the A-G Implementation Task Force. But they also realize that the watchdog role is better suited to preventing abuses than to creating new and better schooling. The members of CEE have begun to create new, collaborative structures that place grassroots organizing groups in relationship with principals and teachers and grant them joint responsibility for school improvement.

Alberto Retana believes that, with a sufficiently energized organizing base, the collaboratives can unleash significant new energy to advance reform. He also sees that there are limits to reforms that work within prevailing structures. What is needed, he argues, is for grassroots groups to organize with an eye to building a broader movement for educational and social justice. Perhaps the most important legacy of the campaign, he reasons, is that it sowed the seeds for this movement building. "We did kind of wake up a generation of activists through this campaign. It is part of their life experience that you can bring a group of folks together, you can use your power to influence policy, and you can see its effects in your life. There are more people who identify with social change and possibility . . . [who have had] an experience that they can apply whenever and wherever they are" (Retana 2007).

Notes

1. The CEE coalition initially called itself the "High Schools for High Achievement Task Force."

2. Luis Sanchez served as the executive director of ICS from 1999 to 2007. Maria Brenes served as the associate director from 2002 to 2007 and presently serves as the executive director.

References

Affeldt, John, Jim Keddy, Solomon Rivera, and Derecka Mehrens. 2007. Now That We Have the Facts: Parents and Students Voice Their Demands for Public Education. San Francisco: Parents and Students for Great Schools.

Alcala, Christian. 2005. Victory for Los Angeles Unified Students. *Eastern Group Publications*, July 1.

Bendixen, Sergio. 2006. Fresh Expectations for State Schools: Immigrant, Minority Communities Aim High. *Sacramento Bee*, August 23.

Blume, Howard. 2000. Top of the Class: The Inside Story of How Roy Romer Got the Job. *LA Weekly*, June 14.

Board of Education of the City of Los Angeles. 2005. Regular Meeting Order of Business. June 14.

Booza, Jason, Jackie Cutsinger, and George Galster. 2006. Where Did They Go? The Decline of Middle-income Neighborhoods in Metropolitan America. In *Living Cities Census Series*. Washington, DC: Brookings Institution Press.

Bradley, Ann. 1993. Amid Uncertainty, Los Angeles Board Approves Reform Plan. *Education Week*, March 24.

Brenes, Maria. 2004. Personal communication with the author. July 23.

———. 2005. East Los Angeles Youth Movement for Educational Justice. *Z Magazine*, September 1.

———. 2007. Interview with the author. September 13.

California Department of Education. 2007. California Basic Educational Data Systems, ed. Standards and Assessment Division.

California Department of Education, Standards and Assessment Division. 2007. California Basic Educational Data Systems.

California State Senate. 2002. *Senate Bill 1731*. February 21.

Carroll, Steven, Cathy Krop, Jeremy Arkes, Peter Morrison, and Ann Flanagan. 2005. *California's K–12 Public Schools: How Are They doing?* Santa Monica, CA: Rand Corporation.

Caughey, John. 1967. *Segregation Blights Our Schools*. Los Angeles: Quail Books.

Caughey, John, and LaRee Caughey. 1973. *To Kill a Child's Spirit: The Tragedy of School Segregation in Los Angeles*. Itasca, IL: Peacock.

Communities for Educational Equity. 2007. Dear Superintendent Brewer. Los Angeles, January 26.

DiMassa, Cara Mia. 2004. Accord Reached on High School for East L.A. *Los Angeles Times*, May 22.

Ettinger, David. 2003. The Quest to Desegregate Los Angeles Schools. *Los Angeles Lawyer* 26 (1): 55–67.

Garcia, Lester. 2004. Personal communication with the author, July 14.

Gonzalez, Gilbert. 1999. Segregation and the Education of Mexican Children, 1900–1940. In *The Elusive Quest for Equality: 150 Years of Chicano/Chicana Education*, ed. J. Moreno, 53–76. Cambridge, MA: Harvard Educational Review.

Haney-Lopez, Ian. 2003. *Racism on Trial: The Chicano Fight for Justice.* Cambridge, MA: Belknap Press.

Hayasaki, Erica. 2005a. College Prep Idea Approved in L.A. *Los Angeles Times*, June 15.

———. 2005b. L.A. Unified to Consider Mandatory College Track. Plan Would Require All Students to Take Courses Needed for Admission to State Universities. *Los Angeles Times*, April 26.

Haydamack, Brent, Dan Flaming, and Patrick Burns. 2005. Labor Market Strengths and Weaknesses. Los Angeles: Economic Roundtable.

Hendrie, Caroline. 1997. Second Thoughts About LEARN Surface in L.A. *Education Week*, May 28.

Heussenstamm, F. K. 1972. Student Strikes in the East Los Angeles High Schools. *School and Society* 101 (March): 182–185.

Kaplan, Aubry. 2005a. Reviving Education: Grassroots Advocates for Public Schools Are Raising Their Voices—and Getting Heard. *LA Weekly*, May 12.

———. 2005b. The New Math of High School Graduation. School Board Passes A-G Requirement. *LA Weekly*, June 23.

Kerchner, Charles. 2007. A Ray of Hope: Politics May Still Save L.A. Schools. *Education Next* 7 (3): 55–57.

Kerchner, Charles, and David Menefee-Libey. 2003. Accountability at the Improv: Brief Sketches of School Reform in Los Angeles. In *A Race Against Time: The Crisis in Urban Schooling*, ed. James Cibulka and William Boyd. Westport, CT: Praeger.

Los Angeles City School District. 1966. *Racial and Ethnic Survey, Fall, 1966.*

Martyn, Kenneth, and Charles Clark. 1967. An Analysis of Comparative Data from Schools in Predominantly Negro, Mexican-American, and Privileged Sections of Los Angeles. Sacramento: California Department of Education, Office of Compensatory Education.

Melvin, Veronica. 2007. Interview with the author, September 5.

Mendoza, Sandy. 2007. Interview with the author, September 6.

Merl, Jean. 2005. Community Activists Promote Education on Eastside. *Los Angeles Times*, February 8.

Meza, Nancy. 2005. Schools Should Challenge Not Appease. *KPCC Newsroom Special: Fixing Our Public Schools*, October 21.

Munoz, Carlos. 1974. The Politics of Protest and Chicano Liberation: A Case Study of Repression and Cooptation. *Aztlan* 5 (1–2): 119–141.

Murray, Bobbie. 2005. Closing the Achievement Gap: L.A. Schools Offer So Few College-track Courses That Many Students Can't Get Them. *Los Angeles City Beat*, April 7.

Nava, Julian. 2002. *Julian Nava: My Mexican American Journey*. Houston, TX: Arte Publico Press.

Oakes, Jeannie. 2002. *Educational Inadequacy, Inequality and Failed State Policy: A Synthesis of Expert Reports Prepared for* Williams v. State of California. www.decentschools.org/experts.php?sub=perr.

———. 2004. *Williams v. State of California* (Special Issue). *Teachers College Record* 106 (10 and 11).

Oakes, Jeannie, and John Rogers. 2006. *Learning Power: Organizing for Education and Justice*. New York: Teachers College Press.

Pitt, Leonard, and Dale Pitt. 1997. *Los Angeles A to Z: An Encyclopedia of the City and County*. Los Angeles: University of California Press.

Radcliffe, Jennifer. 2005. Language, Math Courses Under Study: LAUSD Considering Plan to Set College Minimums. *Los Angeles Daily News*, April 26.

Raftery, Judith. 1992. *Land of Fair Promise*. Stanford, CA: Stanford University Press.

Retana, Alberto. 2007. Interview with the author, September 14.

Sanchez, George. 1993. *Becoming Mexican American: Ethnicity, Culture, and Identity in Chicano Los Angeles, 1900–1945*. New York: Oxford University Press.

Sanchez, Jared. 2006. *A-G: A Tool for Racial Equity*. Oakland, CA: Applied Research Center.

Sanchez, Luis. 2004. Personal communication with the author, July 23.

———. 2005. Our Children Can Learn. *Eastern Group Publications*, April 21.

School Boycotts Not the Answer. 1968. *Los Angeles Times*, March 15.

A School System Is a Terrible Thing to Waste. 1999. *LA Weekly*, October 27.

Sides, Josh. 2003. *L.A. City Limits: African American Los Angeles from the Great Depression to the Present*. Berkeley: University of California Press.

Smith, Mary Lee. 1982. How "Crawford" Began. *Integrated Education* 20 (1–2): 7–10.

Turpin, Dick. 1965. Jones Victory Keeps Liberal Bloc in Control. *Los Angeles Times*, May 27.

Vasquez, Raul. 2004. The Tardy Room Blues: United Students at Garfield High Pushes to Create a More Productive Policy for Late Students. *Eastern Group Publications*, March 11–17.

Webb, Ernest. 1965. Negroes and Mexican Americans in South and East Los Angeles Changes Between 1960 and 1965. San Francisco: State of California, Department of Industrial Relations, Division of Fair Employment Practices.

What Kids Can Do.org. 2003. Toward a Fair Chance at College: In East Los Angeles's Giant High Schools, Students Push for Equity (June): 3–8. Available at www.what

kidscando.org/archives/images/general/youthorganizingcollection.pdf (accessed March 4, 2010).

Wild, Mark. 2002. "So Many Children at Once and So Many Kinds": Schools and Ethno-racial Boundaries in Early Twentieth-Century Los Angeles. *Western Historical Quarterly* 33 (4): 453–478.

10 "Together We Can" in Mobile

A Coalition Across Lines of Race and Class

Brenda J. Turnbull

IN A PROCESS that began with a successful local tax referendum in 2001, residents of Mobile County, Alabama, set a course for improving their public schools. Over a period of years, a large and diverse coalition of Mobilians has maintained pressure on public officials to follow that course. This powerful public consensus would have seemed unlikely a few years earlier in Mobile, which had a history of race, class, and geographic divisions and of low academic expectations for the community's schools and most of its children.

Educators and parents, haves and have-nots, African Americans and whites subscribed to a 2002 "community agreement" that listed the changes they expected to see in school policy and practice. Substantial numbers of committed residents have remained vigilant about progress, repeatedly making their views known to the school board and superintendent. The community agreement has garnered additional resources for the most troubled schools and pressed Mobile's education professionals to grapple with aligning curriculum, assessment, and professional development in an effort to boost student achievement. Support from Mobile's elected leadership is tenuous, but the community coalition owns its school-improvement agenda and continues its work.

The shared vision and sustained activism was achieved after years of strategic groundwork, energetic leadership, and financial support from the Mobile Area Education Foundation (MAEF) and its executive director, Carolyn Akers.[1] MAEF spearheaded a broad-based movement that crossed boundaries of race and social background: affluent and powerful community leaders, residents of poor neighborhoods, philanthropic foundations, policy experts, and more.

In the 1990s, MAEF, whose governing board is made up of Mobile's corporate and political leadership, established its credibility as a charitable benefactor of the public schools but was less assertive in the community or policy deliberations. It supported schools with a mathematics and science initiative, provided recognition and small grants for teachers, and coordinated volunteers.

Below, I describe the process by which MAEF shifted from emphasizing program support to building and sustaining public engagement—engagement that crossed racial and economic lines and has outlasted turnover in the school board and the school superintendency. MAEF itself has used funds from the national Annenberg Foundation and other grants and has enlisted expertise from national networks of advocates for civic engagement and school reform, notably the Public Education Network. Thus, although MAEF has maintained and nurtured a solid connection with the local grass roots, it has also drawn many of its ideas from foundation-supported policy entrepreneurs who work on a national scale.

The Mobile Community and the Challenges of Education Reform

The broad-based community support for school improvement in Mobile has emerged against the backdrop of racial polarization and unequal and inadequate public schooling. Mobile's history of school desegregation dragged out over decades, and divisive rhetoric often typified local education politics.

The Mobile County Public Schools serve a county with a total population of about four hundred thousand. Located in the southwest corner of Alabama, the county has an area of 1,644 square miles, one-and-a-half times the size of Rhode Island. It contains ten incorporated cities, of which the city of Mobile is the largest. According to the 2000 U.S. Census, the county population is 62.5 percent white and 33.4 percent African American, with other races and ethnicities (Latino, American Indian, multiracial, and Vietnamese) each accounting for only about 1 percent. The city of Mobile is roughly half African American and half white, while the suburban and rural areas are majority white.

The Mobile County Public Schools enroll about sixty-five thousand students in a hundred schools. The school system enrollment in 2005–2006 was 50 percent African American, 46 percent white, 2 percent Asian/Pacific Islander, and about 1 percent American Indian and Latino, respectively (National Center for Education Statistics, Common Core of Data). About 16 percent of school-age children attended nonpublic schools, many of them religiously affiliated, in 2005–2006 (National Center for Education Statistics, Private School Universe Survey).[2] The K–12 enrollment in nonpublic schools in Mobile County was 82 percent white.

The drive to attain educational excellence for all in Mobile represents a new perspective on the civic need for a well-educated populace. In interviews conducted in January 2003, several business leaders who were friendly to reform described some of the challenges to mustering community support in an area where more than half of the residents had only a high school diploma, and many of the more-advantaged residents had no connection to the public schools:[3]

> There is a tremendous undervaluing of higher education and K–12 education because of the industrial nature of Mobile. The world is changing, but people continue to hold the same view of education.
>
> We lost so much of the community because people are taking their kids out of public schools.
>
> There was a big battle between public and private school. [But even though] your kids go to private, public education does affect you.

The local economy has historically been more dependent on the natural resources of a deep harbor and abundant timber than on an educated workforce. During World War II, shipbuilding brought a population surge. Since then, Mobile has lost much of its industrial base: shipbuilding declined; Brookley Air Force base closed in the mid-1960s; and pulp and paper plants closed during the 1990s. Currently, one of the arguments for supporting the school system is that the Mobile's economic well-being depends on jobs that require a higher skill level than the jobs that were lost in the twentieth century.

The 2000 census figures show that in Mobile County 76.7 percent of the adult population had finished high school and 18.6 percent held a bachelor's degree or higher. These figures were similar to the statewide percentages (75.3 percent and 19.0 percent, respectively) and those of other Alabama cities such as Birmingham (75.5 percent and 18.5 percent), yet they lagged behind the national averages of 80.4 percent and 24.4 percent.

Race and Education Politics in Mobile

Mobile also has a history of racial division around education. The Alabama Constitution, dating to 1901, mandated school segregation. During the 1950s, new mechanisms were created to perpetuate school segregation in the state in the aftermath of *Brown v. Board of Education*. In 1956, voters approved a constitutional amendment that authorized the legislature to close public schools faced with desegregation. The following year the legislature gave local school boards new authority to block transfer requests from African American families (Pride 2002). Mobile's public schools remained segregated into the 1960s.

In March 1963 the NAACP brought a legal challenge to school segregation with *Birdie Mae Davis et al. v. Board of School Commissioners of Mobile County*. At that time, according to testimony in U.S. District Court, an achievement gap of one year and three months existed between African American and white students in fourth grade. The gap was three years at eleventh grade (Pride 2002, 50).

Although most of Mobile's elites resisted early desegregation efforts, there were exceptions. In 1963, Alabamans Behind Local Education (ABLE), an integrated group with white leadership, organized to support quality, common schools. The call for racial cooperation continued in the early 1970s when the League of Women Voters and the Chamber of Commerce, among other prominent civic organizations, actively supported the Mobile Committee for the Support of Public Education. That group commissioned a public-relations campaign calling for racial harmony (Pride 2002, 116–117). The NAACP president, John LeFlore, counseled peace in the schools and worked in active partnership with the school superintendent.

Some civic leaders' calls for quality teaching and learning in desegregated schools did not prompt commensurate political action. Municipal tax increases for education stopped after *Birdie Mae Davis* was initiated. The school board (called the board of school commissioners), elected county-wide and all white, delayed and minimized desegregation with the rationale that rapid change would be divisive. Interviewed in 1986, Charles McNeil, who had been president of the board, said that the commissioners "thought desegregation was a good thing, it was the law, but they had decided that it had to come slowly if it was to work" (Pride 2002, 41). The judge who oversaw the case, Daniel Thomas, expressed a similar view in a 1996 interview: "I, myself, thought that integration was OK. But I do think that the government and the NAACP pushed it too far. I did my best to slow it down. I did not try to stop it" (Blackledge 1996).

Racially isolated neighborhood schools remained the norm in Mobile in the early 1970s. Largely voluntary desegregation schemes failed to integrate neighborhood schools—and school leaders often permitted white parents to send their children to the predominantly white schools rather than the integrated schools to which they were assigned.

By the mid-1970s, the school commissioners' gradualism lost support from both white and African American voters. In the at-large election of 1974, they were succeeded by school commissioners who fanned the flames of controversy over the schools. Richard Pride describes the 1974 election of Dan Alexander and Ruth Drago in this way:

> [I]t represented the rise to power of people who were not of and selected by the established business leadership of Mobile. The new representatives emerged from and represented the interests of white lower-middle and working-class people, and this represented a substantial departure from the past. (2002, 126–127)

Alexander, who shaped much of the public conversation about education in Mobile until he left office in 1983, used the language of accountability in a way that divided local residents and further weakened any base of support for the schools. With national ambitions, Alexander began to crusade for competency testing of students and teachers. *Time* magazine covered the school board meeting at which he read a note that a teacher had written to a parent—a note filled with errors in spelling and grammar—and demanded that the system identify and remove teachers whose skills were inadequate. Alexander did not couch his criticism in explicit racial terms, but its effect was divisive. African American community members perceived that the teachers likely to lose their jobs under a testing regime would be disproportionately African American. For all Mobilians, the emphasis on student and teacher deficiencies undermined confidence in the school system.

Two NAACP lawsuits filed in 1975 addressed Mobile's system of electing civic leaders, charging that the at-large system of electing county commissioners and school commissioners was at odds with the constitutional right to fair representation. After one court ruling, district-level elections began for the school commission in 1978, and two African American commissioners took their seats.[4] A five-district system was established in the 1980s and has remained in effect through 2007. Two of the districts remain predominantly African American, while the other three are majority white.

The end of the 1980s saw a consent decree in *Birdie Mae Davis* that resulted in the creation of locally funded magnet programs within predominantly

African American schools as well as freestanding magnet schools in African American neighborhoods. The magnet programs and schools attracted white students, but white parents complained about long waiting lists for admission, while some African American parents claimed that their children were ill-served in the new programs (Pride 2002, 224). The consent decree also committed the school system to a major program of facilities improvement. After decades of legal battles and several attempted remedies, in 1997 the courts declared that Mobile had a unitary system (Pride 2002). Over those decades, while the Mobile County population grew modestly, the adjoining, suburban Baldwin County nearly tripled, and enrollment in the Mobile County Public Schools diminished from 77,480 in 1967 to 65,000 at the turn of the millennium (Frankenberg 2002).

Although the courts had declared that Mobile County had a unitary system, racial isolation was the norm in the schools. In 1999–2000, on average a white student attended a school that was three-quarters white, and on average an African American student attended a school that was three-quarters African American (Frankenberg 2002). In addition, 53 percent of African American students attended schools that were at least 90 percent African American, up from 34 percent attending such schools in 1986–1987 (Frankenberg 2002).

Deepening Financial Challenges and a Disengaged Public

By the 1990s, the Mobile schools were in a financial crisis. After municipal tax increases had halted with the advent of the desegregation battles in the 1960s, the school system was in debt and struggling to support basic facilities and services. But the public conversation around reform and two proposed tax referenda, in 1992 and 1999, reflected the skepticism of Mobile's political leadership and electorate about improving the local public schools through new investment.

The 1992 campaign for the tax referendum was marked by disarray among powerful actors. An outspoken superintendent, newly hired from Florida as a reformer, went on the offensive. He blamed the state for underfunding education and sought to lessen the school commissioners' control over personnel decisions. A centerpiece of the improvement he proposed was a major investment in computerizing the district's information systems—probably not the innovation most likely to capture widespread popular support. The superintendent later recalled that many of Mobile's civic leaders expressed skepticism about the need for new funding rather than simple belt-tightening in the central office (Magann 1993).

Mistrust of the school system's spending decisions became a prominent issue in the ensuing debate over a tax referendum. Although the *Mobile Press-Register* had called for more school funding in a January 1992 editorial, it shifted its focus and by a few months later was editorializing for the superintendent's removal. The business community was divided, with some agreeing that more funding was necessary and others pointing the finger of blame at the central office for wasting money and seeking lavish facilities and equipment. Further, a portion of the electorate opposed the referendum because they did not support quality education for African American students (Cherney 1994).

In Mobile, another tax referendum went before the voters in August 1999. It was defeated by a 3-to-1 margin (Holan 2001a), carrying only two of the ninety-three precincts (Catalanello 2001a). Looking back on the defeat, some pointed to the complexity of the ballot language, others to community mistrust of the school system (Holan 2001a). Other analysts from the 1990s highlighted Mobile's lack of civic institutions with the power and capacity to bring diverse constituents together to forge a common agenda.

> Community decision making in this period of Mobile's history does not seem to be a process that invites citizen involvement and builds consensus. What has been demonstrated is manipulation and control, from behind the scenes, by a powerful few. (Cherney 1994)

By 2000, the obstacles to a community coalition for education reform were daunting. Many wealthy people sent their children to private schools and showed little commitment to schools that served poor children. Many still believed that Mobile did not need a highly educated labor force. Racial prejudice continued, as did the concentration of African American children in racially isolated and low-performing schools—despite the nominal success of the *Birdie Mae Davis* suit.

Meanwhile, MAEF was developing organizationally to address a critical and neglected issue: How can a community cross boundaries between the powerful elites, education professionals, and the grassroots organizations? A Mobile Chamber of Commerce newsletter article published in 1998 illustrates both the crossing of boundaries and the different perspectives still embedded on the different sides. Reporting that Executive Director Carolyn Akers had won a national leadership award, the Chamber described MAEF as a charitable enterprise working with educators and with business and civic leaders "to promote business and economic development, charitable activities and enhancement of education programs in Mobile" (Mobile Area Chamber of Commerce 1998). However, the national organization making the award characterized Akers's work in different terms. It recognized that Akers, a white civic leader, was reaching out beyond Mobile's elite: "The judges were most impressed by her demonstrated leadership in working at the grassroots level to bring together the area stakeholders" (Mobile Area Chamber of Commerce 1998). In addition, MAEF had worked with many Mobile teachers in the professional development programs it ran. Looking back in a 2003 interview, Akers commented that the organization had built credibility through more than a decade of work in Mobile: "School employees and the community know that we deliver."

A Moment of Opportunity: The 2001 Tax Referendum

In February 2001, Alabama's governor announced that a shortfall in the state trust fund would force a 6.2 percent cut in state education funds, and another financial crisis faced the Mobile County schools. This time the superintendent, Harold Dodge, riveted the community's attention by announcing that without new funding he would have to eliminate extracurricular activities—and cancel the next fall's football season. The *New York Times* covered the story, quoting Dodge as saying, "I know it might be superintendent suicide. . . . my secretary's fielded more calls than you can imagine from people saying, 'You've lost your damn mind'" (Sack 2001). This cancellation threat appears to have been a tipping point or catalyst for mobilizing sentiment and action. Fortunately for proponents of public schools, the community had enough latent capacity to coalesce around the "Yes" campaign for a tax referendum to take advantage of this moment of opportunity. After the referendum passed, a local political scientist and pollster, Keith Nicholls, said key to the turnaround was that "[t]here was a whole lot more attention because of the sports and bands. . . . The other factors were not as important as fundamentally altering the offerings of the public school system" (Holan 2001b, 1).

Although landowners again opposed a tax increase, proponents of the measure gained a broad base of active support from diverse segments of the community. A Republican state senator who opposed the earlier referendum said, "We've got a crisis in education, so I've got to swallow a bit of a pill and say, 'I've got to do something to fix the education problem,'" and he worked with the Democratic senator to craft the ballot language (Catalanello 2001b, 1).

The "Yes" vote coalition had both deep pockets and community roots. The umbrella Committee for Mobile's Children collected $91,420 in less than one month, almost all of it from business groups and educators' unions (Holan 2001c). The Industrial Development Board of Mobile and the Mobile County Industrial Development Association each donated $25,000, and two school employee unions each contributed $15,000. The powerful Alabama Education Association was on board. The committee retained a local and a national "political and image consulting" firm. Dozens of business and civic groups and associations signed statements of support (Holan, 2001c).

Akers took a leave of absence from MAEF to help lead a community-based campaign for the tax increase. It was a noisy and visible campaign, literally, at the street level: there were parades and public rallies. School principals identified the neighborhood leaders who could be tapped as ambassadors for the initiative. Two business leaders, jointly interviewed in 2003, commented: "It was different from previous attempts by the business community of cramming things down their throats. It was a community-building activity for the schools."

Also different from prior campaigns was the manner in which race was addressed in the public conversation. Superintendent Dodge, himself white, drew criticism in February when the *New York Times* reporter paraphrased him as saying, "many white property owners are reluctant to raise taxes to support a public school system that is about half black" (Sack 2001). As the election neared, he was again quoted, this time in the *Mobile Register,* saying, "a vote 'yes' is a vote against racism," and referendum opponents were reportedly elated, with the head of Citizens for Fair Taxation saying, "Dodge did us a favor today" (Catalanello 2001a, 1).

The referendum passed 56 to 44 percent. Although it failed in 33 of the 38 county precincts, it passed in 51 of 55 precincts in the cities of Mobile and Prichard by 66 to 34 percent (Holan 2001a). Turnout was 46 percent, up from 36 percent in the 1999 referendum (Andrews 2001).

"Yes We Can"

Akers believed that there was a "new climate and strong coalition born out of the VOTE YES Campaign." She envisioned MAEF building capacity and advocating reform at three levels: community leadership from a small advisory group; school system capacity to use data; and coalition building for public engagement.

Akers received a three-year grant from the Public Education Network (PEN) to "create an informed and engaged community." PEN, supported by the Annenberg Foundation, called for a theory of action that combined public engagement and specific school reform goals, "sustained policy and practice," and fostered "the public taking responsibility for public schools." It argued that too many school systems lack accountability to their local constituencies and that the reforms undertaken by school professionals or brokered in back rooms without public engagement are likely to be faddish and ephemeral. It said: "We believe that policy changes can be stabilized when the public is involved in clarifying the problem, diagnosing the causes, developing solutions and monitoring the impact" (Public Education Network 2001, 3).

It ended with a vision of the long-term goal, which was to

create public demand for good public schools and to have this demand actually improve public schools. When we're done, we envision communities with a substantive education agenda making real changes in student achievement. We envision a strong community voice outside the schools—with its own power and constituency—that argues for improvement and helps guide changes. We envision robust community organizations that always are in the process of building new leadership and sustaining involvement. And we envision an accountability system that places shared responsibility for success with everyone in the community. (Public Education Network 2001, 11)

Local education funds (LEFs) in the PEN network are community-based organizations seeking to support and prod their school systems to do a better job of educating poor and disadvantaged children. PEN's new Theory of Action would stretch their capacity to exercise leadership in their communities and galvanize individuals and organizations.

Akers applied several lessons learned from the defeats of earlier tax and reform initiatives. She intended to "go slow to move fast"—that is, to build support that would ensure successful action. She wanted a process in which everyone would get a respectful hearing, not just the business elite but also the concerned residents who had not finished high school. "This is not rocket science," she said, "but it is political science."

Akers agreed with David Mathews (2006) of the Kettering Foundation that effective "civic engagement" distinguished between "a persuaded populace" and "a committed and interrelated citizenry." According to Akers's presentation at a PEN meeting in May 2003,

> This is fourth time I've been involved in public engagement. The first three times were public relations and marketing. [In the past] we may have had 300 people come to meetings and say what they wanted. But this was different. We had 50 kitchen-table conversations. Whatever that community leadership is, they were there. Strong, deep, grass roots leadership.

Building on the momentum of the tax referendum, MAEF used its PEN grant to cast a wide net to engage the public about the public schools. In February 2002, about fourteen hundred Mobilians participated in forty-eight Community Conversations. At more than forty of these Community Conversations, local leaders hosted friends and neighbors in their homes, churches, or community centers across Mobile. Five of the Community Conversations, one in each school board district, were widely advertised public forums.

The hosts for the Community Conversations reflected MAEF's effort to build on existing networks of grassroots leadership, many of them created by MAEF in its previous decade of work. These included students, teachers, and principals who had participated in MAEF programs over the years. In addition, MAEF's network of volunteers, largely from the upper middle class, took part. The network of parents whom principals had tapped to support the "Yes" campaign worked alongside MAEF's infrastructure of supporters.

The conversations were carefully structured in an effort to build commitment and ownership rather than frustration. To this end, Akers drew on a national resource for civic engagement, hiring an outside facilitator and using procedures developed by the Harwood Institute for Public Innovation. MAEF staff recorded what was said in all the conversations.

The first step was to ask people about values in a concrete way, asking what *community* means to them. Some responded that in a community they stand in their front yard and talk with a neighbor. To MAEF, this image contrasted with public discussion in Mobile, which had become fractured and disconnected. An individual, face-to-face connection with a neighbor was an important positive value. Having spoken about a sense of personal connection in their community, the participants were then asked what they had in common with the entire county. They spoke of everything from the water system to the values they held in common.

Akers later commented in an interview: "It wasn't naming problems, though that was a piece of it at the end. It was about establishing connectivity." In interviews, participants and observers said that this process was a great success. Common ground emerged. "From the bayou to the pine trees to the rolling hills, [people] found a consensus on what they want in schools," said a public official. Similarly, another described it as a needed process of "getting people from various communities to understand that their aspirations for their children are the same." A community member put it in personal terms. He described how, beginning with a Community Conversation he attended at his church, he came to trust the process and participate more actively as time went on:

> I stayed involved. I judge organizations on whether they can have an impact, no hidden agendas. Truthful organizations should give out their total agenda. There is no panacea or quick solution, but I agree with most of what [this group is] doing. I hang around to facilitate changes in areas where I don't agree.

Out of these conversations, MAEF selected smaller groups to move the work forward. A group of twenty parents and educators formed a Citizens Advisory Team to study school reform across the country and identify the key issues for reform in Mobile. In addition, a group of fifty "demographically representative" residents was identified from the Community Conversations to participate in further discussions over the summer of 2002 (Mobile Area Education Foundation 2002).

They produced the Yes We Can Community Agreement. The exact wording of this agreement was critically important, as a MAEF board member explained in a December 16, 2003 interview: an editor wanted to smooth the language; instead, the written agreement preserved the exact words of people who had participated in the original Community Conversations. "That's why our agreement has held," Akers said. "People hear their voice in it when they read it. They remember when we talked about it."

What They Agreed On

The agreement is candid in stating its assessment of problems and ambitious in its goals: "A strong economy with high employment," "A stronger commitment to education," "More effective working relationships between community leaders, institutions, and organizations," and "A safe, caring, trusting community." Regarding schools, the statement calls for "High-quality, caring, capable teachers," "A diverse curriculum with high standards in every school," "More equitable distribution of school system resources," and "A learning climate in which everyone—educators, parents, school staff, and community volunteers—does his/her part to support high student achievement"(Mobile Area Education Foundation 2002, 1–2).

Among the problems named are "Needs of all students and the entire community not being addressed," "Inadequate preparation in 'the basics,'" and "Mistrust of information provided by school system and the board." Some conditions that underlie these problems include "Low expectations of our students and schools," "Inequitable distribution of resources," "No sense of ownership in our schools by community," and "Perception of competing self-interests" (Mobile Area Education Foundation 2002, 3).

The agreement continues with, "What needs to happen" and "What conditions need to exist." Here it points to community ownership of the schools, effective instructional leadership for high standards throughout the system, teacher quality, effective school board leaders, a restructured board with more members and shorter terms, and "more positive news" about the schools and school system in the news media (Mobile Area Education Foundation 2002, 3) Finally, it sums up the "target areas" in which to identify and pursue strategies for educational improvement: communications, equity, parental and community involvement, student achievement, school board governance, and teacher quality (Mobile Area Education Foundation 2002, 5).

In 2002, community members brought the Yes We Can agreement to the school board. Members of the Citizen Advisory Team met with board members before a board meeting at which the Yes We Can Community Agreement would be considered. Nearly three hundred community members attended the meeting wearing "Yes We Can" stickers. After endorsing the agreement, a board member later said, "The way Yes We Can was put together, it transcended race, gender, professions. For the school board to resist would have been terrible [for the board]."

Similarly, a community member explained the power of a coalition in addressing the board: "Competing pressures paralyze the system. Yes We Can allows different factions to share the opinion and have one focal point to push issues, instead of a series of fragmented groups making pleas." And a school principal commented,

They responded very positively to the plan. I think there is a common view that people want to see Mobile survive. If we cannot build an equitable education the city will spiral downward economically and the bottom will fall out.

"A Vision Without Action Is a Hallucination": The Strategic Plan

Despite the widespread enthusiasm about the shared vision embodied in the Yes We Can agreement, Akers was nervous. "A vision without action is a hallucination," she is fond of saying. Community members had put their time into demanding change, and they expected to see the school system respond. But the school system had previously started to develop strategic plans, only to abandon them.

Akers was determined that school reform would not be put in the hands of the system; she wanted a community-led process that would be "superintendent-proof and board-proof"(2003). In the fall of 2002, seven citizen-led task forces began working on the highest priorities in the Community Agreement, with the goal of creating a strategic plan to present to the district.

Outside pressures on the school system were mounting. The state of Alabama had been notified in 2001 that it was out of compliance with the federal No Child Left Behind (NCLB) requirement for breaking out the data on student performance by subgroups. Mobile, like the other districts in the state, would have to develop a system for tracking student achievement. In a December 2003 interview, Akers called NCLB's reporting requirements a "two-by-four" that hit the school system and would force achievement problems and inequities into public view.

A white business leader commented in an interview: "Minority and poor students don't get what they need. People are in denial about the problems." An African American civic leader said that the law and the reporting it required would be a "driving force to get everyone to agree. It tells the truth about the results of policies and practices, and some people didn't want to see that." This leader believed that data on the lagging achievement of poor and African American students would command public attention if the system were forced to disclose the data.

Getting "everyone to agree" on a shared school reform agenda was complicated by mounting tensions among the school commissioners, three of whom (two African American and one white) generally supported the superintendent and two of whom (both white) did not. With a divided board, the superintendent was unable to move forward on developing a specific plan—let alone carrying one out—and the powerful citizens who had supported Yes

We Can were impatient. Rather than wait and hope for harmony to emerge on the board, in December 2002, Mobile business leaders set in motion an intervention by the state School Accreditation Committee, which placed the school system on probationary accreditation. This temporary change in status left the board's authority in place but was an embarrassment and a warning to the commissioners. Shortly afterward, a business leader said of the move to involve the state:

> It was the right thing to do, but we took a lot of criticism for it. It was a situation where there was no other choice or avenue. Nobody wanted to do this, it was a last resort. It was an effort to allow the superintendent to do his job. Some board members will never forgive us, others are very thankful.

Having been reminded of the power behind Yes We Can, the board agreed to move forward with strategic planning. It adopted MAEF's suggestion (and accepted MAEF financial support) to engage a consultant in developing a data-driven strategic plan following the priorities laid out in the Yes We Can Community Agreement. The consultant, a former superintendent in Wisconsin named Cheryl Wilhoyte, brought expertise in a particularly complicated planning and accountability approach that had a business pedigree, the Baldrige Criteria for Performance Excellence. With credentials in education and experience in using the Baldrige process, she had credibility with two important constituencies, school system administrators and the business elite. She provided crucial expertise for translating the Yes We Can agreement into a strategic plan with measurable goals and objectives.

The *Press Register* gave favorable coverage to Wilhoyte's first public meeting in Mobile:

> Something happened in the Mobile County public school system this week that employees of more than 25 years said they have never seen. Everyone was getting along. School board members and Superintendent Harold Dodge, whose strained relationship has been a public issue for the last year, sat at tables with 47 educators and community members Wednesday, discussing educational goals and needs.

Community observers agreed that the board had been effectively pressured into participation in strategic planning. A principal said of the board's stance:

> The board was very open to the plan. . . . Reality has hit them that they need to make the community feel welcome.

Another educator said he was seeing

> the two factions on the school board coming together. They recognized that change may happen so they might as well go along. This isn't going away.

Still, some fear remained that, as a civic leader said,

> the school board may retreat and take over the process and shut out the community. If they do, it will lead to war. . . . The school board may be following along just to avoid conflict, hoping that the process will die down.

What emerged from the planning process, at the end of the 2002–3 school year, was a strategic plan closely aligned with the major areas of system improvement that the Yes We Can agreement had called for. Called the PASSport for Excellence (with PASS standing for Public Action Spells Success), it has objectives grouped under the following goals:

1. Student achievement: All children can and will become proficient learners who will graduate.
2. Quality leadership: A highly trained and proficient staff, administration and board will provide excellence in teaching and learning for every student in all classrooms in our schools.
3. Communications/parental and community involvement: We will create a new story about public schools to build and sustain parental and community involvement.
4. Governance: We will establish governance that provides evidence of accountability, trust, compliance, and responsiveness to key communities.
5. Equity: We will ensure that all schools have equal access to needed resources to enable every student to meet high standards.

Early Implementation

It was immediately clear that tight money and money allocation would be a problem.

The community agreement had accused the system of tolerating inequities between urban and suburban schools and between predominantly white and African American schools Overwhelmingly, Mobile's failing schools were heavily African American in enrollment and served high proportions of students in poverty. MAEF said in its application for PEN support that the community had become "numb" to the evidence of failure.

No Child Left Behind, by shining a spotlight on school failure, brought a sense of urgency to budgeting. Under the new strategic plan, the five schools with the lowest performance received extra resources to carry out the reform plans they developed. Called "Transformation Schools," they were slated for intensive intervention. However, the district's 2004 progress report on its plan sought to reassure other schools that they would not lose out, asserting that lessons from the Transformation Schools would be rapidly applied district-wide. Akers described a meeting of a the statewide organization Leadership Alabama, at which a business leader from outside Mobile asked Mobile principals whether they were upset about receiving less financial support than the Transformation Schools. As she described it, a principal's answer was: "I wanted to be in that club, but the district is really doing the right thing, addressing the schools where the need is."

Key to the Transformation Schools were extensive personnel shifts and incentive pay. Principals and teachers were reassigned out of the schools. The incentive-pay plan offered bonuses to teachers and administrators who were willing to work in Transformation Schools and promised additional incentives if student performance improved. MAEF helped enlist the Center for Teaching Quality (CTQ) to develop this plan and to help broker the consent of the teachers' union. The school board adopted this plan in February 2004.

Local networks and consensus building did not reach far enough to prevent active opposition from the Alabama Education Association. But when the state union encouraged every reassigned teacher to file an appeal, the board stood firm, announcing that it would arrive at 7 a.m. to begin hearing the appeals and would stay as long into the night as necessary. Community members attended the board meeting, as Akers later said: "The public was standing behind [the board]. There were Yes We Can folks at every board meeting to say, 'here's what we're so proud of, and here's what you need to do more of'" (Akers 2005).

Districtwide, the use of the Baldrige framework brought an intricate and specialized system of performance accountability, complete with its own vocabulary. A MAEF report to PEN described the unfamiliarity of the business jargon as a temporary impediment:

Terms like "plus-delta," "manage by fact," "results to add/create value," and "reach and stretch goals" had to be learned, understood and applied in order to reach a common understanding for planning and implementation. (Mobile Area Education Foundation 2003, 8)

The complex apparatus of state and local achievement testing was another overlay on Mobile's accountability grid. Alabama has different tests for different subjects and grade levels, and the disaggregation of data required under NCLB yielded dozens of scores, criteria, passes, and fails for each school. In addition, Mobile responded to the testing pressure with additional testing of its own, introducing quarterly administration of criterion-referenced tests as a means of monitoring student progress.

As the professional tools of business and education provided more and more technical means of tracking progress, Akers worried about maintaining connection with the community members who had turned out for the Community Conversations two years earlier. She recalled the woman in a low-income neighborhood who had greeted her with, "No one ever comes here" and had said good-bye with, "When are you coming back?"

One answer to this worry was to enlist another group of professionals, those in the communication field. Collaborative Communications, a Washington firm that worked with LEFs in the PEN policy initiatives, has continued to consult with MAEF. Collaborative conducted a communications audit for the school system and focus groups around the county. Stakeholders—teachers, parents, students, and community members—were surveyed. With advice and assistance from Collaborative, one parent and one teacher from each public school received training as "key communicators" to tell the community about their school's progress. Student-led parent-teacher conferences were introduced as a new means of home-school communication.

To make the welter of accountability information accessible, each school developed and prominently posted a "dashboard" display summarizing its achievement goals, its current status, and its benchmarks for progress. And each administrator, each board member, and each MAEF leader developed a "one-page plan" identifying the goals for which he or she should be held accountable; these plans were available for all to see on the district's website. In this way, both the achievement data and the Baldrige accountability framework were given some transparency for the community.

Thus, within three decades of the reign of Dan Alexander on the board of school commissioners, Mobile was again hearing the language of accountability.

This time, however, proponents made every effort to ground the term in widespread community ownership of a movement—one that had changed its name to "Together We Can," symbolizing the shift from initial organizing to a new phase of ongoing work. They were careful not to use the language of accountability to threaten educators, and they were trying not to undermine public confidence in the school system. This effort has required that MAEF and other reform advocates balance praise for the system's efforts with careful criticism of its remaining weaknesses.

Sustaining the Commitment and Realizing the Vision

From 2004 to 2007, MAEF has provided leadership for Together We Can, the community coalition that maintains pressure on the school system to deliver results and to stay true to the Yes We Can vision. The challenges have been twofold: delivering significant improvement in student achievement does not follow automatically from adopting reforms that have national currency; and the elected officials governing the system have been preoccupied with their own struggles.

Year by year, Mobile schools did better on high-stakes measures of reading and mathematics achievement. The number of schools in "clear" status on the state accountability system (i.e., meeting or exceeding their adequate yearly progress targets) rose from twenty-three in spring 2003 to forty-two in 2004 and sixty-one in 2005. In a wide-ranging *Report to the Mobile County Community on the State of Public Education*, which it published in 2006, MAEF commended the system for its progress. It pointed to the continuing achievement gap, however. It observed that "Education is still the number one issue in this community, particularly as a strategy of economic development" (Mobile Area Education Foundation, 2006, 2), and its first recommendation was that the school system engage the public in continuing conversation with the goal of organizing "a 'public voice' that is focused, sustained and compelling enough to drive the long-term changes needed to ensure high standards and high achievement for every child in Mobile County" (p. 4).

With philanthropic support, and with growing ties to national policy entrepreneurs in education reform, MAEF arranged for several waves of outside scrutiny of the Mobile school reforms. The reports, in general, commended Mobile for undertaking reforms, then expressed concern about the distance still to be traveled in bringing all students to high levels of academic performance. They painted a picture of limited capacity, uneven implementation, and many initiatives overlaid on one another.

For example, along with commendations for hard work by educators and participation by community members, the CTQ reported "mixed results" from incentives used in the process of hiring teachers, "as the incentives were not enough to fill the vacant positions at all schools" (Center for Teaching Quality 2006, v). Curriculum and instruction changes were inconsistently implemented. Collection and analysis of data on student progress proved cumbersome for teachers. The Center concluded that any district-wide application of these schools' reform plans would depend on a clearer understanding of "*what* is essential and *how* schools put those changes into practice," and on "a sustained capacity-building effort" among educators (p. vi). It also pointed to the central office's limited capacity for reform leadership.

In the following year, the Annenberg Institute for School Reform reached similarly mixed conclusions from a review of the Mobile schools, using a process called the Central Office Review for Results & Equity (CORRE). The methods included 34 individual interviews with central office staff, board members, and MAEF staff; and 47 group interviews with a total of 333 principals, teachers, union leaders, support staff, students, parents, and community members. Stakeholders in Mobile participated in the interview process and in observations of classroom teaching and learning. The CORRE team also analyzed the data on student achievement.

The CORRE report pointed to problems in the areas of student performance, equity in opportunities, and leadership from the central office and board. CORRE noted that outpacing the rest of Alabama does not position Mobile's students as high achievers on a national scale. The Alabama state standards in reading and mathematics are among the lowest nationally, it pointed out. The report challenged Mobile to "recognize that 'good' is not good enough" (Annenberg Institute for School Reform 2007, 20). The CORRE report commented that the school system's data showed African American students received far fewer services for gifted and talented students than white students did. It also observed that interviewees were well aware that middle schools and high schools had not matched the elementary schools in their academic improvement.

Among the report's key themes was that the central office focused on "monitoring and compliance" rather than "service and support" (Annenberg Institute for School Reform 2007, 9), imposed a heavy paperwork burden on schools, and conducted school visits that sapped energy rather than adding value. Further, the office had failed to coordinate across its own divisions and did not communicate a clear vision to the schools or the community at large. Finally, the report observed that board members focused on their own districts and did not have shared priorities.

The CTQ and CORRE reviews were the most intensive reviews of progress, but they were not the only ones. With a grant that Mobile's new mayor, Samuel Jones, won from the U.S. Conference of Mayors, the Education Trust visited high schools and audited the rigor of their curriculum. The press release from the mayors highlighted several aspects of Mobile's readiness to move forward with this grant, including the broad base of community support:

> The Mobile proposal exhibited a clear and comprehensive mayoral commitment to education. It also recognized the importance of a central process for planning reform, a feasible plan of action, use of existing community resources, partnering with local universities and businesses, working with a nationally known group, the Education Trust, and using the entire community to ensure sustainability.

The Wachovia Foundation provided support for a team of students (the Superintendent's Advisory Council, which MAEF had set up some years earlier) to survey their peers and report on strengths and weaknesses of the Mobile schools from student perspectives. Although most responding students expressed satisfaction with the preparation they were receiving, they also had criticisms. Most said they would work harder if standards were higher; and many said that discipline was applied unfairly and that adults were not interested in student views (Newell 2006).

A common theme in the outside expert reviews was that of inconsistently implemented initiatives and continuing shortfalls in professional capacity. Perhaps overwhelmed with the dual accountability apparatus brought by Baldrige and test-based accountability, the central office was struggling to convey clear professional direction to schools and instead was passing along a burdensome set of compliance demands. Teachers and administrators alike were finding that professional development opportunities were not necessarily well tailored to provide what they needed when they needed it. Thus, they continued to feel ill-equipped to meet the considerable challenge of raising student performance even to the levels called for by Alabama's tests, let alone higher levels.

Meanwhile, school governance remained troubled and contentious. Dodge, the superintendent, was barely holding majority support. The board decided early in 2006 to terminate his contract but then changed its stance. By the end of that year, however, the board had decided that Dodge would go. The board was embarrassed and distracted that year when one of its members was convicted of driving under the influence and of using public funds to buy Mardi Gras beads. He was briefly jailed, and he lost his board seat.

For the 2007 superintendent search, Akers advocated a highly public, community-driven process. The *Press-Register* agreed, editorializing:

> The Mobile County school board's recent history of micromanagement and appallingly poor decision-making has been detailed in this space many times. The decision to get rid of an outstanding superintendent in Dr. Harold Dodge is just one example. Indeed, the *Press-Register* editorial board does not think the current board is even capable of selecting a new superintendent without help, and has advocated that the members turn that task over to an advisory committee of community leaders. (Bold Plan to Reform Mobile's School Board 2007)

The board, however, did not relinquish control. Its search firm set up a process with some public participation, but the board also conducted a series of closed meetings of pairs of board members, thus circumventing the law requiring it to do business in public.

The new superintendent who took office in January 2008 is a white retired superintendent from Georgia. Both he and the other finalist, a white female superintendent from a small Alabama district, expressed their desire to work closely with the community in Mobile.

MAEF has remained active in convening the public and in supporting education reform. Each spring, it has convened a community education summit with hundreds of attendees. With the PASSport for Success strategic plan, MAEF has been working toward amending the plan based on community views. Thus, before the 2007 summit, MAEF initiated a round of 150 community conversations that drew more than three thousand participants, and it had a survey firm poll a representative sample of the community.

Just before the 2007 summit, Akers published an op-ed in the *Press-Register* exhorting Mobile not to settle for "good" schools. She wove together themes of governance reform, economic development, and broad-based public engagement, saying that improved governance could be achieved by restructuring the school board to include broader participation with shorter terms, by electing effective leaders, by demanding more board accountability, by increasing the transparency of decision-making, and by building the civic infrastructure necessary to keep the public involved and vigilant.

She went on:

We've heard directly from our business community that a qualified applicant pool for our workforce should be one of the "deliverables" of our K–12 school system. The other should be citizens who are engaged in the life of this community. . . . We want our children to prosper in this global economy. (Akers 2007, 1)

About 40 percent of the 560 attendees at the 2007 Summit were teachers or school administrators. Parents and students made up another 20 percent. Business leaders, community-based organizations, the faith community, higher education, and the general public made up the rest. People at the summit used keypads during the day to review and rank various concerns about the schools and options for moving them forward. Most attendees strongly favored restructuring the school board. About half strongly favored reforming high schools "to align with workforce needs." The participants had reservations about high-stakes accountability: almost half said that testing "takes time away from quality instruction," and just over half strongly opposed tying teacher pay to student performance (Mobile Area Education Foundation 2007, 3–4).

Thus, after more than five years of steady public engagement around Mobile school policy, a broad public coalition continued to use MAEF's forums to express and debate views on school improvement. Criticism was openly leveled at the school board, and some steps were under way to restructure it (a process that requires state-level legislation). Mobile had a widespread sense of pride in the schools' progress that did not exist in earlier decades. A sense of commitment to effective public schools for all crossed economic and racial divides.

As the work of school improvement continued, national experts on school reform came to Mobile and praised the schools' progress and the community's engagement but called for higher standards and a more skillfully managed approach to improving teaching and learning. MAEF helped fund their work and gave them access to the system and a platform for their conclusions.

MAEF's role in public engagement demonstrates the possibilities of long-term leadership in a broad coalition for local school reform. Working with business, community-based organizations, schools, hundreds of residents, the media, and national policy entrepreneurs, MAEF has supported a more open engagement process that permits sustained debate among disparate interests. For example, the state-level Alabama Education Association opposed the incentive plan put in place in the Transformation Schools, but local teachers continued to engage with Together We Can.

The Yes We Can Community Agreement and its successor, the Together We Can movement, provided a forum for African Americans and whites to address lingering problems of racism.

The Together We Can coalition demonstrated remarkable persistence, especially in a community that had no shared sense of confidence in its schools before the 2001 referendum, where racial and economic divisions undermined any sense that the public school system could be a valuable public good and where elected leaders often failed to inspire confidence. Grounded in the basic fairness of educational opportunities, the coalition has drawn steady support from residents of Mobile. Whether it can lead the way to still greater educational successes remains to be seen, but its power has been undeniable.

Notes

1. Founded in 1992 (under its previous name of Mobile 2000), MAEF is a local education fund (LEF) that belongs to the national Public Education Network. The LEFs are independent entities, although all have worked closely with their local school systems and most offer resources to their schools. Many LEFs, including the one in Mobile, have strong ties to civic and business leaders. As community-based organizations, they often receive grants from foundations that seek educational improvement but are wary of making grants to public bureaucracies. They differ from local education foundations, however, in raising an independent voice in education policy and services, rather than simply supplementing school system funding.

2. There are no charter schools in Alabama; the state does not permit them.

3. As evaluator of the policy initiatives conducted by fourteen LEFs, I had access from 2001 through 2006 to meetings and reports in which Akers described her work. Along with my colleagues, I was also able to interview Mobile educators and community members during that time, with the promise that individuals we quoted would not be identified by name in our public reporting. Anonymous quotations in this chapter are drawn from those interviews.

4. However, during the ensuing years there were appeals and further rulings in the case; some of the elected commissioners' status remained uncertain; and it was not until 1982 that Mobile received a clear charge to dismantle its at-large system.

References

Akers, Carolyn. 2003. Presentation at a Public Education Network meeting. May.

———. 2005. Presentation at a Public Education Network meeting. May.

———. 2007. Just being good isn't good enough. *Mobile Press-Register*, April 22, Op-Ed.

Andrews, Casandra. 2001. Mobile voters turn out in record numbers. *Mobile Press-Register*, May 16, Section A.

Annenberg Institute for School Reform. April 2007. *Findings and recommendations from the Central Office Review for Results and Equity.* Providence, RI: Author.

Blackledge, Brett. 1996. Focus shifting from integration. *Mobile Register*, January 8, Section A.

A Bold Plan to Reform Mobile's School Board. 2007. *Mobile Press Register*, April 8, Editorial.

Catalanello, Rebecca. 2001a. Landowners say "no" to 12-mill tax option. *Mobile Press-Register*, May 2, Section A.

———. 2001b. New support grows for school tax hike. *Mobile Press-Register*, April 15, Section A.

Center for Teaching Quality. April 2006. *Transforming teaching and learning in Mobile: Understanding reform in MCPSS five transformation schools.* Hillsborough, NC: Author.

Cherney, Paul R. 1994. The hiring and firing of a public school superintendent, Mobile Alabama, 1991–1993, Part 3 of 3. *Mobile Alabama Harbinger*, February 22.

Frankenberg, Erica. 2002. The impact of school segregation on residential housing patterns: Mobile, AL and Charlotte, NC. Paper presented at the Resegregation of Southern Schools conference, August 30, at the University of North Carolina at Chapel Hill.

Holan, Mark. 2001a. Mobile's familiar city, county split evident in vote. *Mobile Press-Register*, May 17, Section A.

———. 2001b. Possible loss of sports helped vote pass. *Mobile Press-Register*, May 16, Section A.

———. 2001c. "Vote Yes" campaign has more money than opponents. *Mobile Press Register*, May 11, Section B.

Magann, Doug. 1993. The power brokers. *Mobile Alabama Harbinger*, June 29.

Mathews, David. 2006. *Reclaiming public education by reclaiming our democracy.* Dayton, OH: Kettering Foundation Press.

Mobile Area Chamber of Commerce. 1998. *The View* (November): 10.

Mobile Area Education Foundation. 2002. *The YES WE CAN Community Agreement: Creating a new public story for Mobile County.* Mobile, AL: Author.

———. 2003. Standards and Accountability Initiative, year two report. Submitted to the Public Education Network. Washington, DC: Author.

———. 2006. *A report to the Mobile County community on the state of public education.* Mobile, AL: Author.

———. 2007. *Preliminary report: Education summit 2007.* Mobile, AL: Author.

National Center for Education Statistics. n.d. Common Core of Data, 2005–06 enrollment data for Mobile County, Alabama. Retrieved from http://nces.ed.gov/ccd.bat/.

———. n.d. Private School Universe Survey: Data 2005–06 school year. Retrieved from http://nces.ed.gov/surveys/pss.

Newell, Jeremiah. April 2006. *The Equity Project student report.* Mobile AL: Mobile Area Education Foundation.

Pride, Richard A. 2002. *The political use of racial narratives: School desegregation in Mobile, Alabama, 1954–97.* Urbana: University of Illinois Press.

Public Education Network. 2001. Theory of action: Public engagement for sustained reform. Washington, DC: Author.

Sack, Kevin. 2001. Cash crunch imperils high school football. *New York Times*, February 27.

11 The Prospects for Public Engagement in a Market-oriented Public Education System

A Case Study of Philadelphia, 2001–2007

Elaine Simon, Eva Gold, and Maia Cucchiara

In fall 2001, Philadelphia was roiling with protest. The mayor, buoyed by student, parent, and union protest, set up office inside the school district, saying he would not leave until the state relented in its initial plan for takeover of the district—which featured handing over up to sixty low-performing schools to a private, for-profit, education management organization, Edison Schools, Inc. The showdown enabled the mayor to successfully bargain with the state to include not only state-appointed members, but city representatives as well in the new district governance structure and to limit, although not eliminate, the presence of Edison Schools, Inc. The public outcry had put the brakes on the proposed large role for Edison in the city, but the door had been opened nonetheless to a new and prominent place for market-oriented reforms in public education in Philadelphia.

IN 2001, Philadelphia became the largest urban district ever to be taken over by a state. The new governance arrangement ushered in an era of complex market-oriented reforms that included a "diverse provider model" of school management, expansion of charter schools, and extensive outsourcing of district functions. With these practices, Philadelphia leaped to the forefront of what was then a still relatively new, but growing number, of school reforms based upon market ideas. This trend toward a market orientation in Philadelphia and other large urban districts was boosted both by federal and local city policies. The passage of the No Child Left Behind (NCLB) legislation supported a variety of market-oriented remedies to school problems, including expanded school choice for students attending "failing" schools and federal Title 1 dollars flowing to private companies for "supplementary services" such as tutoring. Furthermore, municipal leaders across the country looked to revitalize urban centers by attracting corporate business investment and the highly educated workforce these businesses desire. As a result of these converging forces and despite the initial protests, the dramatic shift toward market strategies of education reform in Philadelphia barely registered.

This chapter outlines how the market-oriented ideas introduced by the state takeover, which were affirmed by the NCLB legislation and in line with city's economic development policy, shaped education policy in Philadelphia. We examine the effects of this market-oriented context on public engagement as defined in this volume. With state takeover, Philadelphians have experienced a transition to a fundamentally different landscape of relationships and power with regard to public schools. To describe this new landscape, we trace the changes in public engagement as they played out in a set of interconnected sites—city economic struggles, state politics, public school district policies and practices, and education-focused local organizations. Our study makes visible how policy becomes legitimized by the ideological/economic context, is transformed into a set of practices, and then shapes the experience of differently situated parents, students, and community members trying to maximize public education as a resource for their advancement and well-being.

Though Philadelphia may have been in the forefront of market-oriented reform, a number of other urban school districts across the country are adopting market-based and privatization reform strategies, characterized by high levels of business and corporate influence on public education (Lipman 2002; Bartlett et al 2002; Levin 2001; Richards, Shore, and Sawicky 1996). Much of the research on these reforms, including our own, as well as studies of privatization of other public sectors, indicates that market approaches often narrow the public sphere and limit public involvement (Gold et al 2005; Minow 2003; Bartlett et al. 2002; Sclar 2000; Richards, Shore, and Sawicky 1996). While proponents of market reforms point to their advantages in enhancing individual school choice and entrée for private sector involvement with public schools, in this paper we explore the constraints market reforms impose on collective public action to hold schools accountable. This is particularly critical for an institution whose mission is to serve the broader *public* good and ensure equality of opportunity. (See Jeffrey Henig's Chapter 3 of this book; Schneider, Buckley, and Kucsova 2003; Fuller 2000; see also Margonis and Parker 1999 for a discussion of choice and community control in urban schools).

We draw on a study of civic capacity conducted for a larger investigation of Philadelphia school reform under state takeover (Gold, et al 2007). We argue that the dominance of a market orientation in public policy undermines opportunities for meaningful public engagement that leads to equitable outcomes, even if it does not eliminate all opportunities for interaction. Following the logic of a market orientation, the Philadelphia School District shaped its practices for interaction with the public in ways that favored individual over collective concerns and gave preference to neighborhoods and groups compatible with the city's economic development agenda. As a result, groups using a public engagement strategy to further equity had a more difficult time accomplishing their goals than groups whose initiatives aligned with a market orientation and reflected the city's development plans. What emerges is a cautionary tale about market-oriented education reforms, their effect on public engagement, and the likelihood that they will divert attention from broad community interests, including the needs of low-income, minority, and non-English-speaking students.

Philadelphia: Making the City a Market of Choice

Although there was little obvious interface between the school district and the city, the city's priorities and strategies for revitalization influenced district practices and the way that education groups interacted with the district. Here we describe Philadelphia's strategy for economic growth. Key to the strategy was to attract and retain a highly educated workforce, and that led to targeting particular neighborhoods for revitalization.

Philadelphia today is a city of paradoxes. The October 2005 issue of *National Geographic Traveler* named it "America's Next Great City" and touted its restaurants, nightlife, and colorful neighborhoods (Nelson 2005). According to a 2007 study of the city's economic and civic prospects commissioned by The Pew Charitable Trusts, Philadelphia is "in better shape" than it was in the 1990s and leaders within the city, departing from past downbeat sentiments, expressed optimism about the city's future (Whiting and Proscio 2007). At the same time, Philadelphia also has a 25 percent poverty rate, the highest among the largest American cities (Philadelphia Workforce Investment Board, 2007). Other studies point to a continued decline—in overall population, jobs, corporate headquarters, and wealth (Philadelphia Workforce Investment Board 2007; Fox, Treuhaft, and Douglass 2005; Brookings Institution Center on Urban and Metropolitan Policy 2002), while high levels of crime, particularly gun violence, continue to plague Philadelphia's neighborhoods. So the city teeters between heady promises of revitalization on one side and the tough challenges of poverty, violence, and decline on the other.

Unable to compete with global financial centers, "second tier" cities like Philadelphia, which once built wealth through manufacturing, are struggling to find their economic niches (Hodos 2002; Markusen, Lee, and Digiovanna 1999). The latest formulae for urban re-invention and revival call for cities to re-create themselves as markets of choice for high-tech, medical, and financial knowledge-based industries (Vey 2007; Whiting and Proscio 2007; Florida 2005; Bartlett et al. 2002; Brookings Institution Center on Urban and Metropolitan Policy 2002; Grogan and Proscio 2000). To grow and retain knowledge-based industries, these market-oriented theories claim, cities must attract "knowledge workers" by catering to their preferences for a stimulating urban atmosphere and providing various amenities (Florida 2005; Pennsylvania Economy League 2003).

For Philadelphia, this has meant creating a business-friendly atmosphere, including tax advantages to stimulate downtown economic and residential development and tourism as well as favoring development in neighborhoods outside of the downtown that can appeal to young educated singles and families. Urban historian Michael Katz has written that the elevation of market thinking in guiding public priorities and in defining the role of government has resulted in a fundamental shift in the relationship between government and citizens: "Everywhere [in this current period], the language of the market dominates public policy. . . . According to market logic, benefits should originate with private, rather than public, agencies wherever possible, and competition between providers should be relied on to improve benefits . . ." (Katz 2001, 30). In this market scenario, the citizen's role is as an individual consumer, seeking to take advantage of opportunities afforded by a thriving marketplace. Cities and even neighborhoods then compete for citizens who will choose where to live based on the features locations offer.

During the period of this study, market-oriented strategies and consumer language dominated discussions of development and Philadelphia's future across a range of different actors. The city's official redevelopment program classified neighborhoods by the degree to which residents would "choose" them and targeted certain neighborhoods as ones that, with a little investment, could become "choice" neighborhoods (McGovern 2006). Local leaders hoped to attract or retain middle-class residents, and many interviewees noted that the explosive growth in Center City had created momentum for turning the city around. The city must strive "to retain knowledge workers, retain the vitality of what is the engine for the region's growth, which is Center

City, Philadelphia," explained the leader of a local business organization (see Bartlett et al. 2002 for an extended discussion of the development of the economic "growth" discourse).

The discourse of market-based revitalization was pervasive even among community advocates we interviewed, who saw the attraction and retention of middle-class families as a source of both economic and social stability to the city's many neighborhoods. In the words of one public school advocate:

> Oh, I don't think there's any doubt that Philadelphia needs to retain middle class people. If [there's] anything [that] the '70s and '80s have shown, [it] is that economic isolation is deadly for any kind of community.

The prevailing focus on urban revitalization positioned schools as an important amenity for drawing middle-class residents and the highly prized knowledge workers. Many of those we interviewed felt that the generally poor reputation of local public schools was a primary reason that middle-class families did not choose to live in the city. One education expert expressed sentiments we heard frequently when she said, "I see the development of the city and schools as being interrelated."

With the city prioritizing certain areas, particularly the downtown and a few other "neighborhoods of choice," a select number of places could cast themselves as good bets for public investment. These areas would then have the potential to attract private investment and contribute to the city's development goals. This is the context in which the school reform strategies spurred by state takeover unfolded.

School District Practices: A Market Model for Interacting with the Public

> In what is believed to be the largest experiment in privatization mounted by an American school district, a state panel charged with improving the Philadelphia public school system voted tonight to transfer control of 42 [sic] failing city schools to seven outside managers, including Edison Schools Inc. and two universities.
>
> —Jacques Steinberg, *New York Times*, April 17, 2002

Nationally, market approaches to urban reform and revitalization have penetrated many aspects of governance and urban redevelopment, including policing and social service delivery. Perhaps because public school districts have been tied so closely to serving a public purpose, education has been late in coming to the market transformation. As Paul Grogan and Tony Proscio, the authors of the much-cited *Comeback Cities*, argue,

> In some ways, the new battle over schools is the final frontier of inner city revitalization. All the other incipient positive trends will fall short of their potential if city schools continue to push huge numbers of working- and middle-class families out of the city. . . . If that dreadful "push factor" can be neutralized in time by some combination of charter schools and privatization—force sufficient to drive genuine reform within public schools as well—the ultimate victory might be in the cities' grasp. (2000, 7)

The state takeover and accompanying market-based reforms had been promoted by a conservative state administration. Even some of Philadelphia's Democratic African American legislators, discouraged by the district's persistent financial and academic problems, had crossed the aisle and joined their Republican counterparts to support charter legislation in 1997, as well as the 2001 state takeover and contracting out of many low-performing schools to the private sector. These shifting political alliances at the state level led the way for the takeover and a new market-oriented district leadership (Boyd and Christman 2002).

The state architects of the takeover chose new leadership for the district consistent with its market orientation. The governor selected a businessman from the suburbs to chair the new School Reform Commission (SRC), which replaced the mayoral-appointed Board of Education. The governor's other two appointees came with extensive management experience in the for-profit and nonprofit sectors. In turn, they, along with the two mayoral-appointed commissioners, hired Paul Vallas, formerly the head of the Chicago Public schools, as CEO. Vallas was willing to work within a market scheme, stating pragmatically that he was interested in "what works, whether it's private or non-private" (Dean 2002). The new set of leaders—the SRC and CEO—began their work in an environment marked by a sense of crisis and urgency, rife with multiple and often competing city and state players, and absent clear proposals by educational leaders. This allowed the new leaders—imbued with an entrepreneurial spirit—to implement paradigm-breaking, market-oriented reforms (Boyd, Christman, and Useem 2008).

The new leadership adopted a set of practices that led to a more individualistic, consumer-oriented view of parents and students. These practices opened up some opportunities for involvement, such as traditional volunteer opportunities for parents and partnerships with city organizations that could bring resources to the district. Most opportunities were consistent with the district's new business orientation, with constituents becoming "consumers," "vendors," and/or "audiences." In addition, the district interactions with the public were increasingly mediated by top-down decision making. Below we detail five practices that characterize the district's interaction with parents, civic groups, and the general public around education in this reform era.

Closed-door Decision Making

The school district leadership favored the efficiency of centralization over more inclusive, time-consuming processes of gathering and weighing public input. From the start, the SRC used closed-door decision-making practices that shut out public involvement and limited the ability of public actors to hold the district accountable. For example, in April 2002 when the SRC unveiled a model for school management that involved private-sector providers, there was virtually no public discussion about the criteria for matching providers with specific schools. Similarly, when the contracts with the providers were signed in August 2002, there was no public scrutiny of the standards to which the providers would be held accountable (Christman, Gold, and Herold 2006; Useem, Christman, and Boyd 2006). This scenario presaged a style that was to characterize the SRC during its first five years.

Time and again, the SRC commissioners and CEO Vallas discussed issues among themselves behind closed doors, coming forward only with their decisions. The new leadership also eschewed public debate or oversight, strictly regulating public speaking at SRC meetings to three minutes with the requirement that testimony be submitted several days ahead (Useem, Christman, and Boyd 2006; Gold et al. 2005). An SRC member acknowledged this tendency, noting in an interview that "civic engagement and community involvement" were generally regarded as "softer, might be nice, but not essential." With information scarce about how and why decisions were made, the public was left in the dark, and decision making within the district became the domain of a select few (Useem, Christman, and Boyd 2006; Gold et al. 2005). In addition, the district failed to follow through on its promises to create vehicles for public participation, such as establishing community partners to private providers of school management, "regional parent advisory groups," and regular opportunities to dialogue with the SRC (Cucchiara 2003).

Choice and Customer Service

The district emphasized choice and customer service in many ways. The SRC fully embraced charters, and the number of charter schools rose from forty before the state takeover (2001–2002) to sixty-one in the 2007 school year. Currently, according to school district officials, there are sixty-three charters attended by thirty-seven thousand children. Out of a total of nearly two hundred thousand Philadelphia public school students, 18.5 percent are now served by charter schools. The district also worked to expand educational options among district-run schools, including smaller, themed high schools. Choice was offered to parents as a route to involvement in the schools as consumers in the educational marketplace.

School district leadership also encouraged administrators and staff of district schools to view their primary mission as providing "customer service" to individual students and their families. For some, customer service came to be their way of thinking about what constituted working with the public. Consistent with this emphasis, one district staff member described a set of programs that would allow staff to respond more quickly to individual needs and concerns.

> We've tried to improve our problem-solving of individual family problems with things such as the call center, bully hotline, parent support hotline, and things like that. We had this 24-hour turnaround time to respond to some of these things. We're trying to do better at that.

Contracting Out

After the takeover and the initial introduction of private management of schools, Vallas and the SRC promoted additional outsourcing of core educational functions, including school management (Christman, Gold, and Herold 2006; Mezzacappa 2006; Useem and Rinko 2006). Vallas tied outsourcing to his broader "entrepreneurial" pragmatism (Boyd, Christman, and Useem 2008). The long list of district contractors included individual consultants, corporations, small and minority businesses, universities, educational nonprofits, and dozens of community groups that provided services and personnel to the district in the areas of truancy prevention, after-school programming, parent relations, hospitality and customer relations, and school and community safety (Collins 2006; Dean 2006; Useem and Rinko 2006). The number of individuals and organizations contracting with the district increased from 80 in 2002 to 183 in 2005, when the district spent one-quarter of its budget, or $500 million, on contracts (Useem and Rinko 2006).

While the district had always worked with local nonprofits and universities, its network of relationships increased. District officials, particularly those at upper levels, believed that relationships with external organizations made the district more "open" to outsiders than before. Several staff members noted that many local nonprofit groups began seeking contracts to provide services to the district. One district official spoke of community engagement *only* in connection with the contracting process, implying that the contracts community groups received were the most visible and valued vehicle through which such groups engaged with the schools.

Communicating

At the time of state takeover, the district was a discredited public institution, marked by fiscal and academic crisis and political wrangling between city and state. The SRC and Vallas, wanting to restore confidence and legitimacy, emphasized public relations. In addition to its own communications office, the district hired a public relations firm to help manage the public's perception of Philadelphia's schools, and Vallas began meeting regularly with the local media. As one district official observed of Vallas, he was "educating the people who are communicating to the communities every day about education." Tight management of messages helped maintain overwhelmingly positive media coverage and kept public approval high until a budget crisis erupted in 2007.

Public Engagement in a Market Paradigm

Paradoxically, the district created an impression of interacting with the community at the same time its practices kept a lid on the public's voice in decision making. Over five years the district largely reversed its negative image. Through contracting and partnerships, as well as new charters and public school options, the district increased the number and range of players involved in educating Philadelphia's youth, and its customer service approach created the impression that it was responsive to the needs of families and children. Many in the business and nonprofit sectors began to express cautious optimism, noting that the district appeared more open and less constrained by its old bureaucratic style. However, the negative sides of these practices were building, and they had consequences for relationships with the district's constituencies.

The closed-door decision making of the SRC limited public access to the information it needed for full participation in district reform. Without this information, the public could not monitor contracts and agreements the district made with outside contractors: Were they efficacious, efficient, and fair? (Minow 2003). The district defined public participation narrowly (promoting, for example, the marketplace notion of individual consumers "buying" a product), which discouraged broader public engagement. Finally, some Philadelphians became contractors themselves and, in effect, paid for their participation by giving up a degree of their critical roles or "outsider" perspectives (Bulkley 2007; Gold et al. 2005).

In the section that follows, we look at the on-the-ground experience of local groups working on educational issues in the city to examine the district's shaping of public participation and the results.

Case Studies of Education Involvement in Philadelphia

For this portion of the research, we examined four cases of civic involvement in education in Philadelphia: Downtown Business Improvement District (BID), a business organization; African Americans for School Choice (AASC), a nonprofit African American group promoting school choice; Education Advocates United (EAU), an alliance of local education advocacy and community groups and universities; and Students Empowered, two youth organizing groups.[1] Each of these cases represented a different strategy for interacting with the district. Two of the groups did not employ strategies of public engagement: the Downtown BID used a public/private partnership strategy to gain priority for a particular area of the city, and AASC promoted an individual choice strategy. The two other cases did employ public engagement strategies. The education groups followed an alliance-building strategy, bringing together advocacy, community, service, and school reform organizations. The youth organizing groups followed a community organizing strategy, mobilizing students and community leaders. Below, we discuss how each group's goals and strategies fit (or did not fit) in the city's and district's market-oriented environment. The groups that used public/private partnership and individual choice strategies more easily achieved their agendas, and the groups using public engagement strategies made a smaller impact.

Downtown BID: A Public/Private Partnership Strategy

Downtown BID is one of the country's premier business improvement districts, which for the past nineteen years has promoted the revitalization of Philadelphia's downtown as key to city and regional economic growth. In 2004, Downtown BID launched the Downtown Schools Initiative (DSI),[2] which was designed to provide enhanced school choice as a means of attracting and retaining professional families to the area. The organization argued that without a strategy to attract and retain professionals, it was doubtful that the city could bring in new industry. In addition to increasing school options, DSI succeeded in changing district school admissions policy by giving downtown students priority over other students in admission to high-achieving elementary schools in the area (Cucchiara 2007).[3] The initiative included a marketing campaign and improvements to some downtown schools.

Downtown BID's executive director is a respected Philadelphia figure, often credited as the driving force behind the downtown's resurgence. Independent of partisan politics, he built a network of contacts and allies that included many of the city's institutions, such as the SRC and the school district. Because of his stature and connections, when he approached the district with a proposal to form a partnership, the district responded enthusiastically. District leadership was supportive of DSI also because it forwarded the common-sense view of the role schools should play in city revitalization (e.g., attracting and retaining middle-class families). In addition, association with the Downtown BID conferred prestige and helped to restore the district's credibility within the larger civic and business community, thereby serving a public relations purpose.

Anticipating the controversy it might generate as an initiative favoring a single region of the city and the relatively advantaged population living there, district and Downtown BID leaders moved the initiative rapidly from idea to implementation with minimal public input or oversight. One education advocate called the schools initiative "a lightning rod" for controversy over equity. Sensing pushback from the African American community—even from some of the district's mid-level management—the SRC modified the original plan to temper some of the advantages for downtown parents. For example, they broadened the boundaries of "downtown" to include schools with significant numbers of low-income students, and they called the admissions policy a "pilot" that would eventually be implemented across the city.

Despite these changes, the decision to give priority to downtown families for admissions to highly regarded downtown elementary schools resulted in restricting the number of spots available for low-income and minority students from outside of the area—spots that had previously been available to them. Though the district has not released data on student placements, several district administrators confirmed that no students from outside downtown achieved admissions to the three highest-performing schools through the normal transfer process. In addition, while the initiative brought the resources that professional families can offer to public schools, it marginalized other parents and students in the schools by identifying certain families as more desirable than others (Cucchiara 2007).

Because it is an important organization in the city, representing a key constituency for the long-term growth of the city, Downtown BID was successful in creating a public/private partnership with the district to forward its education agenda. The downtown is acknowledged to be central to the region's growth, and therefore any educational investment that increases the area's vitality is consonant with the city's priorities. The partnership strategy was facilitated by the access the downtown group had to district decision makers and by the Downtown BID's ability to contribute resources and prestige to the district. And district decision makers could accommodate the goals of the Downtown BID because they operated out of public view. By favoring a particular part of the city, however, the district contributed to tensions between neighborhoods about the distribution of district resources and inequities between schools and abetted at least one group's tendency to forward its self-interest over regard for the broader public good.

African Americans for School Choice: An Individual Choice Strategy

The Philadelphia chapter of African Americans for School Choice (AASC) is one of the most active branches of this national membership organization. AASC's mission is to bring equity to black and low-income people in the city by helping to make school choice fair—that is, by providing low- and moderate-income black students with choices comparable to those of students whose families are better off. Arguably, AASC is an expression of a broader social movement—the civil rights struggle to achieve equal rights and opportunity for blacks and, more broadly, all people of color. But in contrast to the civil rights work in the 1950s and 1960s, which mobilized for collective action, AASC works to inspire parents to become effective educational consumers and advocates for their own children. In this way, it embodies the recent turn toward market solutions to social problems.

Nationally, AASC urges the adoption of a variety of mechanisms to enhance school choice, including the controversial voucher strategy. The Philadelphia chapter champions expanding charter school options and state-sponsored corporate tax credits that provide scholarships to private schools for low-income students. It also offers education programs to its members on how to best take advantage of these programs.

AASC was brought to Philadelphia through the efforts of one of the city's powerful black political leaders, a state representative whose district encompasses middle- and working-class neighborhoods. He was one of the architects of the state takeover of the Philadelphia schools and is the Democratic chairman of the Pennsylvania State House Appropriations Committee. He is the founder of a local community development corporation in his district that has made charter schools and school choice an important part of its strategy for restoring economic stability to the neighborhoods it serves. AASC's agenda— to expand education options for African American families—complements the state representative's efforts to counter the decades-old pattern of middle- and working-class families leaving the city when their children reach school age. The organization has also drawn in other political leaders from the black community who share its position on charters.

AASC helps parents across the city learn about options and how to "work the system"; it seeks to give parents more "power" to advocate for their own children and to decide whether to remain in the school system or exit. AASC runs informational workshops for parents, recruits parent volunteers as leaders to recruit other parents, and teaches parents how to effectively lobby for their initiatives. One of its goals was to promote and increase the number of charter schools in Philadelphia.

AASC viewed the SRC approval of a growing number of charter school applications as evidence of its success in creating a "charter-friendly" environment in the district. To a large degree, this success was due to AASC's position in Philadelphia's political field. As one of its board members commented, referring to the organization's political benefactors, "they were the guys who were really behind this whole charter school movement . . . [CEO] Paul Vallas knows he better listen to [AASC]." AASC's stature within the black community was also pivotal to its success. Although the black community does not speak with one voice in support of charters and choice, one AASC board member remarked, "[AASC] has influence in the political arena for initiatives that have to do with school choice. They can speak *for* the black community, [when] it comes to school choice." With blacks making up nearly two-thirds of the city's public school population, the organization represents an important school constituency. AASC's strength, however, derived less from the proportion of the city's black population that it reached than from its political connections. Nonetheless, by adopting policies that were favorable to charter schools, the district gained credibility with an influential segment of the black community.

AASC's approach fit well with the school district's emphasis on parents as consumers and on school choice. Although its leaders insist that the organization is not "anti-public school," they used their political muscle with the state to build momentum for charter schools and expand scholarship funds to private schools for low- and moderate-income families. In other words, AASC's strategy for improving schools relies on informed parents-as-consumers "exiting" low-performing schools, thus forcing those schools to improve or "go out of business." This individual exit strategy differs markedly from a public engagement strategy for improving the city's school system. Of course, *individual charter schools* may encourage public involvement because they provide new opportunities for families and community members to take an active role in their schooling. However, participation at some individual school sites may do little to affect broader policy issues that shape conditions of schools attended by the children of low-income community members.

Education Advocates United: An Alliance Strategy

The local education fund, one of the city's major education nonprofit organizations, convenes Education Advocates United (EAU) as part of its civic engagement program. Established in 2002, the group brings together education, advocacy, university, and community leaders from across the city for a monthly discussion of education issues. Initially, the local education fund hoped that business and civic leaders would also be part of this group, but their participation was modest. Representatives from city government also participated only sporadically. Nonetheless, EAU usually attracted to its meetings between twenty-five and forty participants. The organization was created to increase civic commitment and enhance public engagement in school reform by creating an alliance of organizations.

EAU's identity and purpose evolved over the years in response to the city and district environment. Many participants stressed the importance of coming to agreement as an organization on specific policy positions and engaging in some form of collective action. Others emphasized simply sharing and disseminating information. Initially, the EAU worked toward both aims. One local education fund staff member, for example, described the purpose of the alliance's meetings as "to inform stakeholders on pressing issues in public education and to build a collective voice to influence policy in the school district of Philadelphia and beyond." Reflecting the information-sharing role, another stated, "It was our expectation that they [members] would bring information and would be conduits of [EAU's] work back in their own worlds."

During its early years, when many members viewed EAU as potentially an action organization, the group did arrive at consensus around a small number of issues and mobilized participants to take action. For example, the alliance was an important supporter of the Teacher Equity Campaign, which advocated that the school district equitably distribute qualified teachers across the system. In general, the group commented on district policies through an equity lens and advocated additional state funding for the Philadelphia public schools.

Over time, however, and without any formal decision, EAU's identity as a network that gathers and disseminates information began to dominate. Its meetings became a place where school officials were guest presenters, with the alliance participants in the role of audience or consumers of information about district policies and practices. Analysis of the meeting minutes over the past several years showed a steady decline in actions or consensus decisions and a commensurate rise in presentations by district staff and others. As a result of the frequent district presentations, EAU meetings devoted less and less time to prioritizing issues or coming to agreement as a group on specific issues for action. The organization became, as one local education fund staff member put it, a place solely to "bring members up to speed" on information pertinent to the district.

School district leadership, including Paul Vallas and the members of the SRC, used EAU as a mechanism for communicating with external groups. The school district reported at EAU meetings on policies and plans that were either about to be presented to the SRC or were already in place, in keeping with its practice of communication as public relations. EAU thus came to serve more as a "sounding board" that alerted the district to issues that might generate a negative public reaction, particularly from equity-oriented constituencies, than as an alliance for public engagement.

Why did EAU evolve into an audience for the district instead of a powerful alliance contributing to district policy? The local education fund, which convened the group, and many of the alliance members were partners with and/ or vendors to the district, with contracts for a range of services from curriculum development, evaluation, and student-teacher preparation to after-school programming. Alliance members found themselves torn between two roles: (1) as insiders, assisting the district in implementing programs and reform, and (2) as outsiders involved with the broader school reform community, keeping watch on education issues for the greater public good. Member groups' positions as insiders with bilateral obligations to the district, often defined through contractual relationships, diminished EAU's ability to take public positions.

As early as 2004, some members were concerned about other members who did not want to be publicly associated with criticisms of district policy. One district administrator observed, "so many of these people live off the school district, they're fueled, funded off the district." Reflecting on the compromised position of many EAU members, this administrator went on to argue that it "would be great . . . to get a group of folks who can make decisions about what's best for kids instead of the sustainability of [the education alliance] or of their individual organizations."[4]

The EAU usefully created a "table"—a place for groups to come together—but, with few exceptions, notably around gaining greater city and state funds for the district, it did not become a site for forming an alliance across sectors. Ultimately, the education alliance could not become united and powerful enough to influence the people who were determining district policy.

Students Empowered: A Community Organizing Strategy

The two youth groups that make up Students Empowered have organized Philadelphia students for more than fourteen years, bringing attention and resources to schools in low-income, predominately African American and Latino areas of the city. Here we chronicle the efforts of Students Empowered to bring small high schools to their underserved neighborhoods and to press the school district to support their efforts as part of the district's own small schools initiative.[5] Students Empowered presents a case of public engagement through community organizing. Students Empowered's story is not one of a straight, clear road to achieving the aims of the youth organizing groups—to have new small schools built or renovated in their low-income neighborhoods and resources for planning time and professional development allocated to support them—but one in which there has been, over time, the accretion of legitimacy and a growing number of promises made by the district to meet their demands.

As part of its capital improvement plan, the district promised to build new small schools (or to reconfigure existing large high schools into smaller ones). The district devised a planning process for the high school conversions, but Students Empowered wanted more community and student input. In addition, students from one of its schools had already developed a blueprint for turning their high school into small, thematic schools and hoped the district would incorporate their proposal into its plans. At a public action in spring 2005, which targeted the district's chief academic officer, Students Empowered pressed for a district commitment to a youth- and community-driven school planning process in their neighborhoods.

To gain access and influence, Students Empowered mobilized community allies, including religious and neighborhood leaders, local political leaders, and citywide school reform groups. The youth organizing groups filled what one local politician identified as a "civic gap" or a lack of local adult advocacy for educational reform in their neighborhoods. The youth organizing groups' success in generating neighborhood support can be traced to their ability to convince neighborhood leaders that small schools was a strategy for improving the neighborhood high schools. As one community member reflected, "A high school that works is important to the health of any community, and how can you be one [a healthy community] with this total dysfunctional symbol [the high school] of uncaring?" An early success of one of the groups was the old high school being broken into small themed schools, although this success was undercut by the lack of resources for planning and teacher professional development.

Students Empowered also got support from several Philadelphia foundations, which brought them resources and legitimacy. One local foundation supported Students Empowered in engaging a national architectural design firm with experience in community planning and designing innovative small schools. In summer 2005, the design firm began a community planning process with the youth groups and the local education fund as its partners. The seven-month planning process brought together multiple community leaders, residents, students, and organizations, as well as school principals, teachers and staff, and key central office administrators. The process resulted in a comprehensive report for each site that reflected community assets and a plan for small schools. In spring 2006, the reports and their recommendations were presented to top-level district staff and the SRC, and shared with community and citywide supporters.[6] As a design firm staff member explained, the purpose of the process was to shift the locus of control away from the district and toward the community:

> The question on the table at the end of the day was, "Is the community involved in the district's planning process or is this district involved in the community's process?" From our perspective, it is the last. This is about the district participating in a much broader community planning process that includes education as opposed to the community being involved in the district's process.

Over time, the mobilization of a wide array of groups created the momentum necessary to gain top administrators' attention. As one youth organizer saw it,

> the value of [the design firm planning process] was the amount of community input that went into it. . . . It wasn't the small select group . . . it was 143 people in the neighborhood that came together for a planning process.

While Students Empowered gained recognition as authentic youth groups working for high school change and won promises for small schools, the small schools they achieved lacked resources for planning and start-up comparable to those in more affluent neighborhoods. Finally, in 2008–2009, ground was broken for a new small school in one neighborhood. In another neighborhood, high school planning to restructure into academies got started, though students did not gain district consent to make their new building a campus of small schools. By contrast, the Downtown BID and AASC achieved their goals much more easily. Students Empowered broadened the district's narrow planning process with a community-based and sustained effort in their neighborhoods. The groups got promises of funds for new facilities into the capital budget and gained a seat at the table where the future of high schools was being planned. The next phase is to ensure that the new schools get the planning time, professional development, and other resources needed to make them a success.

Students Empowered had to struggle to make even slow progress. Their base was youth and community networks with limited access to decision-making circles. In addition, their target neighborhoods were low priority in a city that favored growth-oriented policies. In advancing toward new high-quality small schools, the groups were pushing against the city's pattern of investing in re-vitalizing neighborhoods with the potential to attract new middle-class fami-lies rather than communities in which low-income residents were concen-trated. Community organizing methods were necessary to get the district to respond to their demands. Further complicating the task of the youth groups, the institutional structure of the district lacked a clear access point or lever for collective public engagement. In light of the barriers, it is a major accom-plishment that the small schools campaign of Students Empowered has main-tained its momentum over the past six years.

Discussion of the Case Studies and Public Engagement

These case studies represent only a small sample of the myriad organizations involved in education in the city. However, they illustrate the range of types of groups operating and the ways differently positioned groups were able to reach their goals in a market-oriented environment. Groups that relied on strategies of public engagement were at a disadvantage. As a set, the case stud-ies also show the difficulty of crafting a broad citywide reform agenda in-tended to benefit all children in an era when behind-closed-door deals, top-down decision making, a consumer orientation, and city revitalization policies geared to encouraging growth of the middle class dominated. In ad-dition, the case studies confirm the findings of studies of public engagement in other cities:

> The primary obstacles to systemic school reform are not a lack of clever ideas, indifference to education, or a lack of a willingness to try new things. The primary obstacles are political in nature; they are rooted in the fact that vari-ous groups have distinct interests that often lead them to work against each other in ways that dissipate energies and blunt reform efforts. (Stone et al. 2001, 140)

Our analysis of the four cases provides insight into the challenges to public engagement in a privatizing system. First, community-based groups are some-what isolated—from one another and/or from other segments of the civic, community, or business sectors. This isolation is a long-documented tendency in Philadelphia civic life. Organizations and neighborhoods traditionally focus more on their own interests and agendas than on broader, citywide issues. Further, district practices, particularly those elevating choice, customer service, and relationships based on contracting, exacerbated this tendency (Cucchiara, Gold, and Simon forthcoming; Whiting and Proscio 2007; Whiting 1999). The district's market-oriented practices, in other words, did not promote a broad civic process geared toward building a citywide vision and agenda for education reform, but structured relations around individualized interactions. The increase in district outsourcing—though it may have met specific system needs or brought resources, legitimacy, and prestige—reinforced groups working in a bilateral relationship with the district rather than collaboratively around shared interests. And the district's interaction with parents was shaped by its belief in parents as educational consumers, which oriented it to interactions at an individual level—including, but not restricted to, the advancement of a system of school choice. The district's practices, compatible with market ideas for relations between a school system and the public, weakened mechanisms for public participation in reform and the district's role in forwarding an equity agenda.

Second, our case studies show that some groups were better positioned than others to pursue their agendas with respect to the district. In particular, those groups that had political reach or material resources to offer the district, or who could bring the district status or prestige, more easily achieved their goals than groups that did not have such resources and had to struggle for access and a hearing from district leadership through public engagement strategies. Because the district context was characterized by behind-closed-doors decision making, groups that had the ability to reach leaders were much more successful in achieving their goals than groups that relied on public engagement strategies, such as community organizing or alliances. And finally, the expansion of contracting out district functions to external groups "particularized" the role of many groups around narrow functions inscribed in contractual agreements (Bulkley 2007). As the Education Advocacy United case study illustrates, this served to greatly complicate—or even discourage—collective action around mutual interests in relation to the district and school reform.

On the one hand, the state takeover (reinforced by NCLB) pushed the district in the direction of contracting out core educational functions, including the management of schools, and favored the proliferation of charter schools, while the city's development agenda encouraged prioritizing certain sections of the city over others for educational improvement and choice. The outcome was an acceleration of the district's movement toward market-oriented reforms.

Conclusion

In the context of a state takeover pressed by business-oriented elites, a national education agenda that favored market ideas, and a city struggling to appeal to the middle-class, the Philadelphia school district adopted a market orientation that shaped its policies and practices for dealing with the public (Boyd, Christman, and Useem 2008). As the four case studies illustrate, these practices—centralization and top-down decision making, contracting, customer service, communication as public relations, and choice—presented formidable obstacles to public engagement because they favored the spirit of individualism over a collective purpose and they eroded the strength of voices that typically looked after community-wide interests.

Philadelphia, like other large, postindustrial cities, is trying to regain an economic footing and reconcile the tensions between spurring economic growth and assuring social and economic equity. Developing policies that take both of these goals into account requires a broad-based effort that brings many constituencies together around the range of city concerns. Our analysis of the case study organizations paints a picture of an atomized city in which individual, group, and neighborhood self-interest predominated over a sense of interdependence and community. It suggests that where public engagement is curtailed by market logic, unequal patterns of education reform and community development are likely to emerge. Such patterns are troubling, because if city and district leaders do not pay attention to low-income and declining areas within the city, these areas—characterized as they are by high dropout rates; inadequate workforce preparation; and the resulting joblessness, violence, and social dislocation—will continue to perpetuate cycles of poverty and social isolation at the same time that they are a drag on the city's revitalization efforts.

At this writing, there is new district and city leadership in Philadelphia, offering fresh opportunities. City leadership has committed itself to making education a priority, tying education, safety, and jobs together as the critical triangle of issues that must be addressed if Philadelphia is to flourish. The new mayor has tried to identify common ground among constituency groups in the city and across the state. There has been renewed attention by civic leaders and community groups to the need for increasing educational funding and promoting more equitable allocations of resources across the district. Is there reason to hope for more vibrant public engagement and more inclusive education policy in the future? The new district administration has just completed a strategic plan that was developed through a process that provided multiple opportunities for public comment, and the mayor's chief education advisor hired a staffer whose focus is on community outreach. Nonetheless, the assumptions on which district practices are based and their differential consequences for external groups seeking to support and influence the education enterprise remain largely unexamined. The future will tell whether the thrust of the new leadership and the reactivation of the public can overcome the tendency toward individualism and fragmentation that has characterized the market-oriented environment that developed in Philadelphia in recent years.

Notes

1. All names of organizations are pseudonyms.

2. This is also a pseudonym.

3. Historically, students from across the district have applied for admissions to a number of high-performing elementary schools in the downtown. Before DSI, any spots left over after all students from within a school's catchment area had enrolled were opened to students from all over the city who participated in a lottery. Under the new policy, admissions priority is as follows: (1) catchment area students; (2) students transferring under the federal NCLB mandates; (3) students from within the new downtown region; (4) students from the rest of the district. This made it very difficult—if not impossible—for students from outside of downtown to achieve access to desirable downtown elementary schools in the region.

4. We have written elsewhere on the effects of a contracting regime on the independence of community-based organizations (Bulkley, 2007; Gold et al. 2005).

5. The School District of Philadelphia announced an interest in "smaller schools" as early as 2002, but its Small Schools Transition Project was not formally launched until early 2005. In Philadelphia, the School District considers a school of seven hundred students or fewer as small. The youth organizing groups, more in line with national thinking about what constitutes small, have pushed for no more than a hundred students per class, or schools of four hundred students or fewer (ninth through twelfth grades). Since 2003, Philadelphia has created twenty-six small schools, bringing the total number of small district schools to thirty-two. For more on the context for small schools and youth organizing in Philadelphia, see Suess and Lewis (2007).

6. See the New West Philadelphia Community Plan and the Kensington High Schools Community Plan prepared by Concordia, LLC: www.concordia.com/pages/

detail/149/Kensington-HS-Community-Planning-Report and www.concordia.com/
uploads/WPHS%20Community%20Planning%20Report.pdf.

References

Bartlett, Lesley, Marla Frederick, Thadeus Gulbrandsen, and Enrique Murillo. 2002. The Marketization of Education: Public Schools for Private Ends. *Anthropology and Education Quarterly* 33: 5–29.

Boyd, William L., and Jolley B. Christman. 2002. A Tall Order for Philadelphia's New Approach to School Governance: Heal the Political Rifts, Close the Budget Gap, AND Improve the Schools. In *Powerful Reforms with Shallow Roots: Improving America's Urban Schools*, ed. Larry Cuban and Michael Usdan, 96–124. New York: Teachers College Press.

Boyd, William L., Jolley B. Christman, and Elizabeth Useem. 2008. Radical Privatization in Philadelphia: The Role of District Leaders as Policy Entrepreneurs. In *The Transformation of Great American School Districts: How Big Cities Are Reshaping the Institution of Public Education*, ed. William L. Boyd, Charles Taylor Kerchner, and Mark Blyth, 33–59. Cambridge, MA: Harvard Education Press.

Brookings Institution Center on Urban and Metropolitan Policy. 2002. *Back to Prosperity: A Competitive Agenda for Renewing Pennsylvania*. Washington, DC: Author.

Bulkley, Katrina E. 2007. Bringing the Private into the Public: Changing the Rules of the Game and New Regime Politics in Philadelphia Public Education. *Educational Policy* 21: 155–184.

Christman, Jolley B., Eva Gold, and Benjamin B. Herold. 2006. *Privatization "Philly Style": What Can Be Learned from Philadelphia's Diverse Provider Model of School Management*. Philadelphia: Research for Action.

Collins, Tina. 2006. Informal Bidding Process: Cause for Concern? *Philadelphia Public School Notebook* 14 (1). www.thenotebook.org/fall-2006/06525/informal-bidding-process-cause-concern.

Cucchiara, Maia. 2003. The Evolution of Reform: Studying "Community Partnerships" [Electronic Version]. *Penn GSE Perspectives on Urban Education* 2.

———. 2007. Marketing Schools, Marketing Cities: Urban Revitalization, Public Education, and Social Inequality. PhD dissertation. University of Pennsylvania.

Cucchiara, Maia, Eva Gold, and Elaine Simon. Contracts, Choice, and Customer Service: The Institutional Consequences of Educational Marketization. (Forthcoming *Teachers College Record*).

Dean, Mensa. 2002. A Year Later: What's Next in Our Schools. [Electronic Version]. *Philadelphia Daily News*, December 20.

———. 2006. Commission Approves Funding for Parent Truant Officers. [Electronic Version]. *Philadelphia Daily News*, September 21.

Florida, Richard. 2005. *The Flight of the Creative Class: The New Global Competition for Talent*. New York: Harper Business.

Fox, Radhika K., Sarah Treuhaft, and Regan Douglass. 2005. Shared Prosperity, Stronger Regions: An Agenda for Rebuilding America's Older Core Cities. Oakland, CA: PolicyLink and Community Development Partnerships' Network.

Fuller, Bruce. 2000. The Public Square, Big or Small? Charter Schools in Political Context. In *Inside Charter Schools: The Paradox of Radical Decentralization*, ed. Bruce Fuller. Cambridge, MA: Harvard University Press.

Gold, Eva, Maia Cucchiara, Elaine Simon, and Morgan Riffer. 2005. *Time to Engage? Civic Participation in Philadelphia's School Reform*. Philadelphia: Research for Action.

Gold, Eva, Elaine Simon, Maia Cucchiara, Cecily Mitchell, and Morgan Riffer. 2007. *A Philadelphia Story: Building Civic Capacity in a Privatizing System*. Philadelphia: Research for Action.

Grogan, Paul S., and Tony Proscio. 2000. *Comeback Cities: A Blueprint for Urban Neighborhood Revival*. Boulder, CO: Westview Press.

Hodos, James I. 2002. Globalization, Regionalism, and Urban Restructuring: The Case of Philadelphia. *Urban Affairs Review* 37 (3): 358–379.

Katz, Michael B. 2001. *The Price of Citizenship: Redefining the American Welfare State*. New York: Metropolitan Books.

Levin, Henry. 2001. *Privatizing Education: Can the Marketplace Deliver Choice, Efficiency, Equity and Social Cohesion?* Boulder, CO: Westview Press.

Lipman, Pauline. 2002. Making the Global City, Making Inequality: The Political Economy and Cultural Politics of Chicago School Policy. *American Educational Research Journal* 39: 379–419.

Margonis, Frank, and Laurence Parker. 1999. Choice: The Route to Community Control. *Theory into Practice* 38 (4): 203–208.

Markusen, Ann, Yong-Sook Lee, and Sean Digiovanna, eds. 1999. Second-Tier Cities: Rapid Growth Beyond the Metropolis. Minneapolis: University of Minnesota Press.

McGovern, Steven J. 2006. Philadelphia's Neighborhood Transformation Initiative: A Case Study of Mayoral Leadership, Bold Planning, and Conflict. *Housing Policy Debate* 17 (3): 530–570.

Mezzacappa, Dale. 2006. CEP Mystery: Many Pass Through . . . And Then. [Electronic Version]. *Philadelphia Public School Notebook*.

Minow, Martha. 2003. Public and Private Partnerships: Accounting for the New Religion. *Harvard Law Review* 116 (1): 1229–1273.

Nelson, Andrew. 2005. Next Great City: Philly, Really. *National Geographic Traveler* 22 (7): 48–56.

Pennsylvania Economy League. 2003. No Brain—No Gain: Town/Gown Relations and the Competition for Talent. *Greater Philadelphia Regional Review*, Spring.

Philadelphia Workforce Investment Board. 2007. *A Tale of Two Cities.* Philadelphia: Philadelphia Workforce Investment Board.

Richards, Craig E., Rima Shore, and Max Sawicky. 1996. *Risky Business: Private Management of Public Schools.* Washington, DC: Economic Policy Institute.

Schneider, Mark, Jack Buckley, and Simona Kucsova. 2003. *Building Social Capital in the Nation's Capital: Can Charter Schools Build a Foundation for Cooperative Behavior? National Center for the Study of Privatization in Education.* New York: Teachers College, Columbia University.

Sclar, Elliott D. 2000. *You Don't Always Get What You Pay For: The Economics of Privatization.* Ithaca, NY: Cornell University Press.

Steinberg, Jacques. 2002. Private Groups Get 42 Schools in Philadelphia. [Electronic Version]. *The New York Times,* April 17.

Stone, Clarence N., Jeffrey R. Henig, Bryan D. Jones, and Carol Pierannunzi. 2001. *Building Civic Capacity: The Politics of Reforming Urban Schools.* Lawrence: University Press of Kansas.

Suess, Gretchen E. L., and Kristine S. Lewis. 2007. The Time Is Now: Youth Organize to Transform Philadelphia High Schools. *Children, Youth and Environments* 17 (2): 364–379.

Useem, Elizabeth, Jolley B. Christman, and William L. Boyd. 2006. *The Role of District Leadership in Radical Reform: Philadelphia's Experience Under the State Takeover, 2001–2006.* Philadelphia: Research for Action.

Useem, Elizabeth, and Kendal Rinko. 2006. Turning to Outside Organizations to Do More Jobs. *Philadelphia Public School Notebook* 14 (1). www.thenotebook. org/fall-2006/06524/turning-outside-organizations-do-more-jobs.

Vey, Jennifer S. 2007. *Restoring Prosperity: The State Role in Revitalizing America's Older Industrial Cities.* Washington, DC: The Brookings Institution Metropolitan Policy Program.

Whiting, Basil J. 1999. *Philadelphia: Prospects and Challenges at the End of the Decade.* Philadelphia: The Pew Charitable Trusts.

Whiting, Basil J., and Tony Proscio. 2007. *Philadelphia 2007: Prospects and Challenges.* Brooklyn, NY: The Pew Charitable Trusts.

12 Public Engagement for Public Education

Reflections and Prospects

Marion Orr and John Rogers

PEOPLE ORGANIZE TO EXPAND EDUCATIONAL OPPORTUNITY and equalize voice in many ways and under many circumstances. Participants in these public endeavors include youth, parents, community leaders, civil rights advocates, and civic elites. Some join in public engagement as unaffiliated individuals and others as members of community organizing groups. Some follow the lead of nonprofits, alliances, or intermediary organizations. They address a wide range of issues, such as teacher recruitment, school design, educational funding, and much more. They seek changes for small clusters of students or entire student bodies. Sometimes they aim to transform policies at the district or state level. As described throughout this volume, public engagement is often a strategy for building the power and capacity of participants to shape decisions about schooling.

This chapter looks across the varied forms of engagement presented in previous chapters to consider the broad meaning, significance, and possibilities of public engagement for public education. The first section highlights three practices that distinguish *public* engagement from bureaucratic or market responses to reform. The second section examines obstacles to public engagement. In the third section we consider conditions in our present moment that support increased public engagement. Finally, we offer a few thoughts on a research agenda for documenting and informing the next generation of public engagement for public education.

Practices of Public Engagement for Public Education

Three practices are common to many examples of public engagement described in this volume. First, community members join together in response to shared problems. Second, they investigate these problems and learn about possible responses. Third, they act in concert with others to address the problems and build more inclusive, participatory, and powerful publics. Guiding all of these practices is the intention to correct inequalities in schooling and in political participation. These practices differ from bureaucratic or market-based approaches to educational reform. The former exclusively rely on educational professionals to diagnose and address problems. The latter envision community members as educational consumers who prompt systemic change through individual exit rather than collective voice.

The educational and political landscape typically favors bureaucratic or market approaches to reform; thus, public engagement for public education must overcome several structural challenges. Community members often have few opportunities in their daily lives for dialogue that makes them aware of and clarifies common interests. Historical tensions, including a lack of understanding across lines of race, class, or linguistic community, pose additional difficulties. These obstacles are exacerbated by geographic segregation and a lack of public spaces that otherwise might afford opportunities for exchange.

Given these structural challenges, what initiates public formation? Although American education is replete with examples of elites asserting their power on behalf of the most privileged sectors of society, as Dennis Shirley argues in Chapter 2, there are examples of counterpublics asserting the concerns of those who historically have had little role in decision making. Such was the case recently in Los Angeles where residents of neighborhoods poorly served by the public school system joined with one another and then with others across the city in a campaign to expand access to college preparatory curriculum (see Chapter 9). Community members in East and South Los Angeles more eagerly participated in reform as they learned that low-quality education was neither idiosyncratic nor inevitable. They recognized discriminatory patterns in the distribution of learning opportunities, and they saw that these patterns were held in place by a governance structure that failed to represent their interests. By joining together as a public, they expressed common concerns and experienced collective agency.

The quality and robustness of public formation turns on who is participating and in what manner. When a significant proportion of those joining together are middle-class or affluent, collective action may serve to sustain privilege rather than expand access and opportunity. For example, in Atlanta's

Neighborhood Charter School, described in Chapter 4, upper-middle-class parents have been able to secure substantial resources for their children's school, thereby coproducing better services for some while exacerbating systemic patterns of unequal educational opportunities. Further, community members may come together in perfunctory ways that do not draw attention to shared problems. In Chapter 11 we see that community-based organizations in Philadelphia's Education Advocates United have become increasingly reluctant to use their public meetings to question or challenge district officials. Elaine Simon, Eva Gold, and Maia Cucchiara hypothesize that this shift is related to the district's strategy of contracting with these community-based groups for a variety of services. Hence, the authors surmise, the market has intruded on and diminished public activity.

A second practice of public engagement centers on learning, and that requires opportunities for inquiry and openness to new knowledge and understanding. These are participatory activities developed over time in the context of current problems. Participants gain new analytic frameworks and new tools for describing shared concerns that build their public capacity for future endeavors. Learning (as distinct from instruction) in public engagement thus extends beyond "bringing members up to speed" as characterized by the meetings of Education Advocates United. Learning is about recognizing, generating, and communicating new insights.

In Chicago, learning played a central role in the Association of Community Organizations for Reform Now (ACORN) leaders' investigation of teacher quality. Starting with local people who "sensed" that Chicago's West Side schools lacked quality teachers, the leaders developed information-gathering capacities that led to their building a persuasive case for policy change. By talking with policy experts, interviewing principals, and examining administrative data, ACORN leaders confirmed insights with evidence. Guided by their inquiry, the leaders gained tools to make sense of and communicate a critical local problem, both face to face and via the media. They explored the reasons why qualified teachers were distributed unequally and how this problem might be remedied. Over time, the ACORN leaders reframed the issue from inadequate teacher recruitment, to insufficient teacher retention, to the need for a pipeline into teaching for residents of the local community. These transitions reflect ACORN's willingness to follow the evidence that linked educational policy to other issues affecting the community, such as the need for well-paid employment.

What makes learning in the context of public engagement more or less powerful? In Chapter 10, Brenda Turnbull suggests that Mobile's community dialogues supported authentic learning because they were sustained by structures that ensured reflection and inclusiveness. Facilitators encouraged community members to talk about their community as well as their vision for public schools. These conversations led to other public dialogues that afforded participants opportunities to extend what they had learned. Carol Akers of the Mobile Area Education Foundation distinguished these facilitated dialogues from previous efforts that brought together Mobilians to "say what they wanted." For Akers, the practice of learning through public engagement requires more than exchange; it entails the formation of new and shared understandings.

A third practice of public engagement is powerful collective action. Community members are not drawn together by their common interest in abstractions, inquiry, or even "democracy." They experience problems, and they want to solve them. They believe they have too few opportunities, and they want more. Public engagement for public education may produce educational services, generate public commitment for new policies, or direct pressure at recalcitrant officials. In many cases, individuals and organizations coordinate actions within structured campaigns. These campaigns often prompt alliances across neighborhoods and across organizations that serve different constituencies (youth, parents, civic groups, etc.). As Lauren Wells, Jean Anyon, and Jeannie Oakes argue in Chapter 7, such alliances pool the resources of individual organizations, thereby extending their capacity.

How does powerful public action effect change? It can lead to new practices, policies, and structures. Such was the case with the Grow Your Own campaign that developed an entirely new pathway into teaching with appropriate institutional and public policy supports. Powerful public action also can shift the thinking of key decision makers and the broader public. The college access campaign in Los Angeles transformed how school board members and other civic leaders conceived of what quality education is and who deserves it. These ideas in turn have framed the policy dialogue that will shape future decisions. Further, powerful public action can expand the pool of legitimate participants in educational decision making. Hence, the energy and seriousness of Mobile's broad-based and multiracial community dialogues established the political and educational value of a participatory planning process.

Ultimately, the test of public action is whether it responds to the problems that community members come together to address. Does it improve the quality of educational services, redistribute educational opportunities, or promote better educational outcomes such as increased high school graduation and college-going rates?

Beyond current campaigns or policy issues, we should also ask whether and how actions broadly support the development of a more powerful public. In Chapter 4 of this book, Donn Worgs worries that when community members focus exclusively on the coproduction of educational services, they may be less likely to participate in broader public engagement efforts. This is a matter of concern because investments in other forms of public action may yield significant returns for education. According to youth organizer Alberto Retana, one of the most significant outcomes of the campaign for college access is that it built the civic capacity and sense of public possibility of a whole generation of Los Angeles youth.

The Challenge of Building Robust Public Engagement for Public Education

A public engagement perspective encourages actions that provide all students with equal educational opportunity. It is not easy to reconcile this value with the common belief that public schools should stick to preparing students for positions in a highly differentiated economy. In an increasingly bifurcated job market, the stakes are high (Frank 2007). Globalization and the transformation of the national and global economic structures have made superior education and training a necessity in order to thrive in today's world economy. Yet, such high-quality education is a scarce commodity in most U.S. communities. Middle- and upper-income parents, fearing that their children may not retain their affluence, fight to put and keep their children in the limited number of high-quality public schools. Parents of working-class and lower-income students also press for school policies that will enable their children to move up the socioeconomic ladder. However, as we note in the opening chapter, public officials are far more likely to hear and act on the concerns of the affluent than those of poor and working-class parents.

Powerful norms create obstacles for the proponents of public engagement for public education. Hyper-individualism and consumerism shape the way many view schooling. The market orientation encourages the view that "society is best served when each isolated individual has the opportunity to make independent and free decisions—billions and billions of such decisions" (Gecan 2005, 155). Advocates of vouchers and other market approaches to public education are likely to see engaged publics as disrupting healthy market dynamics that depend more on these individual choices than on public deliberation. Survey research shows that this argument resonates with many of the parents of school-age children. Forty-four percent of the parents of school-age children support having the government give parents money to help pay for their children to attend a private or religious school (Phi Delta Kappa International and Gallup 2009). Significantly, today's parents of school-age children constitute a major component of the so-called me generation, who survey researchers have identified as being more focused on one's own immediate interests than on shared responsibility (Twenge 2006).

A second challenge to public engagement lies in the tremendous racial and ethnic change in many metropolitan regions that Jeff Henig describes in Chapter 3. The transitional nature of metropolitan populations—fueled in large part by a huge growth in children with immigrant parents from Mexico, Central America, and the Caribbean—means that many parents have little experience and limited connections with local institutions (Sen 2003). The assumption that shared interests among African American and Latino communities would lead them to work together has not always held true (Vaca 2005). Diversity can create challenges for any attempt at collective activity. Immigration and related issues dealing with legal status and language barriers bring an added dimension to the diversity challenge as well as new vulnerabilities for political participation (Terriquez and Rogers forthcoming). The potential for interethnic tensions over public schools is heightened by the patterns of racial and ethnic neighborhood settlement within and across metropolitan regions (R. Rogers 2006; Gimpel, Lay, and Schuknecht 2003). When racial and class housing segregation is overlaid with the current arrangement of America's fragmented local political institutions in which school systems are divided between suburban vs. city or local student assignment boundaries are either on the affluent part of the city or the low-income part of the city, the challenge for robust public engagement for public education is heightened (R. Rogers 2006; Oliver 2001; Burns 1994).

There are also more localized challenges. For example, at the school site level, research has shown that principals play a large role in whether parents and the community are engaged (Epstein 2001). If educators have an exaggerated sense of professional power, efforts at public engagement for public education can be delayed and derailed. In addition, public education systems are huge bureaucracies, and navigating them successfully is a major challenge. Public schools represent a considerable amount of intergovernmental complexity with local-, state-, and increasingly, federal-level actors involved. The most devoted public education supporters (including many "insiders" who work within the education system) know that developing robust public engagement for public education requires overcoming baffling frustrations. Many urban school systems are under-resourced and have weak capacity to work with community partners (Anyon 1997).

Factors that Support Robust Public Engagement for Public Education

This volume highlights the public purpose of public education—the development of a robust civic community. Contributors to this volume have provided examples of public engagement for public education where the central actors are devoted to giving voice to low-income communities and altering the educational politics and policy decisions that advantage more powerful and wealthier communities. Mark Warren's account of community organizing in Chapter 6 is a clear example. So too is the cross-sector alliance that supported Mobile's reform by explicitly targeting more resources to under-resourced schools in low-income communities. Chicago's Grow Your Own project, led by ACORN and the Logan Square Neighborhood Association, combined community organizing efforts, alliance building, and democratic governance to address a shortage of qualified teachers in low-income communities. The experience of these communities tells us a lot about the factors that contribute to public engagement for public schools.

Dennis Shirley's account of the Reconstruction South reminds us that schools have long been a vital component of the community. People will rally behind their public schools. Survey results show that support for school vouchers among parents of school-age children drops considerably if it means cutting public school funding. The burst of community mobilization spurred when school administrators announce the closing of a local school, though ephemeral in many respects, is an indication that community residents view schools as a significant asset.

Public education is also a local issue. For many people, public engagement starts "at the local level around issues of immediate concerns in their daily lives" (Smock 2004, 242–243). More people in any given community are likely to encounter their public school than any other local institution (except perhaps the church or other religious institution). Because they are central components of most communities, schools can be utilized to draw various community sectors together.

Mark Warren's estimation of the steady growth in the number of community organizations that have added public education to their portfolios suggests that communities are increasingly concerned about improving the quality of public schools. Over the last thirty years, local government powers and functions have eroded in traditional areas of housing, employment and training, and economic and social development. Over the same time, the number of nongovernmental groups working in these areas has grown. They include local nonprofits, voluntary and civic organizations, and other civic advocacy groups. These organizations are potential allies of the proponents of public engagement for public education.

There is certainly a tradition for viewing publics (communities, grassroots groups, etc.) as having an oppositional, adversarial relationship with schools— a discontented minority of parents and students *fighting* for their rights and due services. Today, many observers and educators embrace the view that engagement between publics and schools is of critical social importance. The current support for school reform confirms the general opinion that we should put young people on a path that leads to the mainstream economy and society. The excitement generated by the election of President Barack Obama and his pronouncements about contributing to public service has generated interest across community sectors. In Chapter 4, Donn Worgs describes how community members are increasingly willing to experiment and innovate with charter schools, after-school programs, and other supplementary services to support public education. The chapters on Los Angeles and Philadelphia provide examples of the growing number of student-led organizations across the country working to improve public education. Even provisions of the No Child Left Behind (NCLB) Act, the federal education program promoted by President George W. Bush, are designed to encourage parents and their allies to be involved in their children's school. In short, the national political context is such that organizations ranging from neighborhood groups to national networks, religious congregations and secular organizations, are increasingly inclined to work together to support and improve public schools. The national context is favorable for a focus on public engagement for public education.

Citizens and public officials, supported by scholarly study, are increasingly focused on fiscal disparities, racial and class segregation, and suburban sprawl. Policy discussions often acknowledge and embrace the interconnectedness and interdependence of all publics ranging from traditional elites to newly formed alliances within and between historically underrepresented groups (Pastor, Benner, and Matsuoka 2009; Oliver 2001; Orfield 1997; Rusk 1993). A persuasive case can be made that suburbs would prosper if their leaders worked toward a better-integrated metropolitan region with a vibrant center city (Dreier, Mollenkopf, and Swanstrom 2001).

In Mobile, more than forty years of racial divisions made public engagement for public education a contested terrain. After desegregation, most whites exited the system, putting many of their children into private schools. They also consistently voted against public funds going to support the public schools. Carol Akers of Mobile Area Education Fund helped reverse this trend by connecting diverse community members with one another. She helped forge a broad-based alliance that articulated why the community's business and civic elites, educators, and grassroots leaders should "cross boundaries" and support passage of the 2001 tax referendum for school funding that would improve public education for all students, including schools in concentrated poverty neighborhoods. The public engagement in Mobile strategically articulated the view that the social and economic future of the entire city was connected to how well public schools in the city performed, including the schools attended by students from the city's poorest communities.

Public engagement both builds on and seeks to foster interconnectedness and interdependence. Community members take public action as they recognize that the fate of one's own household is tied to the fate of others. In the age of globalism, the economic interconnectedness of communities has led many more people to call for increased cooperation and collaboration across communities.

Understanding and Supporting Public Engagement for Public Education

The chapters in this volume establish the significance of public engagement for public education and its implications for democracy. Needless to say, we have just scratched the surface of this field of study. There remains much to be learned about how youth and community members come together to learn about and take action on their shared educational interests.

One fertile area for new research is to look at who participates. Across the chapters in this volume, youth, parents, community members, and civic leaders become engaged when they see a role for themselves in addressing shared problems. We need to know more about what triggers this recognition. Are certain conditions critical to this process, such as access to data, strong community leadership, or civic institutions committed to educational improvement? What is the role of organizers, teachers, peers, elders or role models in the community? Why do different people respond differently to the same conditions? How is participation connected to personal political history, cultural understandings, access to childcare and other supports, or work schedule? Do any of these factors lead participants to respond more favorably to particular streams of public engagement?

A related line of research might explore the possibilities for new groups to join public engagement efforts in education. For example, Rogers and Terriquez (2009) studied the interest of low-wage service sector unions in educational reform. Many members of these unions are parents with children attending poorly served public schools. With its ability to deploy significant financial resources, political connections, and strategic capacity, organized labor represents a potentially significant player in educational reform. Similarly, if groups involved in regional organizing for economic justice begin to focus more attention on education, they might bolster educational alliances and expand the possibilities for social movement building (Pastor, Benner, Matsuoka 2009). New research should document the involvement of economically progressive organizations in educational issues as well as the effect of this participation on public engagement in education.

Another line of new research should examine the role of various entities that support public engagement. Powerful public engagement campaigns such as those in Chicago, Los Angeles, and Mobile incorporate research, strategic communications, policy advocacy, and (at times) litigation. Research should focus attention on the organizations that provide this support to grassroots groups. We will want to know what knowledge and tools prove most useful in campaigns and how they are developed. Additionally, it is important to understand what relationships enable productive partnerships between support organizations and grassroots groups and how these relationships are developed over time. Of course, resources are necessary to sustain all of this work, from organizing grassroots groups, to data analysis, to communications campaigns, to mass mobilization. Philanthropic organizations are critical to public engagement, and researchers need to study the role of this important sector. Do certain strategies, for example, targeting support to particular neighborhoods or encouraging collaboration among different groups yield more robust public engagement? Conversely, we need to learn more about the conditions and consequences (as in Philadelphia) when grassroots groups temper their dissent in the hopes of attaining future funding.

Additional research is also needed on the outcomes of public engagement, including evidence about whether and under what conditions public engagement matters. New research on this topic can build on the invaluable work of our colleagues at the Annenberg Institute for School Reform who recently completed a six-year, multisite study of educational organizing (Mediratta, Shah, and McAlister 2009). This study found that effective community organizing led to improved student outcomes, enhanced school-community relationships, and increased policy focus on issues of equity. A next stage for research will be to develop a rubric for assessing robust public participation. Although many educators, community members, and policy members recognize that enhanced participation is an important outcome of public engagement, they need a common metric to document and report on these effects.

Finally, there is a need for research that explores the relationship between public policy and public power. The capacity of community members to join together and take meaningful action is often shaped by government policies on public space, access to information, and formal political participation. Perhaps because research on public engagement has focused attention on the agency of youth and community members, it often has downplayed the importance of public policies in enabling public action. New research should document what Archon Fung (2002) refers to as "public-creating policies" and examine their effect on the depth and breadth of public engagement for public education. It should also consider how the absence of such policies shapes opportunities for public engagement. These policies include: (a) formal accountability structures that ensure parent participation in educational governance; (b) district and state data systems that provide information on opportunities and outcomes across schools; (c) state grants to community-based organizations to support informed public participation; (d) reporting on the quality of public participation (Terriquez and Rogers forthcoming; J. Rogers 2006).

Our hope is that future research across these areas will contribute to the expansion of public engagement in public education. Certainly, such research needs to bring a critical lens to this body of work, questioning the inclusiveness of public engagement activities and the impact of public engagement on conditions and outcomes that the public cares about. Yet, research in the public interest should not be neutral on the potential value of public engagement, just as it should not ignore inequalities in educational opportunities or political participation. New research can prompt the broader community to consider democracy as central to the practice and purpose of educational reform. Further, research can broaden the attention of policy makers from technical questions about schooling to strategies that support the development of informed and powerful publics.

We may well be entering a historic moment when the public and policy makers are receptive to new ideas and new evidence about public engagement for public education. The 2008 presidential campaign unleashed grassroots energy, particularly among America's youth, and brought greater public recognition of community organizing. During the campaign, Barack Obama called for more Americans to become involved in public service, imploring citizens of all ages to rally to the country's needs. President Obama's background as a community organizer, and his unique capacity to cross lines of race, class, and culture, put him in a position to articulate a vision in which people from varied backgrounds and community sectors (religious leaders, civic and corporate elites, suburbanites, city dwellers and average residents) "break their crippling isolation from each other, to reshape their mutual values and expectations and rediscover the possibilities of acting collaboratively" (Obama 2004; see also Obama 1990, 37). Although Republicans ridiculed community organizers during the presidential campaign, community organizing has entered the public consciousness. It could be that more and more people will want to be involved in organizing and look for ways to do so. There is already evidence that more young people are interested in working as community organizers. Community organizations have recently reported spikes in the number of young people applying for community organizing jobs (Rimer 2009). Obama's impact on young people gives us hope that robust public engagement for public engagement could become the norm rather than the exception. We are also hopeful because during the 2008 election millions of Americans got involved in the political process for the first time. This spirit of participation may in the years ahead lift the voices of those often unheard and equalize educational opportunities.

References

Anyon, Jean. 1997. *Ghetto Schooling: A Political Economy of Urban Educational Reform*. New York: Teachers College Press.

Burns, Nancy. 1994. *The Formation of American Local Government: Private Values in Public Institutions*. New York: Oxford University Press.

Dreier, Peter, John Mollenkopf, and Todd Swanstrom. 2001. *Place Matters: Metropolitics in the Twenty-first Century*. Lawrence: University Press of Kansas.

Epstein, Joyce. 2001. *Schools, Families and Community Partnerships*. Boulder, CO: Westview Press.

Frank, Robert. 2007. *Falling Behind: How Rising Inequality Harms the Middle Class*. Berkeley: University of California Press.

Fung, Archon. 2002. "Creating Deliberative Publics: Governance After Devolution and Democratic Centralism." *Good Society* 11 (1): 66–71.

Gecan, Michael. 2005. *Going Public*. Boston: Beacon Press.

Gimpel, James, J. Celeste Lay, and Jason E. Schuknecht. 2003. *Cultivating Democracy: Civic Environments and Political Socialization in America*. Washington, DC: Brookings Institution Press.

Mediratta, Kavitha, Seema Shah, and Sara McAlister. 2009. *Community Organizing for Stronger School: Strategies and Successes*. Cambridge, MA: Harvard Education Press.

Obama, Barack. 2004. *Dreams of My Father: A Story of Race and Inheritance*. New York: Random House.

———. 1990. "Why Organize? Problems and Promise in the Inner City." In *After Alinsky: Community Organizing in Illinois*, ed. Peg Knoepfle, 35–40. Springfield, IL: Sangamon State University.

Oliver, J. Eric. 2001. *Democracy in Suburbia*. Princeton, NJ: Princeton University Press.

Orfield, Myron. 1997. *Metropolitics: A Regional Agenda for Community and Stability*. Washington, DC: Brookings Institution Press.

Pastor, Manuel Jr., Chris Benner, and Martha Matsuoka. 2009. *This Could Be the Start of Something Big*. Ithaca, NY: Cornell University Press.

Phi Delta Kappa International and Gallup. 2009. "Phi Delta Kappa/Gallup Poll of the Public's Attitudes Toward the Public Schools." *Phi Delta Kappan,* September.

Rimer, Sara. 2009. "Community Organizing Never Looked So Good." *New York Times,* April 12.

Rogers, John. 2006. Forces of Accountability? The Power of Poor Parents in NCLB. *Harvard Educational Review* 76 (4): 611–641.

Rogers, John, and Veronica Terriquez. 2009. "More Justice": The Role of Organized Labor in Education Reform. *Educational Policy* 23 (1): 216–241.

Rogers, Reuel. 2006. *Afro-Caribbean Immigrants and the Politics of Incorporation.* Cambridge: Cambridge University Press.

Rusk, David. 1993. *Cities Without Suburbs.* Baltimore: Woodrow Wilson Center Press.

Sen, Rinku. 2003. *Stir It Up.* San Francisco: Jossey-Bass.

Smock, Kristina. 2004. *Democracy in Action.* New York: Columbia University Press.

Terriquez, Veronica, and John Rogers. (Forthcoming). "Becoming Civic: The Active Engagement of Immigrant Parents in Public Schools." In *Critical Voices in Bicultural Parent Engagement: Operationalizing Advocacy and Empowerment*, ed. Edward Olivos and Albert Ochoa. New York: SUNY Press.

Twenge, Jean M. 2006. *Generation Me: Why Today's Young Americans Are More Confident, Assertive, Entitled—and More Miserable Than Ever Before.* New York: Free Press.

Vaca, Nicolas A. 2005. *The Presumed Alliance: The Unspoken Conflict Between Latinos and Blacks and What It Means for America.* New York: Harper Collins.

Contributors

Jean Anyon is professor of urban education at the Graduate Center of the City University of New York. Her work uses political economy to assess the impact of public policy on urban neighborhoods and schools. Her focus has been on the confluence of race, social class, and policy. Among her books are *Ghetto Schooling: A Political Economy of Urban Education*; *Radical Possibilities: Public Policy, Urban Education, and a New Social Movement*; and *Theory and Educational Research: Toward Critical Social Explanation*.

Maia Cucchiara is an assistant professor of educational leadership and policy studies at Temple University and a former teacher and community organizer. Her research focuses on the connections between education policy and practices and broader social, economic, and political processes, such as urban deindustrialization and "revitalization." She is also interested in issues of race and class and schooling and especially the ways race and class shape parental involvement in education. She is currently working on a multisite examination of policies and practices designed to promote urban revitalization by attracting middle-class parents to public schools and on a study of middle-class parental involvement in economically integrated urban schools.

Luis Ricardo Fraga is the associate vice provost for faculty advancement, director of the Diversity Research Institute, and Russell F. Stark University Professor at the University of Washington. He was a member of the American Political Science Association standing committee on Civic Engagement and Education and co-authored *Democracy at Risk: How Political Choices Under-*

mine Citizen Participation, and What We Can Do About It. Dr. Fraga is also co-author of the recently published *Multiethnic Moments: The Politics of Urban Education Reform.* His co-authored book, *Latino Lives in America: Making It Home,* is forthcoming in 2010.

Ann Frost is a graduate student in the PhD program at the University of Washington, Department of Political Science. She studies American politics, with an emphasis on race and ethnicity politics, and the politics of criminal justice. Before beginning her graduate studies, Frost practiced law as a public defender in Snohomish County, Washington. She continues to represent people on appeal from misdemeanor convictions, serves as a judge pro-tem, and teaches law and justice at a local high school.

Eva Gold is a founder and principal of Research for Action. She has served as principal investigator of numerous local and national studies focusing on dynamics among families, communities and schools, including a cross-site national study of community organizing for school reform. Her current research includes a study of youth organizing and the role of student activists in the transformation of low-performing neighborhood high schools in Philadelphia. Her own research is informed by a participatory action research project she led with youth leaders from the organizing groups. Dr. Gold's other research interests include literacies in schools and in communities, civic capacity for school reform, and privatization of public education systems. She is a lecturer in the Mid-Career Program at the University of Pennsylvania's Graduate School of Education.

Jeffrey R. Henig is professor of political science and education at Teachers College and professor of political science at Columbia University. He earned his PhD in political science at Northwestern University in 1978. Among his books on education politics are *Rethinking School Choice: Limits of the Market Metaphor*; *The Color of School Reform: Race, Politics and the Challenge of Urban Education,* named by the Urban Politics Section of the American Political Science Association as the "best book written on urban politics" in 1999; and *Building Civic Capacity: The Politics of Reforming Urban Schools,* named by the Urban Politics Section of the American Political Science Association as the "best book written on urban politics" in 2001, and *Mayors in the Middle: Politics, Race, and Mayoral Control of Urban Schools.* His most recent book is *Spin Cycle: How Research Is Used in Policy Debates: The Case of Charter Schools.*

Sara McAlister is a research associate at the Annenberg Institute for School Reform at Brown University. Previously, she taught at a dual-language elementary school in the Bronx. McAlister holds an MPA in public policy from New York University's Wagner School, an MS in elementary education from Pace University, and a BA in architecture from Yale University. She is a co-author of *Community Organizing for Stronger Schools: Strategies and Successes.*

Kavitha Mediratta is the program officer for education at the New York Community Trust in New York City. Before joining the Trust in 2009, she was responsible for the Youth Organizing and Community Organizing Research projects at the Annenberg Institute for School Reform at Brown University. She has published numerous reports and articles on community organizing for school reform and is the lead author of *Community Organizing for Stronger Schools: Strategies and Successes.* Kavitha has worked extensively with youth, parent, and community organizing groups in New York City and has taught in elementary and middle schools in East Orange, New Jersey; Chicago; and India. Kavitha has a BA from Amherst College, an EdM from Columbia University's Teachers College, and is working toward a PhD in education from New York University.

Ernest Morrell is an associate professor at the University of California–Los Angeles' Graduate School of Education and Information Studies, where he is head of the of Urban Schooling Division. He also serves as the Associate Director for UCLA's Institute for Democracy, Education, and Access (IDEA). For more than a decade, Ernest Morrell has worked with adolescents, drawing on their involvement with popular culture to promote academic literacy development. Morrell is the author of *Linking Literacy and Popular Culture: Finding Connections for Lifelong Learning; Becoming Critical Researchers: Literacy and Empowerment for Urban Youth; Critical Literacy and Urban Youth: Pedagogies of Access, Dissent, and Liberation*; and (with Jeffrey Duncan-Andrade) *The Art of Critical Pedagogy: Possibilities for Moving from Theory to Practice in Urban Schools.*

Jeannie Oakes is the director of education and scholarship at the Ford Foundation. Until fall 2008, she was Presidential Professor in Educational Equity and director of UCLA's Institute for Democracy, Education, and Access (IDEA) and UC's All Campus Consortium on Research for Diversity (ACCORD). Her research focuses on schooling inequalities and the struggle for more socially just schools. Among her many books are *Keeping Track: How Schools Structure Inequality*; *Becoming Good American Schools: The Struggle for Civic Virtue in Education Reform*; *Learning Power: Organizing for Education and Justice*; and *Beyond Tracking: Multiple Pathways to College, Career, and Civic Participation*.

Marion Orr is the Fred Lippitt Professor of Public Policy, Political Science, and Urban Studies and the director of the A. Alfred Taubman Center for Public Policy at Brown University. He is the author and co-author of two books: *Black Social Capital: The Politics of School Reform in Baltimore* and *The Color of School Reform: Race, Politics, and the Challenge of Urban Education*. He is also the editor of *Transforming the City: Community Organizing and the Challenge of Political Change* and *Power in the City: Clarence Stone and the Politics of Inequality*. He is currently engaged in a study of the organizing experiences of the Industrial Areas Foundation (IAF) in various U.S. cities.

Wendy Puriefoy is the president of Public Education Network, a national association of local education funds (LEFs) and individuals working to advance public school reform in low-income communities across our country. Public Education Fund believes an active, vocal constituency is the key to ensuring that every child, in every community, benefits from a quality public education. Wendy Puriefoy, a founding convener of the Forum for Education and Democracy, is a nationally recognized expert on issues of school reform and civil society. Ms. Puriefoy is well known for her passionate advocacy of education equity for poor and disadvantaged children and has written and spoken extensively on the issues.

John Rogers is associate professor of education at UCLA and director of UCLA's Institute for Democracy, Education, and Access (IDEA). He also serves as the faculty co-director of UCLA's Principal Leadership Institute. Rogers studies strategies for engaging urban youth, community members, and educators in equity-focused school reform. He draws extensively on the work of John Dewey to explore the meaning of and possibilities for democratic education today. John Rogers is the co-author (with Jeannie Oakes) of *Learning Power: Organizing for Education and Justice*.

Seema Shah is currently a global research manager for the International Baccalaureate, where she conducts research on student engagement and student outcomes in international education. Previously, she was a principal associate at the Annenberg Institute for School Reform at Brown University, where she co-directed a national study on community organizing and school reform. Over the years, Shah has worked extensively with public schools and non-profit organizations as an evaluator and researcher. She completed a post-doctoral fellowship in mental health policy at Yale University School of Medicine's Consultation Center. She earned a BA in Psychology from Duke University and a PhD in clinical-community psychology from DePaul University, where her dissertation research focused on the acculturation experiences of immigrant and refugee youth. She is co-author of *Community Organizing for Stronger Schools: Strategies and Successes.*

Dennis Shirley is professor of education at the Lynch School of Education at Boston College. Professor Shirley's work in education spans from the micro level of assisting beginning teachers to the macro level of designing and guiding large-scale research and intervention projects for school districts, states, and nonprofit agencies. He is the author of *The Politics of Progressive Education: The Odenwaldschule in Nazi Germany; Community Organizing for Urban School Reform; Valley Interfaith and School Reform: Organizing for Power in South Texas;* and (with Andy Hargreaves) *The Fourth Way: The Inspiring Future for Educational Change.*

Elaine Simon is an anthropologist who has conducted ethnographic research and evaluation in the fields of education, employment and training, and community development. She is co-director of urban studies in the School of Arts and Sciences and adjunct associate professor of education in the Graduate School of Education at the University of Pennsylvania, as well as an affiliated researcher at Research for Action. Simon's perspective on education is informed by her background in urban studies and community development. She has studied and written about the early 1990s Chicago education reform that devolved power to communities and parents, two decades of school reform in Philadelphia, and community organizing for school reform in five cities as part of the Cross City Campaign Indicators Project. Most recently, she has been part of a team examining the effort of a community coalition to influence the terms of the debate about school governance in New York City.

Brenda J. Turnbull is a founder and principal of Policy Studies Associates (PSA). Since 1982, PSA has conducted evaluation, research, and policy analysis on school improvement, youth development, and community engagement.

Turnbull's recent study of local education funds around the nation explores how local communities and organizations that work with them are mobilizing to improve education.

Mark R. Warren is associate professor of education at Harvard University. He is a sociologist concerned with the revitalization of American democratic and community life. He studies efforts to strengthen institutions that anchor inner-city communities—churches, schools, and other community-based organizations—and to build broad-based alliances among these institutions and across race and social class. Warren is the author of *Crossing Over the Color Line: How White Activists Embrace Racial Justice* and *Dry Bones Rattling: Community Building to Revitalize American Democracy.* He is co-author with Richard Wood of *Faith-Based Community Organizing: The State of the Field,* and he also co-edited (with Susan Saegert and J. Phillip Thompson) *Social Capital and Poor Communities.*

Lauren Wells is a research associate at the Metropolitan Center for Urban Education at New York University. She holds a PhD in education from the University of California–Los Angeles, a master's degree in educational leadership from Columbia University, and a BA in English from Temple University. Lauren's research centers around issues of educational equity and justice and are informed by her interests in the dynamics of race, class and power in education, the social and political thought of historically oppressed groups, and community organizing and development. Her scholarly inquiry integrates critical theories of race, theories of political economy, and history. She uses qualitative research methods to understand how those most impacted by educational inequity experience the material conditions of urban schools and communities and to identify solutions to these conditions.

Donn Worgs, is an associate professor of political science and director of metropolitan studies at Towson University. Previously, he worked with the Academy for Educational Development and with a community-based educational program in Washington, DC. His research focuses on education politics and community development. He is currently writing a book that explores the democratic implications of African American communities mobilizing to create or transform educational opportunities for their youth.

Index

Abernathy, Scott Franklin, 67
Accountability, 44; community organizing and, 156–57, 216; in Mobile, AL, 254, 264, 266–68, 272; in new political grid, 61, 63–66, 71
ACORN, 46, 144, 152, 157–59, 161, 163n4, 164n11, 203
ACORN Illinois, 202–26, 303; Grow Your Own (GYO) campaign of, 212–22; *Leave No School Behind,* 208–9, 208t; organizing model of, 203–4; school reform and, 204–12
Action Now, 203, 223n1
Advocacy/advocacy groups, 42–43, 110, 119, 141–42, 177–78, 184
Advocates for Children (AFC), 177
African Americans, 8, 143; Chicago schools and, 205–10; civil rights movement and, 36–40, 143, 188, 194–95; history of education of, 29–33, 36–40; Los Angeles schools and, 230–33; Mobile schools and, 251–56, 263; population shifts and, 55–56, 120–21; school board elections and, 128, 134n6
African Americans for School Choice (AASC), 285, 287–89
Akers, Carolyn, 250–51, 256–61, 263, 266–67, 271–72, 304, 309
Alabama, 2–3. *See also* Coalitions across race and class lines
Alabama Education Association, 258, 266

Alabamans Behind Local Education (ABLE), 253
Albuquerque, NM, 69, 81n11
Alcarcon, Richard, 238
Alexander, Dan, 254
Alinsky, Saul, 142–44, 146
Allen, Fay, 230
Alliance for a Better Community (ABC), 237–38
Alliance for Quality Education (AQE), 161, 176–77, 179–80
Alliances, 16–17, 173–98, 202, 304; challenges of, 186–87, 196n1; community organizing and, 140–41, 158–59, 161; institutional structures and, 180–81; intermediaries and, 183–84; in Los Angeles, 228, 237–42; market-oriented schools and, 289–91; in 1970s and 1980s as, 40–44; nonprofit support for, 181–83; during Progressive Era, 35; revenue-generating funder, 184–86; social movements and, 187–95; theory and action and, 175–79; "top-heavy" nature of, 140–41; types of, 179–80. *See also* Coalitions; Partnerships
Alliance Schools Initiative, 46, 139, 153, 160
Allied Communities of Tarrant (ACT), 45–46
Alvord, John, 31
American Missionary Association, 32
Annenberg Challenge, 205

Annenberg Institute for School Reform
  (AISR), 156, 158, 163n8, 182–83, 269, 311
Anyon, Jean, 35, 47; *Radical Possibilities*, 189,
  192
Asian Americans, 41, 56, 94
Association of Community Organizations
  for Reform Now. *See* ACORN
Assurance Game, 110–12
Atlanta, GA, 105–7
Austin Interfaith, 154

Baker, Ella, 143
Baldrige Criteria for Performance
  Excellence, 264, 266–67
Baltimore, MD, 72, 97–101, 103–5, 112
Baltimore Algebra Project, 92, 145–46
Beam, John, 158
Bell, Terrell, 43
Bendixen and Associates Latino survey, 123
Berkman, Michael, 59
Bertani, Al, 212
Bevel, James, 37
Bifulco, Robert, 103
Bilingual Education Act, 42–43
Bilingual education movement, 194–95
*Birdie Mae Davis et al. v. Board of School
  Commissioners of Mobile County,* 253–55
Birmingham, AL, 37–38
Boston, MA, 145
Boyte, Harry, 10, 91–93, 107
Brady, Henry E., 5
Brenes, Maria, 234–35, 243–45, 246n2
Bridglall, Beatrice, 94
Bronx (District 9), 46–47, 139, 161
Brown, Chris, 158
Brown v. Board of Education, 36, 194–95
Buckley, Jack, 12, 67
BUILD (Baltimoreans United in Leadership
  Development), 97–98, 107
Bureaucracy. *See* Professional educators
Bush, George H. W., 44, 60
Bush, George W., 60, 64

California, 46, 75, 93, 122, 139, 158. *See also*
  Los Angeles, CA; PICO
Californians for Justice, 145–46, 152
Campaign for Fiscal Equality (CFE), 179
Campaign for Sustainable Milwaukee, 190
Capps, Randolph, 57–58
Carvalho, Maria Eulina P. de, 7
Casillas, Maria, 233, 241

Castro, Sal, 232
CEE, 228, 237–45, 245n1
Center for Education Policy (CEP), 183–84
Charlottesville Summit, 60
Charter schools, 66–68, 102–3, 109; in
  Atlanta, 105–7; in Baltimore, 103–5; in
  Philadelphia, 283, 288–89
Chicago, IL, 45, 122, 158–59. *See also* LSNA;
  Teacher quality, improving
Chicago Learning Campaign (CLC), 213–15
Chicago School Reform Act of 1988, 204,
  223n3
Chicago State University, 213–15
Child First Authority, 97–100, 107, 109–10
"Children's crusade," 37–38
Chong, Dennis, 110–11
Churches. *See* Faith-based organizations
Citizen Education Program, 143
Citizens Advisory Team, 261–62
Civic capacity: Alliance Schools and, 46; in
  East Los Angeles, 233–37, 243–45, 305; in
  Mobile, AL, 258–61; in 1970s and 1980s,
  41–42
Civil Rights Act of 1964, 42–43
Civil rights movement, 36–40, 143, 188,
  194–95
Clark, Septima, 143
Class: coalitions and, 250–75; community
  organizing and, 141, 148; public
  engagement and, 6–8, 12–13, 29, 41; test
  scores and, 65
Clinton, Bill, 60
"Club 2012," 94–95
Coalitions: ad hoc, 79–80; in Bronx
  (District 9), 46–47, 139; community
  organizing and, 159; in 1970s and 1980s,
  40–44. *See also* Alliances
Coalitions across race and class lines, 187,
  250–75, 304, 309; implementation and,
  265–73; reform challenges and, 251–57;
  strategic plan and, 263–65; tax
  referendum and, 257–58; "Yes, We Can,"
  258–65
Co-construction, 30–33
Cohen, Cathy, 9
Collaborative Communications, 267
Collective action, 110–11, 304–5; potential
  contributors to, 111
College access, campaign for, 146, 227–49,
  302, 304; CEE and, 237–42; civil
  learning and, 233–37; historical

background of, 229–33; public
  engagement and, 243–45
Commitment, efficacy and, 100–101, 110–12
Committee for Mobile's Children, 258
Commonwealth Institute for Parent
  Leadership (CIPL), 181
Communities for Educational Equity (CEE),
  228, 237–45, 245n1
Communities for Public Education Reform,
  184–85
Community Anti-Violence Project (CAVP),
  89
Community Collaborative for District 9
  (Bronx), 46–47, 139, 161
Community Conversations, 260–61, 271, 304
Community organizing, 16, 92, 139–72,
  312; challenges in field of, 159–61;
  collaboration and, 147–48, 158,
  163nn6–7; contemporary field of,
  144–46, 151–57; cyclical process of,
  148–51, 149f, 163n9; educational reform
  and, 146–48, 151–57, 155f, 163n5, 163n8,
  220–22; expanding the scale of, 157–59;
  as form of public engagement, 140–42;
  funding of, 159–60; history of, 44–47;
  institutionally vs. individually based,
  144–45, 149; market-oriented schools
  and, 291–94; teachers quality in Chicago
  and, 201–26; tradition of, 142–44. See
  also Youth activism
Conjunctures, concept of, 29–30
Consent decrees, 75, 254–55
Context of public engagement:
  contemporary, 52–85; historical, 27–51
Contracting out, 283–84, 291, 295, 303
Contreras, Frances, 122
Coproduction, 14–15, 89–116; as Assurance
  Game, 110–12; after Civil War, 30–33;
  implications of, 108–10; new schools
  and, 101–7; public engagement and,
  90–92, 95, 98, 100, 107, 110–13, 305; in
  supplemental programs, 93–101
CORRE (Central Office Review for Results
  & Equity), 269–70
Cortes. Ernest, 16
Counterpublics, 27, 29, 302
Courts, 74–76, 81n14, 81n16
Crawford v. Board of Education of the City of
  Los Angeles, 231
Cross City Campaign for Urban School
  Reform, 156, 176–77, 205, 213

CTQ (Center for Teaching Quality), 266,
  269–70
Culture: coproduction and, 94, 98; public
  engagement and, 6–8, 127; teacher
  preparation for, 213, 221; test scores and,
  65; tracking and, 230
Cunningham, Christy, 89, 92

Daoud, Annette M., 122
DART (Direct Action and Research
  Training Center), 144, 152
Data analysis capability, 65, 205–10, 303
Democratic governance, 15–16, 117–38; lack
  of, in Los Angeles, 229–34; local school
  districts and, 118–19; during Progressive
  Era, 33–36
Democratic promise: public engagement
  and, 10–13; coproduction and, 108–10;
  social movements and, 194–95
Demographics, shifting, 55–56
Denver, CO, 139
Designs for Change, 205, 213
Detroit, MI, 69, 81n10
Dialogues, public, 260–61, 271, 304
Dillon, Sam, 2
Dingerson, Leigh, 158
Dixon, Denise, 207–9
Dodge, Harold, 257–58, 271
Donors' Education Collaborative, 184–85
Downtown Business Improvement District
  (BID), 285–87
Drago, Ruth, 254
Duncan, Arne, 210

Eason-Watkins, Barbara, 216
East Brooklyn Congregations (EBC), 91–92,
  102
Economy, 4, 11, 41, 69–70, 76
Edison Schools, Inc., 72–73, 276
Education. See Public education
Education Advocates United (EAU), 285,
  289–91, 303
Educational Justice Collaborative (EJC), 173,
  182–83
Education for All Handicapped Children
  Act, 43
Education Law Center (ELC), 183–84
Elections, school board, 127–30, 204–5, 254,
  274n4
Elementary and Secondary Education Act,
  63–64

ELLS (English language learners), 122,
176–77
EMOs (Educational Management
Organizations), 71–73
Empowerment Academy, 104–6
"Engagement gap," 27, 45, 140
Equalizing schools and voice, 3–4; alliances,
coalitions and, 174, 250–75; charter
schools and, 106, 109; in Chicago,
201–26; in Civil Rights Movement, 36–40;
college access and, 227–49; community
organizing and, 44–47; coproduction
and, 91–93, 108–10, 112; in Los Angeles,
227–49, 237–45; market-oriented systems
and, 277–78; in Mobile, 250–75; in 1970s
and 1980s, 40–44; in post–Civil War
South, 30–33; in Progressive Era, 33–36;
public engagement and, 8–10, 13; teacher
quality and, 201–26
Equity, lack of educational, 1–5, 120, 141;
charter schools and, 106, 109; in
Chicago, 205–10; history of, 28–47; in
Los Angeles, 227–33, 241–42; in Mobile,
251–56; unequal voice and, 1–5, 140
Erlichson, Bari Anhalt, 75

Faith-based organizations, 66, 104, 107–8,
144
Familia Initiative, La, 130–31
Federalism, 60–63, 117–18
Flacks, Richard, 37
Flexibility, tactical, 65, 77–80, 176–77, 179
Ford Consortium on Constituency Building
for School Reform, 184–85
Ford Foundation, 158, 160, 213
Fort Worth, TX, 45–46
Fraga, Luis Ricardo, 75
Freedman's Bureau, 32–33
Freedom schools, 38–39, 92

Gamaliel Foundation, 144, 152
Gándara, Patricia, 122
Ganz, Marshall, 16
Gardner, David, 43
Gender and education, 42
Giuliani, Rudolph, 72
Globalization, 4, 11, 76–77, 305
Good Schools Pennsylvania (GSPA), 180–81
Gordon, Edmund, 94
Governance, democratic. See Democratic
governance

Grassroots associations, 193
"Grey Peril," 59
Grogan, Paul, 281
Grow Your Own Teachers Act, 217
Grow Your Own teachers projects: Grow
Your Own (GYO) Illinois as, 217–18,
304; Illinois ACORN and, 212–22; LSNA
and, 180, 202, 213–16

Hallet, Anne, 218
Hamer, Fannie Lou, 143
Hampton, VA, 95–97, 111–12
Hancock, Ange-Marie, 9
Hankins, Katherine, 105–6
Harris-Dawson, Marqueece, 228
Hawaii, 134n2
Hayduck, Ron, 129
Head Start, 194
Henig, Jeffrey, 102, 140
Highland Folk School, 143
Hirschman, Albert O., 66–67
Hispanics, 41, 55–56, 58. See also Latinos
Hochschild, Jennifer, 11
Home schooling, 66
Honig, Meredith, 183
Hornbeck, David, 180
Houston, TX, 5–6, 93, 122
Howell, William, 118
Huizar, Jose, 229, 241, 244
Hyde Square Task Force, 145

IAF (Industrial Areas Foundation), 98,
101–2, 143–44, 152–55; Texas, 46–47, 139,
153, 157, 160
ICS (InnerCity Struggle), 146, 227–29,
234–37, 241
Illinois. See Chicago, IL; Teacher quality,
improving
Immigrants, 7, 34, 57–58, 129, 177, 306
Industrial Development Board of Mobile,
258
Inequality, educational. See Equity, lack of
educational
Institute for Democracy, Education, and
Access (IDEA), 182–83
Institutions of public schooling, 147–48,
302, 307
In-SYNC (Innovations for School, Youth
and families, Neighborhoods and
Communities), 96–97
Interdistrict public choice, 66, 81n9

Interfaith Funders, 151–52
Intermediaries, 145, 158, 160–61, 183–84
InterValley Project, 152

Jefferson, Thomas, 27–28
Jellison Holme, Jennifer, 65
Jones, Samuel, 270

Kari, Nancy, 91–93, 107
Karp, Jessica, 6
Katz, Michael, 279
Kennedy, John F., 38
Kentucky, 61, 180–81
Kentucky Education Reform Act (KERA), 181
King, Martin Luther, Jr., 37–38
Klonsky, Michael, 206

Ladd, Helen, 103
Language and public engagement, 7–8, 58, 126
Lareau, Annette, 6–7
Latino National Survey (LNS), 123–25, 134n5
Latinos, 57, 117–38; administrators and teachers of, 128–29; educational challenges and, 120–27; language and, 7–8, 58, 122, 126; in Logan Square, 201–2; Los Angeles schools and, 39, 230–33, 237; population change of, 120–21; public engagement of, 122–27, 132–34; school board elections and, 127–30. *See also* College access, campaign for; Hispanics
Lau v. Nichols, 42–43
Lawsuits, 75, 253–54
Leadership development, 132, 149–51, 149f
LEARN (Los Angeles Educational Alliance for Restructuring Now), 232–33
Leave No School Behind (ACORN), 208–9, 208t
LeFlore, John, 253
Levine, Charles, 91
Levy, Harold, 72
Lightfoot, Sara Lawrence, 6
Lipsky, Michael, 78
"Little Rock Nine," 36
Local education foundations (LEF), 184, 259, 273n1
Localism, 60–63
Local School Councils (LSCs), 129, 204–5

Logan Square Neighborhood Association (LSNA), 46, 139, 158–61, 180, 201–2, 213–16
Los Angeles, CA, 11, 39, 121, 154–55; college degrees in, 244f; educational governance in, 229–34; income inequality in, 239f. *See also* College access, campaign for
Los Angeles Community Coalition, 145, 228, 242
LSNA, 46, 139, 158–61, 180, 201–2, 213–16

Macedo, Stephen, 119
MAEF, 250–51, 256–57, 260–62, 266–73, 273n1
Magnet schools, 81n8, 254–55
Malloy, Courtney, 102–3
Mann, Horace, 28–29, 31
Market-oriented systems, 42, 102, 276–300, 305–6; alliance strategy and, 289–91; closed-door decision making and, 282–83, 285, 295; community organizing strategy and, 291–94; contracting out and, 283–84, 291, 295, 303; individual choice strategy and, 287–89; public engagement and, 72–74, 277–78, 284–85, 294–97; public/private partnership strategy and, 286–87, 297n3
Mayoral control, 69–71, 76, 81n10–11, 160
McAdams, Donald, 5–6, 11, 93
McNeil, Charles, 253
Medirata, Kavitha, 6
Melvin, Veronica, 238, 242–43
Mendoza, Sandy, 242, 243–45
Meroe, Aundra Saa, 94
Meza, Nancy, 227–28
Miami-Dade County, FL, 122
Milliken v. Bradley, 75
Milwaukee, WI, 190
Mission-oriented schools, 102
Mississippi Adequate Education Program, 139–40
Mobile, AL. *See* Coalitions across race and class lines
Mobile Area Education Foundation (MAEF), 250–51, 256–57, 260–62, 266–73, 273n1
Mobile Committee for the Support of Public Education, 253
Mobile County Industrial Development Association, 258
Moses, Bob, 92

NAACP lawsuits, 253–54
National Center for Schools and
    Communities, 155, 155f
National Council of Education Providers, 71
National Council of La Raza (NCLR),
    183–84
National Household Education Survey Data
    (NHES), 67
Nationalization of education, 61–62
National Network of Partnership Schools
    (NNPS), 105, 113n4
National political context, 308–9, 312
National Training and Information Center,
    164n11, 165n15
Nation at Risk, A, 43–44
"Native schools," 31–32
NCLB. See No Child Left Behind (NCLB)
    Act
Neighborhood Charter School (NCS), 105–7,
    302–3
Neighborhood College, 96
New Song Academy, 104, 107
New York, 41, 72, 91–92, 102, 122; alliances
    and, 161, 176–77, 179–80; Bronx, 6,
    46–47, 139, 161; coproduction and,
    101–2
New York City Coalition for Education
    Justice (NYCEJ), 183
New York Immigrant Coalition (NYIC),
    177
Nicholls, Keith, 257
Nixon, Cynthia, 179
No Child Left Behind (NCLB) Act, 47,
    61–62, 64, 160, 276, 308; Alabama
    noncompliance with, 263, 266–67; SES
    in, 71, 94; teacher quality in Chicago
    and, 201–2, 210–11, 220
Noncitizen voting, 129
Nonprofits, alliances and, 181–83, 193
North Lawndale schools, 202, 207–14, 208t
Nueva Generación Project, 180, 213–13, 216

Oakes, Jeannie, 11
Oakland Communities Organization, 46,
    139, 158
Obama, Barack, 308, 312
Organizing skills. See Leadership
    development
Orr, Marion, 80n1
Ostrom, Elinor, 107
Outcomes, research on, 311
Outputs vs. inputs, 63, 80–81n6

Pacific Institute for Community
    Organization (PICO), 144, 152, 157–58
Padres y Jovenes Unidos, 139, 145
Parent involvement, 103–5, 119, 122–27,
    129–30
Partnerships: community organizing and,
    162, 222; coproduction and, 99, 102–5,
    113n4; in La Familia Initiative,
    130–31; market-oriented schools and,
    286–87; research, 65–66, 205–10, 303.
    See also Alliances
PASSport for Excellence, 265, 271
Patterson Park Public Charter School
    (PPPCS), 104–5, 107
Pennsylvania, 180–81. See also Philadelphia,
    PA
PEN (Public Education Network), 183–84, 259
Perez, Jonathan, 241
Pew Hispanic Center (PHC) surveys, 123–24
Philadelphia, PA, 278–80. See also
    Market-oriented systems
Philadelphia Student Union, 145
PICO, 144, 152, 157–58
Plessy v. Ferguson, 33
Plutzer, Eric, 59
Political grid, new, 52–85; courts and, 74–76;
    federalism dynamics and, 60–63;
    globalization in, 76–77; privatization
    and, 71–74; school boards and, 68–71;
    school choice and, 66–68; standards,
    testing and accountability in, 63–66;
    strategic options in, 77–80; structural
    change and, 54–59
Politics, 12, 40, 101, 119; coproduction and,
    92–93, 100–101, 110–12; inequality in
    participation in, 5–8, 48, 140–41; Latinos
    and, 122–27, 132–34
Population change, 55–56, 58–59, 120–21, 306
Power, 183, 262, 288, 311; in community
    organizing, 149f, 162, 203, 245; unilateral
    and relational, 46, 147–48
Prichard Committee for Academic
    Excellence in Kentucky, 180–81
Pride, Richard, 254
Private schools, 66
Privatization, 71–74, 76, 80–81n6, 160
Professional educators, 3, 64, 69, 302, 306–7
Progressive Era, 33–36, 68
Proscio, Tony, 281
PTA (Parent Teacher Association), 142
Public education: dual role of, 10–11; history
    of, 27–47; urban, 57, 307 (see also by

individual cities); weak institutions of,
147–48. *See also* Equalizing schools and
voice; Equity, lack of educational
Public Education Network (PEN), 183–84, 259
Public engagement: challenges to, 305–7;
defined, 8–10, 12, 14, 195–96; practices
distinguishing, 301–5; support for,
307–12. *See also* Context of public
engagement; Streams of public
engagement
Public formation, 302–3
Public work, 10, 91–93

Queen Street Baptist Church, 96
Quirocho, Alice M. L., 122

Race: alliances, coalitions and, 187, 250–75;
community organizing and, 145–46,
148, 157; educational governance and,
229–33; public engagement and, 6–8, 29,
41, 141; test scores and, 65
Racial transition and politics, 56–58
Radical Possibilities (Anyon), 189, 192
Ramirez, A. Y., 7
Randolph, A. Philip, 41
Reagan, Ronald, 40, 43
Reclaiming Our Children and Community
Project (ROCACP), 97–99, 112
Reconstruction, 32–33
Recruitment of teachers, Illinois ACORN
and, 206, 211, 218, 223n4
Reese, William, 34
Reform. *See* School reform
Regional Congregations and Neighborhood
Organizations Training Center, 152
Relational power, 46, 147–48
Relationship building, 147–50, 149f
Renaissance 2010, 218–19
*Report to the Mobile County Community on
the State of Public Education* (MAEF),
268–69
Republican Party, 44
Research: new areas of, 310–12; partnerships,
alliances and, 65–66, 205–10, 310–11
Research for Action (RFA), 182
Retana, Alberto, 237–39, 243, 244, 305
Rivera, Amanda, 215–16
ROCACP, 97–99, 112
Rodriguez, Nick, 75
Rogers, John, 8, 11, 310
Rognel Heights Cultural Center, 112
Rustin, Bayard, 41

San Antonio School District v. Rodriguez, 60
Sanchez, Luis, 228, 234, 238, 242, 246n2
Sandler, Ross, 75
San Francisco, CA, 75
Sassen, Saskia, 77
Savas, E. S., 72
Schattschneider, E. E., 1, 62
Schlozman, Kay Lehman, 5
Schmoke, Kurt, 72, 97
Schneider, Mark, 12, 67
Schoenbrod, David, 75
School boards, 68–71, 118; elections of,
127–30, 204–5, 254, 274n4; in Los
Angeles, 230–34, 244; in Mobile, 253–54,
262–65, 271
School choice, 66–68, 76, 81nn8–9. *See also*
Market-oriented systems
School districts/systems: democratic
governance and, 117–20; Los Angeles,
229–33; "majority-minority" and
multiethnic, 56–57
School finance, 73–74, 255–61
School officials, 6–7, 108, 130–32, 306–7
School reform, 157, 294, 296, 302; coalitions
and, 148, 250–75; community
organizing for, 139–72; coproduction
and, 100–101, 110–12; youth activism
and, 227–49, 291–94
School Reform Commission (SRC), 281–86,
288, 290, 293
Science, educational policies and, 230
Scovronick, Nathan, 11
Segregation, 29–33, 36–40; in Mobile, AL,
252–56
Shah, Paru, 129
Shipps, Dorothy, 56–57
Small high schools, 291–94
Small Schools Transition Project, 297n5
Small Schools Workshop, 205
Smith, Joanna, 102–3
Smith, Takoura, 242
Social capital, 9–10, 67, 93, 119, 149–50, 157, 177
Social movements, 17–18, 46, 92, 143, 187–96;
cross-sector action and thinking in,
188–91; 1960s emergence of youth in,
36–40
Sommerville, Imogene, 204–5
South Bronx Churches (SBC), 102
South Central Youth Empowered thru
Action, 146
Southern Christian Leadership Conference
(SCLC), 37

Southern Echo, 139–40, 145, 152, 158
Special needs education, 43
SRC, 281–86, 288, 290, 293
Stall, Susan, 16
Standards, in new political grid, 63–66, 71
State involvement, 58–60, 74; Philadelphia
      takeover and, 276–77, 280–81, 295
Stewart, Gwen, 211
Stocker, Randy, 16
Stone, Clarence, 140, 163n6
Streams of public engagement, 13–18;
      alliances and social movements as,
      36–44, 173–98; community organizing
      as, 44–47, 139–72; coproduction as,
      30–33, 89–116; democratic governance
      as, 33–36, 117–38
Strike School Academy, 235
Strolovitch, Dara Z., 9
Structures, institutional, 180–81, 302, 307
Students Empowered, 285, 291–94
Students for a Democratic Society (SDS), 39
Suburbanization, 58–59
Supplemental Education Services (SES), 71, 94
Supplementary programs, 93–101
Swanstrom, Todd, 58–59

Tactical flexibility, 65, 77–80
Talbott, Madeline, 205–6, 208–9, 214, 216–17,
      219–20, 222–23
Teacher pipeline programs, 202, 213–14, 222
Teacher quality, improving, 201–26, 303;
      cultural preparation and, 213, 221; Grow
      Your Own (GYO) campaign and,
      212–22, 304; as lever for systemic
      reform, 205–10; NCLB and, 201–2,
      210–11, 220; recruiting and, 206, 211,
      218, 223n4; teacher turnover and,
      210–12
Teachers' unions, 41, 57, 69, 73; in Alabama,
      258, 266; community organizing and,
      139, 160–61; in Los Angeles, 233, 241
Technologies, tactics and, 78
Terriquez, Veronica, 239f, 240f, 310
Testing, 63–66, 71, 97–99, 112
Texas, 5–6, 45–47, 93, 122, 154
Texas Industrial Areas Foundation (IAF),
      46–47, 139, 153, 157, 160
Thomas, Daniel, 253
"Together We Can" (Mobile, AL), 250–75;
      educational reform challenges and,
      251–57; implementation and, 265–73;

strategic plan and, 263–65; tax
      referendum and, 257–58; "Yes We Can"
      and, 250, 258–65
Tokofsky, David, 229, 242
Transformation and social movements,
      191–92
Transformation Schools, 266
Transforming Education for New York's
      Newest (TENYN), 176–77
Tuscaloosa, AL, 2–3
Tyack, David, 15, 34

UFT (United Federation of Teachers), 139, 161
Unions, labor, 35, 41, 310. See also Teachers'
      unions
United Civil Rights Committee (UCRC), 231
United Mexican American Students, 39
United Students clubs, 234–36
United Way, 242, 244–45
University of Illinois at Chicago, 215–16
U.S. Department of Education, 40, 43, 64

Vallas, Paul, 208–10, 281–84, 290
Verba, Sidney, 5
Virginia Organizing Project, 152
Virginia (state), 94–97, 111–12
Voice, unequal, 1–5, 11–13, 140–41
Voluntarism, 91–93, 142
Vouchers, 66–67, 288, 307

Ward system, 33–34
Washington, DC, 12, 94
Weir, Margaret, 58–59
Wells, Amy Stuart, 65
Wilhoyte, Cheryl, 264
Williams v. California, 237
Wilson, Dante, 98–99
Wohlsetter, Priscilla, 102–3
Wolman, Harold, 58–59
Women organizers, 143
Women's education, 42
Women's movement, 163n2, 194–95

Y. H. Thomas Community Center, 95–96,
      109
"Yes We Can," 258–65
Youth activism, 36–40, 145–46, 227–49,
      291–94, 297n5
Youth United for Change, 145

Zacarias, Ruben, 233